Contemporary Europe

International Library of Sociology

Founded by Karl Mannheim

Editor: John Rex, University of Warwick

Arbor Scientiae
Arbor Vitae

A catalogue of the books available in the **International Library of Sociology** and other series of Social Science books published by Routledge & Kegan Paul will be found at the end of this volume.

Contemporary Europe

Social structures and cultural patterns

Edited by
Salvador Giner and
Margaret Scotford Archer

Routledge & Kegan Paul
London, Henley and Boston

First published in 1978
by Routledge & Kegan Paul Ltd
39 Store Street,
London WC1E 7DD,
Broadway House,
Newtown Road,
Henley-on-Thames,
Oxon RG9 1EN and
9 Park Street,
Boston, Mass. 02108, USA
Set in 10/11 pt Times New Roman by
Kelly and Wright, Bradford-on-Avon, Wiltshire
and printed in Great Britain by
Redwood Burn Ltd
Trowbridge and Esher

British Library Cataloguing in Publication Data

Contemporary Europe: social structures and cultural patterns. –
(International library of sociology).

1. Europe – Social conditions
I. Giner, Salvador II. Archer, Margaret Scotford III. Series
301.4'0094   HN373.5   77–30716

ISBN 0 7100 8790 X
ISBN 0 7100 8926 0 Pbk

Contents

		page
	Editors' Preface	vii
1	The theoretical and the comparative analysis of social structure *Margaret S. Archer*	1
2	Private capital and the state in Western Europe *Gordon Causer*	28
3	Diffusion and crisis of scientific management in European industry *Angelo Pichierri*	55
4	Social democracy and workers' conceptions of power in England and Sweden *Richard Scase*	74
5	Migrant workers in European social structures *Salvador Giner and Juan Salcedo*	94
6	Ethnic problems in Europe *Jaroslav Krejci*	124
7	The intellectuals in contemporary Europe *Michalina Vaughan*	172
8	Changes in social structure and changes in the demand for education *Pierre Bourdieu and Luc Boltanski*	197
9	The religious condition of Europe *David Martin*	288
10	Armed forces and European society *Gwyn Harries-Jenkins*	288
	Index	315

Editors' preface

In the late 1960s our common interest in the study of European society made us aware of the lack of macro-sociological or comparative literature. Wishing to explore the problem further, we organised a series of seminars in 1970, under the auspices of the Graduate School of Contemporary European Studies at the University of Reading, bringing together colleagues who dealt with various aspects of European society on a country-by-country basis. This resulted in the publication of the volume entitled *Contemporary Europe: Class, Status and Power*,[1] which we edited in 1971. In that book, our long introductory essay and the concluding chapter by Professor T. B. Bottomore were addressed to general problems in the fields of class and class conflict, power and social stratification, with special reference to the European continent. In the main body of the book other sociologists[2] presented national studies in which they attempted to answer similar questions from a national perspective, that is, questions about the new class, status and power structures emerging in Europe since the end of the Second World War.

The reception enjoyed by that volume and the encouragement of colleagues prompted us to pursue this initial effort by taking a more thorough look at some of the issues raised there, especially those which had received little attention because of their transnational character. In order to identify those issues and to put them into an analytical perspective, a one-day international seminar was organised at Reading in 1972, again within the framework of the Graduate School, during which a small number of sociologists were able to compare ideas and outline further work to be undertaken. It was then suggested that some of this should eventually be published as a new symposium which would look at European societies across state frontiers, isolating emerging structures, international cultural patterns, and shared institutions, cleavages and conflicts. The present volume, in which several of the original seminar participants have collaborated, is the outcome of this suggestion.

As is explained in the introductory essay, which deals with general methodological and theoretical issues, all other studies in the book attempt to tackle important substantive problems in the life of contemporary Europe: the influence of capital, the changing roles of intellectuals, the economic effects of vast labour migrations, the abiding presence of organised religions and ethnic groupings, the new position of the military, and various other dimensions.

We have been helped and encouraged in the preparation of this volume by a number of friends and colleagues, some of whom we must acknowledge individually. First, we have to mention Professor Stuart Woolf, Professor Hugh Thomas and Dr George Yannopoulos, past Chairmen of the School, who helped us to launch the project; Mrs Patricia Sales who organised the original meeting; and all the members of the Graduate School of Contemporary European Studies at Reading University who supported our work. We also have to thank Professor John Rex for his encouragement throughout; Mr Richard Nice for his help with translation; Ms Joan Hood for her many retypings of the manuscripts; and all those whose interest stimulated our work although their other commitments prevented them from contributing to the present volume, especially Professor Tom Bottomore, Professor Jacques Van Doorn, Professor John Jackson, Dr Steven Lukes, Dr José Maravall and Dr Nicos Mouzelis.

Salvador Giner
Margaret S. Archer

Notes

1 M. S. Archer and S. Giner (eds), *Contemporary Europe: Class, Status and Power*, London, Weidenfeld & Nicolson, 1971; New York, St Martin's Press, 1971; 2nd edn (paperback) 1973.

2 Michael Attalides, Gösta Carlsson, Colin Crouch, Luciano Gallino, John Jackson, Rene König, David Martin, Herminio Martins, Nicos Mouzelis, Pierre Naville, Frank Parkin, Kaare Svalastoga, Michalina Vaughan.

1 The theoretical and the comparative analysis of social structure

Margaret S. Archer

The contributions to this book are all substantive ones, but they also reflect a wider theoretical debate about the analysis of social structure which is now unfolding. Only this latter aspect will be taken up here for it raises some important questions about the place of the comparative perspective in the development of macro-sociology. Historically the founding fathers saw the relationship between theoretical and comparative approaches as one of indispensable symbiosis. In the traditions to which they gave rise this link was maintained, with functionalists placing particular emphasis upon modernisation, Marxists on capitalist and socialist patterns of industrialism, and Weberians on historical bureaucratisation. But the link was somewhat weakened, the intertwining between theoretical frameworks and comparative investigations becoming less intimate in terms of the one leading to the constant revision and reformulation of the other. The contemporary debate represents a further step in this direction in its abandonment of any significant two-way interplay and its concentration on autonomous theoretical issues, or rather problems which are treated autonomously because they have become cut off from comparative sociology. The burden of this paper is to argue for the indispensability of symbiosis and to do so in two ways. First, by examining the contemporary debate about the analysis of social structure to indicate how an important convergence of approaches is being inhibited because links with the comparative have been severed in favour of abstract theoretical models; second, to show how an explicitly comparative orientation can help to overcome this, illustrating the argument by reference to papers in this volume.

From the early 1960s onwards there has been a growing awareness of the underlying *theoretical* compatibility of Marxism and functionalism as first outlined by Van Den Berghe[1] and Lockwood.[2]

1

Recently this affinity has been celebrated by the American Sociological Association in the collective volume on *Approaches to the Study of Social Structure*.[3] It is founded not merely on recognition of the confluence of certain key ideas and concepts – 'contradiction' and 'strain', or 'structural context' and 'structural constraint' – but on the fact that both are concerned with the same kind of *systemic* enterprise.[4] In the two schools of thought the relationship between the component parts of social structure is viewed as being of crucial importance in accounting for the variance in social phenomena. By corollary both are equally concerned to explain three things: the arrangement of the parts in relation to one another, the way in which these emergent structural properties influence actors to produce observed regularities in behaviour, and the circumstances leading to structural change.

In the past these types of concerns set functionalism and Marxism apart from sociological approaches which endorsed the injunctions of methodological individualism. Their common denominator in methodological collectivism[5] was insufficient in itself to encourage *rapprochement* given the salience of sterile debates over consensus and conflict or stability and change, especially in the absence of a prominent school of thought firmly based on individualistic premises. However, developments of the phenomenological tradition with their rejection of objective structural and cultural properties and (concomitant) neglect of macroscopic problems have prompted a closing of ranks among macro-sociologists. For the position taken by both ethnomethodologists and the tougher versions of symbolic interactionism constitute an attack on the problems, subject-matter and methodology which are central to the latter.

By reducing social structure to the product of negotiations, transacted from zero in each new situation, the protagonists of ethnomethodology accept minimal constraints on individual freedom and maximal plasticity on the part of institutions. The result of denying links between situations, experiences and expressions and accentuating the uniqueness of particular contexts is, as Gouldner has noted, that they are not 'interested in why one definition of social reality becomes prevalent in one time or place or group and another elsewhere'.[6] Their lack of concern is consistent with their initial premises – the problem is perfectly uninteresting if situations are perfectly unique – for the answer will lie in the concrete particularities of the contexts and it is after all to their unpurged indexicality that they would have us address ourselves. The very act of generalizing, of attempting to learn from one situation and to apply this knowledge to the next, is considered purely conventional if done by the actor (even though logically a convention requires a precedent) and invalid if attempted by the investigator. Consequently the result of assigning individuals the liberty to make what they will of each situation they confront, unconstrained by past or contemporaneous transactions, is to reveal nothing about the conditions of successful negotiation or about what can be negotiated most easily. The mechanisms of social change, the specification of where and how, are alien to an approach in which all is equally malleable and where the combinations, tactics and attributes most likely to be influential cannot be determined extra-contextually.

Despite their acceptance of decontextualised meanings and search for rules relating experience to expression, the same is true of harder-line symbolic interactionism. Initially it might appear that since social structure, or at least social organisation, is admitted to be trans-situational (due to objectification), it would be possible to link such rules to patterns of social change. However in this approach organisation itself is still a construct and one which has no invariant relationship with objective factors, for the latter have no 'empty and deterministic' influence upon the definitions given to situations. Consequently the rules linking experience of social organisation to interpretation of it and then to subsequent action patterns have little purchase upon empirical reality. It follows therefore that these rules cannot in any way be translated into practical statements about the objective circumstances or conditions under which change is likely to occur. The distance between constructed and empirical reality makes rules relating to the former inapplicable to the latter.

A typical and explicit macro-sociological reaction to these two developments is provided by Coser and is perhaps of additional interest given his early and consistent attempts to bridge functionalism and 'conflict theory'.[7]

At a time when so many of our colleagues have succumbed to what I have called elsewhere 'a veritable orgy of subjectivism', it is most fitting, I think, to re-emphasise that the analysis of objective social structures, rather than exclusive concern with variegated constructions of reality, is the cornerstone of the sociological enterprise. If we are not to give in to a social psychologism that would disregard an outside reality which sets bounds to the strivings and desires of individual actors and retreat into prepotent concerns with individual cognitions, perceptions, and subjective impressions, we have to return to the heritage of Marx, Simmel and Durkheim, which is teaching us that individual striving is not sufficient to free us from the grip of societal constraints. And if we do not wish to limit outselves to queries about how the ethnos thinks, but desire instead to provide instrumentalities for changing society with the help of our interpretation, lasting concern with the

3

stubborn facticity of structural arrangements will have to be in the very centre of our inquiries.[8]

The reanimation of concern about the precise nature and force of structural arrangements was common to macro-sociologists, despite major internal differences over how to conceptualise the social system and which particular relations amongst its component parts should be accentuated.

Moreover, this tendency did not stop short at a realisation of their mutual compatibility and a substantial overlap of approach on the part of those working in the Marxist and functionalist traditions, it also prompted some moves towards theoretical convergence between the two perspectives. Fundamentally these concerned a growing similarity in the way in which the relations between parts of the social structure were conceived of in both schools of thought. This convergence can broadly be summarised as a move away by functionalists from 'mutual determinism', in which every component element universally affects every other, and a corresponding shift by Marxists from 'mono-determinism', where one element consistently has more influence on others than they upon it. Rejection of these extreme and mutually exclusive positions made way for the joint exploration of the relative interdependence or autonomy of parts within the social structure. It also carried with it further implications for a conjoint theory of change, at least in formal terms, based on the common exploitation of the relationship between systems integration and social integration.

Comparative studies and theoretical convergence

As far as functionalism is concerned, there is no doubt that the way was paved for this move by those of its adherents who had been most closely involved with comparative investigations. Here a variety of studies homed in on a basic criticism of the Parsonian assumption that the whole social system must be conceptually constituted prior to the analysis of specific patterns. To them the elements of social structure could not be constituted a priori, that is assumed to be given a particular patterning according to the needs or prerequisites of the social system as a whole. Nor could the examination of the parts primarily be restricted to their contribution to system maintenance or adaptation. In this they were closer to the earlier Mertonian view that the types of functional relationship between parts must be established by empirical research rather than theoretical fiat.

The problematic nature of the relationship between parts came to the fore in studies like Smelser's,[9] which pointed to the unsynchronised nature of changes in different institutional spheres during the process of industrial development, or Eisenstadt's,[10] which concluded that societies may arrive at broadly similar evolutionary stages in terms of differentiation of their major institutional or symbolic orders without sharing the same concrete institutional contours. Anthony Smith's recent critique of the functionalist theory of change[11] abounds with detailed examples of this kind, where authors have recognised the fallacy of equating structural change with institutional problem-solving as if these solutions were given within the system and guaranteed by automatic systemic adjustments. Initially the comparative detection of a lack of mutual dependence between all parts, of incompatible relationships, and of institutional autonomy led to a decreased stress on interdependence, whilst increased importance was placed on equilibration. As Smith has succinctly argued,

> whereas the earlier periods of functionalism highlighted the role of equilibrium and understood the social system as an interdependence of mutually compatible parts, the more recent phase has tended to re-emphasise the fundamental evolutionary framework within which social equilibria function and develop.[12]

Increasingly, however, the debate with other forms of macro-sociology lead certain neo-functionalists not merely to de-emphasise interdependence but to accept it as a problematic. Eisenstadt's current reaction is significant here, for it recognises that the concentration on evolutionary change does not dispense with the problem of structural arrangements.

> The fact that the various aspects of social life upheld by the different approaches seem to be accepted as evolutionary universals of human society does not explain the crystallization of any of their specific concrete types. . . . Hence any given institutional arrangement – be it the formal structure of a factory or a hospital, the division of labour in the family, the official definition of deviant behaviour, or the place of ritual in a given social setting – was no longer taken for granted, as given and derivable from its functional place in the social system; and the different patterns of behaviour that developed in connection with it were no longer examined only or mainly in terms of their contributing to the working of such a setting or of deviance from it. Instead or in addition to the former emphasis, the very setting up of such institutional arrangements was transposed from a given into a problem to be studied in terms of processes of negotiation among the participants in these processes.[13]

5

Nevertheless, as Eisenstadt is quick to point out, widespread recognition of this problematic did not result in a common or immediate theoretical reformulation amongst neo-functionalists. Two major problems had been posed but left outstanding; on the one hand how the parts of society were related to one another and on the other how structural change was negotiated. Recent replies have tackled these questions fruitfully, but in doing so have abandoned theoretical assumptions about mutual interdependence and immanent equilibration, and thus mark a distinct move towards convergence with parallel Marxist reformulations.

Complementary moves have characterised the Marxist tradition and are underpinned by a steady shift away from mono-determinism in the period following the Second International. Such developments have had two distinct but related aspects. On the one hand the general rejection of 'economism', a doctrine which reduces other social institutions to epiphenomena of the economic base and views the relationship between them as both universal and uni-directional, has spelt a loosening up in the conceptualisation of 'base' and 'superstructure'. Instead of the latter 'reflecting' or 'refracting' the former, which assumes a one-way relationship of domination and dependence, their dialectical interplay has been reasserted, and, as a corollary, a greater autonomy has been assigned to the superstructure to allow for it acting back on the base in a bilateral relationship. On the other hand the same question about degrees of autonomy and interdependence has been raised within the superstructure itself, with a radial model of spokes in which each institution is linked separately to the economic hub being replaced by various models of relations between superstructural parts themselves which allow for internal variations in dependence and domination.

Undoubtedly comparative sociological and historical studies have provided the spur to such developments for, as Hobsbawm has argued, 'one of the most characteristic features of contemporary Marxist historiography is the critique of the simple mechanical schemata of an economic-deterministic type.'[14] Comparative analysis of the emergence of different modes of production, and especially the Asiatic mode,[15] raised problems about the structural predominance of the economic sphere especially given the relative autonomy and social pre-eminence of kinship organisation in earlier societies. This question of relative institutional autonomy *coupled with* the notion that their independence could affect the nature of a given mode of production was taken further by Gramsci in his analysis of the state, which was embedded in an attempt to account for the contemporary Italian structure. In turn this signalled a debate about whether the state was the only institution in a position to play this role – and one which has largely been answered in the negative by Western Marxists who have stressed the existence of equivalent cultural phenomena.

In sum, those employing the comparative and historical perspective in Marxism started to address the specific interconnections between the diverse components of social structure whose patterning distinguished one social formation from another. This carried with it an implicit rejection of simple evolutionary schemes[16] where systems were ordered uni-dimensionally, according to the economic element alone. Instead, since all the diverse parts and their relations made for the distinctiveness of particular social formations, then schemes of historical development had to deal with the sequence in which different *social* structures not economic stages, followed one another. In other words, the principles of ordering must be multidimensional. However, because the patterning of each formation is distinctive, any evolutionary schema has to be a multilinear one, for there is no way in which every formation can be arranged hierarchically in relation to every other in terms of development or in terms of chronology. Thus, in direct parallel with the functionalists there has been a shift away from using evolutionary universals as factors which can account for the concrete characteristics of particular societies. Indeed as in contemporary functionalism the problem has been transposed, with more attention now being given to how the parts adhere together in seemingly different formations and are rearranged to give rise to structural change rather than to empirical problems about *historical* transition.

Abstract theory without a comparative perspective

From the neo-functionalist standpoint Gouldner has presented the outline of a systematic theory about the relation between parts which also contains an embryonic account of structural change. It starts from a critique of 'mutual determinism' which constitutes one of the main criticisms that he levels at Parsons. Because the latter regarded interdependence between parts as given and relations between them as reciprocal influences, Parsons begged the question of whether all elements in a system were equally influential in determining the state of the system as a whole or the condition of any of its parts. Gouldner instead advocates a 'stratified systems model'[17] which focusses on the *differential* causal influences of the elements operating together in a system. Since interdependence (termed functional reciprocity) cannot be assumed, Gouldner conceptualises social structures as strung out along a continuum such that at one extreme each element (part of a system) may be involved in mutual interchange with all others, whilst at the opposite extreme, each element may be involved in mutual interchanges with

7

only one other.[18] Why a particular pattern of relationships between parts characterises a given society at any time is not discussed and Gouldner leaves the degree of functional reciprocity and autonomy to be established empirically, being more interested in the consequences than the causes of particular structures.

The potential for change is rooted in the relationship between the parts and is formulated as follows. Any one structure is more likely to persist if it engages in reciprocal functional interchanges with some others; the less reciprocal the functional interchange between structures, the less likely is either structure, or the patterned relation between them, to persist unless compensatory mechanisms are present.[19] The impetus for change thus stems from the most autonomous units, the loci of organised opposition to system controls, whilst the most interdependent elements will tend to be sources of stability. The precise nature of social organisation is then seen as being shaped by the resolution of conflict between these centrifugal and centripetal forces. This of course in turn indicates the generic type of process which at an earlier date presumably gave rise to the initial structure which had to be discovered empirically. Three aspects of this analysis spell movements away from normative functionalism which should be more congenial to the Marxist tradition: the accentuation of conflict as built-in to structural arrangements, the instance that particular parts of the system make different degrees of contribution to systemic stability or change, and the conviction that structural change is shaped by conflictual interaction.

Furthermore, the fact that Gouldner treats interdependence and equilibrium as relatively independent 'dimensions capable of significant variations in degree'[20] – and makes little real use of the latter concept, represents an important departure from the steady state theory implicit in organismic functionalism. Linked to this is an explicit endorsement of society as an open system, where component elements may be partly exogenous and partly endogenous, which thus cuts through the lengthy debate about whether change originates from within or without. Taken together they are indicative of a broader trend amongst neo-functionalists to drop the organic systems model in favour of a cybernetic one which focuses on the structure-elaborating and changing features of the inherently unstable system: on morphogenesis rather than on homeostasis.[21] Whilst the equilibrium or organic model stresses negative feedback effects which restore structure, general systems theory accentuates those positive feedback mechanisms leading to structural elaboration through amplifying deviations from the original structure. And these may be adaptive or non-adaptive in their consequences. Since the amplificatory processes themselves are the results of social interaction, the human actor has been released from his position as a ghost in the machine, an automaton who mediates systemic requirements, to become an active party to social change. This linkage between structure and process, in which the former conditions the latter and is in turn modified by it, brings general systems theory closer to Marx's outlook on history as a dialectical development, in which change originates from conditions immanent in previous structures through the mediation of collective conflict.[22]

Parallel developments can be found in the neo-Marxist tradition, certain recent trends in French Marxism showing them at their most pronounced. For purposes of illustration the work of Althusser and Poulantzas will be used, not because their approaches are assumed to be typical even in France, but because the former specifically addresses the first question about the relations between base and superstructure, seeking to theorise about them rather than leaving them to be determined empirically, whilst in the same vein the latter concentrates on the second question of relationships within the superstructure. Both begin with a clear rejection of 'economism', not merely because it reduces other institutions to epiphenomena and thus dispenses with the need to study them, but also due to its subsidiary assumptions that every change in the social system happens first of all in the economy and that because a part is subordinate to the base it no longer plays a dialectical role. Like Gouldner they are thus concerned with the differential causal (and of course temporal) influence of elements operating together in a system.

Their analyses, like his, revolve around the autonomy and inter-dependence of the component elements. Superstructural institutions are seen as concrete, distinct, and relatively autonomous within the overall structure. Thus the state is viewed as partially independent of the ruling class and the economy: furthermore, independence is a matter of degree (e.g. Fascism is considered the extreme example of the state's autonomy in capitalist society). Within the superstructure both authors underline that the various parts possess a notable autonomy among themselves and draw a very similar distinction between the organised, centralised and interdependent relations prevailing among repressive agencies (government, army, police, judiciary etc.,) when compared with the more flexible and independent relations between cultural agencies (churches, schools, unions etc.,) operating within the same system.[23]

The autonomy assigned to the parts is not in their view contradicted by their simultaneous stress on economic determination 'in the last instance'. Althusser solves this apparent paradox in the following way:

the economic dialectic is never found in a *pure state*, so that in History these instances which constitute the superstructures etc.,

9

are never observed to respectfully make way when their work
is done or to scatter and leave His Majesty the economy
to advance along the royal road of the dialectic. From first to
last, the lonely hour of the 'last instance' never sounds.[24]

Another method of expressing this is that autonomy consists in the
capacity of different parts of society to change in different ways, at
different times, and at different rates from each other. Because of
this social development is not homogeneous but is made up of the
sum of uneven institutional changes, working on different time-
scales, and able to do so because of their relative autonomy. These
surges, lags and temporal discontinuities are characteristic of *every*
social formation because, logically, the last instance never can come.
As with Gouldner the importance attaching to relative autonomy
is in its contribution to social change. This is clear in Althusser's
notion of a 'revolutionary conjuncture': a period in a given social
formation when the specific autonomy of each sphere has given rise
to uneven institutional development and thus to major disparities
between them.[25] This specification of the revolutionary conjuncture,
the site of multiple contradictions, brings them closer to general
systems theory because of its affinities with morphogenesis, and thus
indicates a further area of theoretical convergence. Finally, a distinct
step towards functionalism itself is taken as part of their broader
attempt to trace the different arrangements and displacements of
parts and branches across the full spectrum of social formations.
In answering the charge of merely having advanced a 'multi-factor
approach' which simply charts the practical combinations and per-
mutations of institutional relationships in successive formations,
Althusser defends the *theoretical* nature of his analysis by insisting
on the functional indispensability of institutional changes to the
economy. 'Only this "determination in the last instance" enables
one to escape from arbitrary relativism towards the observed displacements (between institutions) since it gives these displacements
the necessity of a function.'[26] Indeed this particular shift has been
taken a good deal further by Godelier who conceptualises 'base' and
'superstructure' not as structural relations between institutions but
in terms of functions, such that whatever element performs the
function of the relations of production is thus accorded domination
over other parts of that particular social system in his scheme.[27]

Theoretical models without comparative correctives

In the foregoing discussion of neo-functionalist and neo-Marxist
developments I have tried to show how both built upon intervening
comparative work in their respective traditions and display some

convergence in their approaches. However I now want to argue that nevertheless these contemporary theorists are engaging in a type of exercise which separates them off from the earlier trends in both schools, which were firmly rooted in comparative sociology, and which constitute the groundwork of the present debate. Basically it seems that the theorists just discussed are all still seeking (as did traditional Marxists and functionalists) for *universal rules* which will render the patterning of relationships observed in social structures *logical* ones. Now the explanation of structural arrangements is the object of all macro-sociologists, but one can question whether to concentrate on universal rules is the best way of going about it and this is what I shall do in the present context.

The explanation of institutional arrangements is an abstract theoretical exercise for the authors discussed; it is in no way based on empirical generalisation nor thus upon comparative data. Instead both groups take their starting points from the fundamental premises of their respective traditions and these act as the key to the rules that they establish. Both proceed as if a *basic architectonic principle* was known *a priori* and only needed theoretical elaboration and refinement in order to elucidate the universal rules. In criticising this procedure I shall mainly be stressing three undesirable consequences which stem from it: first, and ironically, that this takes both full circle back to the 'multiple determinism' and 'mono-determinism' which they rejected, only to reinstate them in new guises. Second, that this in turn re-establishes mutual incompatability and blocks the prospect for fruitful convergence and interplay heralded by the earlier comparative work in both schools. Finally, that their abstract and ahistorical character renders them unhelpful to those who want to explain a particular structure, variations between them or the the relationship of a particular institution to others, either over time or in different societies . . . in other words to the practical concerns of most macro-sociologists.

Although in both approaches the concepts of interdependence and autonomy are used for discussing institutional relationships within social structures, they in fact define these terms in completely different ways. These differences reflect their adherence to the traditional premises of the schools of thought from which they work. Although unlike Parsons, Gouldner wishes to consider the interdependence of systems parts as problematic not given, he remains a Parsonian in assessing the existence and degree of interdependence *from the point of view of the system*. It is with reference to the *whole system* that parts are assigned high or low autonomy, and with it a different potential for bringing about change. High interdependence is said to exist where each part of the system is engaged in mutual interchange with all others and its opposite, (where each part

11

exchanges with only one other), accords every element 'high functional autonomy'. However each such part is considered to be autonomous because it has the least *number* of relationships of interdependence with other parts. Autonomy then is defined *quantitatively*, in relation to the system and the potential number of interdependencies this could accommodate. It is indeed *functional* autonomy, in the systemic sense of providing few services for other parts of the whole, rather than *operational* autonomy meaning a capacity for self-determination. This becomes clear if instead of defining autonomy quantitatively from the point of view of the whole system it is considered qualitatively in terms of the nature of the relationship sustained with the only element to which it is integrated. An institution may only be interdependent with one other (like education with the Catholic Church in medieval Europe) but it may be so completely subordinate to it that it has no freedom for self-determination. Indeed it may have much less than an institution which has a more reciprocal relationship with several others (like modern education), but thus to Gouldner has lower functional autonomy. In other words multiple determinism has been abandoned as a given, only to become an ordering principle of a rather crude numerical kind. It is an architectonic principle in the sense that it orders the relations among component elements, drawing the boundaries between centre and periphery and distributing the potential for change to the latter and pressure for maintenance to the former.

Furthermore, there are difficulties involved in applying this scheme to study change in social systems, yet Gouldner clearly has hopes about its practical utility. 'It may be that the notion of differential functional autonomy of system parts may provide an analytical tool for the qualitative discrimination of factors contributing importantly to system change'.[28] In fact it is precisely when qualitative considerations are introduced, and Gouldner is sure that they must be, that problems arise. This can be elucidated by comparing the above quotation with his discussion of reciprocity and imbalance, i.e. qualitative aspects of relations between parts. There he confronted two interdependent structural parts (the number of their other independencies was not introduced), and showed how under certain conditions imbalance could develop in their interchange so that one could end serving the other, thus suffering a reduction in operational autonomy. This results from the quality of their relationship. Moreover one of the very conditions under which such an imbalance (and subsequent loss of operational autonomy for one part) is likely to occur is in the *absence* of a third party playing a policing role, with which both were interdependent. In other words here the *lower* the number of interdependencies, the greater the likelihood of losing *operational* autonomy, yet the *higher* the *functional* autonomy is considered to be. Given high functional autonomy this part should contribute to system change: given its low operational autonomy it will be unable to do so. Thus the systemic considerations (quantitative) and the institutional ones (qualitative) give rise to different expectations, unhelpful in practical research and calling for reformulation.

The way in which Althusser and Poulantzas define interdependence and autonomy reflects the tradition from which they work even more obviously. In one sense these characteristics are what they appear, i.e. the dominant institution is the one which subordinates most parts and manifestly displays the most interdependencies, whilst the autonomous elements show the greatest operational freedom.[29] But the relations between them, the very fact that some are dominant, some subordinate and some autonomous is itself determined. So too are the capacities of the parts to develop unevenly according to different time-scales. Thus to Althusser

the fact that each of these times and each of these histories is *relatively autonomous* does not turn them into so many domains which are *independent* of the whole: the specificity of each of these times and each of these histories, in other words their relative autonomy and independence, are based on a certain kind of internal articulation of the whole, and thus a particular *type of dependence* on it.[30]

They are as it were consigned degrees of freedom, just as other parts are allocated dominant roles, in a given social system whose structuration is determined by the economy. Precisely the same notion is voiced by Poulantzas about the superstructure:

each particular form of capitalist State must be referred back, in *its unity*, to important modifications of the relations of production and to important stages of class struggle: competitive capitalism, imperialism, state capitalism. Only *after* having established the relation of a form of State as a unity, *that is as a specific form of the system of State apparatusses as a whole*, with the exterior, can the respective role and mutual internal relation of the 'branches' of the state apparatus be established.[31]

The economy then is the architectonic principle, it places parts in a hierarchical order, assigns an element a dominant position, and later displaces it, and allocates different roles to other parts: its superdetermination consists in, and can only be grasped through, the shifting articulation of the parts with one another which ensures that society as a whole continually provides the non-economic conditions for the reproduction of the mode of production. Neither

author considers that this reduces such institutions to epiphenomena of the economy, since they furnish the conditions for its
existence, but it is hard to resist Miliband's conclusion that such an
approach represents a return to mono-determinism:

> the state is not 'manipulated' by the ruling class into doing
> its bidding: it does so autonomously but totally because of the
> 'objective relations' imposed upon it by the system. Poulantzas
> condemns the 'economism' of the Second and Third Inter-
> nationals and attributes to it their neglect of the state (p. 68).
> But his own analysis seems to me to lead straight towards a
> kind of structural determinism, or rather a structural super-
> determinism, which makes impossible a truly realistic
> consideration of the dialectical relationship between the state
> and 'the system'.[32]

This assessment seems justified, for it is not practically possible to
examine the relationship of one element to another or of one
institution to the system without examining the system as a whole,
the whole and the parts being inseparable. For it is its overall
structuration which determines these relations and thus precludes
any sociological investigation which does not *begin with the system*
but seeks to attribute observed relationships to particular causes.
The latter would be especially fruitless since the system can respond
to an aspect or a change of its environment by displacing its component parts in a number of different patterns. Yet the way in which
the whole operates on the parts is opaque, assumed to be automatic,
and detectable only by its effects – i.e. the very arrangement of
parts which most macro-sociologists are concerned to explain.
There is thus a circularity involved which defies empirical assault.
If we seek to examine the parts (*explanandum*), we are told that we
need to understand the whole as it is organised by the economy
'in the last instance' (*explanans*), but this in turn can only be detected
via the structural organisation itself (*explanandum*). In fact this
circularity operates at two different levels: at the level of the system
as we have seen, but also within the superstructure itself, where the
notion of the state 'in its unity' carries with it exactly the same
implications as the concept of the 'structure in domination'.

In the two traditions of thought basic deficiencies have been
traced back to the fact that their modern exponents begin with the
system itself and seek to isolate a set of universal rules which make
the observed interdependencies between parts appear as logical
ones. Since the rules themselves are simply retranslations of the
traditional premises of functionalism and Marxism it is unsurprising
that the end products are as incompatible with one another as were
their prototypes. In other words, although *formally* these two sets of

abstract theorists are the heirs of the comparative work which preceded them, the revisions which this prompted are *substantively* little more than reformulations which encompass certain key ideas from the intervening period, such as institutional autonomy and temporal discontinuity. This regression has occurred largely because links with comparative sociology have been severed in favour of building abstract theoretical models which in turn do not lend themselves to empirical test or elaboration.

Symbiosis between theoretical and comparative sociology

Alternatively these earlier comparative studies can and have prompted a completely different approach to the analysis of social structure, and ultimately one which seems to hold out more hope of profitable theoretical convergence. Fundamentally this consists in taking the interdependencies which define the social structure as truly problematic. It involves starting from these relationships and examining their patterning in its own right. Here any internal logic of structural organisation will be discovered through them rather than being imposed upon them. Such an approach would be concerned with whether a particular part of society is always related to another over time, whether it is consistently subordinate, whether there are conditions under which it is independent of a third, whether there are clusters of components engaged in reciprocal exchanges or hierarchies of domination and subordination, and above all which of these patternings do not co-exist with others. If systems have a similar logic in their structuration this will emerge from the systematic study of the ways in which their component parts are related.

By definition this kind of approach is both comparative and historical but there is nothing about it which is inimical to either the functionalist or Marxist traditions. Indeed Anderson has lately had occasion to stress the essentially historical nature of Marxist materialism and to devote two comparative studies to the discussion of different types of social structure.[33]

> If the proper designation for Marxism is historical materialism, it must be – above all – a theory of history. . . . Marxist theory is not, despite every laudable temptation, to be equated with a revolutionary sociology. It can never be reduced to the 'analysis of the present conjuncture' in a now fashionable terminology. For by definition, what is current soon passes. To confine Marxism to the contemporary is to condemn it to a perpetual oblivion, in which the present ceases to be knowable once it recedes into the past. Few socialists would dissent from this. Yet the exact statute of history within historical materialism

15

has paradoxically never hitherto been adequately debated. . . . Marxism has in this sense perhaps yet to take with all due seriousness its claim to be a 'science of history'. For the proud title of historical materialism can only be earned by a modest respect for the reality of its two terms.[34]

Importantly in this connection Bottomore has underlined that this enterprise does not reinvoke historical dogmatism.

The general Marxist framework of explanation, in terms of the relation between classes and their connections on one side with the system of material production and on the other side with cultural production, can be used in various ways; and it does not in my view commit us to a single philosophy of history or to a rigid conception of the total historical process.[35]

Certainly, given their underlying belief that particular economic elements are of crucial importance in determining the general form of any society, the Marxist selectively focuses attention on how other institutional orders were related to them over time. Nevertheless there is a considerable difference between this type of exploratory approach which uses the comparative method to establish degrees of interdependence, is open to the discovery of autonomy, or configurations of independent factors, and one which assumes in advance that the same architectonic principle holds for all times and places. Not only is the former open to test whilst the latter is not, but equally importantly the first is capable of specification. It can lead to a series of statements about the conditions under which the economic order influences other spheres most strongly and under which these other institutions display most independence. This potential for convergence at the propositional level is equally clear on the part of those neo-functionalists who have retained their connection with comparative sociology, whether of societies, institutions or organizations, whilst abandoning the organic model in favour of general systems theory. For example, Blau and Buckley have tried to specify the general conditions under which one institution can end serving another. Both specify four conditions under which imbalances in obligations incurred in transactions between two parts produce differences in power, that is the subordination of one institution. Here the conditions of power are defined negatively by the absence of the basic alternatives to it: (i) providing goods/services for the benefits gained, (ii) obtaining the benefits wanted from an alternative source, (iii) securing them by force, and (iv) renouncing the need for them.[36] This type of approach which proceeds from analysis of the qualitative relations between parts, appears to be a real vehicle for theoretical convergence. For the cases delineated by it, (where conditions are present for the emergence of institutional power), could profitably be compared with clear Marxist examples of institutional subordination to the economy or hierarchies of domination within the superstructure, to discover whether these two sets of instances have a common anchorage in the same relational properties.

Furthermore, the explanation of these properties themselves also invites convergence in terms of the social processes bringing them about, and thus accounting for the genesis of the resultant structures. In discussing the four alternatives to power, Blau recognises that:

(i) above, raises problems about the exchange processes that develop and the distribution of resources in a community that governs them and is modified by them;

(ii) leads to the study of competitive processes, of established exchange rates and of monopolisation;

(iii) calls attention to the organisations in which power is mobilised, to political processes and institutions; and

(iv) points to the analysis of common values or the emergence of ideologies.[37] In other words his analytic framework extends an invitation to Marxists to demonstrate whether their particular understanding of the distribution of social resources, of political action, and of ideological consciousness, fill in the background and explain the systematic rather than *ad hoc* patterning of institutional relationships. This confrontation of propositions, as Jonathan Turner argues, is the real stuff from which theoretical synthesis develops rather than cordially vacuuous agreements on the reconcilability of general assumptions.[38]

It is to this type of development that the chapters in the present volume can contribute, for they represent the most open version of this alternative approach to the analysis of social structure. All of their authors start from a substantive concern about the nature and change of a particular part of society rather than from abstract theoretical preoccupations. This leads most of them to adopt a procedure which is rather different from that just discussed, but which is none the less useful to it precisely because of its greater openness.

Those who undertake comparative work from an explicit theoretical stance tend to home in upon and hover around those problems and areas of central concern in that tradition as has just been seen: alternatively those who engage in comparative sociology because of an interest in a substantive area make this central to their analysis. The latter adopt a strategy which is akin to spinning the globe to look at a particular country; this then is the focal point and other areas are examined in relation to it rather than in their own right. Thus a particular institution or collectivity (A) is examined in terms of its relationships with others, for example (AB) (AC) (ABC) (AD) though not mechanically as this suggests, with the aim of formulating propositions about the circumstances under which they are related and why these patternings change. This type of proposition is of course itself theoretical, and is not necessarily restricted to the 'middle range'. However, because of their substance they present the opportunity for a two-way interplay with other propositions, which have been elaborated from a particular school of thought. On the one hand the comparative analyses presented here represent the kind of material which any more general theory must be capable of embracing, by showing how these propositions can be subsumed under higher level ones. It represents a perpetual challenge to any sociological theory which claims a higher level of generality, for it constitutes a source both of refinement and refutation. It can refine and extend because grand theory can be grandly mute about certain problems, (search the founding fathers for a sociology of sport), yet the comparative propositions advanced might be perfectly compatible with existing overarching ones. In this way it helps to work out the various etceteras which are usually attached to the latter, yet are unexplored by them, like some of the undifferentiated statements quoted earlier about 'schools, churches and trade unions'. Even more importantly comparative sociology, undertaken because of a central interest in a particular phenomenon and sifting the mass of data accordingly, actively maintains a logic of scientific discovery because it ensures that the class of potential falsifiers for larger-scale theories is filled in practice rather than merely being 'not-empty' in principle. In other words comparative sociology exerts a continuous pressure towards theoretical refinement and reconstruction.

On the other hand the kinds of regularities and patternings discovered by comparative sociology can point up the utility and necessity of certain kinds of theoretical development and thus invite the elaboration of general theory in certain directions. Thus the open approach to comparative sociology is not only a source of practical refutation but is also a ripe field for bold conjecture. Precisely because it slices through the data at a different angle, (guided by relevance to a specific problem and hypotheses entertained about it), the propositions generated provoke speculation concerning their relationship with others, whether through challenging prior assumptions, revealing gaps in knowledge, confronting previously discrete phenomena, or opening up new areas of debate. A particularly good example of this is provided by Krejci's analysis of ethnic movements which follows. The salience and success of the quest for nationality that he traces in twentieth-century politics almost demands a reconsideration of lines of political cleavage and their relative weightings as well as speculation about relations with class-

18

based politics and contrary tendencies towards centralised decision-making structures.

Taken as a whole, this collection of papers illustrates, in different ways and to different degrees, the contributions comparative sociology can make to theoretical development through prompting refinement, reformulation and speculation.

Of the chapters that follow their authors differ in terms of the parts of society they select and define for comparative analysis. Thus several authors, Martin, Harries-Jenkins, Causer and to a lesser extent Bourdieu and Boltanski take an explicitly institutional approach. Others are specifically concerned with a particular collectivity like migrant workers (Giner and Salcedo), the intelligentsia (Vaughan), ethnic minorities (Krejci), management (Pichierri) and industrial workers (Scase). What they share in common is a concentration on the part selected, an attempt to account for the patterning of its relationship with others in different places and to detect and explain changes in such interdependencies over time.

David Martin's discussion of religion in Europe focuses specifically on the relationship between a structural factor (power at the level of the state) and a cultural one (religious identity, affiliation and organisation) and seeks to explain different national patternings of interconnection between them. The nature of both institutions, together with the history of their interplay is used to account for their contemporary interdependence, autonomy and their mutually supportive or antagonistic roles. Historically he argues that a tight relationship between them at the time of national emergence arose where the Church was the only available vehicle of nationality against foreign domination, whereas the two were considerably more independent when there were several distinctive religions within a national border, each with major followings, for then no religion could carry the national identity whilst the coexistence of several religions worked divisively against it. He argues that this 'set' at a nation's birth exerted an enormous constraining force for the future and then analyses the multiplicity of institutional changes which led to modifications in both the interdependent and independent cases.

Harries-Jenkins engages in a very similar exercise when examining the relationship between the polity and the military. However he concentrates on certain universal European developments within the armed forces, in particular their emergence as bodies of professional specialists and managers, no longer isolated at the periphery of society by their primary involvement in foreign policy, and asks how this international type of institution is related to the various kinds of civil powers. He argues that the superior organisation of

19

the military, their professional attributes, inner-group loyalty, and monopoly of arms, inevitably give the armed forces some domestic political power even where law and constitution emphasise the dominance of civil authority. However, at one extreme he distinguishes countries with virtual political subordination to the military where, given instability, the armed forces manipulate politics by varying their support for different political parties; in the middle are examples of extensive military pressure groups whose political efficacy derives from close links with big business (a military-industrial complex); at the other extreme are countries where the trend towards a completely volunteer army has created a position of political isolation at least among the lower ranks. These are all however cases of variation in the degree of interdependence and in contrast to Martin's analysis of contemporary religions no analagous examples of military autonomy from the national polity are discernable. The military-political links differ in degree rather than in kind and are less complex given the absence of a military pluralism to match that of religious organisations.

Causer's paper is interesting in this connection for he too explores *degrees* of interdependence and in fact starts from the proposition that to say the state in capitalist societies supports the general interests of capital is a virtual tautology. In other words merely to show that there is *a* degree of interdependence between these institutions obscures the complexity (both historical and contemporaneous) of relations between the state and private capital, as it did with politico-military relations. Instead Causer outlines the conditions under which governing elites can pursue policies independently of the interests of capital despite their overall dependence on private enterprise for economic development. The potential for autonomy is greatest where the political structure is authoritarian, retains a patronage system, is still partly run by pre-capitalist elites, has acquired legal and financial controls over business, and where important sections of the labour force are not organisationally integrated into party politics. He also insists that even where the constraints placed on governments by capital are greatest this does not mean that political policy is entirely shaped by business: the relationship is still one of reciprocity not dependence, and he suggests that these qualitative considerations could usefully be conceptualised in a framework stressing exchange and power.

Whilst Causer discusses degrees of interdependence in a relationship which some have interpreted as one of complete dependence, Bourdieu and Boltanski are concerned with the opposite – the detection of an underlying interdependence between parts which superficially appear to be becoming more independent of one another. In examining the interfaces between occupational structure, class

20

stratification and the educational system, they in fact seek to show that the three remain closely linked despite appearances indicating their progressive dissociation. In pointing to the joint transformation of the system of reproduction (in particular the declining significance of direct inheritance) and of the method of appropriating profits (especially the increasing tendency to extract it through salaries) they locate the source of intensified use by the upper classes of educational institutions. This practice ensures the perpetuation of the class as a whole but at the same time conceals it since educational reproduction operates at the level of individuals – the failure of some members of this class obscuring the re-creation of the collectivity. Since the mechanism responsible for the endurance of these institutional connections is the conversion, across two generations, of economic and social capital into cultural capital, Bourdieu and Boltanski are also putting forward a set of propositions having affinities with exchange and power theory.

Other contributions deal less with the interrelationships between social institutions than with the relationship of a particular group to its institutional setting, whether this is to society as a whole or only to certain of its parts. In so doing they are more explicitly concerned with the connections between social and system integration than the first group of authors who mainly concentrate upon the latter. Because of this they address the question of structural and cultural change more directly than those seeking to explain a given pattern of interrelationships. However, at the formal level their procedure is of the same open type, and again consists in moving their particular group to the centre of the stage and examining the way in which it impinges on various institutional spheres and they in turn exert constraining influences upon it. This kind of approach can both inform and test broader theories of change in the same way that those just discussed contribute comparative data and insights to wider theories of structuration.

Krejci's analysis of ethnic problems deals with both sides of the question and he orients his paper around the difficulties encountered by ethnic groups in search of national self-determination (the constraints they meet) and the effects of ethnicity on attempted integration into multi- and super-national associations or confederations (the effects such groups exert). He shows a consistent movement throughout the twentieth century towards acquisition of statehood on the part of ethnic groups, and a commitment to separatism or devolution amongst those who have not yet achieved it, which can override differences of politics, class and religion. The increased salience of ethnicity underlines an enduring problem for Marxist theory which has long been encountered in communist practice. For, as Krejci argues, the strain that ethnicity exerts towards decomposition of the multi-national state is only doubtfully contained by combining federation with the unifying force of a new ideology, particularly when the latter is imposed coercively thus destroying much of its potential for integration. However, he also stresses that the problems created by ethnic affiliation are not confined to the emergence of centrifugal tendencies at times of crisis in Eastern Europe, but represent a series of exigencies affecting the social cohesion of all countries with an indigenous, immigrant or imported ethnic element.

One of the groups included by Krejci is taken up by Giner and Salcedo – the migrant workers. In this particular case the authors deal predominantly with the constraining influences which converge upon these ethnic groups whose reciprocal effects on structural change are largely confined to the unintended. Thus they detail the socio-economic disadvantages accumulated by foreign migrant workers (market fluctuations, wage differentials, official discrimination etc.), which are only offset by the improvement their present position represents over their original situation. From these and other barriers which prevent the integration of the short-stay workers into the host working class, questions arise about their potential for initiating change or exacerbating existing antagonisms. However, despite scattered examples of solidary or particularitistic insubordination, the manipulation of migrant inflows and outflows, together with management of migrant activities, are sufficient to consign most to a role of passive subordination such that the major effect of their employment is a boost to economic development without high costs in terms of social disruption being incurred.

Paradoxically, considering its traditional prestige, Michalina Vaughan presents an analysis of the intelligentsia which reveals it, too, to be severely constrained by modern institutions and increasingly ineffectual in bringing about social change. On the one hand the development of mass education and expansion of white collar occupations have deprived the intelligentsia of its cultural exclusivity, whilst the existence of plural political outlets has largely robbed it of its mission to save society from autarchy. On the other hand the internal cohesiveness of such a group has been weakened by the integrative power of societies which have won the allegiance of some members, and by the economic advantages available which have secured the calculative adherence of others. Together these structural and cultural changes have undermined the intelligentsia as a stratum. They have also underscored its dependence as a distinct and influential group on a social structure displaying considerable institutional discrepancies between the rates of industrialisation, bureaucratisation and educational expansion, such that the limited output of the latter consistently outstripped the ability of the former

22

to absorb it. By comparison the modern intellectuals lack the external social conditions and internal cohesion to guide social change after the manner of the old intelligentsia.

The last two chapters examine different sides of the same coin; with Pichierri analysing changing management strategies for work rationalisation, and Scase investigating workers' conceptions of power in different socio-economic structures. Despite the growing internationalisation of capital, Pichierri shows that management ideologies are sufficiently independent to display differences in social systems whose methods of production are substantially the same. However, in tracing the more rapid decline of the Taylor approach in Europe than the USA, he only partially attributes the shift towards a policy of greater participation in the European organisation of labour to innovatory entrepreneurial attitudes. Equally important were the constraints stemming from strong trade unions, firmly linked to left-wing political parties. Ultimately it is the influence of the unions, especially given the presence of socialists in parliament, which is held to account for the differences between Europe and the USA. In other words the extent to which labour organises and inserts itself into the central political structure in turn conditions the degree to which the organisation of labour can be managed in industry.

Within Europe Scase considers that Sweden differs from Britain in that the self-interests of the economically dominant classes are more restrained because of the greater representation of the labour movement in Swedish processes of political decision-making. Here, however, he is less concerned to demonstrate that political insertion exerts a moderating influence upon management than to show that it intensifies knowledge of and hostility towards inegalitarianism amongst the work force. Thus, in looking at the same institutional connections between unions, polity, and industry, Pichierri is accentuating the negative feedback loop which constrains the latter, whilst Scase is stressing the positive feedback loop which intensifies the awareness and perhaps the action of the former.

Conclusion

In this paper I have sought to demonstrate the indispensability of a continuous interplay between the theoretical and the comparative analysis of social structure. One point should perhaps be stressed in conclusion, namely that the symbiosis between the two is conceived of here as an active analytical exercise, quite distinct from the passive co-existence of both enterprises or from any scanning of the comparative field from within a hermetically sealed theoretical framework. Instead it involves acceptance of empirical adequacy as the ultimate criterion of theoretical explanation (which the latter position rejects) and also a continuous scientific dialogue in which comparative investigation and theoretical formulation are inextricably intertwined (which co-existence neglects).

If passive co-existence is infertile, some of the most arid theorising results from rejecting symbiosis whilst pretending to address comparative sociology. In the case of functionalism this frequently led to the plunder of historical and cross-cultural data in the verificatory search for persuasive illustrations of rigid theoretical constructions. Today there is a strand of Marxism whose violent anti-empiricism renders comparative sociology equally impotent, by reducing it to the fodder from which concepts can be constructed, but against which they cannot be validated.[39] Both insist on the primacy of the theoretical and correspondingly install a one-way traffic with comparative sociology. A neo-functionalism which constructs social systems *a priori* and fits comparative data to them, and a neo-Marxism which replaces objective conditions by abstract constructs, are not likely to draw closer together nor to contribute much to the analysis of social structures.

Notes

1 Pierre Van Den Berghe, 'Dialectic and Functionalism: Toward a Theoretical Synthesis', *American Sociological Review*, vol. 28, October (1963).

2 David Lockwood 'Social Integration and Systems Integration', in G. K. Zollschan and W. Hirsch (eds), *Explorations in Social Change*, Boston, Houghton Mifflin, 1964.

3 Peter M. Blau (ed.), *Approaches to the Study of Social Structure*, London. Open Books, 1976.

4 Cf. P. Sztompka, *System and Function: Toward a Theory of Society*, New York, Academic Press, 1974.

5 I am using this term to refer to all those who endorse descriptive individualism whilst also accepting explanatory emergence, following Brodbeck's definition of these terms. Cf. May Brodbeck, 'Methodological Individualisms: Definition and Reduction', in Brodbeck (ed.), *Readings in the Philosophy of the Social Sciences*, London, Collier-Macmillan, 1968.

6 A. W. Gouldner, *The Coming Crisis of Western Sociology*, London, Heinemann, 1971, p. 391.

7 Lewis A. Coser, *The Functions of Social Conflict*, Chicago, Free Press, 1956.

8 Lewis A. Coser, 'Structure and Conflict', in Blau (ed.), op. cit.

9 Neil J. Smelser, *Social Change in the Industrial Revolution*, University of Chicago Press, 1959.

10 S. N. Eisenstadt, 'Social Change, Differentiation and Evolution', in N. J. Demerath and R. A. Peterson (eds), *System, Change and Conflict*, New York, Free Press, 1967, pp. 229f.

11 Anthony D. Smith, *The Concept of Social Change: A critique of the functionalist theory of social change*, London, Routledge & Kegan Paul, 1973.
12 Ibid., p. 130.
13 S. N. Eisenstadt and M. Curelaru, 'Macro-Sociology: Theory, Analysis and Comparative Studies', *Current Sociology*, vol. 25, no. 2 (1977), p. 44.
14 E. J. Hobsbawm, 'Karl Marx's Contribution to Historiography', in R. Blackburn (ed.), *Ideology in Social Science*, London, Fontana, 1973, p. 282.
15 Cf. D. Giori, *Sul Modo di Produzione Asiatico*, Milan, Franco Angeli, 1972; R. Garaudy (ed.), *Sur le mode de production Asiatique*, Paris, Ed. Sociales, 1969; F. Tökei, *Sur le mode de production Asiatique*, Budapest, Kiado, 1966.
16 Cf. Robert A. Nisbet, *Social Change and History*, New York, Oxford University Press, 1969.
17 Gouldner, 1971, op. cit, pp. 219f.
18 A. W. Gouldner, 'Reciprocity and Autonomy in Functional Theory' in Demerath and Peterson, op. cit.
19 Ibid., pp. 150f.
20 Ibid., p. 155.
21 In the cybernetic perspective such changes of state are seen as necessary and inherent to the operation of complex systems – a property which Buckley terms 'morphogenesis'. This refers to 'those processes which tend to elaborate or change a system's given form, structure or state' and is contrasted with 'morphostasis' which refers to those processes (environmental exchanges) that tend to preserve or maintain a system's given form, organization, or state. (Walter Buckley, *Sociology and Modern Systems Theory*, New Jersey, Prentice-Hall, 1967, pp. 58f.)
22 Put in terms of our earlier discussion, societies and groups continually shift their structures as adaptations to internal or external conditions. Process, then, focuses on the actions and interactions of the components of an ongoing system, such that varying degrees of structuring arise, persist, dissolve or change. Perhaps the first names we think of in the context of such a perspective are those of Marx and Engels, with their view of history as a dialectic process whereby new structures arise out of conditions immanent in previous ones. (Ibid, p. 18)
23 Cf. Nicos Poulantzas, *Pouvoir politique et classes sociales*, Paris, Maspero, 1968, chs 2 and 3; L. Althusser, 'Ideology and Ideological State Apparatuses', in his *Lenin and Philosophy and other Essays*, London, New Left Books, 1971.
   Although to both the arrangement of the parts is viewed as determined – Poulantzas states that within the superstructure 'the condition of possibility of the existence and functioning of these institutions or ideological apparatuses, under a certain form, is the State repressive apparatus itself' ('The Problem of the Capitalist State', in Blackburn (ed.), op. cit. p. 252) – similarly Althusser argues that the organization and articulation of base and superstructure is determined by the economy 'in the last instance'.

24 Author's translation. The original reads

> jamais la dialectique économique ne joue à l'état pur, que jamais dans l'Historie on ne voit ces instances que sont les superstructures etc. . . . s'écarter respectueusement quand elles ont fait leur oeuvre ou se dissiper comme son pur phénomène pour laisser s'avancer sur la route royale de la dialectique, sa majesté économie parce que les Temps seraient venus. Ni au premier, ni au dernier instant, l'heure solitaire de la 'dernière instance' ne sonne jamais.
> (Louis Althusser, *Pour Marx*, Paris, Maspero, 1967, p. 113.)

25 This appears to be the main point of his giving Lenin's analysis of Russia in 1917 (as did Gramsci), as an example of a revolutionary conjuncture, since Lenin concentrated on the cumulation of uneven developments – large-scale industry, techno-bureaucracy, semi-feudal agriculture, autocratic monarchy.

26 Author's translation. The original reads 'seule cette "détermination en dernière instance" permettait d'échapper au relativisme arbitraire des déplacements observables, en donnant à ces déplacements la nécessité d'une fonction' (Louis Althusser, 'L'Objet du Capital', in L. Althusser, E. Balibar and R. Establet, *Lire le Capital*, Paris, Maspero, 1967, vol. 2, p. 46).

27 M. Godelier, *Horizon trajets marxistes en anthropologie*, Paris, Maspero, 1973.

28 A. W. Gouldner, 1967, op. cit. p. 168.

29 This is what enables Althusser to dissociate himself from structuralism. To him the surface-structure is real. Reality is not hidden behind the appearances but is the structured relationship obtaining between the component parts of society. Whereas structuralists attempt to reduce this to abstract models possessing a greater generality, Althusser insists that he wishes to understand concrete reality by means of theory.

30 Author's translation. The original reads,

> Que chacun de ces temps et chacune de ses histoires sont *relativement autonome*, n'en fait pas autant de domaines *indépendants* du tout: la spécificité de chacun de ces temps, de chacune de ces histoires, autrement dit leur autonomie et indépendance relatives, sont fondées sur un certain type d'articulation dans le tout, donc sur un certain *type de dépendance*.
> (Louis Althusser, 'L'Objet du Capital', 1967, op. cit., p. 47.)

31 Poulantzas, 1973, op. cit., p. 248.

32 Ralph Miliband, 'Reply to Nicos Poulantzas', in Blackburn (ed.), 1973, op. cit., p. 259.

33 Perry Anderson, *Passages from Antiquity to Feudalism*, New Left Books, London, 1974; *Lineages of the Absolutist State*, New Left Books, London, 1974.

34 Perry Anderson, *Considerations on Western Marxism*, New Left Books, London, 1976, pp. 109–11.

35 Tom Bottomore, 'Structure and History', in Peter M. Blau (ed), 1976, op. cit., p. 165.

36 Cf. Walter Buckley, 1967, op. cit., pp. 201f.; P. M. Blau, *Exchange and Power in Social Life*, New York, Wiley, 1964, ch. 5.

37 Blau, op. cit., p. 140.

38 When attempts are made to break down these somewhat arbitrary barriers, synthesizers typically attempt to reconcile the *assumptions* (rather than propositions) or two or more perspectives, which, for the synthesizer, reveal more convergence than was heretofore perceived by members of the discipline. Such activity can prove useful if it is followed by a more difficult task: synthesizing the actual theoretical statements that were inspired by the respective assumptions of each of the synthesized perspectives. (Jonathan M. Turner, *The Structure of Sociological Theory*, Homewood, Illinois, Dorsey, 1974, p. 146.)

39 Another more recent and most glaring example of this kind is provided by B. Hindness and P. Q. Hirst, *Pre-Capitalist Modes of Production*, Routledge & Kegan Paul, London, 1975.

2 Private capital and the state in Western Europe
Gordon Causer

Introduction

That the state in capitalist societies operates in such a way as to serve the general interests of the owners of private capital, if only by guaranteeing the legitimacy of the system of private ownership, goes almost without saying. Without this guarantee it is difficult to see how a capitalist economic order could survive. Thus the proposition is virtually tautological – a point often overlooked by Marxists writing on this subject.[1] But it does not necessarily follow from this that there is a ruling class, in the sense that owners and controllers of private capital, by their disproportionate share of political power and influence, are able to direct the social and economic policies pursued by the elements of the state apparatus, or that policies of the state running counter to their interests can be interpreted simply as a 'ransom' paid by capital as the price of retaining its dominant political position, particularly when these policies are often formulated and implemented in the face of vigorous opposition from substantial sectors of business.[2]

Any attempt to formulate a very general description of the relations between the state and private capital tends to overlook the fact that neither 'capitalism' nor 'the state' are fixed and immutable social forms, but display a wide range of historical variation. While the structure of a particular capitalist economy places substantial constraints on possibilities in the political sphere, the historically conditioned form taken by the state power (and, more generally, by the political system) may in its turn shape the options open to capital, and affect the way in which the economy itself develops. As Giddens has pointed out, assertions that capitalism can 'accommodate itself' to a variety of political regimes obscure the different forms taken by capitalism in different societies, and the role played by the form of political regime and the internal dynamics of the political system in conditioning these differences.[3] In addition, the channels of pressure and influence open to capital are themselves conditioned by the form of political regime. In analysing national societies we find that the channels of power and influence open to business, the coherence of the policies pursued by business groupings, the form and extent of countervailing power – and thus the specific extent and modes of exercise of the political power of capital – are subject to substantial variation. In this sense it is true to say, as Finer does, that 'there is in short no political power of private capital as such. There is the political power of British businessmen during a particular period and in particular circumstances; and likewise of American business-men, German, French, Latin American and so on.'[4]

In the first part of this chapter I shall indicate some of the sources of variation in the political power of capital, drawing on evidence from several Western European societies, before going on to consider the significance of post-war developments in supra-national economic and political organisation, and the implications for the general analysis of the power of business in capitalist society.

II Capital and the nation-state

Given the complexity of social and historical forces shaping the development of national societies, and the range of economic and political institutions, it is doubtful if any taxonomy of the factors affecting the power of capital can be wholly comprehensive. But six may be distinguished:

(i) the organisation and extent of common interests among the owners of capital;

(ii) the level of organisation and ideological orientation of the labour movement;

(iii) the power, influence and interests of other social groupings;

(iv) the degree of cohesion and interpenetration of elites;

(v) the concentration and degree of freedom of the economic power of capital;

(vi) the structure of the political system and political regime.

Together, these factors do much to account for the degree of auto-nomy of the state power from dependence on private capital. These six factors are not always easily distinguished one from another, and stand in a relation of mutual conditioning and influence.

(i) The organisation of business interests

There can be little doubt as to the generally high degree of effective-ness of business and capital as a sourse of organised pressure and influence, a fact partly related to the generally high level of political organisation attained by business groups.[5] But just as capitalism is not a monolithic entity',[6] so 'capital' is subject to internal divisions of interest over and above the shared interest in the maintenance of a system of private property and the provision of adequate conditions for the pursuit of private profit. A number of bases for such divisions of interest may be suggested – financial/industrial capital; domestic/foreign market orientation; labour intensive/capital intensive sectors; large/small business; as well as divisions which occur on specific issues.[7] Of these, that of size of firm is one of the most important, size of enterprise being closely related to both relative cost of labour and capital, and market orientation This is not to say that other divisions, notably that between financial and industrial capital, are without significance, though here the long-standing interpenetration of financial and industrial capital in certain societies[8] and the general European trend to growing interpenetration[9] may reduce its importance.

The political power and influence of the large firm is enhanced by its ability to deal directly with the state apparatus,[10] its greater capacity to shift resources and operations between markets, and the frequent domination of the 'peak associations' of business by larger firms.[11] Yet this domination is not always the case. The British Employers' Confederation was for many years dominated by labour-intensive sectors, leading to a relatively 'hard' line on labour relations.[12] The small capitalist and militantly anti-interventionist CGPME was, for a long period, a significant force in the French Confédération National du Patronat Français, reaching a high point of influence in the adoption in 1965 by the CNPF of a policy of economic liberalism and employer paternalism, though declining rapidly in significance with the reorientation of the CNPF from 1969 onwards.[13] Similarly, some authors have seen the Italian Confindustria as dominated for much of the post-war period, at least in the labour-relations field, by the small and paternalistic employers, a position which may also have been altered by recent shifts in policy and organisation.[14] But, even where big business dominates the major interest groups, the very existence of separate organisations of small business can constrain their policies and actions by the threat of open dissension.[15]

However, while it is easy to overstate the degree of consensus and shared interest among business groups,[16] we must recognise that in many cases big and small business may operate in alliance. In certain cases big business 'shelters behind' the needs or interests of small business in seeking to secure wage minima or price controls geared to the situation of the marginal firm rather than to that of the large enterprise.[17] Alternatively big business may actually share the orientations of small business, even where its interests might be better served by the pursuit of different policies – e.g. the lowering of protectionist barriers by the French government after the war, while threatening small rather than big business, was initially opposed by business in general due to the protectionist and output-restrictive attitudes of all French business in the pre-war period.[18] Divergence of both goals and interests is perhaps sharpest in the field of labour relations, where small enterprises tend to remain paternalistic and opposed to trade unions, while the larger enterprises, more able to provide better wages and conditions, and less able to impose their will on a large labour force, have a strong interest in the regularisation of labour relations through the institutionalisation of conflict.

In general, post-war governments in Europe have pursued policies more consonant with the interests of big business than these of small firms, though the Christian Democrat governments of Germany in the 1950s made active efforts to promote small and medium size enterprises in accordance with the economic neo-liberalism of the social market economy.[19] Elsewhere such developments as the promotion of economic concentration by British and French governments in the face of foreign (chiefly US) competition, the 'opening to the left' in Italian government, the partial freeing of industrial relations from government regulation in Spain, the establishment of the conditions of increased international trade, and so on, have tended to favour the interests of enterprises in the more concentrated and advanced sectors of the economy, and have often conflicted with the aspirations and interests of small business. Yet in each case factors other than the interests of big business have played a major part in these decisions – the influence of the French technocrats of the Plan in promoting the rationalisation of French business; the need of the Christian Democrats to retain their dominant political position in the face of declining electoral support, and the changes in Catholic attitudes during the papacy of John XXIII, in facilitating the opening to the left against widespread (though not complete) business opposition; the influence of Opus Dei (which cannot be regarded simply as a business pressure group, despite its business ties), the goal of maintaining an authoritarian state in changed political and economic circumstances and Franco's manipulation of the supports of his regime to maintain his position in the liberalisation of the Spanish economy; the role of the movement for European unification in promoting the EEC; and so on.[20]

The essential point is that business and capital are not homogeneous groups, and that the interests that all share in common may be limited. The extent to which business can present a united front affects its capacity to influence decisions – e.g. the French CNPF was unable to play a significant role in the discussions on the formation of the EEC due to internal divisions, and similar instances have been reported in Germany and the UK. Likewise level and form of business organisation may affect the capacity to exert influence. This was clearly recognised by British industry when, in the face of a unified trade union movement, and a new level of government intervention in the economy based on formalised tripartite policy discussion, three formerly separate organisations merged to form the Confederation of British Industry.[21]

Finally, the level of concentration in the economy, and the relative balance between large and small enterprises is itself significant, in that the greater the level of concentration of economic power, the greater are the possibilities of concerted actions by substantial groupings of business which constrain the options open to the state power and other potential countervailing forces.[22]

(ii) The organisation and orientation of labour

While it is tempting to locate the relative strength of the counter-vailing power of labour in the degree of unionisation in a society, the political orientation of the unions and their linkages with political parties are at least as significant. Three points are relevant in analysing the implications for the power of business.

First, if business possesses a significant source of leverage through its 'surrogateship' role – its provision of goods and services which would otherwise have to be provided by government (see section (v) below), sections of labour possess an analagous power through the capacity to withdraw labour and impair the normal functioning of society.[23] Despite the generally weaker bargaining position of the worker, the potential effectiveness of this source of power is clearly indicated in recent times by the success of the 1974 strikes of coalminers in Great Britain and public service workers in West Germany, in both cases leading governments to breach existing policies of wage restraint. Indeed, if the imposition of incomes policies in general can be seen as indicative of the power of business,[24] the limited effectiveness of these policies in the absence of trade union support, and their frequent tendency to collapse, can be seen as indicative of the power of labour.[25]

Second, the power potential and mode of its exercise is related to the extent/strength of ties between political parties and unions, and particularly to the degree to which associated parties have the possibility of gaining office, and the extent to which they remain dependent on coalition allies. Attention has rightly been drawn to the way in which Social Democratic governments when in office tend to act as much as regulators of the labour movement as its agents,[26] but while there is considerable truth in this, it is not wholly the case, as is indicated by the extention of worker rights by German Social Democratic governments, and the repeal of the Conservative

Industrial Relations Act by the British Labour government.[27] Much will depend here on the orientation of the unions themselves. It may be that in countries where historical circumstances have tended to blunt worker and union militancy (e.g. the Netherlands, W. Germany, Sweden) working-class movements are more likely to turn to the use of electoral politics to secure gains – thus, on the one hand, increasing the possibilities of influencing and participating in political decision-making while, on the other, increasing the possibilities of being drawn into a general elite consensus.[28]

Third, the effect on the power of the labour movement of ideological/religious divisions is problematic, for while it renders concerted action difficult (and the association of growing co-operation and increasing success in the Italian labour movement in the late 1960s indicates the importance of this)[29] the experience of Sweden, West Germany and (to a lesser extent) Great Britain indicates that a unified labour movement may more easily be integrated into a dominant consensus. At the same time, the presence of labour sections within predominantly conservative parties can act in some measure as a counter-balance to the dominance of business – e.g. the role of Catholic trade unions in supporting the reformist wing in the Italian Christian Democrat party,[30] and the influence of the workers' wing in the German Christian Democratic party, and especially in the party's Social Affairs Committee.[31]

(iii) Other significant power groupings

Peasants and small farmers. The agrarian sector, like business, displays divisions of organisation and interest, notably in societies such as Italy and France where a substantial pre-modern agricultural sector persists alongside modern capitalist agriculture. The resultant relations between agricultural groups, business and the political system are consequently complex, but three ways in which the agrarian sector may affect the interests of capital may be outlined.

First, agrarian groups, by the successful pursuit of their goals, may act against the interests of business, even where business does not directly oppose them. Thus in France (and in the EEC in general) successful pressure of farmers for protectionist policies and an extensive price support system through the artificial raising of food prices runs counter to the interests of business in the maintenance of cheap food prices to keep down the wage demands of organised labour.[32]

Second, and associated with this, is the significance of agrarian groups in conservative (especially Christian Democratic) parties as an interest which the formulators of policy must take into account.[33]

33

Third, and related to this, is the fact that the agrarian organisations can, at least where there is a substantial agrarian sector, provide alternative sources of financial and other supports for these parties. Thus, in Italy, the attempt of the Confindustria to re-establish its privileged relationship with the Christian Democrats after the failure of its pursuit of an independent political role, was thwarted by the party's development of new sources of support, including the Coltivatori Diretti (small and medium farmers).[34]

At the same time business and agriculture, both inclining toward a conservative viewpoint, may prove allies in many circumstances[35] but this should not obscure the fact that even here the success of the influence of business can be conditioned by its need for alliance with other groups.

Pre-capitalist elites. By reference to pre-capitalist elites I do not want to imply that these are groups which necessarily disappear or lose their elite position in capitalist society, but that they are groups which more typically act as autonomous sources of power in pre-capitalist (or semi-capitalist) social formations. I shall discuss three such groups here – traditional agrarian elites, military elites and religious elites.

1) TRADITIONAL AGRARIAN ELITES. While disappearing wholly in the fully developed capitalist economic order, these groups retain their significance in so far as the traditional agricultural sectors in which they predominate persist. Their political influence in societies such as Italy and Spain[36] is of interest here in so far as, by impeding the modernisation of the social order, they prevent the development of a fully capitalist economy, and, by providing alternative sources of political support for conservative parties and administrations, shape the orientation and policies of government. In this context we may mention the continuing underdevelopment of the Italian south which, while benefiting northern industry by providing a source of cheap labour, at the same times tends, at least in the long term, to generate a more militant labour force than would otherwise be the case, and to hamper the development of an internal mass consumer sector, and hence orients Italian business to the societies of northern Europe;[37] and the continuing predominance in much of post-war Spanish government of elites drawn from traditional sectors, giving rise to attitudes of resentment and estrangement on the part of Spanish business.[38] However, perhaps of more direct importance is the role of pre-capitalist groups and social formations in shaping the present political structures of societies – a point which will be developed further below.

2) THE MILITARY. While the leadership of the military remains a significant elite group in advanced capitalist societies,[39] its direct intervention in politics is more typical of pre-capitalist or semi-capitalist societies. The role played by the military depends on the historical constellation of forces and circumstances in a national society, and its impact on state–capital relations and the form of capitalist development will be similarly variable. Thus the part of the armed forces in bringing de Gaulle to power in 1958 is significant, in the main, for the impact of the Gaullist regime on French political institutions and social and economic policy; the seizure of power by a predominantly petit-bourgeois military group in Greece was significant for the way in which the junta's absence of any coherent economic policy, its inherent distrust of business and its heavy reliance on foreign investment inhibited the development of indigenous Greek capitalism; while the close ties of business with the military were a factor in the development of a more modernised capitalism in Spain. In the Spanish case military mistrust of cabinet domination by the technocratic Opus Dei and the exploitation of grievances over pay by Falangists and right-wing conservatives, together with the problems of political unrest following on the partial liberalisation of industrial relations, played a part in the reimposition of a more authoritarian political order and the eclipse of Opus Dei in government circles, thereby hampering the development of a fully modernised neo-capitalist order.[40] More recently, events in Portugal have indicated the significance of the military as an autonomous locus of power in societies which, if not fully capitalist, none the less possess substantial capitalist sectors.

3) RELIGIOUS ELITES. While the typical effect of religious institutions has rightly been seen as sustaining the existing order,[41] this is not the whole picture for disagreements on the form of this order may bring the political weight of religious circles (most significant in those countries with Christian Democrat or other church-affiliated parties) into conflict with the goals of business. The effect of shifting attitudes in Italian catholicism in facilitating the opening to the left has already been referred to,[42] and in general the reformist orientation of social Catholicism – as expressed for example by the Centre des Jeunes Patrons (subsequently the Centre des Jeunes Dirigeants des Enterprises) in France, may bring a section of Catholic employers into conflict with their fellows.[43] More generally, the measure and type of integration of the elements of the political system with religious institutions may act as a significant conditioning factor with regard to the balance of political forces. This point is perhaps most clearly illustrated in the Netherlands, where the system of Protestant, Catholic and liberal and socialist secular *zuilen* or

'pillars', each with its own set of associated institutions, played a significant role in promoting an especially close interpenetration of elites and a pattern of institutionalised accommodation between elites. This interpenetration and accommodation (involving governmental, business and labour elites) may help explain the long-term success of Dutch wage-restraint policies in the 1950s, just as the breakdown of the pillarised structure from the late 1950s onwards may be associated with the declining viability of such policies.[44]

(iv) Cohesion and integration of elite groupings

Of significance here are both the extent of mutual interpenetration of the elite groupings in society, and the degree of formalised modes of consultation and co-operation between them. This is a larger subject than can be adequately dealt with here but in the context of the political power of business, two points should be made.

First, there are substantial national differences in the degree of interpenetration between the worlds of business and finance and the sectors of the state apparatus. Thus the level of involvement of men of business backgrounds in cabinets and legislative assemblies shows substantial national variations, having been generally very low in Spain and Greece, exceptionally high in the Netherlands and of a relatively moderate level in most other Western European societies.[45] Likewise, the pattern of movement from the state administration to private industry, commerce, etc, is not a universal feature of capitalist society, reaching its highest level in France, but conversely being fairly rare in Italy, the differences reflecting the different characters of the state bureaucracy.[46] (In the context of Italy, it should be noted that there is substantial overlap of personnel in the private sector with those in the public sector of the economy.)[47] Furthermore, the principal modes of access by interests in general, and business in particular, to the state apparatus vary according to the relative significance of these sectors – thus in France, with the weakness of the legislature during the Gaullist period, access to the bureaucracy has been of more significance, while in Italy and West Germany, where the legislature and parliamentary committees can play an important role in the formulation of policy, access to these may be of equal (and in Italy possibly greater) significance.[48] As the relative capacity of business groupings and other interests to gain access to the different sectors of the state apparatus may vary, this may be of particular significance to the outcome of individual policy-decisions.

Second, the extent to which the interest groups of organised labour are integrated within a national political elite may be significant, both in enabling trade unions to exercise effective counter vailing power to that of business, and in affecting the degree to which trade unions are integrated within a general consensus and thus likely to exercise such power. (The two effects are not necessarily contradictory, as the relative involvement of trade unions may affect the precise form which the consensus takes.) The role of joint labour-management-government bodies for the discussion of economic policy (such as the British National Economic Development Committee, the Dutch Social and Economic Council, and the Swedish Economic Planning Board) may be particularly important here, though their very existence is likely to be dependent on the degree of elite integration in society, which may facilitate or hinder such developments. Thus in the French planning process the technocrats of the plan were to a considerable degree able to select for consultation those who displayed a general sympathy for the goals and objectives of the plan, thus substantially avoiding the formalised interest group consultation which might have given a greater weight to the unions and to those business elements (represented in the CGPME) most opposed to state intervention. A similar pattern characterised Spanish efforts at planning. In contrast, the necessity of securing TUC involvement in the planned tripartite direction of the British economy, and the general preference of Whitehall for consultation of formalised bodies, led to a strictly 'interest group' mode of representation in the NEDC (especially after the accession of the Labour government in 1964), which inhibited the development of planning in accordance with the French model.[49] Similar bodies have been able to operate with formal representation in Sweden and the Netherlands due to the high level of elite integration in the former, and the long-established pattern of formalised accommodation grounded in the *zuilen* system in the latter.[50]

(v) *The economic power of capital*

Much, though not all, of the political power of the owners of capital derives directly from their control over substantial economic resources, and in particular from what Finer has called their 'surrogateship' role – the fact that much of what industry produces is 'in the public interest', and would otherwise have to be provided under government auspices.[51] The extent to which this power potential is in fact realised is dependent not only on the degree to which the owners and controllers of capital are willing to use economic sanctions (and hence on the political culture of the society and the attitude to the particular government in power)[52] but also on the measure of restraint placed on its use by legal or de facto limitations. While the extent of these limitations is itself an outcome of the balance of political forces in society, it has in its turn consequences for this balance. Thus while the concentration of control over economic resources in fewer hands, and their linkages through such means as holding companies and interlocking directorships[53] confronts governments with consolidated blocs of economic power, the control of such concentrations by anti-monopoly legislation and laws prohibiting (as in Italy) or limiting (as in West Germany) interlocking directorships might shift the balance of bargaining positions. (The significance of interlocking directorships has been queried with the argument – based on empirical study—that, due to their non-executive role and the very multiplicity of their director- ships, those involved possess little effective control over business activity, having a predominantly legitimating function. It might, however, be possible to accept this and still argue that such directors can act as agents and intermediaries on behalf of their companies in the pursuit of particular goals in the wider social and political environment.[54])

There are of course possibilities of evading the limitations placed by governments on concentrations of economic power, and Western European governments in particular have been confronted by the ambiguities of pursuing a policy of limiting concentrations of economic and market power, while simultaneously protecting and promoting such concentrations in the face of growing competition from foreign enterprises. In addition several societies (notably France and the Netherlands) have a long tradition of a benign government attitude towards cartels and concentration, and even in West Germany, where the neo-liberal doctrines of the social market economy enjoined vigorous state action, the 1957 act was allowed to be seriously modified by business pressure.[55] The paradox here is that the more governments seek to limit the incursion into national economies of multi-national enterprises over which they have limited power, the more they are compelled to build up domestic concentrations of economic power which, by virtue of their size and the increasing multi-nationalism of their operations, themselves become less amenable to government control.[56]

At the same time governments possess other resources which may enable them to place limitations on the actions of enterprises, and to shape the direction of the development of the economy. There is no space here to go into the multiplicity of controls, aids, incentives, etc, which governments may use to influence the direction of the economy, but as a most striking instance we may cite the role played by the weakness of the French capital market, and the consequent control of the government over the bulk of investment resources, in enabling the planners to promote the extensive modernisation and rationalisation of the French economy in the post-war years, and the more recent attempts to use the plan, by selective use of incentives, as a device to promote government policies.[57] Generally speaking, the more business has the capacity to finance itself independently of government, through self-financing or provision of alternative sources of funds (as, for example, in Germany by the banks[58]), the less control government has, even potentially, over its activities.

Similarly, the greater capacity business has to shift its resources between sectors, and even more importantly, between countries, the greater becomes the dependence of government on business for the realisation of its own goals. This is seen at its most acute in countries such as Greece, which are heavily dependent on foreign capital and have limited means of attracting it, but has become particularly important in other economies as the growth in the volume of international trade increases the significance of balance-of-payment considerations.[59] Faced with payments problems, an actual or threatened 'flight of capital' becomes a major constraint on government action, compelling policies to restore business confidence. This is most dramatically illustrated by the flight of capital from Italy in 1963/4 impelled by the accession of the centre-left government and its nationalisation of electricity, and compelling the government to abandon plans for establishing taxation on a more equitable basis.[60] Again governments possess the formal means of dealing with this through exchange-control mechanisms, but, as Hirsch has pointed out, this is difficult to enforce without the consent of the holders of capital themselves, and this is least likely to be forthcoming for precisely those governments of the left-of-centre who are most likely to use this device. Faced with these problems governments are compelled to seek the support of international bodies who may make the pursuit of policies likely to restore business confidence a condition of assistance.[61]

Thus, while on the internal political front the governments and administrations of capitalist societies are frequently able to act contrary to the political demands of business, the impact of the growing multi-nationalism of the economy presents increasing constraints on their ability to do so. I will return to this point in section III.

(vi) The political structure

In capitalist societies, given the 'surrogateship' of business, and the heavy dependence of government on business for the realisation of its own objectives, the 'natural' situation is for the policies of government to be heavily constrained by the goals and interests of business. Yet, within this general constraint, there may be a range of options open to government, and this range of options, and those which are chosen, is conditional, not only on the factors which have been outlined so far, but also on the historically developed structure of both the political regime and the broader political system. This is most apparent in authoritarian regimes, and those with greater or lesser vestiges of political patronage structures. Thus Franco and his governments were able to maintain a largely autarchic, protectionist policy (favourable to the interests of small business) from the end of the Civil War to 1958, and to shift thereafter to a policy of limited liberalisation in the economy and labour relations, favouring the interests of big businesses more able to cope with international competition and collective bargaining. But while the continuing development of this trend would probably have served the interests of the bigger enterprises (including the foreign firms who moved into Spain on a large scale after 1958) by fostering the trend to a fully modernised society and economy with reasonably well-regulated labour relations, the *political* repercussions, with demands for change spilling over from the economic to the broader political sphere, led to a halting of the trend, and the eventual decline in the political influence of the principal agencies of economic (though not political) liberalisation, the technocrats of the Opus Dei. This is not to say that the situation in Spain was in any way positively disadvantageous to business, but that the principal changes in the general orientation of the economic policies of the Franco regime had as much to do with the problems of maintaining an authoritarian political order and the varying strategies used in pursuing this goal by Franco himself, as with the interests of, and pressures exerted by, business.[62]

The persisting influence of the politics of patronage is best seen in Italy where, despite the radical changes of the twentieth century the political parties still bear the marks of the origin of the political system in parties of 'notables' and their followers linked to a predominantly rural patronage structure. Thus today they remain characterised by highly organised factions associated with particular figures, and there remains extensive use of both the state bureaucracy and the parastatal agencies of the public sector as structures of patronage.[63] Thus the Christian Democrats, despite close early ties with the Confindustria, were able to free themselves from direct dependence on the bulk of organised business by the establishment of alternative bases of support, not only in the Coltivatori Diretti, but also in the state agencies, notably the Ente Nazionale Idrocarburi.[64] (It is an interesting corrective to the view that the financial resources of business are necessarily a means of access to political power to note that, in the period when the Confindustria shifted the bulk of its financial support from the Christian Democrats to the Liberal Party, the electoral share of the latter steadily declined.)[65] Yet at the same time the elements of the political system have constrained the Christian Democrats from using their relative autonomy from business interests to promote the widespread modernisation of Italian capitalism and Italian society beyond the tentative reforms of the early centre-left government. The very bureaucracy which was established as a mode of conferring patronage remains an inhibiting factor on development, constituting a drain on investment resources, a source of political opposition to modernisation and, in its complexity and inefficiency, fails to provide the state with the necessary instrument to promote large-scale and active government intervention.[66] Likewise, the extensive public sector, partly by virtue of the dependence of the dominant party on it, rather than vice versa, is inadequately controlled by government for its use as a co-ordinated policy instrument.[67] (In Italy, as in Greece, the absence of a modernised bureaucratic administration, and the persistence of significant relations of patronage in the political systems, with the opportunities for corruption and arbitrary application of policies implied by this, have prevented the state taking a very positive role in shaping or, in the case of Greece, developing the institutions of modern capitalism).

In this respect Italy differs sharply from France, where a long historical tradition of centralised government and *dirigisme*, coupled with the existence of a highly skilled elite administration and the possession of power resources such as control over extensive investment capital, enabled government to play an active role in the shaping and development of the economy in the post-war period, despite the existence of substantial sectors of business hostile to change.

In fully liberal-democratic regimes, such as Britain, West Germany and Sweden, governments with a popular mandate confront substantial and generally well-organised forces of private capital. Paradoxically, their apparently firmer grounding in popular support (which might be thought to enhance their power *vis-à-vis* concentrations of private economic power by giving popular legitimation to their demands) may in fact serve to increase the dependence of such governments on private capital. Given the dependence of such governments for the retention of power on the continuing support of the electorate, and the fact that electorates tend to hold the government responsible for their economic well-being or otherwise,[68] there will necessarily be a greater pressure on government to retain business 'confidence' and to encourage those private sector activities which are seen as conducive to the maintenance of economic prosperity. Thus the power derived by capital from its surrogateship role will tend to be enhanced by the subjection of the government to popular election. In a somewhat similar fashion governmental attempts in such societies to bring private economic decision-making

41

under more democratic control through planning mechanisms are likely, in the long run, to increase the dependence of governments on private business, as a major source of the information required for planning and a major agency in effecting the objectives of the plan.

At the same time, however, it should be recognised that the existence of such regimes facilitates the development of more powerful and effective trade union movements, and that in all of the societies mentioned above, social democratic parties, which have more or less special links with the labour movement, have entered into government. While this may plausibly be seen as having blunted the radical potentialities of these labour movements, it has also to be recognised as enhancing their capacity to influence specific policies. Hence differences between these societies in certain important respects are to be explained at least in part by the character of the labour movement, as well as by the general constraints imposed by the existence of a capitalist economy. Thus the much greater legal regulation of industrial relations in both Sweden and (especially) West Germany as compared with Britain is less a reflection of the relative power of business in these societies than of differing orientations on the part of their labour movements.[69] In Sweden, in contrast to Britain, the pattern of industrial development has been such as to foster and facilitate the regulation of industrial relations by centralised employers' associations and trade unions, whilst the long-standing political ascendency of the Social Democratic Party has encouraged the unions to pursue their ends as much by political as by industrial means.[70] Similarly, in West Germany a rationalised trade union structure, organised in the post-war period on industrial lines, permitted the predominance of regulated centralised bargaining, while the pre-war experience of inflation and social breakdown has acted as a continuing restraint on industrial militancy. Furthermore, the joint activity of employers and unions in resisting the post-war allied attempts to break up German industrial power, and the association of the 'social market economy' with the beginnings of the economic miracle, blunted the anti-capitalist orientations of German unionism, while a legal structure which operates to the general disadvantage of labour has been accepted at least in part out of a respect for the law engendered by the experience of Nazism.[71] In Britain, in contrast, the labour movement has remained suspicious of external intervention in its organisation and the conduct of its business, such suspicion arising in part from the fact that, due to the relatively high level of unionisation and shop-floor organisation, British unions have been able successfully to promote members' interests with little need to appeal to external agencies. In consequence, the struggle by unions to retain their autonomy has been a major factor in post-war British politics, furnishing several instances of the capacity of the unions to overturn government policies (notably with respect to the 1971 Industrial Relations Act and the Conservative government's incomes policy of 1974) and leading (following the estrangement of the Labour Party and unions over the former's plan for industrial relations legislation in 1969) to a growing influence of the unions in the Labour party by the mid-1970s.[72]

While it would not be true to say that these differences have made the British Labour party a more anti-capitalist party than its Swedish or West German counterparts (none display in any sense a systematic and coherent anti-capitalist philosophy) it is fair to say that, at least in the field of labour relations, the British Labour government has been less willing (or less able) to make or support policies which are unequivocally in the interests of capital, and that this must be related to the character of its associated trade union movement.

Of course, the differences between these societies are secondary, in a sense, to the general existence of a pro-capitalist consensus in all of them, in which the trade unions and social democratic parties are more or less integrated. But this does not mean that they are without significance or that they do not affect the ways in which the national capitalisms of these countries develop. Even where policies advocated by the unions may be argued to benefit the interests of capital – e.g. co-determination in Germany as a means of integrating workers in a capitalist consensus – these cannot be explained simply by the political predominance of business, but are often vigorously opposed by it. Nor does the fact that policies will tend to be formulated within broad parameters set by the dependence of governments on the private economic sector mean that the policies can be automatically deduced from that dependence.

III Supra-national political and economic organisation

The multi-national corporation[73] represents an even greater concentration of economic power than the large firm confined predominantly to the national market, and those who control it generally enjoy an even greater freedom of action in the disposal of their capital as, despite various attempts by national governments at regulating the inflow and export of foreign capital[74] their dependence on these firms for developing advanced sectors of production and providing employment limits the possibilities of regulating inflow, while the multi-national company generally has the capacity (through such devices as international intra-company transfer pricing, intra-company loans, leads and lags in trading payments, fees and royalties to parent companies) to shift its financial resources with only limited

43

constraint from national governments.[75] Further, the presence of multi-national companies can exacerbate the balance-of-payment constraints mentioned earlier, in that, as part of the normal 'hedging' operations carried out with liquid funds, they may move out of, and thus weaken, already weak currencies.[76] Despite this, most Western European governments, especially those with semi-developed capitalist economies, have generally welcomed multi-national companies for the new employment and the possible economic benefits they bring.[77] Concern is generally expressed at the take-over of existing firms by foreign capital rather than at the establishment of new enterprises.

However, while the multi-national company, for the reasons outlined, stands in a strong bargaining position *vis-à-vis* national governments, the position is subject to variation, in as much as firms may be committed to investment in a particular area, due to its possession of particular resources, and because, once capital is invested, the firm has a vested economic interest in remaining in production for a certain period.[78]

As has already been indicated, the principal response of European governments to the growing incursion of foreign multi-nationals has been to promote concentration among their own national industries to provide effective competition, thus creating greater domestic concentrations of economic power.[79] The same ambiguity of response has been seen in the European communities where the demands of competitive policy have had to be set against the goal of growing concentration of European enterprises to meet US competition.[80] Indeed, the EEC itself, while in one aspect opening up the possibilities of European competition to the US enterprise by providing a large 'domestic' market for European firms, at the same time provides an enhanced means of access (by the establishment of European subsidaries) to US enterprises themselves.

Despite the creation of a 'European' market, there are grounds for scepticism as to any generalised 'European' orientation and commitment to unification *per se* on the part of most European business, despite the general, if pragmatic, commitment of the national associations in the Union des Industries de la Communauté Européenne (UNICE) to the principle of unification – a pragmatic orientation illustrated by business opposition to community-level collective bargaining, feared as a means of harmonising pay and conditions upwards.[81]

Indeed, while there is general consensus that business groups in general constitute one of the most powerful political interests at community level, they share with most other interests a preference for operating primarily at national level.[82] In this they recognise the reality of the domination of community decision-making by the

Council of Ministers, and the primary importance of securing support for their interests at the national level. In addition, the problems facing any peak association in reconciling members' interests are multiplied at the international level, with rivalries of national capitalisms compounding other divisions of business interests. The same applies, though to a lesser extent, to the specialised industry associations. Many firms have preferred to work through these and (in the case of large firms) in direct relation to community authorities, rather than through UNICE. Banking groups are more supra-nationally minded, and have secured significant successes at community level, notably in getting banking exempted from the community's anti-cartel provisions.[83]

Despite its supra-national status, the EEC plays a limited role as a regulator of business activities. While it has had some measure of success in dealing with cartels and in changing certain national policies toward cartelisation,[84] its contribution to systematic economic planning remains limited.[85] In general the Treaty of Rome is less '*dirigiste*' in its orientation than the Paris Treaty which established the ECSC, and was thus able to secure a greater (though still somewhat reluctant) support from the business groups which had opposed the latter. Yet, while the decision-making process in the Community has had limited impact (with the exception of certain fields, notably agriculture) on national policy-making,[86] it has served to bring about certain shifts in attitude, notably the acceptance by German industry of the desirability of some measure of economic planning, consequent on their involvement in UNICE.[87] In general, given the persisting nationalistic orientations of member states, and the growing problems of pursuing common policies, doubts must be expressed as to the EEC's capacity to act as a significant counter-balancing agency to the powers of multi-national business.[88] Indeed, given the general commitment to the promotion of economic concentration of European business (action on concentration has been very limited compared with action on cartels[89]) the community tends to build up the concentrations of economic power, rendering control more difficult. Proposals for a European Company, and the general goal of free movement of capital, are similarly likely to increase the constraints on the freedom of action of national governments.[90]

In sum, it may be said that the growing trend to the internationalisation of trade, enterprises, and capital markets[91] tends to diminish the amount of freedom of the state from the constraints imposed by the existence of the capitalist economy, and that there is little indication that the EEC in its present form can act in any very substantial way as a regulator of private economic interests, nor that it is likely to develop in ways facilitating this.

45

IV Conclusions

At the beginning of this chapter I suggested that the proposition that the state in capitalist society supports the general interests of capital is a virtual tautology, which fails to illuminate the complexity of the relations between the state and capital. In this brief, and necessarily selective, survey I have indicated some of the variables that enter into the determination of the degree of political power exercised by business, with particular reference to the extent to which the controllers of government policy are able to free themselves from the constraints on their freedom of action imposed by their dependence for the economic development of society on a system of private productive enterprise. As a very broad generalisation, we may say that this potential for autonomy is at its greatest in societies with authoritarian systems of government or those in which substantial structures of political patronage exist; where pre-capitalist elites retain a significant influence; where the economic autonomy of business remains weak; and where substantial sectors of the labour force remain unintegrated within a general socio-political consensus. In these circumstances the political elites are in a better position to pursue policies independently of the interests of capital and often (though not always, as the case of Italy indicates) to play a major role in the shaping of the patterns of development of the capitalist economic order. Conversely, the more we approach the classic patterns of liberal democracy, the more constraint we observe placed by capital on the activities of government – though this is not to suggest that business groupings are able wholly to dominate the governmental policies of these societies.[92] The reasons for this state of affairs are complex, but three in particular may be mentioned. First, the tendency to a greater integration of the labour movement in the general socio-economic system, which tends both to enhance its influence and constrain the ends for which this influence is used. Second, the growing economic prosperity of these societies in the post-war period, coupled with the enhanced influence of labour and the possession of modernised administrative machinery, has fostered the provision of an extensive range of welfare benefits and the general regulation of social and economic development, thus reducing the grounds for opposition to the dominant order. (Compare the effects of the lack of such control in Italy.) And third, the state in these societies finds itself confronted with greater and more cohesive blocs of economic power due to the greater level of economic concentration.

Yet one may doubt whether even in these societies we may speak of a 'ruling class', and several Marxist writers have recognised the problem by arguing that the role of the capitalist state is to serve the interests of the dominant class by pursuing its long-term economic and/or political interests in situations where that class is temporarily or chronically incapable of recognising where its interests lie and/or organising collectively to pursue them.[93] This raises problems of why the controllers of the state apparatus act in this way, and why business groups oppose them in so doing. And, indeed, if this interpretation of the role of the capitalist state is correct, then the last thing the owners and controllers of capital should do is to rule or to attempt to exercise disproportionate influence on the political process. I lack the space here to explore these paradoxes, but would briefly suggest that at the heart of the problem lies the fact that many Marxist writers share a basic assumption with many pluralists, that the activities of the state apparatus are to be explained largely by sources of pressure external to that apparatus, whether it be through the balancing of a multiplicity of external influences or subservience to one. But the members of the government and bureaucracy may have goals of their own, ranging from the desire to implement a particular policy to the simple desire to retain power.[94] The analysis of the specifically political power of business must concentrate on the degree to which the goals of government or administration are congruent with the interests of the different sectors of business, thereby recognising that, just because a policy serves the interests of a group, it is not necessarily a result of the pressure of that group;[95] a consideration of the constraints imposed on government action by the economic power, organisational strength, etc, of business; an examination of the countervailing constraints in the hands of the policy-makers; and an analysis of the extent to which other significant interests enter into the process. While we lack an adequate conceptual apparatus to generalise about these relations, the considerations outlined in this paper would suggest that the most useful line of development may be through a development of those theories of power which centre around the concepts of exchange and dependence.[96] Over and above this, of course, is the more general question of why, even where state and labour elites oppose many of the immediate interests of business, there is still a general tendency to accept the legitimacy and 'given-ness' of the capitalist social and economic order. The question has in recent years increasingly been answered by reference to notions of 'cultural power', 'hegemony' or 'manipulated consensus'.[97] Indeed there are signs that this is now becoming a principal line of argument for those who wish to assert the predominance of the power of capital in modern Western societies.[98] Leaving aside the problem of how such concepts are to be used in empirical studies, and the fact that the mechanisms through which cultural power is exercised or consensus manipulated have only been specified in very general terms, it can be argued that, even if these concepts point to real and significant phenomena, they are probably able to account only for the broad outlines of the social and economic system, and not the specific balance of political forces and their relative influence. This paper has concentrated on questions of the latter type and, as even this brief survey indicates, there is no way in which the distribution of political power in post-war Europe can be seen as a simple correlate of the presence of a capitalist economic system.

Notes

1 But see Ernest Mandel, *Late Capitalism*, London, 1975, p. 496.
2 These propositions are argued most persuasively in Ralph Miliband, *The State in Capitalist Society*, London, 1969. Miliband's argument and method are cogently criticised in Ivor Crewe, 'Studying Elites in Britain' in I. Crewe (ed.), *British Political Sociology Year Book, vol. 1: Elites in Western Democracy*, London, 1974, pp. 38–41.
3 Anthony Giddens, *The Class Structure of the Advanced Societies*, London, 1973, pp. 174–5.
4 S. E. Finer, 'The Political Power of Private Capital', pt 1, *Sociological Review*, vol 3 (1955), p. 292.
5 Gerard Braunthal, *The Federation of German Industry in Politics*, Ithaca, 1965, p. 34; Management Counsellors International, *European Labour Relations in the 70's: An Overview*, Brussels, 1972, pp. 7, 126, 194; Geoffrey Ingham, *Strikes and Industrial Conflict*, London, 1974, ch. 4.
6 Giddens, op. cit., p. 175.
7 For specific examples see Braunthal, op. cit., pp. 257–62, 265–70; S. E. Finer, 'The Political Power of Private Capital' pt 2, *Sociological Review*, vol. 4 (1955), pp. 5–30; J. Szokoleszy-Syllaba, *Les Organisations professionelles françaises et le Marché commun*, Paris, 1965, pp. 283–91; Jean-Jacques Bonnard, 'Planning and Industry in France', in Jack Hayward and Michael Watson (eds), *Planning Politics and Public Policy*, Cambridge, 1975, p. 107.
8 Salvador Giner, *Continuity and Change: The Social Stratification of Spain*, Reading, 1968, pp. 27–8; Ricardo Soler, 'The New Spain', *New Left Review*, vol. 58 (1969), p. 10; Geoffrey Denton, Murray Forsyth and Malcolm Maclennan, *Economic Planning and Policies in Britain, France and Germany*, London, 1968, pp. 68–72.
9 Jean Meynaud and Dusan Sidjanski, *L'Europe des affaires*, Paris, 1967, pp. 111–13.
10 Ibid., pp. 103–10; George H. Kuster, 'Germany', in R. Vernon (ed.), *Big Business and the State: Changing Relations in Western Europe*, London, 1974, p. 71.
11 Braunthal, op. cit.; Stephen Blank, *The Federation of British Industries in Politics*, Farnborough, 1973; H. W. Ehrmann, *Organised Business in France*, Princeton, 1957.

12 H. A. Clegg, *The System of Industrial Relations in Great Britain*, Oxford, 1970, pp. 130–3, 406–12; I. C. McGivering, D. G. J. Matthews and W. H. Scott, *Management in Britain: A General Characterisation*, Liverpool, 1960, pp. 94–8.

13 Philip M. Williams and Martin Harrison, *Politics and Society in de Gaulle's Republic*, London, 1971, p. 147; J. E. S. Hayward, *Private Interests and Public Policy: The Experience of the French Social and Economic Council*, London, 1966, pp. 103–4; Jean-Daniel Reynaud, 'France', in Solomon Barkin (ed.), *Worker Militancy and its Consequences, 1965–75*, New York, 1975, p. 306; Michael Watson, 'A Comparative Evaluation of Planning Practices in the Liberal-Democratic State', in Hayward and Watson, op. cit., p. 471.

14 Luciano Gallino, 'Italy', in Margaret S. Archer and S. Giner (eds), *Contemporary Europe: Class, Status and Power*, London, 1971, p. 101; G. Giugni, 'L'autunno "caldo" sindicale', *Il Mulino*, vol. 19 (1970), pp. 32–3, cited in Raphael Zariski, *Italy: The Politics of Uneven Development*, Hinsdale, 1972, p. 215; but cf. Jean Maynaud, *Rapport sur la classe dirigeante Italienne*, Lausanne, 1964, pp. 73–4; Joseph la Palombara, *Interest Groups in Italian Politics*, Princeton, 1964, p. 288; and, for more recent developments, Pietro Merli Brandini, 'Italy' in Barkin (ed.), op. cit., p. 106.

15 John P. Windmuller, *Labour Relations in the Netherlands*, Ithaca, 1969, pp. 242–6.

16 Miliband, op. cit., pp. 156–7.

17 Meynaud and Sidjanski, op. cit., pp. 135–8; Windmuller, op. cit., p. 246; Joachim Bergmann and Walther Muller-Jentsch, 'The Federal Republic of Germany', in Barkin (ed.), op. cit., p. 247.

18 Ehrmann, op. cit., pp. 288–90; John Ardagh, *The New France*, Harmondsworth, 1973, ch. 2; Eric Cahm, *Politics and Society in Contemporary France*, London, 1972, pp. 454–6; John Sheahan, *Promotion and Control of Industry in Post-War France*, Cambridge, Mass., 1963, ch. 10.

19 Denton, *et al.*, op. cit., p. 64.

20 On French planning see Sheahan, op. cit.; J. M. and A. M. Hackett, *Economic Planning in France*, London, 1963; S. S. Cohen, *Modern Capitalist Planning: The French Model*, Cambridge, Mass., 1969; Denton, *et al.*, op. cit., esp. ch. 3; Andrew Shonfield, *Modern Capitalism*, Oxford, 1965, chs 5, 7, 8; Yves Ullmo, 'France' in Hayward and Watson, op. cit., pp. 22–51. On the 'opening to the left' in Italy, see Jon Halliday, 'Structural Reform in Italy', *New Left Review*, vol. 50 (1968), pp. 73–92; Michaele Salvati, 'The Impasse of Italian Capitalism', *New Left Review*, vol. 76 (1972), p. 33; Norman Kogan, *A Political History of Post-War Italy*, London, 1966, chs 12–13; Giuseppe Mammarella, *Italy after Fascism*, Notre Dame, Indiana, 1966, pts 4 and 5. On the development of Spanish capitalism see Charles W. Anderson, *The Political Economy of Modern Spain*, Madison, 1970; Max Gallo, *Spain Under Franco*, London, 1973; Stanley G. Payne, *Franco's Spain*, London, 1968, ch. 3; Fred Whitney, *Labour Policy and Practices in Spain*, New York, 1965; Jon Amsden, *Collective Bargaining and Class*

Conflict in Spain, London, 1972; Soler, op. cit. On the movement for European integration see Ghita Ionescu (ed.), *The New Politics of European Integration*, London, 1972; Michael Hodges (ed.), *European Integration*, Harmondsworth, 1972.

21 Blank, op. cit., chs 6, 8; Shonfield, op. cit., p. 154.

22 Ingham, op. cit.; Walter Kendall, *The Labour Movement in Europe*, London, 1975, pp. 201–2

23 S. E. Finer, 'The Political Power of Organised Labour', *Government and Opposition*, vol. 8 (1973), pp. 391–406; Jack Hayward, 'Comparative Conclusions' to pt II of Hayward and Watson, op. cit., p. 216.

24 Miliband, op. cit., p. 81.

25 Andrew Martin, 'Is Democratic Control of Capitalist Economies Possible?', in Leon N. Lindberg, Robert Alford, Colin Crouch and Claus Offe (eds), *Stress and Contradiction in Modern Capitalism*, Lexington, 1975, pp. 31–2. For a useful overview of European incomes policies see Lloyd Ulmann and Robert J. Flanagan, *Wage Restraint: A Study of Incomes Policies in Western Europe*, Berkeley, 1971.

26 Miliband, op. cit., pp. 99–102.

27 On German employer resistance to co-determination, see Richard F. Bunn, 'Co-determination and the Federation of German Employers' Associations', *Midwest Journal of Political Science*, vol. 11 (1960), pp. 278–97; and Herbert J. Spiro, *The Politics of German Co-determination*, Cambridge, Mass., 1958.

28 On West Germany see Kurt Sontheimer, *The Government and Politics of West Germany*, London, 1972, chs 2 and 6; Bergmann and Muller-Jentsch, op. cit. For Sweden see Kurt Samuelsson, *From Great Power to Welfare State*, London, 1965, chs 4 and 5; Martin, op. cit.; Ingham, op. cit.; Casten van Otter, 'Sweden', in Barkin, op. cit., pp. 194–234. On the Netherlands, Windmuller, op. cit.; Bram Peper, 'The Netherlands', in Barkin, op. cit., pp. 118–53. For a general overview of the development and orientations of European unions, see Kendall, op. cit.

29 Gino Giugni, 'Labour Relations in Italy', in Management Counsellors International, op. cit.

30 Zariski, op. cit., p. 214; Kogan, op. cit., pp. 106–10; La Palombara, op. cit., pp. 248–9.

31 Braunthal, op. cit., pp. 99–102; William Safran, *Veto-Group Politics: The Case of Health-Insurance Reform in West Germany*, San Francisco, 1967.

32 Michel Drancourt, *Les Clés du pouvoir*, Paris, 1964, p. 188; Jean Meynaud and Dusan Sidjanski, *Les Groupes de pression dans la communauté européenne*, Montreal, 1969, pp. 36–7.

33 Braunthal, op. cit., ch. 14; Sontheimer, op. cit., p. 105.

34 Meynaud, op. cit., pp. 78–80; La Palombara, op. cit., p. 310.

35 See the analysis of the voting patterns of business and agrarian groups in the French Social and Economic Council given in Hayward, op. cit., pp. 44–52.

36 Meynaud, op. cit., pp. 78–80; Gallino, op. cit., pp. 99–110; Juan J. Linz and Amando de Miguel, 'Within-Nation Differences and Comparisons: The Eight Spains' in Richard L. Merritt and Stein Rokkan

(eds) *Comparing Nations: The Use of Quantitative Data in Cross-National Research*, New Haven, 1966.

37 F. Roy Willis, *Italy Chooses Europe*, New York, 1971; Anthony Sampson, *The New Europeans*, London, 1968, p. 391.

38 Juan J. Linz and A. de Miguel, *Los empresarios ante el poder publico*, Madrid, 1966, cited Anderson, op. cit., pp. 71-2.

39 Miliband, op. cit., pp. 129-38.

40 Gallo, op. cit., pp. 86-7; Stanley G. Payne, *Politics and the Military in Spain*, Stanford, 1967, pp. 435-6; Salvador Giner, 'Spain', in Archer and Giner, op. cit., pp. 146-7; Joaquin Romero Maura, 'After Franco, Franquismo? The Armed Forces, the Crown and Democracy', *Government and Opposition*, vol. 11 (1976), pp. 35-64; J. M. Maravall, 'Modernisation, Authoritarianism and the Growth of Working-Class Dissent: The Case of Spain', *Government and Opposition*, vol. 8 (1973), pp. 432-54.

41 Miliband, op. cit., pp. 198-205.

42 Halliday, op. cit.; Mammarella, op. cit., pp. 318-19.

43 Ehrmann, op. cit., pp. 188-9; Williams and Harrison, op. cit., pp. 147-8. On reformist strains in Catholicism in general see J. P. Chausseriaud, *La Partie Democrate Chrétienne en Italie*, Paris, 1965, and R. E. M. Irving, *Christian Democracy in France*, London, 1973.

44 Arend Lijphart, *The Politics of Accommodation in the Netherlands*, Berkeley, 1968; Christopher Bagley, *The Dutch Plural Society*, Oxford, 1973; Bram Peper, op. cit.

45 Windmuller, op. cit., p. 256; Braunthal, op. cit., ch. 7; Meynaud, op. cit., pp. 14-16; Juan J. Linz, 'An Authoritarian Regime: Spain', in E. Allardt and Y. Littunen (eds), *Cleavages, Ideologies and Party Systems*, Helsinki, 1964, pp. 333-4; Keith R. Legg, *Politics in Modern Greece*, Stanford, 1969, p. 308; Jean Meynaud, *Nouvelles Études sur les groupes de pression en France*, Paris, 1969, pp. 186-7; W. L. Guttsman, *The British Political Elite*, London, 1963, pp. 363-4; Andrew Roth, 'The Business Background of M.P.'s in John Urry and John Wakeford (eds), *Power in Britain*, London, 1973, pp. 131-3; W. L. Guttsman, 'Elite Recruitment and Political Leadership in Britain and Germany since 1950: A Comparative Study of M.P.'s and Cabinets', in Ivor Crewe, op. cit., pp. 89-125; R. W. Johnson, 'The British Political Elite, 1955-72', *Archives Européennes de Sociologie*, 14 (1973), pp. 35-77.

46 La Palombara, op. cit., pp. 379-80.

47 Paul Ferris, *Men and Money*, Harmondsworth, 1970, p. 50. On Italian public enterprise in general, see M. V. Posner and S. J. Woolf, *Italian Public Enterprise*, London, 1967.

48 La Palombara, op. cit., p. 222; Safran, op. cit., *passim*; Braunthal, op. cit., ch. 8; Williams and Harrison, op. cit., pp. 145-6.

49 Shonfield, op. cit., chs 5, 7 and 8; Anderson, op. cit., pp. 165-6; H. W. Ehrmann, 'French Bureaucracy and Organised Interests', *Administrative Science Quarterly*, 5 (1960-1), pp. 542-3.

50 Lijphart, op. cit., *passim*; cf. Windmuller, op. cit., chs 3, 6.

51 Finer, 1955, op. cit.

52 Ibid., pt 2.

53 Michael Barratt Brown, 'The Controllers of British Industry', in Urry and Wakeford, op. cit., pp. 73–116; Denton *et al.*, op. cit., pp. 68–72; P. Kraemer, *The Societal State*, Meppel, 1966, p. 70.

54 R. E. Pahl and J. Winkler, 'The Economic Elite: Theory and Practice', in Philip Stanworth and Anthony Giddens (eds), *Elites and Power in British Society*, Cambridge, 1974, pp. 102–22; cf. J. H. Westergaard and H. Resler, *Class in a Capitalist Society*, London, 1975, pp. 163–4.

55 Braunthal, op. cit., ch. 11; Meynaud and Sidjanski, op. cit., pp. 54–5.

56 These policies are detailed in several of the papers in Vernon, op. cit., and in Hayward and Watson, op. cit., esp. pt II.

57 Denton *et al.*, op. cit., p. 104; Peter Coffey, *The Social Economy of France*, London, 1973, p. 88; J. E. S. Hayward, 'Interest Groups and Incomes Policies in France', *British Journal of Industrial Relations*, vol. 4 (1966), pp. 165–200; Raymond Vernon, 'Enterprise and Government in Western Europe', in Vernon op. cit., p. 7; J. E. S. Hayward, 'State Intervention in France; The Changing Style of Government-Industry Relations', *Political Studies*, vol. 26 (1972), pp. 287–98.

58 Denton *et al.*, op. cit., pp. 68–72; Ferris, op. cit., pp. 78–86; Michael Kidron, *Western Capitalism Since the War*, Harmondsworth, 1970, p. 22; Graham Hallett, *The Social Economy of West Germany*, London, 1973, pp. 37–8.

59 Kidron, op. cit., p. 44.

60 Ferris, op. cit., pp. 58–9; Mammarella, op. cit., p. 353.

61 Miliband, op. cit., p. 154; Fred Hirsch, *Money International*, New York, pp. 172–3.

62 Payne, op. cit., *passim*; Amsden, op. cit., *passim*; Soler, op. cit., pp. 9–10; Maravall, op. cit.

63 Jean Meynaud, *Les Partis politiques en Italie*, Paris, 1965, ch. 1; Kogan, op. cit., pp. 59–62; La Palombara, op. cit., ch. 4; Romano Predi, 'Italy', in Vernon, op. cit., pp. 45–63.

64 Dow Votaw, *The Six-Legged Dog: Mattei and E.N.I.*, Berkeley, 1964, chs 3–5; Charles E. Dechert, *Ente Nazionale Idrocarburi*, Leiden, 1963, ch. 5; P. Frankel, *Mattei: Oil and Power Politics*, London, 1966, *passim*.

65 Zariski, op. cit., p. 214; Kogan, op. cit., p. 110; cf. Meynaud, 1969, op.cit., pp. 195–6, for similar evidence from France.

66 See Gianfranco Pasquini and Umberto Pecchini, 'Italy', in Hayward and Watson, op. cit., pp. 70–92.

67 Salvati, op. cit.; Giuseppe Sacco, 'Italy after the Miracle', *New Society*, vol. 541 (1973), pp. 348–51.

68 See, e.g., D. Butler and D. Stokes, *Political Change in Britain*, London, 1969, ch. 2.

69 Otto Kahn-Freund and Bob Hepple, *Laws Against Strikes*, London, 1972; van Otter, op. cit.; Bergmann and Muller-Jentsch, op. cit., esp. pp. 253–6.

70 Larry Hufford, *Sweden: The Myth of Socialism*, London, 1973; Samuelsson, op. cit., pp. 272–83; Ingham, op. cit., ch. 4; Martin, op. cit.

71 Sontheimer, op. cit., p. 102; Bergmann and Muller-Jentsch, op. cit.

72. J. F. B. Goodman, 'Great Britain', in Barkin, op. cit., pp. 39–80.

73 Among the vast literature on this subject, we may mention as being of particular relevance here; Raymond Vernon, *Sovereignty at Bay*, New York and London, 1971; Louis Turner, *Invisible Empires*, London, 1970; Hans Gunter (ed.) *Transnational Industrial Relations*, London, 1972; H. R. Hahlo, J. Graham Smith and Richard W. Wright (eds), *Nationalism and the Multinational Enterprise*, New York, 1973; Alfred Kamin (ed.), *Western European Labour and the American Corporation*, Washington, 1970; Ernest Mandel, *Europe versus America? Contradictions of Imperialism*, London, 1970; Rainer Hellman, *The Challenge to U.S. Dominance of the International Corporation*, New York, 1970; Michael Hodges, *Multinational Corporations and National Government*, Farnborough, 1974.

74 Hellman, op. cit., ch. 3; Gilles Y. Bertin, 'Foreign Investment in France', in I. A. Litvak and C. J. Maule (eds), *Foreign Investment: the Experience of Host Countries*, New York, 1970, pp. 105–22; Helmut C. Coing, 'Germany and the Multinational Enterprise' and Paul Leleux, 'France, Belgium, EEC and the Multinational Enterprise', in Hahlo *et al.*, op. cit., pp. 87–100, 101–35.

75 Robin Murray, 'Capital and the Nation-State', *New Left Review*, vol. 67 (1971), pp. 106–8; Dennis Kavanagh, 'Beyond Autonomy? The Politics of Corporations', *Government and Opposition*, vol. 9 (1974), pp. 52–3.

76 Vernon, op. cit., pp. 133–4.

77 Felix De Luis and Emilio Canseco, 'Foreign Investment in Spain', in Litvak and Maule, op. cit., pp. 338–54; Legg, op. cit., pp. 239–40; Jean Meynaud with P. Merlopoulos and G. Notaras, *Les Forces politiques en Grèce*, Lausanne 1965, pp. 421–48; Harry G. Johnson, 'Economic Benefits of the Multinational Enterprise, in Hahlo *et al.*, op. cit., pp. 165–70.

78 B. C. Roberts, 'Factors Influencing the Origin and Style of Management and their Effect on the Pattern of Industrial Relations in Multi-National Corporations', in Gunter, op. cit., pp. 131–2.

79 Hellmann, op. cit., *passim*; Meynaud and Sidjanski, 1967, op. cit., pp. 199–200.

80 D. L. McLachlan and D. Swann, *Competition Policy in the European Community*, London, 1967; D. Swann and D. L. McLachlan, *Concentration or Competition: A European Dilemma?*, London, 1967.

81 Roger Blanpain, 'Efforts to Bring About Community-Level Collective Bargaining in the Coal and Steel Community and the EEC', in Gunter, op. cit., pp. 290–6.

82 Meynaud and Sidjanski, 1969, op. cit., chs 1, 18; Werner Feld, 'National Economic Interest and Policy Formation in the EEC', *Political Science Quarterly*, vol. 82 (1966), pp. 392–411; Werner Feld, 'Political Aspects of Transnational Business Collaboration in the Common Market', *International Organisation*, vol. 24 (1970), pp. 209–38; Dusan Sidjanski, 'Pressure Groups and the European Economic Community', *Government and Opposition*, vol. 2, (1967), pp. 397–416.

83 Meynaud and Sidjanski, 1969, op. cit., p. 484.

84 McLachlan and Swann, op. cit., ch. 7.
85 Denton *et al.*, op. cit., ch. 12.
86 Helen S. Wallace, 'The Impact of the European Communities on National Decision-Making', in Ionescu, op. cit., pp. 196–214.
87 Ibid., p. 210.
88 Joseph S. Nye, 'The Strength of International Regionalism', in Gunter, op. cit., p. 63; Vernon, op. cit., p. 16.
89 McLachlan and Swann, op. cit., chs 7, 8.
90 On the proposals see Karl Gleichmann, 'The Proposed European Company Law: Implications for Industrial Relations', in Management Counsellors International, op. cit.
91 Murray, op. cit.; cf. Richard N. Cooper, 'Towards an International Capital Market?' in John H. Dunning (ed.), *International Investment*, Harmondsworth, 1972, pp. 231–7; Kavanagh, op. cit.
92 Christopher J. Hewitt, 'Elites and the Distribution of Power in British Society', in Stanworth and Giddens, op. cit., pp. 45–61.
93 Paul M. Sweezey, 'Has Capitalism Changed?' in S. Tsuru (ed.), *Has Capitalism Change?* Tokyo, 1961, p. 88; Nicos Poulantzas, *Political Power and Social Classes*, London, 1973, *passim*; Manuel Castells, 'Advanced Capitalism, Collective Consumption and Urban Contradictions', in Lindberg *et al.*, op. cit., p. 178.
94 Charles-Albert Michelet, 'France', in Vernon op. cit., p. 106; Colin Crouch, 'The Ideology of a Managerial Elite: The National Board for Prices and Incomes, 1965–70', in Crewe, op. cit., p. 78.
95 Meynaud, 1969, op. cit., p. 383; Crewe, op. cit., p. 39.
96. Peter M. Blau, *Exchange and Power in Social Life*, New York, 1967; Richard Emerson, 'Power-Dependence Relations', *American Sociological Review*, 27 (1962), pp. 31–41; Roderick Martin, 'The Concept of Power: A Critical Defence', *British Journal of Sociology*, 22 (1971), pp. 240–56. See also Finer's discussion of 'Socio-Economic leverage', Finer, 1973, op. cit., p. 393.
97 John Urry, 'Introduction', pp. 4–5, in Urry and Wakeford, op. cit.; Steven Lukes, *Power*, London, 1975.
98 See Westergaard and Resler, op. cit., pt III, esp. pp. 142–4.

3   Diffusion and crisis of scientific management in European industry

Angelo Pichierri

Objectives and limits of this study

The first part of this paper will examine some characteristics of scientific management, with special reference to manufacturing and in particular manual work, some aspects of its diffusion in Europe, and some now 'historical' experiments on and hypotheses about how to correct or even by-pass this type of work organisation. The second part will consider the factors which recently seem to have provoked a radical crisis in scientific management, together with the latest proposals and attempts at innovation made in America and in Europe.

There is already a vast amount of literature on this subject and it will be freely drawn upon in this article, which does not specially aim at originality. It will not, however, be merely a 'bibliographical survey' or an 'anthology of case evidence'. Instead, an attempt will be made to bring out from existing material certain elements which shed light on the problems to be considered in the conclusion: first, the question of the relationship between ideologies and organisational models, both in business practice and in formulation of theories of the social sciences; and second, the question of the possible independence and originality of certain European experiments in the context of Western industrialised capitalism.

On both of these questions it is hoped not so much to arrive at definite conclusions as to indicate a number of hypotheses for study, and research directions not yet sufficiently explored.

Scientific management

Characteristics of scientific management

The stress on the technical division of work does not start with modern industry and is not characteristic of it alone, but is already evident in

capitalist manufacturing. However, in the course of the development of modern industry, the technical division of labour is carried to
the extreme and takes on particular connotations since its principal
point of reference is no longer the activity of the worker, but the
operation of the machine of which the worker is a simple appendage.[1]

This process comes to completion after the first phase of development of capitalist industry (Phase A, that of the skilled workman)
in which the organisation of production presents no problems for
the owner-managers of the enterprise, since this is almost wholly in
the hands of the workers themselves, whose work is judged on the
basis of results.

In the mass-production phase, however, the worker's tasks are
rigorously determined beforehand on the basis of criteria of rational
organisation.[2] The current terms for this are 'scientific management',
or 'Taylorism' or 'Taylorian organisation', and in this paper we
too shall follow this habit to some extent. But as Touraine
observes,

> . . . l'histoire professionnelle de l'industrie entre 1914 et 1940
> est dominée par l'extension du travail spécialisé, c'est-à-dire
> directement soumis aux impératifs de la production en grand
> série. Avant 1914, l'organisation du travail prônée par Taylor
> et ses disciples avait préparé ce mouvement. Cependant les
> expériences de Taylor portaient sur des tâches proprement
> manuelles, peu ou pas mécanisées – transport de gueuses de
> fonte, pose de briques – soit sur le travail aux machines
> considéré dans ses aspects proprement techniques. Le taylorisme
> représente donc une première phase de l'organisation de
> travail, antérieure à l'organisation des ateliers consacrés à la
> production en grande série, seconde phase que symbolise le
> nom de Ford.[3]

The work of Taylor and his followers therefore either precedes or
is contemporary with the organisation of work of the assembly-line
type, Industrial practice has developed in a fairly independent way
compared with Taylor's teachings, and for a certain period in the
development of capitalist industry, it would probably be more
accurate to speak, as Gramsci does, of 'Fordism' rather than 'Taylorism'. (In 1932, the characters in Huxley's *Brave New World* swear
'by Ford', and not 'by Taylor'.) It must be clearly understood that,
when we use expressions like 'Taylorism' 'Taylorian organisation'
and 'scientific management', we now refer to a much wider range of
phenomena than that covered by specific reference to Taylor's work:
i.e. the phenomena to which Friedmann has applied the term
'rationalisation' and which as an entity Touraine consigns to
'Phase B' in the evolution of factory work.

' In the preceding phase, as we have said, the organisation of manufacturing work did not constitute a problem for the (factory) management, whereas in the phase of rationalisation the 'design' of the workers' tasks becomes one of the basic concerns of the business hierarchy: Taylorism is a current of thought and a set of techniques which provide instructions on the 'best' way to put such a design into practice.

Within the scope of this paper, the principal characteristics of this 'rationalised' organisation are considered to be the following:

(i) The emphasis on the division between intellectual and manual work; and between the task of preparation, programming and management of work and the actual carrying out of that work.

(ii) The breaking up of the working cycle into increasingly simple and more fragmented tasks.

(iii) Assembly-line work ('a type of organisation of work in which the various operations, reduced to the same length, are carried out without any interruption between them and in a fixed order in time and space').[4] The breaking up of work into simple movements and operations, which in itself is 'Taylorian' in the strict sense, is necessarily prior to the assembly line.

(iv) The chain of command of a hierarchial and military type, the result of the removal of autonomy from the workshops, of the increase in the number of employees and of the need for co-ordination imposed by the assembly line.

The major ideological implications of this type of organisation are the conception of man as *homo economicus* and the interpretation of his interests in individual rather than collective terms, thereby excluding the work group, the social class, and the trade union.[5]

The principal conditions which make this organisation possible are the existence of a predictable market for the product, capable of absorbing mass production, and of a labour market characterised by an abundant unqualified, unskilled, inexpensive, politically reliable labour force.[6]

The spread of scientific management in Europe

The spread of *travail en miettes* and, more generally, of the kind of organisation of manufacturing work which can, following convention, continue to be called 'scientific', has taken place at various times and rates in different countries and industrial sectors. These rates have been determined by the appearance in each case of the two conditions mentioned at the end of the previous paragraph.[7]

Whilst advanced fragmentation of work was already manifest in the textile industry in Europe at the end of the nineteenth century, (connected with the existence of a large market for these products, including the colonial market, and of an abundant supply of labour of rural origin), in the United States by contrast the development of the car industry, the area *par excellence* of assembly line work, was marked by an expansion in the absorption capacity of a 'rich' market and by the existence of a mass of new immigrant workers, unskilled and non-unionised, together with the open-shop policy and the anti-union policies of the management.

'Taylorism' in its strict sense was first put into practice in Europe relatively early: first in 1905 at Hopkinson's in England, then in the next few years in France, especially at Berliet and Renault – apparently in a particularly brutal way ('without any attention to Taylor's warnings on prudence', writes Friedmann). At Renault, in 1912 and 1913, the introduction of the new system of time control and of the new type of payment on the amount produced piecework caused notorious strikes.[8]

But the spread of the new techniques of organisation was considerably accelerated by the two world wars, which 'artificially' created the necessary conditions for the application on a large scale of the assembly line: the mass demand for certain products (arms, munitions, vehicles, but also, for instance, textile products), and following the mobilisation of the majority of males of working age, a need to draw upon unskilled labour, such as large numbers of Italian women who were recruited for engineering factories, often in heavy industry, during the war.[9]

Even if the introduction of techniques of scientific management in the course of the First World War represents a process which was in many ways irreversible, the end of the war and of the mass demand for certain products placed considerable difficulties in the way of an extension of this rationalisation, especially in Europe. The fundamental differences between the European and American markets were clearly brought out in the work of the Third International Congress on the Scientific Organisation of Work held in Rome in September 1927. Besides, as Friedmann observes, in the period between the two wars the evolution towards more complex and progressively more self-sufficient economies favoured the more intensive exploitation of technical equipment and the national labour force.[10] In this contradictory situation we should bear in mind that, even though in the period between the two wars there were memorable cases of protests against the more brutal versions of scientific management, such as the Bédaux system (even in Fascist Italy), nevertheless in this same period, both in America and in Europe there were declarations of support by unions for its introduction at least in principle, not to mention the earlier statement by Lenin about the progressive aspects of Taylorism.

The first International Congress attended by countries interested in scientific management took place in Prague in 1924; in 1925 the Comité International pour l'Organisation Scientifique du Travail was formed. The introduction of techniques of scientific management during the First World War and also in the period between the wars, bore, however, the stamp of imported American models and methods, especially those of Ford.

The reaction of the labour unions to the introduction of Taylorism, both in America and in Europe, was emphatically negative: for one thing, Taylorian organisation in its extreme form presupposes the absence of trade unions. What scientific management meant ideologically to American employers when it was first introduced is clearly illustrated by Bendix:

> The open-shop campaign went hand in hand with the rise of the scientific management movement. In their attack upon the trade-unions, American employers came to make their own absolute authority within the plant so central a tenet that the compliance of the worker became ideologically a far more important value than his independence and initiative. Scientific management went a step further in the same direction. It proposed to study each work performance in order to ascertain scientifically the 'one best way' of doing each task. And it made the results of such enquiry into a set of rules which each worker had to follow to the letter if he was to earn the premium offered for increased output.[11]

Amongst the noisiest protests made by the American unions, was the 'Hoxie enquiry' of 1915, which brought out the hostility of the workers towards the system in thirty-five factories listed by Taylor himself. But this reaction of the unions, like so many others, was based essentially on defence of the 'trade', and these were usually lost causes, both because the destruction of the individual trade was inevitable, and because the leading workers of the new phase of development of industry were, at the beginning at least, almost by definition not members of unions.

It was this 'European' aspect of union reaction which moved Gramsci to write:

> The struggle which is going on in America ... is still for the ownership of the individual skilled trade, and against 'industrial liberty', and therefore similar to the struggle which took place in Europe in the Nineteenth Century, although under different conditions. The labour union in America is more the corporate

expression of the ownership of the skilled trade than anything else, and hence the fact that industrialists want it to be suppressed has a 'progressive' aspect.[12]

The 'correctives' of scientific management

The history of attempts to improve the conditions of workers made by enlightened employers is as old as that of methods of industrial production. Pre-Taylorist initiatives of this sort, throughout the nineteenth century both in Europe and America, comprised attempts to find remedies for the 'evils of industrialisation' rather than specific answers to the damage caused to the workers (whether physiological, psychological or professional) by the rationalisation and fragmentation of work. It was the spread of Taylorism and Fordism which gradually brought about the need for precisely this kind of solution. In Europe, the most original example is probably the development of industrial psychology and psychotechnics: where a strong impulse towards change was given by the First World War (during which the Industrial Fatigue Research Board was founded in England). According to Baritz, in Europe, where unions were more mature and psychologists and managers more open, great efforts were made to convince the workers of the usefulness of certain psychological devices which could, for instance, be applied to the selection of personnel; whereas in America such links between psychologists and workers were totally absent.[13] In the United States, the most important development was the human relations movement of the late 1920s, which aimed to correct and integrate scientific management, giving equal consideration to the 'logic of efficiency' particular to management, and the 'logic of feelings' particular to the worker, and thereby substituting for the *homo economicus* inseparable from Taylorism an overriding concern for the informal work group.

Both of these movements appear as 'correctives' to the predominant system of work organisation, upon which they have had only minimal and, so to speak, peripheral influence. Psychotechnics has, for instance, modified certain aspects of Taylorist mechanicism and assembly-line work, by studying the cycles of the working day, for example, and introducing breaks, while the human relations movement has introduced, at the level of the work group, certain elementary forms of participation in decision-making (a forgotten offshoot of the experiments of Mayo, now taken up by some of his followers).[14] The psychology and psychotechnics which originated in Europe had some degree of success and influence in the United States, although within the limits outlined by Baritz. As to the human relations movement, this has turned out in many instances to be a textbook example of the uncritical importing into Europe of American models, since it is not in fact so much a question of real organisational models as of ideologies and manipulative techniques.

Automation as a stage beyond 'travail en miettes'

The realisation of the negative aspects of scientific management brought about the adoption of certain corrective measures, (sometimes presented as such, but sometimes purveyed as panacea for all the ills of industry), and also triggered off a large number of forecasts that the organisation of work based on fragmented and repetitive tasks was out of date, especially from the 1950s onwards.

The belief which spread from the United States was that the phase of fragmented work and of the 'de-skilling' of the workers was being left behind by the complete automation of the process of production. According to one current of thought, of which Drucker was one of the most typical representatives, automation would at one and the same time increase the number of people employed, their incomes, their skills and also the productivity of firms.[15] There was however no lack of pessimists[16] who foresaw technological unemployment, the downgrading of skills and a stepping up of automatic centralisation in factory organisation. However even the pessimists thought that the 'industrial revolution' which automation represented was already at hand or even under way. Expectations of this sort, more ideological than scientific, yet coming from the country where the process of production was most highly developed, spread widely in Europe, even in places where the industrial situation scarcely justified it. A good example was the slavish use in Italy of the term 'automation' in years when what was really happening was the change to fragmented and assembly-line work. The way industry has developed since then has largely given the lie to any 'optimistic' hypotheses, both as regards the ways automation has spread and the effects it has on industrial skills.

Until a few years ago, automation had often made unbelievable steps forward, but it has developed in an irregular and contradictory fashion, and certainly not one which turned the 'automatic factory' into a widespread reality. The effects of this on work skills are difficult in the extreme to interpret. It is probably more accurate to speak of substantial changes in the criteria for judging such skills rather than of upgrading or downgrading. At all events it seems hazardous, to say the least, to speak of upgrading in the case of a traditionally highly skilled worker who moves on to work at a machine tool with numerical controls, not to mention the effects of automation on the working role of many white-collar workers. The way that Phase B of manual labour is being superseded is seen in

61

fact in a whole series of innovations which are not only technological but often organisational in the main.

Attempts to overcome the crisis

Factors leading to crisis in scientific management

In recent years the traditional organisation of manufacturing work, and more generally the mechanistic type of factory organisation[17] have reached a crisis. In the large American and European factories, the symptoms of this crisis have been greater difficulty in controlling the labour force (turnover, absenteeism, wildcat and other strikes, sabotage), a worsening of the quality of products (or at least an increase in the costs involved in checking the quality), and third, difficulties which firms face in keeping up with changes in the market and encountering them with sufficient elasticity.

The reasons for this crisis and for the organisational changes which have been made to meet it, are many, but they can probably be traced back principally to the two kinds of structural factors which we have had occasion to emphasise before: changes in the market of the product and in the labour market. In the first category of changes come the difficulties of selling many goods, the shortened average life of products, and interference in the market or in the products by such things as safety regulations or anti-pollution measures, etc. In the second category comes the strengthening of the bargaining power of certain categories of workers who are particularly in demand because of their age, sex, schooling or psychophysical characteristics.

In this phase, subjective cultural and political changes in the new generations of workers carry considerable influence, and make them far less willing to accept the traditional forms of authority; equally influential are the changes in the organisational structure, the political orientation, and the demands of the union bodies. The conflictual orientation of the labour force can be considered as a third variable which, together with the state of markets for the product and that of the labour market, brings about a crisis in the traditional organisation of industrial labour.

The subjective changes and those in union politics, as well as the degree of industrial conflict are functions of the workings of the labour market.[18] It is, however, doubtful that the state of the labour market *alone* explains the development of workers' conflictual propensity. In a preliminary examination we propose to distinguish between conflict behaviour of a mainly individualistic and spontaneous type (for instance absenteeism), which reflects fairly faithfully the degree of bargaining power of the worker in the labour market, and, on the other hand, conflict behaviour of a collective and organised variety (strikes and collective bargaining) which reflects the characteristics of union organisation and the level of political consciousness attained, and which is affected only indirectly by changed circumstances in the labour market.[19]

All the changes indicated above have served to bring gradually to light the excessive rigidity of the factory which is organised on traditional lines, and have made the behaviour of the labour force increasingly difficult to monitor and to predict. The most advanced factory managements, which tend at the same time to be those most exposed to the demands of the *turbulent environment*[20] are responding to this state of affairs by putting forward a whole series of changes in the organisation of manufacturing work, of which examples will be given below. In the United States these changes are seen very much as the response of 'enlightened' factory management to a *turbulent environment*. The cultural changes in the labour force are a part of this *environment*, but the workers and their organisations do not put forward explicit demands about the organisation of work.

In certain European countries, however, important changes in the organisation of work have stemmed at least in part from union action. This has been brought about by provoking a crisis in parts of this organisation, by demanding its abolition or transformation, and by bargaining over it with the factory management (a conflictual form of transformation which in Italy is typical), or on the other hand by co-operating with the management, and when necessary with governmental bodies, in bringing about the change (negotiated change, as in Norway). In both cases, the participation of unions in changing the organisation of work represents a significant turning point both in European experience and in the present phase of industrial history, compared with the time at which assembly-line work was introduced, when unions had far fewer means of analysis and forecasting at their disposal and far less opportunity for active intervention rather than of bargaining over the effects of certain innovations after they had been introduced.

One more thing should be considered before we pass on to analyse specific examples of the transformation of manufacturing work. We have tried to show, while analysing the passage from Phase A to Phase B of manual labour, that certain important transformations in factory organisation can to some extent be traced back to changes in the market of the product and the labour market. If this is so, we do not believe it can be maintained that, in the present economic crisis, possible organisational changes affecting manufacturing work can be viewed by students or by labour militants as 'luxury' problems of secondary importance, compared with the

basic questions of pay and employment. On the contrary the economic crisis will accelerate organisational change (as well, of course,
as technological change) which many factory managements will
probably tend to present to the working class and its organisations as
a *fait accompli*. The incentives towards change arising from the
market situation are already increasing even in sectors which
apparently were, until recently, stable (the most notable example
obviously being the current difficulties in the motor industry).

As to the labour market and its repercussions on the subjective
characteristics of workers, recent periods of great economic difficulty,
both in Europe and America, have shown that certain cultural
changes in the labour force are apparently irreversible: not even the
crisis and the spectre of unemployment seem capable of completely
reviving in the worker the characteristics of *homo economicus*.

Attempts to overcome the crisis

In examining past and current experiments aiming at some sort of
transformation of manufacturing work, (whether on a psycho-
physiological or a professional or simply a survey level) we can
distinguish in a preliminary analysis three separate strands: one of
'participation', one of 'job design', and one of the application of theories
of 'socio-technical systems'. It is necessary to stress at once that this
distinction and the classifications which derive from it are made
largely on a provisional basis and for convenience; especially as in
the most advanced experiments (those which involve the creation
of autonomous working teams) 'participation', 'job design' and
'socio-technical systems' are woven together often quite inextricably.[21]

In a more detailed analysis than that which follows it would
perhaps be possible to classify with greater precision the various
innovatory experiments on the basis of the kind of objectives which
the innovator has (whether he is aware of them or not). Here,
however, we will merely point out that in the case of organisational
changes, as opposed to technological change, the *immediate* objectives can usually be construed in terms of a quest for greater factory
integration on various levels, rather than a quest for increased
productivity.[22]

In the less advanced interpretations of 'participation' in factory
decision-making we find that decisions already taken are simply
communicated to the workers, or at most they are consulted more
or less formally on decisions which principally affect them: this is
typical of the experiments which were part of the human relations
movement, or which stem directly from it. The more advanced
firms come close to a complete restructuring of the tasks of control,
programming and manufacturing at the level of the individual

worker or team of workers, and consequently involve the need to redefine the role of manager. In these cases, participation tends to overlap with experiments in job design and socio-technical systems. It is perhaps worth noting that some quite advanced experiments in participation were taking place in Europe during the period when the human relations movement had become most widespread in the United States. Before the Second World War, the most interesting example is probably the Bat'a shoe factory in Czechoslovakia, where we find not only welfare and productivity initiatives of a standard paternalistic nature, but also the introduction at shopfloor level of autonomous work teams. But experiments of this kind, which depend on the personality of the individual entrepreneur, are isolated cases which do not constitute a 'movement'. Job-design experiments aim to design or redesign the place of work, taking into account not only the needs and demands of the whole organisation but also the personal and social needs of the worker. They do not therefore consider technology as something fixed, but as a working variable which can be changed.

We shall not refer here to cases of job rotation and job enlargement, which do not constitute a change in technology or in organisational and hierarchical structure, but simply alter the allocation of tasks which themselves remain essentially unchanged. Such cases have by now a relatively long history, beginning with IBM in the 1940s, and they can be considered largely as 'correctives' to traditional Taylorian organisation. They are, however, extremely important as symptoms of the fact that the fragmentation of work has now reached the point where, even from the factory management's point of view, its returns are diminishing. Job enrichment, however, in as far as it restructures actual functions performed by the individual worker or work team, (functions like manufacturing, programming and control), represents a real innovation in the traditional organisation of manufacturing work. There are by now many examples of job enrichment in the United States (in particular the experiment at ITT) and in Europe as well, notably at Philips, IBM France, and ICI. The ICI case is of special interest because work enrichment has also involved white-collar workers and one particular case of enrichment of factory work, that of nylon spinners, was actually conducted in accord with the trade union.

In Italy we have instances of direct intervention by unions in the formulation of measures aimed at the restructuring of tasks and at job enrichment in the case of Italsider and especially of Olivetti. In the agreement signed on 5 April 1971 by the Olivetti management and the engineering unions, the firm undertook to make the most of the professional capacities of mass production workers by allowing them to move on to tasks requiring higher skills by means of the following initiatives: (i) restructuring of tasks with the aim of widening and enriching the contents of work; (ii) more internal mobility through the use of workers in different jobs leading to higher professional skills; (iii) the introduction of new techniques and new production methods; (iv) the employment of personnel who have been working for some time on the assembly line on new and more complex products; (v) streamlining of the professional contents of certain tasks.

The movement for job design is of American origin. In the face of the growing costs incurred by traditional organisation given the current turbulent environment, it represents an attempt to make work more stimulating and to make the organisation itself more elastic and flexible. From the ideological point of view, the supporters of job design have insisted above all on the need to raise the psycho-physiological and professional level of work. At the beginning at least, before close links were formed with the movement for socio-technical systems there was no concern, or at most only secondary concern, about the level of control and of factory democracy. Besides, as we have seen, it is only in a few European cases that job design (and how to apply it) has been the subject of bargaining and transactions between factory management and workers' unions.

The idea underlying the theory of socio-technical systems is that a technological system and a social system co-exist in the factory, running in parallel yet interdependent, but capable of being optimised jointly.[23] The practical applications of the theory of socio-technical systems generally lead to great emphasis being placed on autonomous teams of workers:

> The contribution of socio-technical systems to work design is in the conception of autonomous group structure as appropriate to sophisticated modern technology. Autonomous groups are effectively leaderless teams of employees working together in the completion of the group's primary task. By definition, *occupational roles* are more central to the work process than are *jobs* in autonomous groups. The self-co-ordination and co-operation required among members, and the use of multiple (and even redundant) skills, as well as formation of composite teams, makes role content rather than job content the central concern of socio-technical systems.[24]

The setting up of these groups is usually accompanied by some kind of organisational transformation of the individual job: job rotation, enlargement, enrichment. In any case real job enrichment which *only* involves the individual place of work is virtually inconceivable, as is shown by those cases where autonomous groups

66

of workers have been set up without any reference to the theory of socio-technical systems (ITT, Texas Instruments, Philips). The application of methods evolved by the Tavistock Institute and the use of job design criteria are characteristic of the Norwegian experiment, carried out jointly by the government, employers' associations and the unions. In the case of the Scandinavian 'factory micro-democracy', the workers' team agrees on a certain output with the management, and then has considerable freedom of decision-making in the pursuit of this objective. Contacts with the management are maintained by an elected member of the team; the factory management retains the task of integrating the efforts of the teams, and of providing each team with the necessary inputs, in terms of raw materials, tools and information.

The theoretical origins and also the major practical applications of this approach based on the theory of socio-technical systems are therefore specifically European. Right from the beginning, the ideology which has dominated this approach has been that of 'industrial democracy'. What this has meant in practice is the discovery of an area of interest in reform shared for a period at least by both the employers' and workers' organisations, and the realisation that these interests could be pursued in collaboration with state intervention and with technical assistance from groups of social scientists.

Organisational models and ideologies in the United States and Europe

Organisational models and ideologies

A striking characteristic of the innovatory moves to which we have referred is the dominance of initiative from the factory management, even in cases where it is also stimulated or conditioned by intervention of the workers' organisations. Corresponding to the economic and social changes in industry promoted by the factory managements, we regularly find changes in the ideologies concerned with work and authority, as has been brilliantly demonstrated by Bendix. Even the experiments outlined in the previous paragraph have an important ideological content: the currents of thought they stem from and the images they present of 'manager' and 'worker', are themselves in many ways becoming ideologies of factory management just as Taylorism and human relations had been before them.

Normally cases of change in job content involving greater responsibility, self-regulation, complexity and variety in the job tend to be described so as to bring out improvements in motivation with its subsequent reduction in absenteeism, turnover and disputes and its increase in performance.

This particular attitude, which is common to studies of management and of 'behavioural science' reveals in two ways its ideological orientation: firstly because the improvement of 'working life' is seen as a means of obtaining increased performance rather than an objective of social value; and secondly, because this kind of approach ends up by suggesting that the new way of working stems from a voluntary action aimed principally at improving job motivation.[25]

Along with the ideological elements, however, we also find real changes in work organisation, in forms of control, and in technology. During the most recent phase in the evolution of large industry, the organisational innovations have received much more publicity than the technological innovations, the former constituting a series of ideological messages; a situation almost the reverse of that which existed when the ideology of automation was most widespread. Indeed in some cases at least we can even formulate the hypothesis that the ideological insistence on certain organisational changes (such as participation or job design) serves the latent function of 'concealing' organisational changes of another kind (like the introduction of 'breathers' between the various phases of the productive cycle and the decentralisation of production until it resembles putting-out work), or technological innovations which are often cases of partial automation.

Over and above the conscious motives mentioned, the structural reasons for the change stem from developments in the market of the product, in the labour market and in workers' propensity towards conflict. It seems that the history of industry shows how, in the long term, the organisational transformations occurring in response to environmental changes cannot but jointly affect both manufacturing work (by manual and office workers), management activity, and the organisational structure of the whole concern. Here perhaps can be found the key to understanding the relationship between ideology and structural transformation in instances of change such as those given in the previous section. When this 'innovation' affects only the manufacturing level, or the macro-organisational or management level, we must presume that the method of manipulation and the ideological aspect are predominant: this is true on the one hand of proposals like job rotation, and on the other of the many prescriptions provided by experts and consultants in factory management.

It is not difficult to discover the mirror image of this statement in the social sciences which have as their aim the analysis of organisations (sociology of industry, of work, of organisation, management sciences, etc.). Authors who have dealt with manual labour or with the formal organisation of the firm have tended to proceed almost totally independently from each other. Perhaps the most significant example amongst the latest work in the field, is provided by the research of Alain Touraine and of Joan Woodward.[26] Both were working at the same time, both give a determining role to technology in their studies, and both end up by proposing schemes of evolution which have striking similarities. In Touraine's work however, his lucid analysis of manual work is surrounded by a void as regards information on the social structure of the whole firm; and in Woodward's study, manual work only appears in a very abstract and indirect way. As to 'managerial' writers, even the most intelligent ones only provide abstract prescriptions which in principle are considered to be applicable to any type of firm, or indeed any kind of organisation, which in turn is only possible if the analysis concentrates on some indeterminate managerial activity.

We can perhaps go one stage further, and formulate the hypothesis that the ideological elements in theory and the manipulative elements in practice are most evident where the analysis and practice inside the firm are least integrated with an analysis and practice which involves the social system in which the firm is situated. This would help to explain why formulae such as job rotation, job enlargement, and job enrichment are becoming official ideology for American management whereas the theory of socio-technical systems and its applications does not approach this position as far as European management is concerned. Whilst the former ideas deal basically and almost exclusively with problems surrounding the conditions of the work place and the psychological motivation of the worker, the latter theory poses questions about the relationship between the place of work and the social system, particularly by the use of concepts like 'internalized environment'.[27]

On one level we have encountered ideological deformations occurring because of the gap between analysis (and practice) of manufacturing work, and analysis (and practice) of the factory organisation as a whole, and also because of one of these two elements being considered in isolation from the other; on another level therefore we encounter ideological deformations occurring because of the gap between analysis (and practice) concerning the social system and analysis (and practice) of factory organisation, and also due to the exclusive consideration of only one of these two elements.

Unless he makes an integrated analysis of the factory system and the social system, the social scientist, like the trade unionist, may be led to ignore the fact that the superseding of Taylorism in certain firms can be accompanied by its wider diffusion in other areas and sectors, as well as by real forms of paleo-capitalist regression like the putting-out system. On the other hand he may be led to under-estimate the risk that meeting very advanced demands in the field of labour organisation will only affect a fraction of the working class which is then destined to become an aristocracy rather than a vanguard. In addition, a stress on analysis and demands relating to the social system does not in itself make the theory and practice any more revolutionary: in capitalist countries, limiting claims to wages and employment can lead to shelving the problems of labour organisation indefinitely; in socialist countries the change which has occurred in the social relations of production has been and still is an ideological excuse for not facing up to these very problems.

American hegemony or 'polycentrism'?

Taylorism and Fordism first developed in the United States, and were, for a certain period at least, very much an import into Europe: those engineers who tried to put the 'Taylor system' into effect in 1912 at the Renault factory at Billancourt had come back from a spell with United Steel. However, there do not appear to be grounds for believing that the workers' and unions' reactions to the intro-duction of rationalisation were of a different nature in the United States and in Europe: the reaction in both sprang from a defence of the psycho-physical integrity of the worker and of individual skills, which rationalisation was destroying.

Since the Second World War there have arisen some interesting differences between the United States and Europe, notably in the case of innovations aiming to supersede the Taylorist organisation of labour. The existence of strong unions linked to socialist parties in government certainly helps to explain what has happened in Great Britain, (the Tavistock Institute first intervened not only at Glacier, but in the newly nationalised coal industry), and in Norway (with a tripartite plan for industrial democracy). In Italy, and to a lesser extent in France, the existence in the opposition of strong trade unionists is certainly conditioning, if not determining, the trans-formations which are under way. In the last analysis, the influence of the union organisations, and the climate created by the presence of socialists in government strike us as distinctive features, compared with the United States, of the European countries where events relevant to this paper have occurred.

Another distinctive feature, only alluded to above, concerns the more marked tendency for European entrepreneurial ideologies and practices to affect the social system outside the factory. With parti-cular references to the ideology of co-operation in the first phase in the process of industrialisation in certain European countries, it has been observed that:

the ideology of co-operation takes on particular features on the continent of Europe: unlike what can be seen in the United States, this ideology does not merely concern itself with the stability of the relations of production, but seems to embrace the social arrangements themselves as a whole. Consequently this ideology is not exclusively based on the opportunities for agreement between the parties arising from the objective functioning of the productive apparatus, but also exposes itself in institutionalised forms of participation by the workers in the life of industry, (for instance, profit-sharing worker shareholders, consultative committees etc.).[28]

These differences have not yet been sufficiently studied whether from an historical or sociological point of view, and we believe they merit more thorough investigation, especially in terms of their political implications. They should not however be overestimated. The process of the internationalisation of capital has gradually increased in many respects, and yet these differences are still seen in the context of social systems whose method of production is substantially the same. From this point of view we urgently need an analysis and an appraisal of the role which the multi-national companies play in the homogenisation and diffusion of technological and organisational innovations in different countries, bearing in mind that in this period the technology and organisation which the multinationals tend to export, in the less developed areas at least, are probably of a markedly 'Taylorist' sort.

In the field of applied social sciences, perhaps the most interesting symptom of a process of current re-homogenisation is provided by the close links, even the convergence, which is becoming apparent between the American job-design movement and the European movement for socio-technical systems and for factory democracy. This convergence can be seen in the works of those most directly concerned, and in the fact that some of the most noted exponents of these different trends are now working side by side in promoting certain important innovatory experiments.[29]

Notes

1 K. Marx, *Das Kapital*, vol. 1, part IV.
2 A. Touraine, *L'Évolutiondu travail ouvrier aux usines Renault*, CNRS, Paris, 1955; A. Touraine, 'L'Organisation professionnelle de l'entreprise', in G. Friendmann and P. Naville (eds), *Traité de sociologie du travail*, Paris, Armand Colin, 1961, vol. 1.
3 A. Touraine, 'Le travail ouvrier et l'entreprise industrielle', in A. Touraine (ed.), *La civilisation industrielle*, Paris, Nouvelle Librairie de France, 1961, p. 20.

4 Touraine, 1955, op. cit., p. 39.

5 A. Anfossi, *Prospettive sociologiche sull'organizzazione aziendale*, Milan, Franco Angeli, 1971, part 1.

6 A. Pichierri, 'Fasi tecnologiche ed evoluzione professionale: l'uso dello schema di Touraine nel caso italiano', *Quaderni di Sociologia*, vol. XXII (1973), no. 3.

7 We can consider many of the examples of early mechanisation and early introduction of assembly-line work cited by S. Gideon, *Mechanization takes Command*, Oxford University Press, 1948, parts III and IV, in this light.

8 G. Friedmann, *Problèmes humains du machinisme industriel*, Paris, Gallimard, 1954, part III.

9 B. Caizzi, *Storia dell'industria italiana dal XVIII secolo ai giorni nostri*, Turin, UTET, 1965, p. 426.

10 Friedmann, op. cit., introduction.

11 R. Bendix, *Work and Authority in Industry*, New York, Harper & Row, 1956, p. 274.

12 A. Gramsci, *Note sul Machiavelli, sulla politica e sullo Stato moderno*, Turin, Einaudi, 1955, p. 317.

13 L. Baritz, *The Servants of Power*, Middletown, Wesleyan University Press, 1960, ch. 3.

14 P. Blumberg, *Industrial Democracy. The Sociology of Participation*, London, Constable, 1968, chs 2 and 3.

15 See for example the articles of P. Drucker published in 1955 in *Harpers' Magazine*.

16 F. Pollock, *Automation. Materialien zur Beurteilung der ökonomischen und sozialen Folgen*, Frankfurt am Main, Europäische Verlagsanstalt, 1964, parts II and III.

17 We use the term 'mechanistic' in the sense employed by T. Burns and G. M. Stalker, *The Management of Innovation*, London, Tavistock, 1961.

18 With reference to the Italian situation this view is coherently developed in M. Paci, *Mercato del lavoro e classi sociali*, Bologna, Il Mulino, 1973.

19 We have in mind especially the case of the Fiat works in Turin: in a period of serious economic difficulties for the firm, absenteeism and turnover are dramatically reduced, whilst strikes, both general and departmental remain remarkably frequent.

20 F. Butera, *I frantumi ricomposti*, Padua, Marsilio, 1972, ch. 3.

21 For the cases quoted in this section we have drawn on the following: *Tecnologia, sistemi organizzativi, qualificazione. Esperienze innovative in Europa*, Rome, Intersind-Arpes, 1973; *Le trasformazioni dell'organizzazione del lavoro esecutivo*, Ivrea, Olivetti – Servizio Ricerche Sociologiche e Studi sull'organizzazione, 1972; L. E. Davis and J. C. Taylor (eds), *Design of Jobs*, Harmondsworth, Penguin, 1972; Butera, op. cit.; 'Mutamento dell'organizzazione del lavoro e egemonia', *Economia e lavoro*, vol. VIII, no. 1 (1974).

22 For a similar interpretation, but one which refers specifically to the technology of information, see A. Luciano and E. Saccomani, 'Usi diversificati delle tecnologie dell'informazione: sistemi informativi e

problemi di integrazione', in *Razionalità sociale e tecnologie dell'informazione*, Milan, Comunità, 1973, vol. II.

23 F. E. Emery and E. L. Trist, 'Socio-technical systems', in C. W. Churchman and M. Verhulst (eds), *Management Science, Models and Techniques*, Oxford, Pergamon, 1960, vol. II.

24 Davis and Taylor, op. cit., pp. 17–18.

25 F. Butera, 'Contributo all'analisi di variabili strutturali che influiscono sul mutamento dell'organizzazione del lavoro: il caso Olivetti', *Studi organizzativé*, 1973, vol. 1, p. 3.

26 A. Touraine, 1955, op. cit.; J. Woodward, *Industrial Organisation. Theory and Practice*, Oxford University Press, 1965.

27 Emery and Trist, op. cit.

28 G. Baglioni, *L'ideologia della borghesia industriale nell'Italia liberale*, Turin, Einaudi, 1974, p. 75.

29 Davis and Taylor, op. cit.

4 Social democracy and workers' conceptions of power in England and Sweden[1]

Richard Scase

Of the many social factors which affect workers' images of society, there are two which are among the more important. First, the immediate experiences of everyday life.[2] Second, the influences generated by the mass media and the other institutions which contribute to the interpretation of events, occurrences and social structures.[3] Parkin, adopting the terminology of contemporary academic sociology, has argued that in capitalist society there are three 'meaning systems', each of which interprets the nature of social reality.[4] He refers to these as the *dominant*, the *subordinate* and the *radical*. He suggests that the *dominant* meaning system endorses existing structures of economic, social and political inequalities.[5] The *subordinate* meaning system fulfils a similar function; although it is generated by various work and community milieux within the working class, it promotes an 'accommodative' response to inequality.[6] The *radical* meaning system, by contrast, does not endorse the existing social order. Instead, based upon the working-class political party, it 'purports to demonstrate the systematic nature of class inequality, and attempts to reveal a connectedness between man's personal fate and the wide political order'.[7] Parkin is not suggesting that this meaning system generates a level of consciousness which brings about revolutionary changes in the structure of society; he is merely stating that it creates an awareness of existing inequalities. Whether or not this will develop into political action is problematic and subject to variable empirical circumstances.

Sociological studies that have been conducted in Britain since the war suggest that of these meaning systems, the *radical* has been the least influential. A number of investigators have shown that not only the Labour party but also large sectors of the trade union movement have given little emphasis to the grass-roots participation of rank-and-file members and to radical political socialisation.[8]

74

Consequently, there has been a tendency for structural inequalities to remain largely unchallenged and for there to limited knowledge among the English working class about inequalities generated by the socio-political system.[9]

In Sweden, labour unions and the Social Democratic party have achieved a higher degree of 'penetration' among industrial manual workers than their equivalent institutions in Britain; that is, as measured by membership statistics and voting behaviour.[10] Has this, then, provided the basis for the development of a more broadly based *radical* meaning system to the extent that industrial workers are more knowledgeable about existing patterns of economic and political inequalities? Elsewhere, I have tried to demonstrate that values relating to the Swedish working-class movement have created a heightened awareness of economic inequalities; at least by comparison with English workers.[11] But has this generated greater resentment towards the socio-political system? On the one hand, it can be argued that it has if only because Swedish workers, subject to the socialising influences of the working-class movement, would be more likely to be informed of the means whereby economically dominant groups exercise power in society. But, on the other hand, it could be that these same influences, although creating an awareness of economic inequalities, have generated a 'false' consciousness about the exercise of power in society. Thus, the Labour movement may have led workers to believe that it is the organised working-class movement as represented by the Social Democratic party and the labour unions, which has come to exercise the most influence. In fact, there is some evidence to suggest that this was the case in Sweden during the 1950s. In a study of two industrial communities, for example, Segerstedt and Lundqvist asked, 'Which class do you think is the most influential in Sweden?' Among male manual workers, almost one half of those identifying themselves as 'working-class' stated their 'own' social class, while only a third mentioned 'another' class.[12] Do such attitudes still persist, or do workers now have a more 'realistic' assessment of their position within the power structure? In other words, has the organised working-class movement in Sweden reinforced 'false' attitudes about the exercise of power in society or has it now generated a heightened awareness of power inequalities? Either way, the implications are likely to be important both for the development of social democracy and for the future of capitalism in Sweden.

The method

In order to test these ideas a series of interviews was conducted with manual workers employed in two Swedish and English engineering factories in the spring of 1970. These factories were similar in terms of both their technologies and products. The samples were chosen randomly from all those between the ages of 25 and 54. They consisted of fairly 'typical' workers; work careers were well established, and they were likely to be married, with children.[13] The response rates were 87 per cent for the Swedish sample and 73 per cent for the English, producing 122 completed Swedish schedules and 128 English schedules, upon which the present discussion is based. Obviously the findings cannot be regarded as representative of all English and Swedish manual workers since the samples were very small and chosen from only two factories. But the responses can be regarded as *indicative* of wider social patterns.

The results

The respondents were asked a number of questions in order to investigate the degree to which they felt the respective working-class movements had exercised influence in society to produce benefits for industrial manual workers. Thus, the 122 Swedish and the 128 English workers were asked 'Do you think that employment conditions have improved for factory workers since the war?' An overwhelming majority of both samples claimed that they had: 93 per cent and 98 per cent of the total Swedish and English samples

TABLE 4.1   *'In what ways do you think they (employment conditions) have improved?'*[1]

Improvements in:	Swedish workers		English workers	
	No.	%	No.	%
Physical conditions – noise, lighting, ventilation	37	33	103	82
Work tasks	64	57	44	35
Manager/worker relationships	5	4	11	9
Welfare benefits	17	15	3	2
Shorter working hours	30	27	27	21
Wage rates	39	35	13	10
'Social justice' and 'equality'	26	23	4	3
Other and non-classifiable responses	9	8	9	7

[1] Asked of those 113 Swedish and 126 English respondents who claimed that employment conditions had improved. Since most workers mentioned more than one factor, the figures add to more than 100 per cent. In this and the following tables, the decimal figures have been rounded to the nearest 'whole' number.

respectively. These respondents were then asked, 'In what ways do you think they have improved?' The coded responses are shown in Table 4.1.

Among those of the Swedish sample who felt that employment conditions had improved, 57 per cent mentioned 'work tasks', making such comments as 'the new machinery has made work easier', 'the jobs are not so tiring now', and 'you don't have to carry things about so much today'. A further 33 per cent referred to improvements in the physical conditions of the factory, while 35 per cent mentioned improvements in wage rates. But as many as 23 per cent suggested that there was now more 'social justice' and 'equality' in the workplace. Among these responses there were a number of statements which suggested that 'the individual has more rights now than before', 'managers treat the workers more on equal terms', 'there is less of a division between white-collar workers and the rest of us'. By contrast, 82 per cent of the English workers referred to improvements in the physical conditions of the workplace, 35 per cent to better 'work tasks', 21 per cent to shorter working hours, and only 3 per cent to 'social justice' and 'equality'.

Those respondents who considered that employment conditions had improved for factory workers since the war were then asked: 'What do you think is the major factor which has brought this about?' The coded answers are presented in Table 4.2:

TABLE 4.2 *'What do you think is the major factor which has brought this about? (Improvements in the employment conditions of factory workers)*[1]

Major factor	Swedish workers		English workers	
	No.	%	No.	%
Trade unions	55	49	59	47
Social Democratic/Labour party	23	20	1	1
Management	7	6	36	28
Technological change	13	12	19	15
Other and non-classifiable responses	14	12	10	8
Don't know	1	1	1	1
TOTAL	113	100	126	100

[1] Asked of the 113 and 126 Swedish and English workers respectively, who considered that employment conditions had improved since the War.

Although both samples gave equal significance to the role of trade unions, there were important differences in their other

77

responses. Whereas 20 per cent of the Swedish respondents claimed that improvements in employment conditions had been brought about by the efforts of the Social Democratic party, only one of the English workers mentioned the role of the Labour party. At the same time, as many as 28 per cent of the English, but as few as 6 per cent of the Swedish workers, attributed improvements to the efforts of management. Consequently, Table 4.2 suggests that more than two-thirds of the Swedish workers compared with less than one-half of the English respondents attributed improvements in their conditions of employment to the activities of the Labour movement; that is to the efforts of trade unions and the Social Democratic party. In other words, it appears that the Swedish workers were more likely to regard the Labour movement as a force for reform in the workplace; they perceived that it was this which had brought about improvements rather than the 'goodwill' of management.

The greater legitimacy of the Labour movement among the Swedish respondents – particularly that of the Social Democratic party – was confirmed by their answers to a number of questions about their standard of living. Swedish enquiries conducted during the 1950s found that industrial workers tended to attribute improvements in this to the efforts of the Labour movement. Dahlström, for example, when he asked: 'What factors do you think explain the increase in living standards over the last 50 years?' found that

TABLE 4.3 *'What do you think has brought this about?' (the increase in the standard of living)*[1]

Factor mentioned	Swedish workers		English workers	
	No.	%	No.	%
General improvements in trade and business	11	9	12	10
Social Democratic/Labour party	61	52	8	6
Trade unions	10	9	37	29
'Worker demands'	—	—	10	8
'Full employment'	16	14	13	10
'Higher wages'	8	7	26	21
Other and non-classifiable responses	11	9	19	15
Don't know	—	—	1	1
TOTAL	117	100	126	100

[1] Asked of the 117 Swedish and 126 English respondents who claimed that the standard of living had improved.

approximately 50 per cent of all the manual workers in his sample claimed that they were a consequence of the activities of Labour unions.[14] Similarly, Segerstedt and Lundqvist found that almost 23 per cent of their respondents attributed improvements in the living conditions of workers to the role of the Social Democratic party, and a further 44 per cent to the efforts of labour unions; they found that these institutions were mentioned to the same extent by both manual and non-manual workers.[15] In the present enquiry, the respondents were asked: 'Do you think that the standard of living for people like yourself has improved in this country since the war?' In both samples, an overwhelming majority of workers stated that it had; 96 per cent and 98 per cent of the Swedish and English respondents respectively. These workers were then asked: 'What do you think has brought this about?' Their coded replies are shown in Table 4.3.

As Table 4.3 suggests, a far higher proportion of the Swedish workers mentioned the Social Democratic party as the major reason for the improvement in living standards than of the English respondents who referred to the Labour party: 52 per cent compared with 6 per cent. Even when the figures are combined for those workers who mentioned the Social Democratic/Labour parties, trade unions and 'worker demands', it is clear that these accounted for as many as 61 per cent of the replies of the Swedish sample, but for 43 per cent of the English respondents. But it is also interesting that only 9 per cent of the Swedish, compared with as many as 30 per cent of the English workers, referred to the role of trade unions. One possible explanation for this could be that the Swedish workers tended to make a distinction between 'work' and 'society' as institutional orders. Consequently, when they referred to the working-class movement in their replies, they tended to mention trade unions in their comments about the factory, employment and working conditions, and the Social Democratic party in their attitudes about society. In other words, they regarded the Social Democratic party and the labour unions as interrelated institutions and referred to either of these according to the institutional context about which they were being invited to comment. But clearly, the Swedish sample regarded the working-class movement as a major agent of reform, bringing about general improvements in living and working conditions. The English workers, by contrast, were less likely to perceive the Labour party and trade unions in these terms.

In view of these findings, were the Swedish workers more likely than the English to conceive of themselves as members of an influential social group? To enquire into this, those workers of both samples who recognised the existence of social classes – 118 and 119 of the Swedish and English respondents respectively – were asked, 'Which are the major classes in this country today?' and then 'Which class, do you think, has the most influence over things today?' The responses are shown in Table 4.4.

TABLE 4.4 *Which class do you think has the most influence over things today?*[1]

Labels mentioned by respondents in describing the class structure		No. of respondents mentioning specific classes in their descriptions of the class structure		No. of respondents stating that this specific class 'had the most influence'		Percentage of respondents mentioning a specific class and who also stated it 'had the most influence' $\frac{(2)}{(1)} \times 100$	
		Swedish workers	English workers	Swedish workers	English workers	Swedish workers	English workers
1 'Upper', 'top' 'higher classes'		24	89	15	49	63	55
2 'The wealthy', 'the rich' 'those with plenty of money'		14	19	11	7	79	37
3 'Social group I'		57	—	47	—	83	—
4 'Middle class'		19	90	5	18	26	20
5 'White-collar people'		20	1	9	—	45	—
6 'Educated people'		5	1	5	—	100	—
7 'Social group II'		56	—	6	—	11	—
8 'Social group III'		47	—	4	—	9	—
9 'Working class'		46	89	6	37	13	42
10 'Ordinary people'		2	2	—	1	—	50
11 'Lower class'		2	21	—	1	—	5
12 'The poor', 'the lower paid'		7	8	—	1	—	13
13 Negative evaluation		10	1	—	—	—	—
Don't know		—	—	10	5	—	—
TOTAL		—	—	118	119	—	—

[1] In the first column, most respondents mentioned more than one class. Thus, the figures add to more than the total number of respondents in each of the samples. The labels listed in this column are those *actually used* by respondents.

From Table 4.4 it is clear that a majority of both samples who mentioned an 'upper' class, considered that it exercised the most influence in society. At the same time, 83 per cent of the Swedish workers claimed 'Social group I' had the greatest degree of influence, together with 79 per cent of those who referred to 'the rich' in their descriptions of the class structure. By contrast, only 37 per cent of the

English respondents who mentioned 'the rich' shared the same opinion. They were more likely to mention the 'working class'; no less than 42 per cent of the English workers who had used this 'label' considered that it exercised the most influence in society, compared with only 13 per cent of their Swedish counterparts. In fact, of the 47 Swedish workers who mentioned 'Social group III' in their descriptions of the class structure, as few as 9 per cent felt that it was the most influential group in society.

The respondents were then asked: 'Why is this?' (that this class has the most influence over things today). Since some of the classes were mentioned by only a very small number of respondents, those considered to be most influential by the two groups of workers were allocated, for the purposes of this analysis, to three categories – A, B and C – in the following manner:

Upper, top, higher class ⎫
The wealthy, the rich ⎬ A
Social group I ⎭

Middle class ⎫
White-collar people ⎪ B
Educated people ⎪
Social group II ⎭

Social group III ⎫
Working class ⎪
Ordinary people ⎬ C
Lower class ⎪
The poor ⎭

Table 4.5 indicates that 76 per cent of the Swedish respondents attributed the influence exercised by category A, that is the 'upper class', 'the rich', and 'social group I' to economic factors. Hence they claimed that 'money talks', 'those with the money take the decisions', 'it's their wealth which makes them powerful'. Among the English workers there were also respondents who referred to economic factors of this kind; for example, 52 per cent did so in their comments about the classes grouped in category A. But there was a far greater tendency for them to give examples of 'influence' which appeared to be unconnected with economic characteristics. Hence, they often made statements such as 'they are the born leaders', 'they have always taken the decisions', and 'they occupy the powerful positions'. The Swedish workers, by contrast, appear to have regarded the 'influence' exercised by these groups to be determined by the economics of the marketplace. If a high proportion of the English respondents (42 per cent) considered the 'working class' to exercise

TABLE 4.5 'Why is this'? (that this class has most influence over things these days)

Responses	Category mentioned as the 'Most influential'											
	Swedish workers						English workers					
Suggesting:	Category A (N-73)		Category B (N-25)		Category C (N-10)		Category A (N-56)		Category B (N-18)		Category C (N-40)	
	No.	%	No.	%	No.	%	No.	%	No.	%	No.	%
Economic factors	55	76	5	20	—	—	29	52	2	11	—	—
Activities of trade unions	—	—	2	8	2	20	—	—	—	—	24	60
'Majority of people'	—	—	4	16	4	40	—	—	3	17	9	23
Specific examples of influence	9	12	6	24	—	—	24	43	7	39	1	2
Other and non-classifiable responses	9	12	8	32	4	40	2	3	4	22	4	10
Don't know	—	—	—	—	—	—	1	2	2	11	2	5
TOTAL	73	100	25	100	10	100	56	100	18	100	40	100

TABLE 4.6 *Respondents' conceptions of whether their 'own class' or 'another class' exercised the most influence*

	Class mentioned as the most 'influential'											
	Swedish workers						English workers					
Respondents' self-placement in class placed in category:	'own'		'another'		total		'own'		'another'		total	
	No.	%	No.	%	No.	%	No.	%	No.	%	No.	%
A	—	—	—	—	—	—	—	—	—	—	—	—
B	9	22	32	78	41	100	7	30	16	70	23	100
C	10	13	65	87	75	100	38	40	57	60	95	100
Other and non-classifiable responses	1	50	1	50	2	100	1	100	—	—	1	100
TOTAL	20	17	98	83	118	100	46	39	73	61	119	100

83

the most influence in society, it is evident from Table 4.5 that they felt this to be a consequence of the activities of trade unions. Thus, trade unions were mentioned by no less than 60 per cent of those workers who claimed that the classes included in category C exercised the most influence over things.[16] At the same time, a further 23 per cent felt the classes in category C exercised the most influence because they were 'the majority of people', 'most people in the country' and 'the greater proportion of the country'.

Although Tables 4.4 and 4.5 describe the respondents' views about which classes exercise the most influence in society, they do not specify the respondents' own class self-placements. Consequently, from these tables it is not possible to ascertain whether they perceived their 'own class' or 'another class' to exercise the most influence. Such an analysis is presented in Table 4.6.

As Table 4.6 suggests, more than twice as many of the English respondents as of the Swedish workers considered that their 'own class' exercised the most influence: 39 per cent compared with 17 per cent. At the same time, no less than 40 per cent of the English workers compared with only 13 per cent of the Swedish respondents in category C felt their 'own class' exercised the most influence. In other words, it is clear that the Swedish workers were far less likely than their English counterparts to regard themselves as members of the 'most influential' group in society. This is a surprising result in view of the conclusions of the study conducted by Segerstedt and Lundqvist.[17] How, then, can the difference between their findings and those of the present study be explained? Furthermore, how is it possible to account for the differences in the attitudes of the English and Swedish workers?

Discussion

One possible explanation for the differences could be the development of feelings of relative deprivation which seems to have occurred among Swedish manual workers since the late 1960s.[18] The Social Democratic party and the labour unions have emphasised, particularly over recent years, the persistence of 'objective' patterns of economic inequality in society and the need for these to be reduced. It would be surprising, therefore, if feelings of relative deprivation which these policies appear to have generated did not affect attitudes towards the distribution of power in society, particularly in view of the fact that the Swedish respondents overwhelmingly attributed the influence of the 'upper class', 'the rich' and 'social group I' to economic factors.[19] Furthermore, it is possible to suggest that the Swedish respondents' awareness of the influence exercised by these groups was a function – if only partly – of their greater commitment to the

Social Democratic party, certainly, by comparison with the English workers' attachment to the Labour party.[20] In successive general elections, the Social Democratic party, with the support of the labour unions, has emphasised the need for the election of Social Democratic governments so that wage earners can be protected against the interests of 'big business'. Hence, the Swedish labour movement has stressed the importance of its role in society as a 'check' against the economic self-interests of modern capitalism. Consequently, if 'democracy' is to be preserved, according to Social Democratic electoral appeals, it is necessary for the political apparatus of the state to be 'isolated' from the control of financial and industrial interests; this can only be achieved by electing Social Democratic governments.[21] In other words, the appeals that have been put forward by the party and the trade union leadership have emphasised the class basis of political power, and possibly, if only partly as a result of this, Swedish manual workers – as illustrated by the attitudes of the respondents – have become more aware not only of economic inequalities, but also of power differentials as they exist in contemporary Sweden.

Therefore, it is possible to suggest that the organised working-class movement in Sweden has provided the basis for the development of a *radical* meaning system which has created a greater awareness of power inequalities than that which exists in Britain. Certainly, the attitudes of the two samples – admittedly of very small numbers of workers – indicate that this may be the case. If further empirical enquiries substantiate on a more general and representative basis the findings of this highly limited study,[22] then these attitudes could have important implications for working-class commitment to the organised Labour movement as well as for the long-term development of social democracy in Sweden. But, although the adherence of the movement to a *radical* meaning system seems to have heightened the level of socio-political awareness among working-class supporters, the institutions of capitalism continue to generate structures of power and privilege within which industrial manual workers are deprived and exploited. Accordingly, because of the incompatibility of *radical* norms with capitalist economic institutions, it seems appropriate to consider social democracy in Sweden as subject to strains so that, over the long term, two possible outcomes can be expected. On the one hand, disillusion with the leadership of the organised Labour movement could become widespread among industrial manual workers so that there is a shift in support for more 'right-wing' political parties. Alternatively, there could be increased demands by the rank-and-file for the leadership to adopt more radical policies in relation to existing patterns of ownership and control.

Although Sweden and Britain are both capitalist countries, it is not to be assumed that they have exactly comparable power structures. One of the most systematic empirical studies of the relationship between the political state and private capital in modern Western societies has been undertaken by Miliband.[23] He argues that in such countries economic elites are interconnected so that they constitute a dominant economic class. This class, he claims, has more influence than any other class and exercises a decisive degree of political power. Although the structure of power in Britain, and particularly in the early 1970s when there was a Conservative government in office, may be of the kind described by Miliband, it is difficult to argue that such circumstances prevail to a similar degree in Sweden. Most certainly there is a dominant economic class which primarily represents the interests of private property, but it is doubtful whether it can be regarded as a ruling class in the sense of explicitly dominating the formal state political apparatus. If successive Social Democratic governments have done little to destroy the parameters and the mechanisms of contemporary capitalism, they have restricted the degree to which privately owned economic interests have dominated the exercise of political power. Therefore, since the war – and especially during the 1960s – they have passed legislation which has not only 'protected' the interests of employees but also increased their representation in formally prescribed decision-making processes. For example, laws have been introduced which have increased the job security of workers and restricted traditional managerial prerogatives in relation to hiring and firing. Other laws have attempted to increase the participation of industrial manual workers and of lower grade white-collar employees in decision-making at industry, company and plant levels. Similarly, other legislation has been enacted which has aimed to protect the interests of consumers and clients against the potential abuses of private and public bureaucracies. Furthermore, the development of these laws has been such that it has become increasingly difficult for privately owned wealth and assets to be transmitted from one generation to the next. Although Labour governments in Britain have pursued comparable policies, they have been less comprehensive than in Sweden. In these ways, Social Democratic governments have represented the interests of industrial manual workers to a far greater degree than has been the case in Britain. If, then, both countries are to be regarded as similar types of capitalist society, in the sense that they are both dominated by economic classes which overwhelmingly own and control the means of production, they must also be seen as different to the extent to which the self-interests of these classes are 'restrained' by the representation of the Labour movements within their respective political decision-making processes. In other words, the development of the working-class movement in Sweden has tended to reduce the degree to which economic dominance has been 'converted' into political control. Thus, a comparison of political developments in Britain and Sweden would suggest that although they possess a number of features common to all capitalist countries, they also have a number of important differences. As Runciman has argued, it is possible to categorise societies in terms of whether they are 'capitalist' or 'socialist' but this should not lead to the assumption that there are no differences between countries within these socio-economic systems.[24] Consequently, it can be argued that in Sweden, the Labour movement has forced the state to exercise a greater degree of control over privately owned institutions than in Britain, although it has not – as yet – explicitly and fundamentally challenged the dynamics of Swedish capitalism. However, because the growth of a well-organised working-class movement in Sweden has led to the development of a power structure which represents the interests of industrial manual workers to a greater extent than in Britain, it does mean it is in a better position to alter existing patterns of ownership and the relations of production. The distribution of income, earnings and wealth in Sweden has been, and continues to be, primarily determined by the private ownership of the means of production, and by national and international forces of supply and demand. But in the long term, the legitimacy of Swedish capitalism could be breaking down if only because of the way in which the Labour movement's ideological commitment to egalitarianism has heightened workers' awareness of economic and power inequalities.

However, this does not seem, as yet, to have generated demands for a drastic restructuring of society according to principles which would be more favourable to the industrial working class. At the most it seems, so far, to have generated feelings of resentment. Why, then, have there not been greater rank-and-file pressures for a radical restructuring of society and for the abolition of the institutions of private property? In order to offer some kind of answer to this question it is necessary to consider changes in the ideological themes of the Social Democratic party during different periods of the twentieth century.

Since its inception in the latter part of the nineteenth century, the primary objective of the Social Democratic party has been to create a more egalitarian society.[25] But the *means* whereby this objective could be achieved have been subject to considerable debate within the party and the basis for the revision of policies at different points of time. Thus, it is possible to identify phases in the history of the party when the abolition of private property was considered essential if egalitarian goals were to be achieved, while at other times it has been argued that such goals were compatible with capitalism and attainable within the parameters of such a society. The first period can be considered to have lasted until the end of the First World War, when the public ownership of the means of production was seen to be the only method whereby greater economic and political equality could be attained. The second phase can be regarded as lasting from this time until the early 1930s when, during a decade of minority governments, the party pursued 'pragmatic' and short-term policies which were more concerned with solving current economic crises than with pursuing long-range radical, socialist objectives. It was in the 1920s, according to Tingsten, that the predominant ideology of the Social Democratic party became de-radicalised, rejecting the necessity for socialising the means of production for the attainment of egalitarian goals. The party was then elected to government in 1932 and during a third period – which lasted for approximately thirty-years – reformist and welfare policies almost completely dominated the objectives for-mulated by the leadership of the working-class movement.[26] Thus, it was considered by the leadership of the Social Democratic party that the development of the welfare state, the application of Keyne-sian economics and the regulation of economic activity by a system of government controls and stipulations were sufficient to guarantee that the wealth created by capitalism could be distributed according to criteria of social justice and equality. However, during the early 1960s there was a further shift in Social Democratic thought when there were reappraisals of the degree to which party goals could be achieved within the parameters of capitalist society. Consequently, it is possible to delineate a fourth stage in the development of Social Democratic thinking which has persisted until the present. Therefore, since the early 1960s, more radical measures have been contemplated and the party has re-adopted a more positive attitude towards state ownership of the means of production. In this way, it has again recognised that public ownership provides an important instrument whereby the traditional ideological goals of the party can be achieved.

Thus, the development of the Swedish Social Democratic party suggests that a process of de-radicalisation, in the sense of rejecting the extension of state ownership and control and the representation of working class interests in society, cannot be seen as an inevitable feature of working-class parties in capitalist societies in the manner suggested by Michels.[27] At certain stages in its history it may be necessary for such parties to pursue less radical policies for the purposes of obtaining widespread electoral support, but at a later period of time the heightened expectations of the rank-and-file may force the leadership to adopt more radical objectives. Whether such shifts in ideological parameters are initiated by changes in the attitudes of leaders, or by the leadership responding to perceived changes in the attitudes of its supporters is problematic. Michels, for example, suggested it was the attitudes of the leadership which determined the policies of working-class parties, while Tingsten, on the other hand, has claimed that the rejection of policies which advocated the public ownership of the means of production by the Swedish Social Democratic party during the 1920s was primarily a consequence of the leadership's response to the immediate demands of rank-and-file members.[28] For example, he claimed that during this period the party membership was more concerned with immediate policies which would reduce the level of unemployment, raise real wages and provide a minimum provision of social security than with restructuring ownership and control in society. Consequently, it is difficult to identify the bases for changes in Social Democratic policies in terms of whether they originated from the leadership or the mass-based supporters. But it does seem that once party objectives have been formulated, the working-class movement in Sweden has enjoyed a considerable degree of success in retaining the commitment of its membership. Whether this allegiance will continue in the future will largely depend upon the extent to which rank-and-file supporters perceive that the leadership has been successful in achieving the movement's explicitly stated goals. The ideological commitment to egalitarianism by the party appears to have been conducive to the generation of attitudes which could have important implications for the long-term development of the Swedish working-class movement, particularly in generating widespread feelings of relative deprivation and resentment. Such attitudes could lead to an increased recognition among workers of the inherent contradictions between the movement's goals and the existing socio-economic structure. However, so far these contradictions have been successfully accommodated by the Social Democratic party's adopting a number of tactics for the purposes of legitimation, of which the following are but two of the more important.

In the first place, the party claims to have improved opportunities for workers' children by reforming the educational system,[29] and to be currently pursuing policies which will ultimately break down existing economic inequalities.[30] But at the same time, it has legitimated its relationship with the Swedish working class by emphasising the improvements in the standard of living which have occurred since the 1930s. This argument has been strengthened by the adoption of two sets of comparisons, each of which are frequently used in Social Democratic debate – the one, historical and the other, trans-national. In terms of the first, the party has always presented itself as an instrument of progress and change. Thus, for the purposes of political rhetoric, history has often been categorised in terms of two eras – the 'old' and the 'new' Sweden.[31] Consequently, 'old' Sweden is described as consisting of widespread inequalities, injustices and acute deprivations which have only been removed as a result of the achievements of the working-class movement. According to the arguments, the Social Democratic party and the Labour movement have created a 'new' society in which remaining inequalities and injustices are being removed. In this way, the pre-Social Democratic era of Swedish history has become linked with notions of injustice and deprivation. Indeed, the descriptive categories used for these 'types' of society are different; for the discussion of inequality in 'old' Sweden the terms 'upper class' and 'working class' are used, while for the Social Democratic analysis of 'new' Sweden, socio-economic categories are described in terms of social groups I, II and III.

The second set of comparisons emphasises the advantages of industrial manual workers in Sweden over those of workers in other countries.[32] For these purposes, Britain and the United States are most frequently chosen. Britain is used in order to demonstrate the equality of Swedish society and the socio-economic advantages of Swedish manual workers. Journalists in newspapers, radio and television describe Britain by reference to the attitudes and behaviour of the upper and working classes, with the implication that it is a country at a similar level of development to that of 'old' Sweden. At the same time, the United States is used in order to emphasise the high standard of the Swedish urban environment, the 'progressive' attitudes of Sweden towards developing countries and the lack of 'corruption' in Swedish political life. If then, Britain, the United States and other Western countries are characterised by glaring injustices and 'reactionary' political regimes and if, at the same time, socialist countries are regarded as failing to protect individual and civil liberties, then Sweden must – according to the arguments – be the most egalitarian and the most democratic country in the world. These achievements, so it is claimed, have been brought about by policies pursued by the leadership of the working-class movement.

These, then, are but two examples of the arguments used by the Social Democratic party in order to maintain its legitimacy with rank-and-file supporters. In these ways it has been possible for leaders of the Swedish Labour movement to conceal – if not always successfully – some of the inherent contradictions between an ideological commitment to egalitarianism and a capitalist productive system. By the use of cross-national comparisons, the attempt has been to demonstrate that the Labour movement has achieved a considerable degree of equality. If there are persisting inequalities in Sweden these will be removed, according to the appeals of the leadership, provided that continued support for the movement by rank-and-file members is forthcoming. But such appeals tend to reinforce the tensions which exist between ideology and material infrastructure. If efforts by the party leadership to accommodate these strains become less successful in the future, then the Social Democratic party may either lose its broadly-based support among industrial workers or be increasingly forced to adopt radical policies towards existing patterns of ownership and control.[33]

Notes

1 This chapter is an edited version of chapters 6 and 7 of my *Social Democracy in Capitalist Society*, London, 1977.

2 See, for example, the articles in M. Bulmer (ed.), *Working Class Images of Society*, London, 1975.

3 For a useful discussion of these see J. Westergaard and H. Resler, *Class in a Capitalist Society*, London, 1975, pt III.

4 F. Parkin, *Class Inequality and Political Order*, London, 1971.

5   The concept of a dominant value system derives from Marx's celebrated statement that 'the ideas of the ruling class are, in every age, the ruling ideas'. This proposition rests on the plausible assumption that those groups in society which occupy positions of the greatest power and privilege will also tend to have the greatest access to the means of legitimation. That is to say, the social and political definitions of those in dominant positions tend to become objectified and enshrined in the major institutional orders, so providing the moral framework of the entire social system. (Parkin, op. cit., pp. 82–3.)

6   In so far as it is possible to characterise a complex set of normative arrangements by a single term, the subordinate value system could be said to be essentially *accommodative*; that is to say, its representation of the class structure and inequality emphasises various modes of adaptation, rather than either full endorsement of, or opposition to, the *status quo*. (Ibid., p. 88.)

7 Ibid., p. 97.

8 See, for example, J. Goldthorpe, D. Lockwood, F. Bechhofer and J. Platt, *The Affluent Worker: Political Attitudes and Behaviour*, Cambridge, 1968.

9 This was almost certainly the case until the early 1970s. Since then, government economic policies have probably increased, at least to some extent, working-class awareness of economic inequalities. For a discussion of the consequences of national income policies for the development of attitudes of this kind, see J. Goldthorpe, 'Social inequality and social integration in modern Britain', in D. Wedderburn (ed.), *Poverty, Inequality and class structure*, Cambridge, 1974.

10 For a statistical documentation of this point see Scase, 1977, op. cit., ch. I.

11 R. Scase, 'Relative Deprivation: A comparison of English and Swedish manual workers', in Wedderburn (ed.), op. cit.

12 T. Segerstedt and A. Lundqvist, *Människan i Industrisamhället*, Stockholm, 1955, pp. 287–93.

13 For detailed description of the two samples see Scase, 1977, op. cit., ch. 3. Funds for the enquiry were provided by the Centre for Environmental Studies, London (Research grant RAP 127).

14 E. Dahlström, *Tjänstemännen, Näringslivet och Samhället*, Stockholm, 1954, pp. 97–9.

15 Segerstedt and Lundqvist, op. cit., pp. 335–6.

16 It is, however, important to mention that many of these respondents perceived this influence to be illegitimate. A number of them claimed that 'trade unions were too powerful', 'that they held the country to ransom', and 'they had gone too far'.

17 Segerstedt and Lundqvist, op. cit.

18 R. Scase, in Wedderburn, op. cit.

19 See Table 4.5 on p. 82.

20 Measured, that is, by voting statistics. See Scase, 1977, op. cit., ch. I.

21 This was particularly the case in the party's 1970 and 1973 election campaigns.

22 Seeman, for example, in a study of workers' attitudes in Sweden, found that the experience of alienation at work was not generalised to non-work situations. He found that workers who were alienated in the workplace were not less knowledgeable or less engaged in political matters; on the contrary, they demonstrated a degree of political and social integration not found in similar studies conducted in the United States. See, M. Seeman, 'On the Personal Consequences of Alienation at Work', *American Sociological Review*, vol. 32 (1967).

23 R. Miliband, *The State in Capitalist Society*, London, 1969.

24 W. G. Runciman, 'Towards a Theory of Social Stratification', in F. Parkin (ed.), *The Social Analysis of Class Structure*, London, 1974.

25 For a discussion of this, see H. Tingsten, *The Swedish Social Democrats*, New Jersey, 1973.

26 Except for the late 1940s when there was a prolonged debate about the party's attitude towards public ownership.

27 R. Michels, *Political Parties*, New York, 1962.

28 Tingsten, op. cit.

29 Educational reforms, Social Democratic appeals and their consequences for working-class attitudes are discussed in R. Scase, 1977, op. cit.

30 See R. Scase, in Wedderburn op. cit.

31 This division is generally expressed in terms of *Förr i Tiden* and *Nuförtiden* so that they should appear as quite distinct historical eras.

32 This and the following comments are derived from the author's personal experience of the interpretation of news and current affairs by

party spokesmen in the Swedish mass media over the past ten years; particularly in the radio, television and the press as represented by reports in *Dagens Nyheter*, *Expressen* and *Aftonbladet* – the largest selling daily newspapers in Sweden.

33 In September 1976, after this chapter was written, a general election was held in Sweden resulting in the return of a centre-conservative coalition. However, in this election the Social Democratic party lost only one per cent of its share of the votes. Recent opinion polls show an increase in the level of support among industrial manual workers for the Leadership of the labour movement, and since the 1976 election, the Social Democratic party has formulated a series of radical policies for implementation when it is returned to office.

5 Migrant workers in European social structures

Salvador Giner and Juan Salcedo

I Labour migrations and social structure: problems of interpretation

The temporary or definite settlement in the more industrialised European countries of a great number of workers either from the south of the continent or from overseas has been an event of great importance. By the early 1970s there were well over 10 million foreign labourers, mostly unskilled, whose presence has inevitably affected the most diverse elements in the host countries: government agencies, employers, trade union organisations, political parties, economic plans, and, above all, the life of the people who came into daily and direct contact with the newcomers, their fellow-workers and their neighbours. A number of wide-ranging social processes have been influenced by this phenomenon: economic growth, employment trends, wealth patterns, urban segregation and ghetto formation, to name but a few. The chief protagonists of the entire event, the migrant workers and their families, have been of course those who, confronted with the more acute and varied problems, have had their lives most drastically affected.

This chapter is concerned with a sociological interpretation of the set of problems brought about by labour immigration in north-western Europe. Apart from our own limitations and from those imposed by the vastness and complexity of the aspect, the task is made more difficult by the absence of a proper theory of migration in the social sciences.[1] In order to achieve some clarity, this chapter will concentrate its attention chiefly on one subject, namely, that of the class nature of the immigrant collectivities and their position within the patterns of conflict and order which are to be perceived in the contemporary host countries of Europe. Thus, a number of issues will have to be ignored[2] while others, often very important, will only be brought in to illuminate the argument.

94

The elucidation of the class situation of the migrant workers and their role in the set of social conflicts and problems brought by their presence is far from easy. Answers will largely depend on whether the analysis of such situations assumes (a) that the migrants form a mere stratum within a single working class – whose internal differentiating features are thus secondary to their common 'true' interests – or (b) that they are essentially and even dangerously alien collectivities – alien especially to the working classes themselves – only connected to the host society through certain links of labour and wages, backed by a number of legal provisions, but with no cultural, ethnic or *Gemeinschaft* links with that society. As we shall see, several sociological studies have adopted assumption (a), whereas (b) is more typical of a number of political groups whose hostility towards the immigrants is quite plain. The first notion often reflects the received wisdom of the left, and has many corollaries – such as the idea that the migrant population reinforces the capitalist system in so far as the rest of the working classes refuse to be aware of the common nature which they all share, and to act accordingly. Otherwise stated, the working classes of the host countries suffer from a form of acute 'false consciousness' and therefore fail to develop a brotherhood of class, common identification, or 'consciousness of kind'. The second notion is, of course, sponsored by reactionary tendencies within trade unions and within the more openly xenophobic political movements. This last position appears thoroughly vitiated from the start and will not be discussed, but the conventional opinion of the left[3] deserves some scrutiny and, as we see it, much correction.

For one thing, one cannot expect the working classes of affluent Europe to develop a 'brotherhood of class' with those immigrants who fill positions in the social division of labour which they themselves reject as 'lowly', especially if this is combined with the fact that their internal diversification, along lines of status, power and indeed, class, is very great. That all workers – from the highest paid to the humblest labourer – 'ought to' possess a sense of solidarity is a moral question of doubtful relevance in the present analysis. It is obvious, though, that even in Marxist terms they cannot do so as long as capitalism and the welfare state continue to flourish, for their combined success is reflected in the strengthening of the multiple stratification of the manual working population as well as in the creation of great wage differentials and a very uneven distribution of risks such as the likelihood of unemployment.[4] To ask complete solidarity and brotherhood towards the foreign migrants from such a diversified working class begs the question and ignores the real strengths of a mixed economy which is firmly linked to the ruling classes and to the political, trade union, and cultural elites of Western

Europe. Under the present circumstances, then, skilled manual workers and technicians cannot be expected to show towards unskilled foreign labourers the attitude of brotherhood and solidarity that they do not show to their own unskilled fellow-citizens, as their struggle to keep (or even to increase) wage differentials patently shows.[5]

An important change in attitudes – both from governments and from social classes – will only come about under a number of pressures.[6] One of the most important is bound to be the strife generated by foreign workers themselves in so far as they organise, protect or make their voice effectively felt in the world of labour relations or in the wider realms of civil society. Under the present circumstances their presence may be a factor increasing the degree of class conflict and social unrest in Europe. This is turn may ultimately facilitate, rather than hinder, the achievement of some of their aims of equality and non-discrimination.

II Some basic facts

A serious hindrance in the study of international migrations is the doubtful quality of the data available for the purpose. Data are reliable neither at the international nor at the national levels. Definitions about who exactly is a migrant or how migrants are registered are unclear or lacking. These difficulties may be summarised in the following four points:

1 The only data which are reliable are those which refer to 'assisted' or official migration.[7] Assisted migration is, of course, only part of the total volume of migration. It is very hard to know with even a minimal degree of accuracy what is the relationship between total and assisted migration. Then the quality of data varies enormously from country to country. When data are available they frequently refer to new migrants and ignore the previously existing stocks of foreign workers already living in the country. Often no distinctions are made between economic and political migrants or refugees, and their respective age, sex and occupational composition.

2 Many migrants have not been described as such because they are officially described as students, tourists, *au pairs*, etc. Yet it is obvious that many of these join the work force and share in the community life of the countries concerned just as migrant workers do.

3 There is a grave lack of information about political refugees and their employment patterns despite the fact that their number and importance are considerable, both in North America and Europe.

4 When accurate data do exist, they are often not directly comparable between countries.[8]

With these observations in mind we shall now present a brief account of the main features exhibited and effects produced by the phenomenon of labour migration in the host countries.

(i) Origins of international labour migrations in contemporary Europe

Vast labour migrations – that is, migrations across state boundaries, for the purpose of finding work and earning more, and not necessarily with the intention on the part of the migrant of leaving his country for good – are far from characteristic of the European situation after the end of the Second World War. Yet, it was in the political and economic climate created by its aftermath in Western Europe that they became a regular feature of its social life. They were of course preceded by a wave of forced migrations of a different nature, of truly gigantic proportions, which may nevertheless have had some psychological effects favourable to the later labour migrations. Thus, during the war, in 1944, Germany employed almost 9 million foreign workers, of which 1·8m. were prisoners-of-war and the rest slave labourers or hired foreign workers. At its end about 30 million people had to be repatriated and many millions had to find new homes. Thus 6·5 million *Volksdeutsche* were driven out of Eastern countries, and Germans were expelled from the Oder and Posnania, while Poles were transfered from Soviet-occupied territory into Old Poland; 100,000 Italians left Istria to the Yugoslavs; and preceding all these and other groups, more than half a million Spaniards had crossed the Pyrenees at the end of the Civil War, in 1939, many of them settling in France.

The recovery of the Western European economy after the war is said to be the chief reason for the steady rise of migrant workers from the less developed parts of the continent.[9] While this is patently true, there have been other factors which have been systematically overlooked by serious observers. We may list three at least. First, there is *demographic growth*. This was considerable in the years after the war, especially in Southern Europe, where life-expectancy made great strides. Thus, the southern half of Italy, in the early 1950s with less than 40 per cent of the country's total population, furnished 66 per cent of its total demographic growth. Second, there were *the landslide effects of internal migration*. In some countries migration from the countryside reached exodus proportions, for a variety of reasons, even producing – as in Spain – urbanisation without a corresponding rate of industrialisation. This in turn produced an overspill effect as unemployed ex-peasants began looking for work abroad. Third, there were *political factors encouraging migration*. This was officially encouraged in Yugoslavia and Spain – in order to

97

strengthen their respective economies – but against the official policy of Portugal before April 1974, where great numbers of peasants would leave clandestinely, and at great risk and discomfort to themselves to seek work in France and elsewhere, thus avoiding being sent to colonial wars or as 'settlers' in dangerous colonies. This latter aspect of migration is of course connected with new forms of gangsterism and illegal trade in men and manpower which has been flourishing in several countries, without much effective opposition from governments concerned.

(ii) Volume and intensity of the labour migrations

Tables 5.1, 5.2 and 5.3 may be useful in providing an idea of the general rhythm, fluctuations and some key features of the foreign work force in a number of European countries over the years examined.

TABLE 5.1 *Long-term immigrant flows to several countries of Western Europe, 1962–1974 (main host countries only)*

	Migrants (thousands) in the years:									
Countries	1962	1963	1964	1965	1966	1967	1968	1969	1972	1974
Austria	6	5	6	6	6	6	10	13	—	—
Belgium	—	66	79	73	71	64	57	55	5[2]	—
Denmark	28	26	27	30	30	—	27	—	25[2]	30[1,2]
France	113	115	153	152	132	107	93	—	120	65
Germany (FR)	649	574	699	839	746	431	686	701	303[1]	—
Netherlands	51	43	55	65	69	44	54	66	16[2]	—
UK	68	47	224	206	219	225	221	206	35[2]	—

[1] 1973.
[2] Proceeding from non-EEC countries.
— without data.

Sources: UN *Demographic Yearbook 1970*, New York, 1971, table 25; *Le Monde* (Paris) 23 January 1974; *La Vanguardia* (Barcelona), 11 September 1975.

(iii) Occupational distribution by sectors

Once again, the limitations inherent in the data at hand severely limit the study of the occupational structures of migrants. We now face an additional problem: the actual occupational patterns of migrants within public administration bodies or in private firms are unclear.[10] It is well known, however, that immigrants are employed in two main fields:

TABLE 5.2 *Stocks of foreign workers by main host and emigration countries (thousands)*

Host country		Turkey	Yugoslavia	Greece	Italy	Portugal	Spain	North Africa	Total
Germany (FR)	1968	4	32	6	248	172	270	333	1,260
	1972	450	435	264	384	57	174	394	2,159
France	1968	4	32	6	248	172	270	333	1,260
	1972	22	65	10	590	600	650	1000	3,500
	1975	—	—	—	—	—	—	—	4,128
Austria	1972	22	154	0·6	1·6	—	0·3	18	197
Switzerland	1969	6	17	5	386	—	89	132	636
	1972	—	—	48	298	—	123	—	612
Belgium	1968	8	1	6	70	3	27	66	182
	1972	11	—	7	85	3	35	—	217
Netherlands	1969	16	3	1	10	12	12	25	80
	1972	21	9	1	10	—	15	—	75

Sources: This is a simplified version of the table presented by S. Paine (1974), p. 26; for France 1975, *The Economist*, 31 January 1976, p. 50; M. Teresa Iza, 'El exodo espanol a Europa' in *Cuadernos para el Dialogo*, no. XL, May 1974.

TABLE 5.3 *Migrant foreign workers in the EEC[1] by general recruitment area circa 1970*

	Migrant workers from: (thousands)		
Countries of the EEC	*EEC[1]*	*Rest of South Europe and North Africa[2]*	*Total*
Luxembourg	25	5	30
Italy	9	21	30
Netherlands	23	57	80
Belgium	104	78	182
France	262	798	1,060[3]
Germany	424	1,151	1,575
TOTAL	847	2,110	2,957

[1] The 'Six', not the 'Nine'.
[2] Spain, Greece, Turkey, Portugal, Yugoslavia, Algeria, Morocco and Tunisia.
[3] Estimation by a survey.

Source: EEC *Documentation Europeenne, 1970*, Bruxelles, 1970, vol. IX.

1 As industrial workers, mainly in building, public works, mechanical and engineering jobs. In these branches of activity migrants are near (but certainly not equal) to the status of native workers on the lowest rungs of the industrial occupational system.

2 As marginal workers, in jobs rejected by native people, found chiefly in great concentrations of population, with low wages and very low status, and often associated with some kind of social stigma.

Workers in the 'industrial' situation are more at the mercy of market fluctuations (i.e. come closer to belonging to the 'industrial reserve army' provided by the migrant pools of labour force in Southern Europe and overseas) whereas workers in the more 'marginal' situation find jobs which can only be explained by patterns of prejudice in combination with welfare-state policies. Thus, though unemployment in Great Britain has prompted strong government protection against excessive labour immigration, Spaniards and Portuguese – both from non-EEC countries –can easily find work in the catering, hospital and hotel industries simply because the native work force prefers to go on the dole rather than taking up such kinds of employment. As unemployment sharply rose in 1974 and 1975 the situation continued to be the same. In France, for instance, immigrants amounted to 7·7 per cent of the total population by 1976, but made up 8 per cent of its labour force, and 12 per cent of the nearly 1 million unemployed, while 90 per cent of them were manual workers.

In the light of all this it seems clear that the host countries' economic and cultural demands determine the unskilled nature of the migrant population. The very common idea that foreign workers are by definition unskilled, illiterate, and unprepared for any serious job, has its origins in precisely these demands, and not in the true make-up of the migrant population, and especially of the local communities from which this population stems. (Incidentally, the serious brain-drain of skilled workers and professional talent suffered by Greece and Spain should underline this point. So too, should the presence of the Pakistani and Indian doctor in English hospitals, an all too familiar figure.) Tables 5.4 and 5.5 may help illustrate these comments.

TABLE 5.4 *Five major sectors of migrant employment in several countries and years*

France 1968	%	Germany 1968	%
1 Building and Public Works	30·0	1 Building	23·2
2 Engineering and electrical goods	12·4	2 Engineering	19·1
3 Agriculture, forestry, fishery	8·7	3 Hotel and Catering	11·8
4 Commerce	8·6	4 Clothing	6·1
5 Personal services	4·7	5 Commerce	4·9

Switzerland 1966[1]	%	Great Britain 1966	%	%
			Men	Women
1 Clothing	63·2	1 Miscellaneous services	20·5	26·0
2 Textiles	52·6	2 Engineering and electrical goods	10·5	6·4
3 Stone and earth (6)	51·7	3 Professional and scientific services	9·6	23·3
4 Rubber and plastics	44·9	4 Distributive trades	8·4	12·9
5 Metal Industry	42·8	5 Construction	6·9	—

[1] Proportion of migrant workers to total workers in these industries.

Source: Adapted by us from Stephen Castles and Godula Kosack, *Immigrant Workers and Class Structure in Western Europe*, London, Oxford University Press, 1973, pp. 62–78.

(*iv*) *Market situation*

The migrants' market situation may be described under three different headings.

1 '*Free labour*' occurs when the worker is not legally tied to any one employer and may change jobs without leaving the country.

TABLE 5.5 Socio-economic characteristics of immigrant workers in several countries and years (%)

Socio-economic characteristics	France 1967	Switzerland 1960	Germany 1968 Men	Germany 1968 Women	Great Britain 1966 Men	Great Britain 1966 Women
Engineers and managers	1·2	[1]	[1]	[1]	12·3	5·5
Supervisory personnel and technicians	1·7	[1]	[1]	[1]	7·8	2·3
Non-manual workers	3·4	15·0	8·0	12·0	12·4	37·9
Skilled manual	25·2	25·0	20·0	3·0	28·5	11·1
Semi-skilled manual	36·6	37·0	36·0	30·0	24·8	37·6
Unskilled manual	31·9	23·0	34·0	53·0	4·8	4·8

[1] Without accurate information.

Source: Adapted by us from Stephen Castles and Godula Kosack, Immigrant Workers and Class Structure in Western Europe, London, Oxford University Press, 1973, pp. 79–90. Data for Great Britain have been re-elaborated by us for purposes of comparability.

This is not the normal situation among foreign workers in Western Europe during their first period of stay (from four to twelve or fifteen years) in the host countries. The relationship between employer and employee involves a multiple subordination of the latter to the former, as expulsion from the country will follow expulsion from the job in most cases. This relationship is also extremely important in the resocialisation of the migrant in the dominant patterns of the new country.

2 *'Unfree' labour* occurs when the employer recruits workers only for specific jobs and for a limited period of time. Workers are treated in this case 'as a commodity and not as citizens' (Moore, 1975, p. 5). At the end of the 'unfree' labour period workers are repatriated (usually within three months) in the case of the majority of non-EEC migrants in industries in Switzerland and Germany.

3 *Illegal labour* occurs when workers cross frontiers through unofficial channels and without proper registration papers. Many false students and pseudo-*au-pair* girls fall within it, apart from the labourers smuggled into certain countries (Portuguese to France, Pakistanis to England, etc.) with the help of criminal organisations and the connivance of employers.[11] There seemed to be about six hundred thousand illegal immigrants *plus* their families in the EEC countries in 1974.[12]

(v) Official policies towards the immigrants

As essential element of the overall situation examined here is formed by the set of policies carried out by the several governments, public bodies, trade unions and certain privately sponsored organisations towards foreign labourers. Despite some differences, governments, employers' organisations and trade unions often find large areas of agreement and very frequently listen to each other in the elaboration of their respective official policies towards the immigrants. This could not be otherwise for they serve – rhetoric apart – largely complementary interests in the same economic system and are not prepared to introduce the changes in the political *status quo* which would be needed if the immigrants were to be fully integrated in their host societies.

(a) *Governmental policies.* The existence of the EEC provides a certain degree of homogeneity among nations in this area, though no unified policy exists. After the 1973 energy crisis Federal Germany has been trying to persuade the EEC Commission to adopt a unified policy for all member countries to restrict inflows of non-EEC migrants[13], but its efforts have not yet been successful.

One country of emigration, Italy, would appear to enjoy special advantages through its membership of the Community, and another, Ireland, through its special arrangements with the United Kingdom established well before both countries joined the EEC in 1974. Yet numerous bilateral agreements often offset such advantages. Spain, for instance, is not a member of the EEC and has perhaps suffered economically from it – for political reasons – but in so far as the prosperous industrial countries needed her work force, ample facilities for recruitment were granted to them by her government.

The salient feature of government policies everywhere is simply that there is no coherent general policy established by any government aiming at the legal, political, economic and cultural equalisation of the rights of the immigrants. One finds, instead, either official declarations of intent, or a number of uneven provisions in the field of welfare, schooling, right to send remittances, and so on. Perhaps because immigrants do not vote, among other reasons, the formulation of a coherent policy, which would include serious steps for their protection and social promotion, is by-passed in electoral campaigns. In fact, governments' paramount preoccupation is the regulation of the immigrant population, that is, the maintenance of an 'optimum number of immigrants' at each stage of the economic conjuncture. Therefore systematic education and training of immigrants for skilled work and higher paid jobs would contradict the needs of the capitalist economy for a given pool of an unskilled work force, with low wages and placed conveniently outside the trade-union world, that is, incapable of putting adequate and effective pressure on governments and employers alike. Most revealing in this context are those measures regulating the control and repatriation of workers when the economic events are unfavourable. Sudden expulsions and repatriations – attempted or completed – are directed particularly against immigrant leaders who pose a threat to the established trade-union organisations by setting up their own immigrant unions. In such cases collusion between government and unions is quite evident despite disagreement in nearly every other field, as occurs in France under Giscard.[14] Governments, of course, do not expel their own citizens when excessive unemployment arises, but they do so with foreign workers, especially with those whose minimum number of years of residence has not been completed. Since, as we have pointed out, one of the characteristic features of European migrations has been the short length of stay of the migrants, a very sizeable section find themselves at the mercy of repatriation, often by simply losing one job and, with it, their resident's permit.[15] In turn, the threat of being laid off by an employer hangs like Damocles' sword over their heads. The authors have interviewed non-EEC European immigrants in England who live in fear for four years, till they can move about and look for other jobs in the market. During that period they are completely tied to their employer,[16] a situation which occurs, of course, in accordance with Home Office rules.

In this connection, it is interesting to note that, more often than not, official bodies looking after foreign workers[17] do not possess enough autonomy in their decisions and budgets, and depend entirely on governmental instructions. The main criteria inspiring those instructions are the achievement of full employment, economic development and the provision of an adequate work force for depressed and undermanned industries or regions as well as for those which are earmarked for development.

Under modern welfare-state conditions and the constant criticism provided by political opposition parties, responsible journalists and pressure groups, governments and employers' organisations often make efforts to cushion the negative effects of sharp falls in foreign employment or rises in repatriation. Thus, the Bonn government ban on the recruitment of workers from all countries outside the EEC (November 1973 and still in force in 1977) was accompanied by a move by the employers to offer workers compensation for voluntary redundancy. Though such an offer was not labelled as being intended for foreign workers, it was clearly made with them in mind. Yet in spite of repatriation and compensation, general unemployment in West Germany was higher for foreign workers at the end of 1974 than for national workers.[18]

Usually, government efforts to improve the condition of the immigrants go hand in hand with measures to regularise, restrict or diminish the number of immigrants, both legal and illegal. This double-edged policy has attempted to meet the increasing demands of the immigrants for better treatment and more rights[19] as well as the pressures exerted by anti-immigrant political groups. One favourable result of this in some countries, such as France after 1968 and Great Britain after the 1962 Immigration Act, is that permanent settlement with the families joining the initial migrant has increased, though the overall inflow has been reduced (S. Paine, 1974, p. 7). Family settlement is an incipient trend, however. As we pointed out earlier, the enforcement of a system of temporarily employed labour has meant that the host economies have enjoyed the supply of a very flexible pool of labour-power without incurring all the additional social costs which arise when dependants are admitted and people must be trained while young or looked after when retired.

(b) *Trade-union policies.* Like governments, trade-unions in the host countries have been slow to react in any significant way to the inflow of immigrants. A measure of this slowness is given by the fact that the first trade-union discussions and substantial reactions to migration only began to take place in the early 1970s. It was as late as 1973 that a conference of European and Mediterranean unions – representing both native and migrant workers – explicitly demanded improvements in legislation, housing and active co-operation between workers of all kinds. Migrants themselves – perhaps for reasons which are too obvious to need detailed explanation – have also been very slow at organising themselves in any effective form, save that of limited mutual help or leisure institutions along ethnic lines. Thus, the first Pan European Migrant Workers Congress took place as late as the end of 1974, in Holland (Moore, 1975, p. 20). A loose federation of local organisations may one day arise from this, though no international body with any significant powers was foreseen at the meeting.[20]

On the whole, many migrant workers – perhaps well over two-thirds – lie outside the world of unions, like many poorly paid native workers, but are far worse off than they (Moore, 1975, p. 20); they are discriminated against on ethnic grounds, they lack the freedom to bid for jobs in the open labour market, they have fewer chances for adequate training leading to promotion, and they are isolated because of linguistic and ethnic barriers. It could be said that, in spite of all this, they are not really discriminated against by the unions, for unions look after their own members and not after other workers – whether their own co-nationals or not – who are outside their membership. This observation is indeed correct, though it shows exactly what the nature of contemporary European trade unions is, despite ideological statements to the contrary made either by unions belonging to the ILO or by those which are controlled by several Communist parties in Western Europe.

Observers of the hostile – or rather mutedly hostile – reaction of the European unions to the immigrants point out that established industrial labour forces and their organisations have always been antagonistic to the influx of substantial numbers of workers from abroad or from other regions in the fear that it may spoil the ever-present struggle for better wages. This seems to be a normal reaction and Castles and Kosack are right when they point out that

> the protectionist attitude of workers towards new immigrants cannot . . . be ascribed to racialism and xenophobia. If workers in Western Europe today fear that immigrants will be used for undercutting wages and conditions, for strike-breaking, that immigrants may even make them redundant, they can draw on long and bitter experience (Castles and Kosack, 1973, p. 119).

Despite all this, to varying degrees trades unions have not only accepted foreign workers as members but actually encouraged or allowed them to form their own organisations. This has not occurred independently of international and national party politics – social democratic unions inspiring and financing social democratic migrants' organisations, or communist ones doing the same along their own lines – but it has taken place in all countries discussed,[21] and apart from its effects upon the local situation, it is bound to have important consequences in countries such as Spain and Portugal, where free trade unions have been absent during the two decades of migration under scrutiny.[22]

(c) *EEC policies.* The Common Market policy is based on the *principle* of free circulation of workers, though this principle is limited by certain considerations such as 'limitations by reasons of public order, security or health'.[23] Such limitations are, *de facto*, a political weapon in the hands of the politicians for restricting the movements of workers across political boundaries.

One of the most important limitations for the worker is the fact that he cannot move from one country to another to look for a job; free movement (travel, meals, lodgings) is very expensive for a worker (not for a professional). In this sense workers' movements are not free, but conditioned by employment agencies, government offices and other institutions of control. The only freedom of the worker consists in either *accepting* the contract which is offered by an employment agency, or remaining in his country of origin. At a second stage, when the worker is in the host country, he can move to another firm or job 'if the conditions of the labour market are favourable' – but not in all countries. Because of this, the importance of the employment offices becomes very great. They are a tool in the hands of the governments or unions of the host countries. The freedom of migration appears to depend largely on the general forces of the economic system. In addition to this there exist a number of institutions sponsored by certain countries of emigration whose aim is the political surveillance and control of the migrants.[24]

(vi) *Wage differentials*

There is a grave dearth of data about how native and migrant workers compare as to their respective wage-scales or incomes for the same job performed. The reason is that such comparisons would not always be legally possible; at any rate, official statistics about an illegal state of affairs are inconceivable. However, private conversation and enquiries about the problem in Germany and France show that such differences do exist. *Ceteris paribus* (occupation, seniority, social security, etc.) the wage difference between native

107

and immigrant may be as high as 30 per cent. The size of the gap is in indirect relationship to the legal situation of the foreign worker. When his or her legal situation is fully on a par with that of the natives, wages are finally equal or near the national average for the kind of job performed. However, when the contract is illegal, as occurs with vast numbers of foreign workers, we are confronted with typical cases of blatant exploitation by unprincipled employers. If we then take into account that often workers are paying off their debts to illegal traders in international labour, as well as the fact that they are easy prey for 'Rachmanism' and criminal housing practices, we shall be able to imagine with some degree of accuracy both the complexity and the gravity of this situation.

(vii) Some macro-economic effects

The cost-benefit analysis of migrants in individual terms is difficult enough. Its macro-economic counterpart is considerably more complicated, if we are to take into account which institutions, social groups, and collectivities benefit from the increased wealth made available by the labour of migrant workers.[25]

It is evident from the above figures and data that the immigrant labour force presents a set of characteristics which make it distinctive for its 'cheapness' to the host economy. Apart from some very limited expenses such as recruitment agencies in the countries of emigration, language schools, where they exist, and so on, the maintenance of the immigrant worker is much cheaper to the governments and local authorities, and other bodies involved. (Even some of these costs can be written off. Thus, in so far as recruitment agencies demand certificates of good health and physical fitness, their minimal cost is enormously offset by the savings incurred by hiring only able-bodied men in their prime.)

There are many aspects of the situation which underline the advantageous nature of foreign labour for the host economy. A few can be pointed out.

(a) Unemployment does not always mean that the migrant worker is entitled to a subsidy while he is out of a job, but rather that he or she is forced to return to the country of origin, no matter what the economic situation may be there.

(b) The demand on housing and social overhead capital by the migrants is smaller. Thus many married workers live in host countries without their families. (In Germany, in the early 1970s, 82 per cent of male Turkish workers were married, but 54 per cent were without their wives; as for Greek workers in the same country, 78 per cent of whom were married, only 61 per cent of the latter had their wives with them (Yannopoulos, 1974, p. 11).)

(c) In connection with this last point, but in a somewhat different sense, the temporary nature of the stay and the much smaller size of the migrants' families means that the pressure on health services, schools, retirement benefits, and the like is bound to be considerably smaller than that created by the native workers. Initial training and education of the workers – some of which is necessary even for the most unskilled – is not paid by the host society. The cost of all this cannot compare in any sense with travel expenses which are sometimes paid by firms and governments. Tables 5.6 and 5.7, which give the age structures of the immigrant workers, and show how many of them are in the prime of their life, do not need any comment. Notice, though, the enormously advantageous proportions in the case of France and the comparatively equitable figures for the United Kingdom.

(d) The number of workers without labour permits actually performing tasks at very low wages cannot be accurately calculated, but it is obvious that cheap labour thus obtained is an important factor in the production of large profits. Combined with this is the keenness of both clandestine and officially recognised foreign workers in doing overtime, also for fairly low wages.

(e) No matter how relatively small the capital stock owned by the workers of the host countries, it is clear that immigrants 'come to the country without any capital stock' and that therefore the immigrant community 'will not be in a position to share' in its products (Yannopoulos, 1974, p. 12). It can be safely assumed that only a very small number of immigrants invest their savings in the host country, as their saved earnings tend to either be channelled through remittances to their families back home or to the creation of a small capital stock for investment when they return, e.g. to build themselves a house in their village, or buy some land.

(f) The propensity to save has a direct effect on a country's rate of growth. Since the very sizeable immigrant labour forces have a much higher propensity to save than the native wage earners, it is obvious that they will influence both rates of spending and of national investment in a favourable way for the host country. Migrant labour therefore acts as a deflationary force, through its propensity to save (S. Paine, 1974, p. 14, quoting Böhning).

(g) Finally, foreign workers partly 'take away from the native population the burden of cyclical unemployment' (Yannopoulos, 1974, pp. 16–17). The figures and tables we have presented so far show that drops in the numbers of foreign workers follow the fortunes of the national economies. Labour permits are or are not renewed according to the state of the labour market, and precise instructions are also given to recruitment agencies according to labour-market fluctuations. The role of the foreign labour force as an 'industrial reserve army' is quite clear.[26]

TABLE 5.6 Distribution of immigrants to several countries of Western Europe by age groups in 1969 (%)

Country	Under 14	15 to 24	25 to 44	45 to 64	65 and over	Total (thousands)
Belgium	27·1	23·0	33·4	7·2	2·7	(55)
France[1]	—	34·4	59·2	5·4[2]	0·8[3]	(93)
Germany[1]	12·2	29·4	46·0	8·8	3·2	(686)
Netherlands	20·8	23·8	46·2	7·4	1·4	(67)
UK	17·1	35·5	35·5	6·8	2·1	(206)

[1] 1968.
[2] Only 45 to 54.
[3] 55 and over.

Source: UN Demographic Yearbook 1970, New York, 1971, table 25. We have chosen 1969 as representative of the peak years of the migratory period under consideration.

TABLE 5.7   *Proportion of male immigration to several countries of Western Europe, in the age group of 25 to 44 and in the total (1969)*

Countries	% of males in the following groups	
	25–44	*Total migrants*
Belgium	71·3	61·2
France[1]	85·6	81·6
Germany[1]	69·1	63·2
Netherlands	67·8	60·6
United Kingdom	58·6	51·2

[1] 1968.

Source: UN *Demographic Yearbook 1970*, New York, 1971, table 25.

III Integration, conflict and labour migrations

From the sociological standpoint the migratory issues examined here pose certain basic questions, namely: To what extent has social integration occurred? To what extent has social conflict been created or exacerbated? How have power groups, social classes, and affected institutions reacted to the migrants?

A unified and meaningful answer to these central questions is not easy, but some clarification may be achieved if we first distinguish between two different levels of response by the migrants to the host society, and vice versa. These we shall respectively call 'class integration' and 'political subordination'. The level of *class integration* is given by the degree to which a collectivity of migrants has entered into the established class system of a country. Thus, a group of immigrants whose ethnic habitat and life patterns are distinctly segregated from all those of the host society can be said to possess a very low degree of class integration. Such group is 'marginal' in more senses than one to the society for which and in which it nevertheless works. By contrast, the level of *political subordination* is given by the degree of acceptance and accommodation shown by the immigrants to the established institutions through which conflicts are solved in the host societies *and* to the predominant structure of domination. Thus a group of immigrants whose trade union, electoral and civic behaviour is very poor or non-existent and combines with a high degree of conformity to its overall situation can be said to possess a very high degree of political subordination.[27]

With these distinctions in mind we shall be able to distinguish four main types of migrant response to the host society, thus:

111

Integration and conflict of migrants

Political subordination

		+	−
Class integration	+	(a) Positive assimilation	(c) Solidary insubordination
	−	(b) Passive subordination	(d) Particularistic insubordination

(a) *Positive assimilation.* This process occurs when a long stay in the host country, intermarriage, effective acculturation, and other related phenomena act upon the migrants till they are more or less part of the host society. It is characteristic of the traditional type of migration, where the migrants stayed for good in the 'new country' or 'second homeland'. Of course, the notion of complete assimilation must be discarded altogether as either naive or grossly ideological, but some form of assimilation – in the economic, class and political structures of the host country – does take place, as not only studies of American, Canadian and Argentinian societies have shown but also surveys of European countries, past and present. Thus, the large Spanish and Italian element in several areas of Southern France, which came into that country either for political or economic reasons well before the migrations analysed here, has been largely absorbed into French society and fully shares its patterns of mobility, class, politics and occupational change. To give only one historical example, the same occurred long ago with the eighteenth-century Bavarian settlers of Andalusia. Of course, it cannot be assumed that this pattern can easily apply to that section of the migrant population which is coloured or possesses some strong ethnic identification traits such as the Muslim religion, as is the case with West Indians in England, Indonesians in the Netherlands, and Algerians in France. [28]

Despite the inaccuracies of the official data it can safely be assumed that the new patterns of migration do not, on the whole, favour positive assimilation. It is impossible to put forward a figure of 'assimilated' migrants – though it is probably higher than imagined for countries culturally akin, such as Spain and France – but it is obvious that the unprecedented patterns of migration pointed out above, reinforced by the new transport facilities of modern times, which allow periodic and effective contact with the countries of origin, all work against traditional forms of assimilation. [29] Assimilation is therefore an important, but essentially marginal, phenomenon within the entire social process of post-Second World War migration in Europe.

(b) *Passive subordination.* This has been the most frequent case throughout the migratory period analysed: it consists of a lack of integration into the class system of the society combined with a generalised acceptance of the domination and authority patterns found at the state, enterprise and community levels.

The fact that the bulk of the migrants belong to the unskilled population does not mean that they belong to the lower classes of the host societies: they are in too many senses *outside* society: ethnic, language and cultural barriers separate them from other workers (as, has been abundantly shown, do wage barriers), and the fact that they can be and are effectively taken out of the economy – sent back home – only stresses this point. A number of studies consistently fail to see this fact, and therefore are guilty of serious misinterpretation when introducing notions such as 'class consciousness' and 'solidarity' in this particular context. The migrants are often 'imported' by the economic system on a basis that perpetuates and reinforces their being aliens; they are hired labour, borrowed personnel, and remain so. This may sound extreme, but the analysis of the particular work situation, market-bound life and residence patterns of the migrant communities leaves no room for a less drastic appraisal. By the same token, all this points directly to the high complexity of working-class social structures, which do not lend themselves to sweeping and romanticised generalisations. The European 'proletariat' as a unified, solidary, revolutionary force waiting to be swept by a sudden wave of single-minded 'class consciousness' simply does not exist as long as the general economic and political conditions thus far described or referred to continue to operate in Western Europe.

(c) *Solidary insubordination.* The overwhelming predominance of the 'passive subordination' pattern among immigrants does not preclude other forms of response. One of them is the kind of revolt against the system of domination which does imply a substantial degree of class integration. This occurs when both the immigrant working classes and those of the host country make common cause in their demands *and* challenge the economic and political systems in which they live and work with a certain degree of consistency. Now, under conditions of high employment, economic growth, and high out- and inflow of migrant workers, this has hardly occurred in Western Europe in recent times. When an economic crisis approaches that could trigger such a process, migrants' returns escalate, and recruitment comes to a standstill; the migratory processes that could aggravate tensions is brought to a halt.

André Gorz speaks for the wishful-thinking left when he states that it is 'no coincidence that in May 1968, when ... a total challenge was made by the masses in France, unity between "national" and "foreign" workers flowered spontaneously'.[30] It certainly was no coincidence, for the revolutionary wave which both the Gaullist government and the French Communist party so skilfully stifled did create conditions of solidary insubordination. They were ephemeral, though, and allow no critical observer to generalise from them. On the contrary, it can be empirically proven that explicit and important large-scale movements towards the blurring of class barriers between the two working classes have been all too rare and always too short-lived to be considered as the norm.

(d) *Particularistic insubordination.* Together with solidary insubordination – though more frequent than the former kind of challenge to the established rules – particularistic insubordination is also less common than passive subordination. This occurs when a given migrant collectivity engages in some form of overt and fairly organised rejection of the system of domination originally accepted when the migration took place, and when that rejection is neither co-ordinated nor previously accepted by other workers. (Other workers and their organisations may in fact disapprove of it, though *ex post facto* recognition may ensue in some cases.) Like in the case of solidary insubordination, but in a more acute form, this may lead to serious reprisals, that is, expulsion from the host country. Since this form of insubordination involves by definition immigrant workers alone, these are easily singled out as clear 'culprits' in the labour disputes or other forms of conflict within this category and become highly vulnerable to disciplinary measures.

Particularistic insubordination is sociologically very interesting because it shows the ways in which authorities and employers react when immigrants try to transform their particularly weak legal, organisational and economic position as well as the ways in which trade unions are forced to face a situation which they have not foreseen in their established policies.

IV Some concluding remarks

The four possible types of migrants' response to their class, economic and political environments have, of course, a limited explanatory power. Their possible interest lies in their capacity for clearing the ground for a more adequate description of the migrant social universe. Subsequent explanation would have to take into account not only those combinations of factors which give rise to each type of reaction, but also look at the historical fluctuations and changes of emphasis from one case to the next. This last point has some importance in view of the fact that until now most students of the phenomenon seem to single out one type as *the* decisive aspect in the entire migratory process. Some for instance (Rose, 1972) are openly inclined to emphasise assimilation (case a); others (Gorz, 1970) opt for solidary revolts (case c) as most important; still others find that passive subordination is only a case of 'false consciousness', as is particularistic insubordination in so far as the native workers do not join the migrants in their demands. The shortcomings of such partial explanations of the migrant workers' social behaviour towards the power, authority and economic structures of the host societies can perhaps be traced to the fact that each author (or current of opinion) analyses the whole complex situation with the help of only one perspective. Let us explain this.

There are, basically, two standard versions of the migrants' situation. They are used both by social scientists and by politicians and the public at large, though the former understandably try to use a more sophisticated language in their assessments. The first version (which can be called the 'conservative' version) claims that immigrants are better off in the new countries. If they were not, the argument goes, they would simply go back. The more enlightened supporters of this view acknowledge that there are discomforts in the life of the immigrant, even that in some cases discrimination or unlawfuly low wages come into the picture, but they insist on the primacy of the overall advantages of migration for those who have opted for it. All this would basically explain the widespread pattern of conformity amongst the migrants, though certainly not those in which they show a rebellious attitude to their social setting. The second one (which can be called the 'radical' version) claims that immigrants are subject to countless indignities in the host countries, that they have left their own under unbearable economic and political pressures and that they are overexploited. Though the argument that the capitalist or neo-capitalist system keeps them subservient is hackneyed, it is certainly not irrelevant. It tends to ignore the migrants' own account of their situation, and the migrants certainly express the view that they are much better off than in their own societies in a number of fundamental ways. We ourselves have not emphasised this aspect of the situation until now – without which a full picture is not possible – but this is essential if a satisfactorily balanced understanding of the problem is to be achieved

Each of these two explanations looks at the problem from one single perspective, and ignores the other. The truth of the matter seems to be that the migrant lives simultaneously in two sets of social universes, with two corresponding sets of reference groups. Exceptions apart he sees himself as better off than his national equals (those landless peasants, say, he left back home) and sees himself as worse off than the local people who 'ought' to be his peers – the

115

local unskilled or skilled workers, as the case maybe. Empirically, he is right on both counts. His decision to leave is connected with a desire to improve his lot; to live up to his sense of self-dignity by being able to send money back home to a hard-pressed family; to save up for a flat or a house on his return; to show everyone that he can wrest himself free from local oppression and succeed in the world. The achievement of these aims in turn requires submission and subordination to the rules of the game he finds in another society, where he is certainly in many senses, overexploited, marginalised and discriminated against. In this connection, however, there is a set of responses which have often been ignored by both sides of the argument and yet which protect and encapsulate the migrant against too much indignity, thus reinforcing his patterns of conformity: the development of a community culture along ethnic lines in the areas where he settles.[31]

The coexistence of at least two sets of reference groups in the migrants' view of their social universe can go a long way to explain the four main patterns of response. The analysis of anomic situations leading to the high rates of mental illness recorded among migrant workers[32] could also be carried out in the framework of the confusion produced by class, status and cultural conflicts at the personal level amongst those who are too torn to opt for one of the two characteristic decisions of the migrants, either to stay in the new countries forever, really to settle down, or, as is typical of the contemporary situation, to return home after several years. Apart from the specific case of the seasonal worker, the temporary nature of the stay also goes a long way to explain conformity, at least as much as do the wage and market patterns of the neo-capitalist mode of production with all its welfare-state-supporting practices.

Reference group theory, though, is not enough to finish a picture which is left incomplete by the mere economic interpretation of migrant flows, even when the latter is presented in an adequate framework which class and power analysis provides. The fluctuations and changes in the history of labour migrations must be considered in conjunction with the underlying processes which have been taking place in contemporary Europe in all areas concerned. The Schwarzenbach 'initiatives' against so-called *Überfremdung* in Switzerland did not appear mechanistically the day that country's immigrant labour force grew to one-third of the entire Swiss labour force. The project for a general *Loi de l'immigration* in France did not finally reach an advanced stage in 1975 because the French government had suddenly woken up to the needs of the four million aliens in the country.[33] Portugal, in its decades of despotic right-wing rule, was not averse to migration to Europe because it shunned foreign currency, nor did Yugoslavia under Tito and Spain under Franco follow the opposite policy because they thought that remittances were the only and overriding reason for the open-door criterion. Migrant communities in North-Western Europe have not inexplicably waited till the early 1970s to make their demands felt through strikes, petitions, cultural activities and pressure on the media. All these varied instances, and many others, need specific explanations through sets of circumstances which cannot be generalised to the whole, or even to parts, of the European continent. Thus the imperial shackles of pre-1974 Portugal, the abandonment of Fascist-like programmes of economic autarchy in Spain, the internal policies of the League of Yugoslav Communists, they are all as vital to explain the rhythms, intensity and direction of the migrations as the 1973 energy crisis and its subsequent developments.[34] Time itself, and the socialisation processes undergone by the migrant communities, would help explain their greater militancy and increasing demands since the late 1960s. It is not only that new forms of strife have arisen (or been intensified) throughout our continent and that inevitably migrant workers must be affected by them, but that the migrant communities – in spite of the rapid turnover of individuals – are better equipped for communicating and making their voice felt without mediation in the host societies; migrant social traditions, networks, mutual aid and political know-how are now much more established than they have ever been before.

All these features, combined with the new political and economic developments which have been taking place in Europe after 1973 – the fall of Southern European dictatorships, the enlargement of the EEC, the energy crisis – are bound to have important repercussions on the life of migrant workers. Some of these can already be detected, such as the stabilisation or diminution in the stocks of foreign labour, changes in the availability of unskilled work in the traditional areas of emigration,[35] the passing of laws for both the control and the welfare and the civil rights of the migrants, the further development of schooling and other services to the migrants, the realisation by the xenophobic elements in several societies of the 'need' for a foreign work force. Such 'need' cannot easily be attributed to the 'evil' aspects of monopoly capitalism or any such construct. Thus it is obvious that so far the little-explained labour migrations occurring within Eastern Europe and the Soviet Union take quite similar forms and produce several similar effects to the ones so far examined. States, under every existing political system, possess the right to regulate imigration flows in order to protect what they believe to be the economic interests of their own citizenry. Often well-meaning and humane social critics forget that such rights will always be exercised and must therefore be treated as an invariant. This has nothing to do, of course, with the fact that social justice must be

117

seen to be done to the migrant workers in the host countries. Whatever the future of labour migration, it is clear that without it much in the modern structures of inequality, class conflict, economic growth and political life of the modern European world would have been very different. In fact, the migrant foreign worker with his problems, his anxieties and his search for a better and more dignified life is the most vivid illustration of what is still wrong and what is indeed right in contemporary Europe.

Notes

1 Despite the numerous studies on migration, and detailed analyses of 'pull' and 'push' effects upon the affected populations, an *integrated* theory of migrations, which would take into account cultural, political, socio-psychological, as well as class and market conditions, is still wanting. Such theory ought to focus especially on how decisions about moving are made by the prospective migrants and on their own definition of the socio-economic situation and their chances in it. Cf., however, J. B. Lansing and E. Mueller (1971), and J. Jackson (1969). For accurate accounts of migrants' definitions of their situation and of the migratory process generally cf. J. F. Marsal (1969) and A. Sayed (1975). For a detailed critique of the basic assumptions of 'push-pull' theories as mere projections of gravitational physics into social phenomena cf. J. Salcedo (1976).

2 Among them there are some of sociological relevance which deserve more attention from social scientists. Such are, for instance, the question of the effects of the returned migrants to their countries of origin – on this, see A. Pascual (1970) – the national or ethnic, as opposed to the state, origin of the labour force, and the correlation between this and the jobs performed; the patterns of status and income differentials of each national collectivity in each host country; the different rates of acculturation and 'assimilation' by group and country; the comparative political behaviour and trade union militancy of each collectivity; etc. Another dimension largely left unexplored in this paper is 'ethnic' and race relations. While we reject the race-relations approach which assumes that all migrants are easily integrated in the social structure of the host country *except* coloured or ethnically very distinct ones and ignores the economic and political basis of the entire process, we consider the more sophisticated approach to race relations emerging in works such as John Rex (1970) far more useful. However, the limited scope of this paper does not allow us adequately to integrate this aspect of contemporary research into it.

3 The most characteristic statement being contained in S. Castles and G. Kosack (1973a).

4 For a perceptive treatment of working-class consciousness, cf. M. Mann (1973).

5 Addressing themselves to a related problem the authors of a study on trade unionism and stratification appositely say:

the literature surveyed . . . never confronts the central questions. . . .
Under which conditions and for which reasons do workers,
whether manual or white-collar, come to see themselves as
socially connected with interests in common, and under which
conditions are those interests perceived to involve a confrontation
with the existing social order? G. Bain, *et al.* (1973) p. 157.

6 Among these pressures the campaigns of enlightened social critics,
film-makers, journalists, politicians and other opinion leaders cannot
be ignored, though, for obvious reasons, their efforts cannot be
considered in this essay.

7 For information on characteristic official inexactitudes, clerical errors
and miscalculations cf. J. Power and A. Hardman (1976), p. 7.

8 Castles and Kosack in their painstaking study collect a number of
tables by occupation and country which are accurate enough, and yet
hardly comparable (Castles and Kosack (1973b), pp. 62–93). The *UN
Yearbook* uncritically relies on data made available by each government in their official communications.

9 For issues related to this problem compare the opposite views of C. P.
Kindleberger (1967) and J. P. de Gaudemar (1976).

10 It is not as relevant to know in which type of industry a man or woman
works, as the exact nature of his job. There are statistics that tell us
how many foreigners work in 'Broadcasting and transmission' but we
do not know whether they are professional broadcasters or lift opera-
tors and night cleaners. The latter is more probable, of course, but it is
obvious that through this kind of guesswork no serious study can be
carried out.

11 The most important case in the last years was the migration of Portuguese workers to France (more than 800,000 in ten years). Paris had, in
1974, the greatest concentration of Portuguese in the world, after Lisbon
and Oporto (See *Le Monde* 14 April 1974).

12 According to a 1974 Report by the EEC (J. Power and A. Hardman
(1976), p. 24), this figure amounts to 10 per cent of the legally employed
foreign manpower.

13 J. Franceschi, Deputy to the French Assembly, Socialist Party,
declares:

There is . . . 'peu d'empressement à vouloir mettre sur pied une
politique globale de l'immigration donnant aux quatre millions de
travailleurs étrangers, et à leurs familles, qui vivent sur notre sol
le statut social correspondant aux services qu'ils rendent à notre
développement et à la solidarité que nous leur devons' ('Le budget
des immigrés: une illusion de plus', *Le Monde*, 7 November 1975,
p. 34).

14 See *Le Monde*, 18–19 April 1976 and following days, for reports on the
scandals caused by summary expulsions of numerous foreign labour
leaders from French soil.

15 According to *Le Monde* (14 December 1974, p. 3) as many as 40 per
cent of Spanish workers in Europe were ready to return to their
country 'by the end of the month' due to the non-renewal of their

labour contracts under the new economic situation and the non-membership of Spain in the EEC. Even though such a massive and sudden return did not entirely materialise, these figures themselves and the fear of mass dismissals plays an important part in the acceptance of low salaries and the lack of unionisation.

16 The telling expression used among Spanish workers in England when referring to the final permit to change jobs after four years is *ser libre*, to 'become free'.

17 Such as the French *Secretariat d'Etat aux immigrés*, the German counterpart of which appears as the *Bundesanstalt für Arbeit*, or the Swiss federal *aliens police*.

18 *The Times*, 28 January 1975.

19 As after the Renault strike in France in April 1973. The Ford strike at Cologne and that of North Africans in France at the end of August 1973 were important in raising governments' awareness of migrants' plight – at least Parliaments debated it – during 1974 and 1975 sessions.

20 Around 1972 it would appear that 30 per cent of foreign workers in Europe were in unions, (J. Castles and G. Kosack, 1973b, p. 131). Their share of posts of responsibility and union offices must be very low indeed in proportion to their numbers and this latter feature probably helps explain why unions are generally not hostile to the recruitment of foreign workers as members.

21 For reasons of space no detailed account can be given of the diverse policies in this respect. However, see J. Castles and G. Kosack (1973b) pp. 127–52.

22 We are not concerned with this phenomenon here. Yet, see A. Pascal (1970).

23 Article 58 of the Rome Agreement.

24 The Spanish government, for instance, maintains an office for help and assistance to the foreign migrants (IEE) in the host countries (Germany, Switzerland, France), which until 1977 had a parallel political mission of surveillance and control of the activities of migrants.

25 Normally cost-benefit analyses at the macro-economic level focus on the 'national economic advantage' produced by immigration (cf. L. H. Klassen and P. Drewe (1974), pp. 86–92), and study such things as subsidies, migrants' propensities to save, etc. by blatantly ignoring the crucial question of who gets what amounts of the wealth created by the immigrants. In spite of a notable degree of mathematical sophistication, these studies are flawed by their refusal to tackle such questions. An exception to this can be found in G. Yannopoulos (1974).

26 The character of 'industrial reserve army' appears, for instance, in comments such as this, which appeared in the *Guardian*, (11 July 1975):

> The new Government restrictions (in Switzerland), which come into effect at the beginning of August and last for a year, allow the Government office responsible for immigrant workers to hold in reserve several thousand work permits. These will be used for contingencies in trades where foreign workers are still badly needed.

27 This distinction bears some similarity to notions put forward by D. Lockwood (1964), and N. Mouzelis (1974), but refers to a less general level of enquiry.

28 It is in this area, of course, that the race relations approach, combined with conflict theory and a multi-causal analysis of migration, may make some contribution. Cf. J. Rex (1970) on 'Discrimination, exploitation, oppression and racialism', pp. 116–35.

29 Several studies point out that the assimilation and integration of Spaniards is much more difficult in, say, Germany, than France, where language barriers are weaker and styles of life differ less. G.L. Diaz-Plaja (1974), G. Hermet (1974), A. Rose (1972) give a standard optimistic view of the assimilation process, often using entirely arbitrary tables, indices and interpretations. See esp. Rose, p. 394.

30 A. Gorz (1970), p. 31.

31 Much work has been done on this however since W. I. Thomas and F. Znaniecki's (1918) classic first appeared. Yet, studies on migrants in Europe tend to ignore the cultural factor, as if it were not structuring the whole situation.

32 A very important consequence of loneliness and lack of integration of migrants is the high incidence of mental illness. A recent report of two Spanish psychiatrists shows a bigger incidence of some mental diseases such as depression, delirium or psychopathologies than in the native population. The problem is of such importance that many governments (e.g. the Dutch) have been studying programmes establishing some sort of 'cushion' to protect immigrants from culture shock. See, for instance the study of Tejeiro and Ajuriaguerra, 'Problèmes psychopathologiques de l'immigration espagnole à Genève' (1967), or the article by John Cunningham in the *Guardian*, 30 January 1973 about the survey. In some few cases the culture shock may take constructive and original forms of expression, such as theatre (see *Le Monde*, 12 December 1974).

33 The 'boom' of xenophobic movements in Germany or in the German cantons of Switzerland can be explained in terms of both the traditional xenophobia of some strata of German people and by the existence of a real national problem in the case of Switzerland. In effect, in this country more than a third of workers are foreigners with a higher birth rate than nationals. If there is no integration (very possible) the number of foreigners could, in the next two decades, become superior to that of the inhabitants of the country. For the nationalists the solution is the expulsion of foreigners. Xenophobic feelings in France are often based on the 'arguments' that the 4,128,312 foreign workers of 1975 will have multiplied to 8,000,000 by the year 2000 (*The Economist*, 31 January 1976, pp. 51–2). In connection with this France's more liberal policies in admitting workers' families (by comparison with Germany) has created 'social problems' for the French which West Germany has avoided, i.e. has confined them to the immigrant population itself.

34 Thus the projected Democratic Congress of Spanish Emigrants (1976) could not have been prepared until the death of General Franco

(ABC, Madrid, 28 April 1976). Events such as this must be explained through the concrete situation of a given country, and cannot be generalised to the whole of Europe.

35 In this connection we can speak of a 'two-step flow of migration', developed in some Southern European countries. For example, while Spain was still sending many migrants abroad, great numbers of unskilled Moroccan workers crossed the Straits in order to work on Spanish motorway building and other public works.

Bibliography

Note This bibliography includes all sources directly quoted in the text as well as a number of references which are relevant to problems of migration in European society and are mentioned here as a guide to further information.

ABADAN, N. *et al.* (1972), 'Les travailleurs immigrés', special issue of *Sociologie du travail*, no. 3.

BAIN, G., COATES, D., and ELLIS, V. (1973), *Social Stratification and Trade Unionism*, London, Heinemann.

BARBICHON, G. (1962), *Adaptation and Training of Rural Workers for Industrial Work*, Paris, OECD.

BAUCIS, I. (1972), *The Effects of Emigration from Yugoslavia and the Problems of Returning Emigrant Workers*, The Hague, Nijhoff (European Demographic Monographs, no. 2).

BÖHNING, W. R. (1972), *The Migration of Workers in the United Kingdom and European Community*, Oxford University Press and Institute of Race Relations.

BRAECKMAN, C. (1973), *Les étrangers en Belgique*, Bruxelles, Les éditions vie ouvrière.

CASTLES, S. and KOSACK, G. (1973a), 'The Function of Labour Immigration in Western European Capitalism', *New Left Review*, no. 73, May–June, pp. 3–21.

CASTLES, S. and KOSACK, G. (1973b), *Immigrant Workers and Class Structure in Western Europe*, Oxford University Press and Institute of Race Relations.

Cetedim (1975), *Les Immigrés*, Paris, Stock II.

Cuadernos para el Diálogo (1974), 'Los emigrantes', Special Issue no. XL, May.

DANIEL, J. L. (1975), *La traité des pauvres*, Paris, Fayard.

DIAZ-PLAJA, G. L. (1974), *La condición de emigrante*, Madrid, Educisa.

GAUDEMAR, J. P. de (1976), *Mobilité du travail et accumulation du capital*, Paris, Maspero.

GORZ, A. (1970), 'Immigrant Labour', *New Left Review*, no. 61, pp. 28–31.

HERMET, C. (1967). *Les espagnols en France*, Paris, Editions ouvrieres.

HERVO, M., and CHARRAS, M. A. (1971), *Bidonvilles*, Paris, Maspero.

Hommes et migrations/Documents, Paris, Etudes Sociales Nord Africaines (ESNA).

JACKSON, J. (ed.) (1969), *Migration*, Cambridge University Press.

122

KINDLEBERGER, C. P. (1967), *European Post-War Growth: The Role of Labour Supply*, Harvard University Press.

KLASSEN, L. and DREWE, P. (1974), *Migration Policy in Europe: A Comparative Study*, Westmead, Saxon House (1st edn 1973).

LANSING, J. B. and MUELLER, E. (1971), *The Geographic Mobility of Labour*, The University of Michigan, Survey Research Center (1st edn 1967).

LOCKWOOD, D. (1964), 'Social Integration and System Integration', in G. K. Zollschan and W. Hirsch (eds), *Explorations in Social Change*, London, Routledge & Kegan Paul, pp. 244–57.

MANN, M. (1973), *Consciousness and Action Among the Western Working Class*, London, Macmillan, BSA Monograph.

MINCES, J. (1973), *Les travailleurs étrangers en France*, Paris, Seuil.

MOORE, R. (1975), *Migrant Workers, Social Stratification and the Economies of Western European Societies*, BSA Conference, mimeographed.

MARSAL, J. F. (1969), *Hacer la América*, Buenos Aires, Instituto de Tella.

MOUZELIS, N. (1974). 'Social and System Integration: Some Reflections on a Fundamental Distinction', *British Journal of Sociology*, vol. XXV, no. 4, pp. 395–409.

PAINE, S. (1974), *Exporting Workers: The Turkish Case*, Cambridge University Press.

PASCUAL, A. (1970), *El retorn dels emigrants*, Barcelona, Nova Terra.

POWER, J. (1974), 'The New Proletariat', *Encounter*, September vol. XLIII, pp. 8–22.

POWER, J. and HARDMAN, A. (1976), *Western Europe Migrant Workers*, London, Minority Rights Group.

PRINGLE, P. (1974), 'Paying Guests', *Sunday Times Magazine*, May.

REX, J. (1970), *Race Relations in Sociological Theory*, London, Weidenfeld & Nicolson.

RODRIGUEZ LOPEZ, A. (1974), 'El emigrante y la enfermedad mental', *Triunfo*, no 623, 7 September, pp. 15–18.

ROSE, A. (1972), 'The Integration of People', in M. Hodges (ed.), *European Integration*, Harmondsworth, Penguin (1st published USA 1970).

SALCEDO, J. (1976), *Movimientos de población en la región de Madrid*, Autonomous University of Madrid, mimeographed.

SALOWSKY, H. (1973), 'Economic impact of foreign labour', *Intereconomics* no. 2, pp. 59–62

SAYED, A. (1975), 'El Ghorba: le mecanisme de reproduction de l'émigration', *Actes de la recherche en sciences sociales*, no. 2, March, pp. 50–66.

TEJEIRO and AJURIAGUERRA (1967), 'Problèmes psychopathologiques de l'immigration espagnole à Genève, *Triunfo*, October.

THOMAS, W. I. and ZNANIECKI, F. (1974), *The Polish Peasant in Europe and America*, New York, Octagon Books (1st edn USA, 1918–1920).

VILLA, L. E. de la (1974), ' "Die Gastarbeiter" en España', *Gentleman*, no. 13, April, pp. 89–93.

YANNOPOULOS, G. (1974), *Immigration from the Mediterranean Countries and its Impact on the Economies of the European Communities*, University of Reading, mimeographed.

6   Ethnic problems in Europe
Jaroslav Krejci

Sociologists often tend to underestimate the primary role of ethnic problems. Those problems with which they are acquainted relate to countries where races with different civic rights and different educational and economic levels live together, and so they are more often than not inclined to look at them as basically social or class problems which can consequently be solved by changing their socio-economic determinants.

Yet a careful observer cannot overlook the fact that there are still situations where language, cultural heritage and historical memory weigh than the individual's or group's position in the spectrum of social stratification. This is especially the case in Europe, where immigration of people of other than European races and civilisations is still, with a few exceptions, a marginal phenomenon, and where most ethnic problems arise from time-honoured endogenous roots, from the quest for national identity and self-determination.

These desires and sentiments are often considered vague and irrational. The whole question of nationality and interrelated emotional attitudes is found highly complex and something which almost evades precise conceptualisation; therefore there is an increasing tendency to relate ethnic aspects and issues to the more perceptible and supposedly rational trends of political and economic development, or philosophical thought. Although there are some good reasons for the above practices, I nevertheless consider it worth while focusing attention on the ethnic problems in their own right. Whilst they are a part of a multi-faceted social reality, they represent quite a distinct complex which, in certain circumstances, may become of primary relevance for a particular society or geographical area.

If the ethnic problems are to be singled out, some conceptual issues have to be clarified. The adjective 'ethnic' can be understood as a synonym for national, or as one possible aspect or type of nationality, depending on the definition of 'nation' and on the criteria used for its identification.

As is well known, the concept of nation has acquired different meanings in particular cultural areas of Europe. In the West, especially in English- and French-speaking countries, nation is understood in geographical rather than ethnic terms. The basic identification mark is a politico-territorial formation – the state – which by definition is supposed to be a sovereign body. In Central and Eastern Europe however, the state or statehood on the one hand and nation or nationality on the other, are quite different concepts. Statehood implies citizenship, nationality implies ethnic affiliation irrespective of citizenship. Here the basic characteristic of nationality is seen primarily in language and its connected culture.

Recently, however, this difference has been somewhat blurred. On both sides there are increasing exceptions to this rule which point to the development of a more complex, rather multi-dimensional pattern. In the last three decades ethno-linguistic sentiments and desires have been re-emphasised in several West European countries. In Central Europe separate statehood, irrespective of linguistic and cultural ties, also became an alternative criterion for national identity. Not only has the Austrian sense of national identity *vis-à-vis* its German neighbour been strengthened, but new focuses of separate consciousness have emerged in the two post-war German states.

In anticipation of continuing convergence between the two concepts of nation we can list five common objective criteria for its identification: territory, state (or similar political status), language, culture and history. When positive answers to all these criteria coincide there can be little doubt about the identification of a particular society as a nation; then usually a sixth, the subjective criterion of national consciousness, is also present. But there are situations where some, or even most, of the objective criteria are missing and yet the community feels itself a nation.[1] Whether the rest of the world, especially its interested neighbours, is or is not willing to acknowledge the group in question as a separate nation is, in the long run, irrelevant. The subjective factor of consciousness is the ultimate factor which eventually decides the issue of national identity.[2]

This phenomenon and its pattern of development is well known: intensified communication and imitation processes, the latter originating in some focal strata and spreading from there both to higher and lower levels of the social stratification system. As the scope of this diffusion depends on the intensity of contacts (Durkheimian 'moral density'), the ethnic differentiation of kindred people increases with the decreasing intensity of contacts, which in their turn result from geographical or, in the broadest possible sense,

125

social conditions. The focal strata of national consciousness are as a rule amongst the top power elite. There are however numerous cases where the originating focus of national consciousness has developed in opposition to the power elite. This has happened when the power elite of another ethnic origin became superimposed on the people in question, or when their own native elite embraced a foreign culture and language, and the counter-elite, consisting mainly of writers, poets, teachers, parsons etc., awakened the more or less lukewarm population to a national consciousness different from that of the ruling stratum. To borrow Milyukov's terms, only through these processes of communication and imitation does 'ethnographic material' acquire consciousness and become a 'nation'.[3]

Most European nations can be identified by all six aforementioned criteria; consciousness, language, culture, history, territory and statehood. There are, however, several types of anomalies, some of which are more or less harmless, i.e. they do not exert disturbing influences on the given societal structure and relationships; some of them however, tend to be dysfunctional and, combined with other adverse circumstances, even disruptive.

In order to assess the nature and scope of these anomalies, the contemporary position of individual European ethnic groups or nationalities, whether generally recognised or only claiming recognition, has to be scrutinised with respect to all the defining characteristics. It is not enough to ascertain whether the particular defining mark is present or not, but also its quality or type. This is especially important for different types of political status (different degrees of sovereignty or self-government) and for different conditions contributing to the sense of national identity.

All defining marks or characteristics can be conceptualised as three or four basic (standard) types of that characteristic. This makes up a taxonomy where the six defining characteristics (territory, political status, history, culture, language and consciousness) are amplified into twenty-two types in the following way:

1. *Territory.* There are three basic alternative relationships of an ethnic group to a geographical area:
   (a) the main body of the ethnic group lives in *compact* settlements in the respective territory;
   (b) the group lives *mixed* with another in the respective territory;
   (c) the group has no country of its own and is scattered over a wider area (*'diaspora'*).

2. *Political status.* There are four alternatives with respect to this:
   (a) sovereign *state;*

(b) equal position of respective nationality with others within a federation or unitary state with adequate local self-government; both these cases may be, in our taxonomy, labelled as *federated* status, i.e. federated with respect to ethnic issues;

(c) *autonomous* status within a federation or unitary state;

(d) no status or self-government at all, labelled '*none*'.

3. *History.* In our taxonomy this is conceived mainly in political terms, and is assessed in terms of the degree to which it can be related to the respective ethnic group, i.e. whether or not the latter had, over a long period of its history, a state or similar political formation of its own. If it had its own territorial political framework then the question is whether its history was more or less continuous or whether it had been interrupted by a prolonged incorporation into an alien territorial political framework. If an ethnic group shared its political history with another, as for instance the Catalans with the Spaniards in the Aragonian kingdom, or Slovaks with Magyars in the Hungarian kingdom, then the position can be classified as *unrelated*. The alternative positions then are: (a) '*continuous*', (b) '*interrupted*', (c) '*unrelated*' and (d) '*none*'.

Related political history, whether continuous or interrupted, is also assumed in cases where there was a plurality of states in the territory of the respective nationality, most of which contributed to the promotion or upholding of national tradition and/or consciousness, as in medieval Germany or Italy and the twin Romanian principalities of Wallachia and Moldavia.

4. *Culture.* In the case of culture the point is to determine the primary basis of the particular culture; whether it is (a) *language,* (b) *religion,* (c) *political conditions,* irrespective of whether past or present, or possibly (d) a special *way of life.*

5. *Language.* As the existence of one's own language is not a necessary condition for national identity, the basic alternatives are whether the group possesses its own language or whether it shares it with another group. If it has its own language, then it may be relevant to the strength of national consciousness whether that language has developed into a literary form or remained more or less in a state of spoken vernacular (dialect) only. If it has developed into a literary language then there may be a relevant question about whether it has a long, more or less uninterrupted tradition, or whether it has become developed or used for literary purposes only recently, since approximately the period of intense nationalism in the nineteenth century. The alternative characterisations then are (a) *old*, (b) *new*, (c) *dialect* and (d) *shared* (literary language shared with another ethnic group).

127

6. *National consciousness.* As this reflects the salient characteristics of the nationality, a typology can be drawn up with respect to these characteristics. In our scheme the following alternatives are envisaged: (a) *ethnic*, if the basis is language and its connected culture, (b) *political*, if the basis is a separate political unit (state) the significance of which is supported either by historical tradition or by a particular socio-economic system and (c) *both*, if ethnic and political elements are so closely intertwined that it would be arbitrary to consider one of them more important.

Religion is not presumed to be a sufficient cause of or reason for national consciousness. Wherever it has assumed the role of being the main differentiation mark between what otherwise appear to be kindred people, it seems to be rather as a substitute for another determinant. It is a rallying point for those who either have abandoned another, more pertinent, expression of ethnic identification such as language (Jews, and Ulstermen of both denominations), or, who having lost their special political status of belonging to the dominant group within an empire, which had been horizontally stratified in religious communities, cannot accommodate themselves within a differently patterned framework (Serbo-Croat-speaking Muslims in Yugoslavia).

As is generally the case, this typology can be applied to individual situations with different degrees of precision. A certain margin for possible error in judgment has to be anticipated. There is however, much less scope for arbitrary decisions if each characteristic (variable) is considered separately than if one attempts to draw a more general compound taxonomy combining several variables into one concept. Therefore a tabular form of presentation, giving each characteristic the possibility of separate assessment, is preferred in this chapter. Specific nuances or qualifications can be then registered in the footnotes. There are, however, some relevant circumstances which may remain unnoted.

One particular difficulty may arise from doubts about whether or not a particular ethnic community enjoys a true sovereignty or genuine autonomy. Given the absence of any precise criteria for answering this question, a rather formal criterion has to be applied in the tables; the nuances and intricacies of real positions have to be left over to the commentary. Another problem may arise from the difficulty of ascertaining whether a particular language became a literary one and whether this happened in the nationalistic atmosphere of the last two centuries or was an earlier development. This question may be highly controversial, especially if few written documents have been preserved from earlier periods. The translation of the Bible into the particular language can be considered, however, as a quite reliable yardstick. Whenever this happened in times when the

Bible was the main reading matter (i.e. before the period of Enlightenment), the respective language can be classified as an old literary one.

A further possible margin of uncertainty arises with respect to national consciousness which, being a matter of subjective feeling, can be shared by individuals in different degrees. It would be most useful if we could assess the respective strength (intensity) of this consciousness among individual strata of population. However, as the necessary information is not available, we have, in my opinion, to work with the quite plausible hypothesis that the existence of a developed national consciousness can be taken for granted with respect to all European ethnic groups. Only in cases where the respective ethnic group has for a long time been subject to political and cultural preponderance of another ethnic group (as, for example, the Bretons and the Welsh) may there then be a question of how far the particular communal consciousness has become superseded by the sense of belonging to the wider national community (French and British respectively).

Even if Europe is conceived of in its narrowest geographical confines (with the eastern frontier on the Ural mountain range and the Manych lowlands, and excluding the Caspian coast, inhabited by Asian nationalities of Kazakhs and Kalmyks), sixty-nine ethnic groups can be identified. These groups are, of course, of very different magnitudes, from several tens of thousands to hundreds of millions; this diversity may also be a factor of particular sociological relevance. Therefore, in our tables, an indication of the numerical strength of each nationality is added to the six characteristics.

For the convenience of the reader, Europe has been divided into five geographical areas, each of which reveals a different stress on, or pattern of, individual defining marks and their sub-types. These areas are (1) West; (2) North; (3) West Centre and South; (4) East Centre and (5) East. The Centre is divided between the East on one side, and West and South on the other, according to the political criterion. Nationalities living in countries whose governments profess Marxism–Leninism as their state doctrine are presented in the fourth table, whereas all other countries of Central and Southern Europe are placed in the third. The East includes only nationalities whose main corpus lives in the European part of the USSR. The numerical strengths of their populations however, refer to the USSR as a whole. All characteristics refer to the end of 1977.

There is yet one important factor, which the tables do not indicate: namely the type and magnitude of 'fragmented' ethnic groups. These are parts (fragments) of nations detached from their main bodies in the nation-states and living in states dominated by other nationalities. This special case of ethnic minorities will be considered at a later point.

129

TABLE 6.1 Western Europe

	1 Territory	2 Political Status	3 History	4 Culture	5 Language	6 Consciousness	7 Population (million)
Alsatians	compact	—	unrelated	language	shared & dialect	ethnic	1·4
Basques	compact	—[1]	unrelated	language	old	ethnic	0·8
Bretons	compact	—	interrupted	language	old	ethnic	1·0
Catalans	compact	autonomous[2]	unrelated	language	old	ethnic	6·0
Channel Islanders[3]	compact	autonomous	continuous	politics	shared & dialect	ethnic & political	0·12
Corsicans	compact	state	unrelated	language	shared & dialect	ethnic	0·25
English	compact	state	continuous	language	old	ethnic & political	45·0
French	compact	state	continuous	language	old	ethnic & political	50·0
Irish	compact	state	interrupted	religion	shared & old	ethnic & political	3·5[4]
Manx	compact	autonomous	interrupted	politics	shared	political	0·06
Portuguese	compact	state	interrupted	language	old	ethnic & political	9·0
Scots	compact	autonomous[5]	interrupted	politics	shared[6]	ethnic & political	5·5
Spaniards	compact	state	continuous	language	old	ethnic & political	28·0
Welsh	compact	—	interrupted	language	shared & old	ethnic	2·7

[1] As 1978 begins, discussions on Basque autonomy are being actively pursued.

[2] From 5 October 1977, subject to the approval of the forthcoming constitution, but not covering the whole of the Catalan speaking area.

[3] Norman population of Guernsey and Jersey.

[4] Including Catholics in Northern Ireland; from the ethnical point of view the approximately 1 million Protestants can be considered as a particular branch of Scottish or English or combined British nationality. Their characteristics would be: territory – mixed; self-government, none at present; political history – continuous; culture – based primarily on religion; language – shared; consciousness – mainly based on political history coupled with religious affiliation.

[5] In contrast to the Welsh, Scots are classified as an autonomous ethnic group because Scotland's union with England is based on a kind of constitutional contract which enabled Scotland to preserve a wide range of legal and cultural peculiarities and which, within the common political institutions, can more easily be altered than in certain cases of autonomous or federated status of some ethnic groups elsewhere.

[6] Gaelic being spoken by under 2 per cent of Scottish population and not being a common Scottish issue, is not considered relevant for identification of Scottish nationality.

TABLE 6.2 *Northern Europe*

	1	*2*	*3*	*4*	*5*	*6*	*7*
	Territory	*Political Status*	*History*	*Culture*	*Language*	*Consciousness*	*Population* (million)
Danes	compact	state	continuous	language	old	ethnic & political	5·0
Faroese	compact	autonomous	unrelated	language	new	ethnic	0·03
Finns	compact	state	interrupted	language	old	ethnic & political	4·3
Icelanders	compact	state	interrupted	language	old	ethnic & political	0·2
Lapps	mixed	—	—	language	new	ethnic	0·05
Norwegians	compact	state	interrupted	language	new & old[1]	ethnic & political	4·0
Swedes	compact	state	continuous[2]	language	old	ethnic & political	8·0

[1] Virtually two languages: the rigsmål, used mainly in cities, is a newly adapted form of Danish; the landsmål, used mainly in the countryside, is the old dialect adapted for literary purposes.

[2] The rule of Danish kings in Sweden was not so extensive as to justify the view that the continuity of Swedish statehood had been interrupted.

TABLE 6.3 West-Central and Southern Europe

	1 Territory	2 Political Status	3 History	4 Culture	5 Language	6 Consciousness	7 Population (million)
Austrians	compact	state	continuous	political	shared	political	7·5
Belgians: Flemings	compact	federal	unrelated	language	shared	ethnic & political	6·0
Walloons	compact	federal	unrelated	language	shared	ethnic & political	4·0
Dutch	compact	state	continuous	language	old	ethnic & political	13·0
Frisians[1]	compact	autonomous	unrelated	language	old	ethnic & political	0·6[1]
Furlanians[2]	compact	autonomous	unrelated	language	dialect	ethnic	c. 0·5[2]
Germans[3]	compact	state	continuous	language	old	ethnic & political	60·0[4]
Greeks	compact	state	interrupted	language	old & new[8]	ethnic & political	8·6
Italians[5]	compact	state	continuous	language	old	ethnic & political	54·0
Luxembourgeois	compact	state	continuous	political	shared & dialect	political	0·35
Maltese	compact	state	unrelated	language	new & shared	ethnic & political	0·32
Swiss: Germans	compact	federal	continuous	language	shared & dialect	ethnic & political	4·2
French	compact	federal	continuous	language	shared	ethnic & political	1·2
Italians	compact	federal	unrelated	language	shared	ethnic & political	0·8[7]
Raetians	mixed	federal	unrelated	language	old	ethnic & political	0·06
Turks	compact	state	continuous	language	new[9]	ethnic & political	4·5[6]

[1] In the Netherlands only; East and North Frisians in the Federal Republic of Germany are no longer considered as a separate nationality but as a population speaking dialects like other ethnic sub-groups of the German nation.

[2] Including Ladins (c. 20,000) living as a tiny minority in the autonomous province of Trentino-Alto Adige. Furlanian and Ladin languages are considered by some linguists as Italian dialects, by others, together with the Romansh (in Switzerland) as a separate group of Raeto-Romance languages.

[3] The differentiation between ethnic sub-groups identified by distinct dialects and/or autonomous regions is also not considered. It is assumed that such a regional consciousness, even in the most explicit case of the Bavarians, does not exceed the general framework of the German nation with its common literary language and ethno-political consciousness.

[4] Including West Berlin but excluding migrant workers.

[5] Neither Sicilians nor Sardinians can, in the light of our indicators, be considered as separate ethnic groups. Recently, however, a movement claiming separate nationhood for Sardinians on linguistic grounds is gathering momentum. Aostans and German-speaking people of the South Tirol are considered as parts of French and Austrian ethnic communities respectively.

[6] European part of Turkey (minus its non-Turkish population) plus Turkish minorities in Bulgaria, Greece and Yugoslavia.

[7] Including Italian guest workers.

[8] The spoken vernacular (demotic) is used increasingly for literary purposes alongside the official 'Kathareusa' which is more in line with ancient tradition.

[9] With respect to many Persian and Arabic elements in the pre-nineteenth-century Turkish.

TABLE 6.4 *East-Central Europe*

	1 Territory	2 Political Status	3 History	4 Culture	5 Language	6 Consciousness	7 Population (millions)
Albanians	compact	state[1]	unrelated	language	old	ethnic & political	3.6[2]
Bulgarians	compact	state	interrupted	language	old	ethnic & political	7.7
Croats	compact	federal	interrupted	religion	shared	ethnic & political	4.5
Czechs	compact	federal	interrupted	language	old	ethnic & political	9.6
Germans (GDR)	compact	state	unrelated	political	shared	political	16.9[3]
Gypsies	diaspora	—	—	life-style	dialect	ethnic	c.2.0
Hungarians	compact	state	interrupted	language	old	ethnic & political	12.3[4]
Macedonians	compact	federal	unrelated	language	new	ethnic & political	1.2
Montenegrins	compact	federal	continuous	political	shared	political	0.5
Poles	compact	state	interrupted	language	old	ethnic & political	33.0[5]
Romanians	compact	state	interrupted	language	old	ethnic & political	18.5
Serbs	compact	federal	interrupted	religion	shared	ethnic & political	8.4[6]
Slovaks	compact	federal	unrelated	language	new	ethnic & political	4.5
Slovenes	compact	federal	unrelated	language	old	ethnic & political	1.7
Sorbs (Lusatians)[7]	mixed	—	unrelated	language	old	ethnic	0.07
Yugoslav Muslims[7]	mixed	autonomous[8]	unrelated	religion	shared	political[9]	1.7

[1] And autonomous region in federal Yugoslavia.
[2] Of which 1.3 million in Yugoslavia.
[3] Not including about 2.7 million Germans living in the USSR and other East-Central European countries.
[4] Including 2.7 million in Romania, Czechoslovakia and Yugoslavia.
[5] Not including 1 million Poles living in the USSR.
[6] Including 0.3 millions who declared themselves Yugoslavs.
[7] Officially recognised as separate nationality.
[8] In view of being the largest ethnic group in Bosnia-Hercegovina which is one of the six republics constituting the Yugoslav federation.
[9] In the sense of being a community whose identity was created by political circumstances. Type of communal consciousness similar to that of Protestants in Northern Ireland.

General
Unlike Yugoslav Muslims, the Pomaks (Bulgarian Muslims) were not recognised as an ethnic group. Similarly, the remnants of Jews in East-Central Europe are considered as a religious minority only. Before the Second World War, however, there were more than 4 million ethnic Jews in that area. In some countries they could even declare Jewish nationality at the censuses.

TABLE 6.5   Eastern Europe (European part of the USSR)

	1 Territory[1]	2 Political Status	3 History	4 Culture	5 Language	6 Consciousness	7 Population (million)[2]
Bashkirs	mixed	autonomous	unrelated	language	new	ethnic	1·2
Belorussians	compact	federal	unrelated	language	new[3]	ethnic	9·1
Chuvashs	compact	autonomous	—	language	new	ethnic	1·7
Estonians	compact	federal	unrelated	language	old	ethnic	1·0
Jews	diaspora	—[4]	—	religion	shared & old[5]	ethnic	2·1
Karelians[6]	mixed	autonomous	—	language	new	ethnic	0·15
Komi	mixed	autonomous	—	language	new	ethnic	0·5
Latvians	compact	federal	unrelated	language	old	ethnic & political	1·4
Lithuanians	compact	federal	interrupted	language	old	ethnic & political	2·7
Mari	mixed	autonomous	—	language	new	ethnic	0·6
Moldavians	compact	federal	interrupted	language	new	ethnic & political	2·7
Mordovians	mixed	autonomous	—	language	new	ethnic	1·3
Russians	compact	federal	continuous	language	old	ethnic & political	129·0
Tatars	mixed	autonomous	interrupted	language	old	ethnic	5·9
Udmurts	mixed	autonomous	—	language	new	ethnic	0·7
Ukrainians	compact	federal	unrelated	language	old	ethnic & political	40·7

[1] Territory is classified as mixed wherever the share of the respective ethnic group does not exceed 50 per cent of population in the corresponding republic or autonomous region.

[2] Figures refer to the population who, within the territory of the USSR as a whole, declared themselves as belonging to the particular nationality at the 1970 census. Their number may differ considerably from the population in the corresponding republics or regions.

[3] Belorussian language established its identity in the sixteenth and seventeenth centuries, but only became widely used for literary purposes after 1917.

[4] Jewish Autonomous Region is in the Far East of Asia; it has barely 0.2 million population, over 80 per cent of Soviet Jews live in the diaspora.

[5] Yiddish. In Central Europe Yiddish was widely used from the sixteenth century, but is now mainly confined to the USA and USSR.

[6] Karelian is a Finnish dialect which, for political reasons, is considered a separate language.

TABLE 6.6 Summary of classification of European nationalities (no. of communities)

Defining characteristics	Type	Geographical Areas					Europe as a whole
		Western	Northern	West Central & Southern	East Central	Eastern	
Territory	compact	14	6	15	13	8	56
	mixed	—	1	1	2	7	11
	diaspora	—	—	—	1	1	2
Political Status	state	5	5	8	6	—	24
	federated	—	1	6	6	7	20
	autonomous	4	—	2	2	8	16
	none	5	1	—	2	1	9
History (political)	continuous	5	2	8	1	1	17
	interrupted	5	2	1	7	3	18
	unrelated	4	2	7	7	5	25
	none	—	1	—	1	7	9
Culture base	language	10	7	14	10	15	56
	religion	1	—	—	3	1	5
	political conditions	3	—	2	2	—	7
	special way of life	—	—	—	1	—	1
Language	old	7	4	5	8	6	30
	new	—	2	1	2	9	14
	old and new	—	1	1	—	—	2
	dialect	—	—	1	1	—	2
	shared	2	—	5	5	—	12
	combined[1]	5	—	3	—	1	9
Consciousness	political	—	—	1	3	—	4
	ethnic	7	2	3	2	10	24
	both combined	7	5	12	11	6	41
Totals		14	7	16	16	16	69
of which with less than 1 million population		4	3	6	2	4	19

[1] Combination of a literary language (own or shared) with a dialect.

Table 6.6 gives summarised information on the regional distribution of sixty-nine European ethnic groups or nationalities. It shows that the most frequent types of individual characteristics are (a) the compact settled territory and (b) language as the basis of the culture; fifty-six groups have been classified in both of these categories. Religion provides the basic identification of an ethnic group *vis-à-vis* its neighbours in five cases and a special (more or less nomadic) type of life in one or two particular cases (depending upon whether Lapps, who in the table are characterised by language, are added to Gypsies). In the remaining seven cases the bases for a certain cultural differentiation from the main ethnic body, with whom the language is shared, are political conditions, namely the existence of a separate state.

Thirty ethnic groups can be identified by a time-honoured literary language; fourteen by a language which only became used for literary purposes in modern times. Two nations (Greeks and Norwegians) each have two literary languages and in two cases (Furlanian and gypsy Romany) the literary usage of a language seems not to have fully developed yet. Nine ethnic groups are in a sense bilingual: they speak both their own special dialect and a language which they share with another ethnic group. In twelve cases the language of the respective group is the same as that of kindred people in another, usually neighbouring, state.

Looking at it from the political angle, in 1976 only twenty-four ethnic groups had a state of their own. If nationalities who share a state with other nationalities on at least formally equal terms (our category of federated status) are included, the number increases to forty-four; of these, however, five are virtually branches of broader ethnic groups (Flemings, Walloons, Swiss Germans, Swiss French, Swiss Italians) with whom they share their literary language and from whom they differ almost only because of their separate statehood.

With regard to political history the position is also variegated. Only in thirty-five cases can the political history prior to the nineteenth century be related to the respective ethnic group. Of these in only seventeen cases was this history more or less continuous (a more or less sovereign political body or bodies encompassing the greater part of the ethnic group); in eighteen cases there was a prolonged interruption by foreign domination. In twenty-five cases the political history was related to a body which was as a rule multi-national, the unifying factor of which was usually a dynasty. In nine cases no political history in any proper sense of the term can be traced before the twentieth century.

National consciousness can be classified in forty-one cases as based on both ethnic and political identification. In twenty-four cases a prevalence of ethnicity in the national consciousness could be ascertained; only in four cases was the national consciousness primarily due to political circumstances and development. This category increases to six cases if the Swiss and Belgians, whose ethnic aspects of consciousness are stressed in internal rather than external relationships, are included.

On the whole the tables amplify what was anticipated, namely that consciousness is the only ever-present factor of national identity; yet it has to be combined with some objective characteristics. If we look at the problem from this angle, we can identify only two ethnic groups which have, at least within the European context, no political and territorial basis (i.e. where there is no type of self-government and no political history) and whose collective consciousness is wholly based on a particular type of culture. In the case of Jews it is based primarily on religious tradition, in the case of Gypsies on a special more or less nomadic way of life.

The difference in the nature of European nationalities becomes more significant, if they are scrutinised by regional breakdown. Most political nations (identified in our tables by the political base of their culture) are in Western and Central Europe. Of the nine ethnic groups without any status of self-government, five are in the West, one in the North, two in the East Centre and one in the East. In contrast to this, the three Western parts of Europe have a high number of ethnic groups with continuous political history. On the other hand, in the East and East Centre, there is only one ethnic group with continuous political history in each of them. These are paradoxically the greatest and the smallest nationalities: Russians[4] and Montenegrins.

As the East comprises the European part of Soviet Russia alone, there is only one state there which is composed of seven federated republics and eight autonomous republics or regions. The quality of the federated status and the extent of the autonomy will be discussed later. In this context they have to be accepted at face value: they provide an institutional framework at least for the linguistic identity of individual ethnic groups. The federated type of self-government is also importantly represented in the East Centre, West Centre and South. It is non-existent in the West and North.

Federation is, in many ways, advantageous where different nationalities live in mixed or intertwined settlements. In Europe there are eleven ethnic groups which cannot claim a certain territory for themselves because they share it with another nationality. Seven of them are in the USSR and only four of them comprise more than one million people. Northern Ireland can be added to this category as a special case.

All the aforementioned differences are due to particular historical developments in individual areas of Europe. This, however, does not fall within the focus of our study: our concern is with the present position, especially with respect to the possible eufunctional or dysfunctional consequences of individual combinations. On the strength of our contemporary and past experience we can identify a certain scope for dissatisfaction which can be ascertained by the absence of some types of characteristics in our tables.

The absence of individual characteristics is most significant in the case of statehood and language, the two main pillars of what may be called full national status. As is well known, the lack of a nation's own language is a phenomenon which does not produce any difficulty in international or rather interethnic relationships. Although there are cases when a government would like to see more frequent use of national language, at the expense of a language shared with another nation (this is most conspicuous with the Republic of Ireland), this endeavour does not result in any particular tension within the society. On the other hand the lack of self-government is, as a rule, strongly resented by many members of the respective ethnic group. This dissatisfaction primarily affects those nations which have no type of self-government for the group as a whole (such as Basques, Bretons, etc.). Their grievances are usually centred on linguistic matters: school education in the native language, its usage in offices, mass media, etc. Together with this is usually linked the demand for more equality, such as access to jobs, both in public and private employment and sometimes greater consideration for the economic development of the area is sought.

But grievances are often voiced by ethnic groups which possess some kind of federated or autonomous status but are dissatisfied with its extent (for example Scottish or Croat nationalists) or with its practical implications (Ukrainians and Baltic nations in the USSR or German-speaking Tirolese in Italy). Here grievances tend to concentrate on the desire for more participation in decision-making, extension of the competence of autonomous authorities, possibly in all spheres of societal life.

On the whole, one can see strong pressures towards a full nationality status whose ultimate manifestation would be the establishment of a sovereign state. So far there is, on the strength of centuries of experience, only one multi-national country in Europe where the centrifugal longing for separate statehood can be considered to have been overcome by common consciousness of a federated community, and this is Switzerland. Belgium, with a tradition of barely one hundred and fifty years of statehood, can only be given the benefit of the doubt. The experience of Soviet Russia and Yugoslavia is too short to allow any definite conclusions. Nevertheless, they represent two outstanding attempts of how to stop the decomposition process by combining federation with the unifying forces of a new ideology.

The importance of an adequate solution to ethnic problems can best be seen from a short glance into the not-too-distant past. Looking at the whole of Europe and following its development during the last hundred years or so we realise that it was mainly ethnic differences, national aspirations and rivalries which divided Europe and evntually brought her to the terrible cataclysm of two world wars. No selfish interest of capitalists, or financial or governmental manipulation alone could have unchained such a tremendous holocaust as did nationalistic attitudes and rivalries between 1914 and 1945. Moreover, in spite of a sophisticated and well-organised attempt by the Marxist movement to overcome national antagonisms and to promote the international solidarity between the 'have-nots', the new proletarian loyalties collapsed whenever they were confronted with dilemmas resulting from national rivalries. So it happened both in 1914 and 1939.

In 1914 most socialist members of parliament in countries declaring war, who a few months previously had solemnly promised to do their best to prevent a European conflagration, voted for the war credits and approved the war policies of their respective governments. In 1939, the Germans, a third of whom a few years before voted for one or the other Marxist party, gave, by their disciplined obedience, support to their autocrat for the conquest of Europe. In 1941, the still more autocratic Marxist-Leninist leader of the 'fatherland of socialism', had to declare the 'Patriotic War' in order to stimulate the war effort and so help his country to survive the combined effect of the tremendous Nazi striking power and the lack of genuine loyalty of his subjects to his system.

Since then we have witnessed many times how national loyalties have prevailed over any international consciousness, whether liberal or proletarian. This has been especially conspicuous in Eastern Europe. Immediately after the war the Communist parties, in their bid for exclusive power, tried to saddle the nationalistic horse and to show themselves as the best representatives of the respective national traditions and aspirations. Most of these parties eventually succumbed to the domestic political culture, distinct from that of the country which they had to consider their example, and it was only the interference of the Russian armies which brought them into line with the Soviet leadership. For contemporary Yugoslavia the national menace from outside is the main force behind the national unity of its constituent parts.

If there is any decline of nationalistic feelings, it is rather in the West. There the terrible lesson of the past has produced a certain malaise and weakened the uncompromising nationalistic attitude in favour of a greater awareness of social rather than ethnic differences. Yet in those countries which have so far escaped agitation among their ethnic minorities or which have prevented development of institutions which might have helped the minorities to some degree of self-determination, the ethnic problem continues to be acute and, in the recent decade, has even gathered momentum.

Countries which until recently were considered safe from the menace of internal strife such as France and Great Britain (excluding Northern Ireland) are being confronted with the vigorously presented claims of ethnic groups whose existence has long been considered as a matter of marginal relevance. And a country with such a well-established political tradition as Britain, whose stability has been envied by many Europeans, is getting alarmed by the prospect of devolution of some central government powers to the historical constituent parts of the United Kingdom.

Looking at the past two hundred years, we realise that Europe has experienced a conspicuous trend towards greater political self-determination (self-government) of ethnic minorities. The romantic idea of nation as a primary socio-cultural value, conceived at the turn of the eighteenth/nineteenth centuries, gained a tremendous impetus from the French Revolution. Nationalism as a means of collective self-assertion spread over the whole of Europe. Gradually it took over the integrative role of religion and/or of dynastic loyalties. The pace of this process varied from country to country and also with respect to social groupings and strata, according to the progress of the secularisation of spiritual life. The intellectual vanguard of this secularisation was the Enlightenment. However, its cold rationalism left an emotional gap which, within the framework of secular values, romanticism was eventually able to fill. In promoting the Sacred Fatherland in the place of the Holy Church, nationalism of the romantic period was able to satisfy a deep socio-psychic need which neither the men of Enlightenment nor rationalists of any other period were capable of understanding.[5]

Consequently, a principle was promoted that any ethnic group of whatever type of identification is entitled to have its own state and that each state has to be based on one such ethnic group or nation.[6] It was several decades before this idea could be realised on a large scale, but its strength can be deduced from the fact that it was in principle accepted by powers which later were to become antipodal forces of the world's political constellation. Both the American President on the one hand and the leaders of the newly formed Soviet Union on the other were keen to heed this principle in their respective politics; the former in the peace negotiations after the First World War, the latter in reshaping the Russian empire into a federation based on ethnic units.[7] A similar federalisation of the Habsburg Empire had been sought in vain before that war by some Social Democratic leaders.[8]

Before the First World War there were in Europe sixteen sufficiently populous ethnic groups with a fairly well developed national consciousness (despite differences in degree) which had no state of their own or even a reasonable degree of autonomy for the entire group. These nations, in alphabetic order, were Albanians, Basques, Bretons, Catalans, Croats, Czechs, Estonians, Irish, Latvians, Lithuanians, Poles, Slovaks, Slovenes, Tatars, Ukrainians, and Welsh. After the peace settlements which followed the war, there remained only four such nations, namely the Basques, Bretons, Catalans and Welsh.

In 1910 (before the two Balkan wars which preceded the First World War) there were three nations the greater part of whom did not live in their national state: Greeks, Serbs and Romanians. In 1920 there was no nation in such a position. In 1910 there were in Europe two empires (Austro-Hungarian and Ottoman), whose leading nations constituted a minority in their respective population. In 1920 there was no such case. In 1910 there was one empire, the Russian, in which, including Asian territory, the leading nation numbered about a half of all inhabitants. In 1920 Russia was transformed into a formally multi-national federation and five nations managed to secede from her completely and establish sovereign states for themselves (Poles, Lithuanians, Latvians and Estonians who had no autonomy in pre-war Russia and Finns who enjoyed a considerable degree of self-government).

As a result of redrawing boundaries and of some transfers of population (the latter happened on a much lesser scale than in and after the Second World War) the percentage of populations belonging to ethnic groups (nations) without state or self-government in Europe as a whole, decreased from about 25 per cent in 1910 to about only 4 per cent in 1930.[9]

The Second World War resulted in further adjustments in favour of the principle of ethnic self-determination. The share of ethnic groups and minorities without any type of self-government dropped to below 2 per cent of the total European population. Yet these adjustments were undertaken in quite a different spirit from those following the Balkan wars and the First World War. Between 1913 and 1923 the issue was almost exclusively that of redrawing the boundaries. Only between Greece and Turkey and between Greece and Bulgaria was there a significant exchange of population .About 2 million people altogether had to leave their homelands and settle in countries of their co-nationals. The redrawing of boundaries affected approximately 78 million people.[10]

During and after the First World War it was also possible to ascertain, on the strength of previous censuses, political activity, and elections, the attitude of the respective population regarding the state to which they preferred to belong. In a few cases plebiscites were even organised.[11]

Adjustments after the Second World War consisted both in large-scale transfers of populations and in territorial changes. On the whole about 20 million people moved, and permanently settled in new homelands. Of these more than half were Germans who were expelled from East-Central European countries such as Czechoslovakia and East German territories annexed by Poland and the USSR, and less than half were Poles, Czechs and Russians who settled in their place. About 15 million remained in the ceded territories. Cessions affecting more than 13 million were in favour of the USSR.[12] Territories ceded by Germany to Poland[13] had to compensate the latter for provinces taken over by the USSR. The remaining beneficiaries of territorial changes were Yugoslavia, Greece and Bulgaria,[14] though to a much lesser extent.

During the post-war period, with waning prospects for the re-unification of divided Germany, a new ethnic problem began to emerge. For those who are prone to understand nationality largely in political or even socio-economic terms, a question arose; whether statehood, coupled with the different political and socio-economic separate systems of West and East Germany, does not bring about the development of two separate nationalities. Since communication between the two Germanies is limited as a deliberate policy of the East German authorities, and as the systemic differences are far reaching and affect the everyday life of citizens in the respective German states, there are favourable conditions for the development of some kind of separate consciousness. Whether this happens or not, depends on many circumstances, not least upon the attitudes of the political and cultural elites in the two Germanies.[15] As the crystallisation of national consciousness is a long-term process, it cannot be expected that this issue will be decided in our lifetime or perhaps even in the next few generations.[16]

The ethnic developments taking place between 1913 and 1948 may be summed up with the help of the following balance sheet: on the asset side there were ethnic groups which totalled approximately 80 million people (70 million after the First World War, 10 million after the Second World War) which improved their political status in the sense of achieving national self-determination. (Since then the number of most of these groups has increased further as a result of the excess of births over deaths.) The main beneficiaries were the Western and Southern Slavonic nationalities, Romanians, Italians, Greeks, French and for the period between the two world wars, also the Baltic nations.

On the liability side, in purely ethnic terms, there remained after both wars about 6 million people who belonged to the pre-war ruling nations (Hungarians, Turks, and Germans, where these were not evicted) and were ceded with their territories to the newly created nation-states and so became subject ethnic groups (minorities) in their turn. As a result of the Second World War there were also 8 million members of nationalities who had to renounce their independent statehood and accept, without any electoral consultation, a federated status within the USSR (Baltic nations and Bessarabian Romanians – Moldavians).[17] So against about 80 millions who, as nations, attained a higher political status, there were about 14 million whose status declined. The political status of approximately 12 million people who were forcibly resettled has not changed as far as the ethnic aspect is concerned. As a rule, these people were transferred to the countries of their kin.[18]

Yet, as these rearrangements were due to the wars, casualties and losses of population have also to be taken into account. With respect to Europe alone, over 40 million soldiers and civilians were killed as a result of war and related actions (over 8 million in the First and over 32 million in the Second World War). To these figures tens of millions of wounded, imprisoned and displaced persons have to be added. During and after the Second World War there were large bodies of ethnic groups which were forcibly transferred (as already mentioned), together with political refugees and inmates of concentration and labour camps (in Nazi Germany these were mainly political opponents and members of the persecuted ethnic groups, in the USSR they were unreliable persons, especially from the newly acquired territories, and returning prisoners of war).

One can rightly ask whether all the above-mentioned improvements in nationality status were worth this terrible price. The Second World War especially, with the ideological embattlement displayed by the totalitarian regimes, produced a staggering disaster toll. Secular religions of modernity with their excessive stress on collective achievements, supported by the unprecedented striking power of technological warfare, have carried a high price, which in relative terms (i.e. in proportion to absolute numbers of population) have only been superseded by a few of the most devastating military campaigns in past history.

So not only had an excessive price to be paid for the adjustment of the political to the ethnic map of Europe, but also some nationalities were left out of the readjustments and some had even to suffer new injuries. The remaining and newly created ethnic problems can be divided into four categories:

first, ethnic groups who still lack any kind of self-government (home rule);
second, ethnic groups who are dissatisfied with their present status of self-government;

third, fragments of ethnic groups who were, against their will, detached from their main ethnic body and had to accept an alien rule (were incorporated into other nation-states);
fourth, a quite new category of ethnic problems which has been created by large-scale migration of individuals who left their homelands for political or economic reasons and settled in considerable numbers in countries of another language and culture.

In Tables 6.1 to 6.5, we have identified, in the whole of Europe, nine ethnic groups without what may be considered a kind of self-government status. However, as has been said already, only five of them are of sufficient size and possess a compact territory and so thus may be considered as candidates for improved political status, they are: Alsatians, Basques, Bretons, Corsicans and Welsh.[19] Together they represent about 6 million people. To this list the case of Languedoc-speakers ('Occitanians') in southern France and Gallicians (Gallegos) in north-western Spain may be added but their respective movements for linguistic emancipation, let alone self-government, do not seem to be widespread enough to justify inclusion in our considerations.[20]

All of these aforementioned groups live in time-honoured nation-states of Europe (France, Spain and Great Britain), nation-states which in many ways became prototypes for other nationalities who built states of their own much later. Moreover, as a result of an unprecedented colonial expansion the literary languages of these three nations became widely used in vast areas beyond their political boundaries.[21]

In that sense all these three nations have a unique position in Europe, a position with which, up to a point, only the Russians can be compared. They are the basic pillars of wider, in a sense supra-national, cultures. Speaking the language and participating in the whole culture related to this language can more easily foster cosmopolitan feelings than if one's own outlook is locked in a culture and language with a narrowly circumscribed horizon. It is easy to put forward the following proposition: 'Let us be cosmopolitan while speaking my language.' This is an assumption which, whether one knows it or not, implies more than acceptance of language as a means of communicating with each other. With it is usually linked a particular intellectual and artistic tradition which in its turn implies a certain way of thinking, preference for certain values, habits, etc.

Although many sociologists may dislike the idea because it does not fit their specialist tools of perception and explanation, Salvador de Madariaga's brilliant essay on the three leading West European nations – English, French and Spanish – still provides an unmatched insight into the concrete relationship of language with ways of thinking and evaluating.[22] For those who have tasted the social and intellectual milieu of different nations, there can be little doubt that European ecumenism or cosmopolitism would acquire somewhat different features according to which language and intellectual tradition provided its basis.

Further, for members of a nation, whose status of independence is taken for granted and whose state embraces a wider territory than that inhabited by their co-nationals (in the ethnic sense), it is also easier to shift the stress of national consciousness to issues other than those of collective self-determination. In such conditions Lord Acton could well develop his 'Whig' theory of nationality which, in contrast to the concept prevailing on the European continent, stressed individual liberties rather than the collective freedom of ethnic groups irrespective of their own political regime.

From the position of those who possess superior national status the claims of small ethnic groups such as Bretons or the Welsh for linguistic emancipation may seem ridiculous; so, in the nineteenth century, appeared many similar claims of Western and Southern Slavonic nations. These of course came forward with their demands at the right time, on the tide of romanticism and nationalistic feelings prevailing almost everywhere in Europe. Yet even without the intellectual backing of romanticism, or as some argue, Kantian philosophy,[23] the quest for the full exercise of national identity of those who speak a particular language remains a meaningful goal.

The contemporary reawakening of nationalism among some ethnic groups, not only in Europe but also in other parts of the world, is due primarily to dissatisfaction with their political status. Economic conditions are usually secondary; while they may strongly accentuate or even stir resentment, these shortcomings are supposed to be solvable by a greater degree of home rule or independence rather than by changes in the society as a whole.

So, for instance, Corsican nationalism has been reawakened by the immigration of French refugees from Algeria (resulting from the solution of another ethnic problem), whose energy and entrepreneurial spirit has put the native Corsicans at a disadvantage and made their inferior social status more apparent. Therefore Corsicans, who ethnically are more Italian than French, demand more vehemently than before to have the island for themselves and for that purpose claim a satisfactory level of self-government.

The potential of stateless nations for obtaining some type of self-government is unequal. As the situation appears at the beginning of 1978, it seems most likely that Welshmen are on the verge of obtaining it. (The Scottish issue, to be discussed later on, has been included in point 2 of our list of problems.) The scope for using Welsh in

Wales has already been expanded considerably since the Welsh Language Act in 1967. The problem, however, is that approximately three-quarters of Wales's inhabitants do not speak Welsh but English. Their national consciousness seems to be a combination of regional (Welsh) and national (British) loyalty, perhaps in a way similar to that of inhabitants of individual *Lands* within the Federal Republic of Germany or cantons within the Swiss Confederation.

The hopes of the Basques and Catalans in Spain are also rising. The democratisation of the Spanish monarchy is hardly imaginable without some kind of self-government and cultural self-determination for nationalities who have already enjoyed some home rule for a short period (during the Spanish Republic in the late 1930s). Even in the last years of Franco's rule Catalans and Basques gained some ground for using their respective languages in private schools and mass media. Towards the end of 1975 the Spanish government made it legal for Basques, Catalans and other Spanish citizens to use their native regional language in many official dealings and in all cultural affairs. On 5 October 1977 Catalonia was granted an autonomous status which has yet to be implemented in practice. A similar status is envisaged for the Basque country.

The situation in France seems to be least hopeful for ethnic minorities. There the tendency to consider the non-French languages as mere dialects (patois), which are good only at the cultural level of folklore, is the main obstacle to admitting their languages in schools, offices and mass media.[24] Also, the particularly vigorous blend of political and ethnic national consciousness of the Frenchman is a strong impediment to substantial concessions towards centrifugal tendencies even if these may involve only 6 to 7 per cent of the total population of France. The twenty-one regions, each covering two to six *départements* created in 1964 and provided with more authority since then, were devised to meet the needs of administrative decentralisation mainly in the field of economic and social (in the narrow sense) matters, and not the requirements of the ethnic minorities or the call for some type of genuine home rule.

Another category of unsolved ethnic problems is ethnic groups with unsatisfactory self-government, from their point of view.

In the West there is only one ethnic group which, at the time of writing, can, with some qualifications, be included in this category, namely the Scots. As has been mentioned in the notes to the respective tables, Scots were classified as an autonomous ethnic group for the following reasons:

(a) Scotland's union with England is based on a kind of constitutional contract which, as contemporary development indicates, can be altered in Scotland's favour by adequate pressure exerted through common political institutions;

(b) Scotland has preserved a wider range of local and cultural peculiarities than other countries with formal autonomy or federated status have achieved.

Scottish national consciousness can hardly be described in simple terms. It seems to me that Scottish feelings in this matter can be viewed rather as a spectrum of nuances strung out between two poles: exclusive Scottish national consciousness on one end and, on the other, British national consciousness combined with different degrees of affection for Scotland as a region. A similar strongly articulated two-tier consciousness can be observed in Bavaria, whose home rule, however, is amply borne out by the federal constitution of West Germany.

At the time of writing this chapter the combined attitude seems to prevail. Yet in view of the continuous increase of votes cast for the Scottish National Party, which stands for much more autonomy, if not full independence, an increase of those whose national consciousness is primarily Scottish can be assumed. The electoral switch, however, was so abrupt (from 11·5 per cent in 1970 to 21·9 per cent in February 1974 and 30·4 per cent in October 1974) that it may well reflect occasional dissatisfaction as well as a more gradual shift in the hierarchy of loyalties. As more self-government for Scotland is the stated policy of each of the three main British parties, and as legislative change has already been initiated by the government, a substantial move in that direction seems almost certain. The only question is, how many Scots will be satisfied with the eventual outcome, and to what degree?

All the other ethnic groups with a kind of self-government in their territory, but one which is not considered adequate by many of their members, are in Eastern or East-Central Europe. Most of them live in the USSR. Here also belong the three ethnic groups whose independent statehood attained after the First World War was changed into a federated status on the eve of the Second World War.

As the problems emerging in the Soviet Union are basically due to the peculiarities of the Soviet system, a few words have to be said on the official Soviet position *vis-à-vis* ethnic problems. The USSR is a country where a grandiose attempt has been made to reorganise a society dominated by one particular nation into a federation of ethnic groups united not only by a common institutional framework but also by a common ideology which, in contrast to ideologies with similar functions in the past, is thoroughly secular and, as it is claimed, scientific.

Within this framework it seemed possible to allow individual ethnic groups a certain degree of self-determination. Thus the Ukranians and Belorussians, whom the Tsarist regime considered as members of the all-Russian nation, were now allowed to foster their

147

separate languages and national consciousness. Moreover, all non-Slavonic nationalities, especially the small and under-developed groups with rather religious (Islamic) consciousness or without any awareness of being a nation in a modern sense, were encouraged to develop their own languages and ethnic identity. In the first instance even Muslims, who until then mainly used Arabic or Persian languages for literary purposes, with the corresponding type of calligraphy, were permitted to introduce Latin characters for their native Turkic–Tatar languages as the Anatolian Turks had done earlier. However, in order to impede the spread of pan-Turkic feelings, the Soviet leadership in the 1930s forced these nations to substitute Cyrillic for the Latin characters. Similarly Moldavians, a detached fragment of the Romanian nation, whom the Soviet government recognised as a separate nationality, had to abandon their traditional Latin script and adopt the Cyrillic.

This shift characterised the changed position. Even with an efficient ban on other competing ideologies, Marxism-Leninism was not strong enough to assume the integrative function for the new federation. Neither could the state, party, and police apparatus, with their tremendous coercive potential, substitute for the role of spontaneous integrative tendencies. Attraction exerted by the main ethnic bodies abroad on the detached ethnic groups within the USSR had to be checked by divisive measures.[25] More support from below was looked for in the integrative potential of the past. Its basis was eventually found, in spite of Lenin's warnings,[26] in the traditional national consciousness of the Russians, who constitute more than half of the population of the USSR (in the 1970 census, 53 per cent).

The possible centrifugal tendencies of the non-Russian nationalities are efficiently checked by the exclusive domination of the Communist party with all its power concentrated in the Politbureau at the top. Although Article 72 of the Constitution of the USSR grants every Union republic the right to secede from the Union, such an act is practically inconceivable. The decision to this effect would have to be passed by the majority of the Supreme Soviet of the respective republic, which being composed predominantly of the members of the Communist party have to vote according to the line adopted by the All-Union leadership in Moscow. As all Union republics are specified by name in Article 71 of the Constitution, secession from the USSR implies a constitutional change which according to Article 174 requires the approval of two-thirds of both houses of the Supreme All-Union (federal) Soviet; this is not only composed mainly of party members but also leaves the representatives of any would-be dissident republic in a helpless minority. The constitutional rights of individual republics to enter into direct contractual and diplomatic relationships with countries outside the USSR (Article 18a) are illusory for the same reasons. (All the aforementioned articles refer to the new 1977 Constitution; the 1936 Constitution contained identical provisions in articles 17, 13, 146 and 18a respectively.[27])

In many respects the Soviet Union became a direct continuation of the Russian Empire. Great personalities of Russian history, whether men of culture or the military, became looked upon as national heroes of the whole Soviet Union. Historical personalities of other nationalities in the Soviet Union are acknowledged only so far as their activity has been friendly towards Russia. Even if, in the official view, Tsarist Russia is regarded as inferior to the Soviet Union, in comparison with her neighbours in the past she is considered as the best alternative partner which the smaller nation could have joined.

The dominant position of the Russians is also supported by the ideological argument that this nation has earned the merit of being the first to build socialism. Therefore, not only other Soviet nationalities but also other 'socialist' nations, i.e. nations ruled by Communist parties, have to acknowledge the primacy of the USSR. A positive attitude towards the USSR is considered a test of proletarian internationalism as opposed to cosmopolitism which does not make a distinction between socialist and non-socialist nations. In view of a divided world, proletarian internationalism has to be promoted in a two-fold pattern: solidarity with every Communist-dominated country as a whole (with the possible exception of those ruled by heretics); in all other countries, solidarity with co-Marxists, with the proletariat and possibly with the oppressed ethnic groups and developing nations. Moreover, internationalism conceived in these terms, does not exclude development of, and even strong support for, patriotic feelings, as long as these feelings are in line with the basic policy or rather strategy of the 'fatherland of socialism'.

Marx himself created a precedent for such an attitude when he evaluated the struggle for political emancipation of individual European nationalities according to whether they followed what in his eyes were progressive or reactionary trends. For him also, the attitude towards Russia, then Tsarist, was crucial in this respect but in the opposite direction. Therefore Marx supported the national aspirations of Poles and Hungarians, but disapproved of the struggle of the Czechs and Southern Slavs. Stalin simply reversed this position. Referring to one of Lenin's statements on political strategy, namely that the various demands of democracy, including self-determination, are to be approved or rejected according to the needs of the general democratic (now general socialist) world movement Stalin concluded:

This is the position in regard to the question of particular national movements, of the possible reactionary character of these movements – if, of course, they are appraised not from the point of view of abstract rights, but concretely, from the point of view of the interests of the revolutionary movement.[28]

This is the basis of 'proletarian' internationalism, in contrast to 'bourgeois' nationalism, or even worse, cosmopolitism, which is supposed to be a non-differentiated, colourless feeling of people who have little attachment to any nationality. Consequently, the would-be independent nationalists and people with cosmopolitan attitudes are subject to different measures of discrimination or even persecution.

The position of the Russian nation within the USSR is appositely characterised by the first verse of the new Soviet national anthem which, in 1944, in the full swing of the Great Patriotic War under Stalin's auspices, was substituted for the original anthem of the USSR, the International. The words read: 'The Great Russia welded forever together the indissoluble union of free republics'.

In building their own system in one particular country first, a country with particular features which very much influenced its nature as the fatherland of socialism, Marxist-Leninists created in the USSR an indissoluble blend of ideological and ethnic loyalty. Soviet Russia became not only a bulwark of a particular brand of Marxism but also a great power in her own right, a power dominated by one nation, the Russians. Consequently, the other nations who joined the league or who were brought to do so by force, not only had to accept the lead of the Soviet Union but also give her requirements (whether political or economic) priority over their own interests. This of course deprived the established Marxism-Leninism of its potentially supra-national integrative capacity.

The process of disintegration of pro-Soviet loyalties within the whole Communist bloc from Central Europe to the Far East is well known. The fate of communism in individual countries very much depends on how far it has been able to identify itself with the particular interests of that country. And then there are countries, such as Poland, where it has in traditional religious affiliation a formidable foe which can still claim to be the most significant cultural determinant of national identity.

The lesson so far is that ethnic affiliation and associated national consciousness has also proved to be the most decisive element of social cohesion and source of loyalty in the Communist-dominated part of the world. This development can be demonstrated in other Communist-ruled countries confronted with specific ethnic problems, such as Yugoslavia and Czechoslovakia.

Yugoslavia is in many ways the most interesting sociological laboratory. There, attempts are being made to find out how to reconcile several pluralistic aspects (especially in economy and culture) with the exclusive rule of one political party, which nevertheless allows for a certain scope of differentiation within its ranks. Another no-less-ambitious attempt is to induce a viable co-operation between several ethnic groups with different national consciousnesses, although from the linguistic point of view they are closer to each other than are the dialects of many other European nations who have no problems of that kind.

Ethnic differentiation of Southern Slavs ('Yug' means south in Serbo–Croat) is due not only to the different political formations – the historical states of Croatia, Serbia, Bosnia, Montenegro and also for a time in the distant past, Carinthia – but additionally because these states developed within the context of three different civilisations; each of them was based on a particular religion and associated culture: Catholic, Orthodox and Islamic.

The complexity of Yugoslav ethnic problems can be seen from the following list of her internal dividing lines. Yugoslavia is a country of six federated republics (Serbia, Croatia, Bosnia–Hercegovina, Slovenia, Macedonia and Montenegro) five regional languages (Serbo-Croat, Slovenian, Macedonian, Albanian and Hungarian), three religious traditions (Roman Catholic, Greek Orthodox and Ottoman Islamic), two types of writing (Cyrillic and Latin) which are both used in the most common of the five languages (spoken by three-quarters of the population), thus dividing it into two additional variants (Serbian and Croatian). To complete the mosaic, one has to add, within the Serbian republic, the autonomous region of Kosovo and the autonomous province of Vojvodina.

All these overlapping differences have to be overcome by a federal system (which as far as possible would meet individual ethnic requirements) combined with the integrative force of one political party operating on the basis of one world view. This, although derived from the same theoretical basis as in the USSR, has developed a more cautious, in a way more tolerant, approach to divergent views.

As religious affiliation in Yugoslavia has acquired a particular connotation, and as the merger of religious and ethnic identity creates the most powerful blend of communal consciousness,[29] the Yugoslav Communist leadership is first trying to dissolve this blend. The stress is laid on its ethnic element at the expense of religious aspects which can be substituted, it is believed, by the Marxist world view. As a result of this strategy Yugoslav Muslims, living mainly in Bosnia–Hercegovina, were recognised as a separate ethnic group although they have neither their own language, nor alphabet, nor

151

are they compactly settled on a clearly circumscribed territory. Unlike some other Communist countries such as neighbouring Albania, the Yugoslav policy towards churches relies more on their gradual 'withering away' rather than on direct repression.

Yet industrialisation combined with enhanced horizontal and vertical mobility bring new problems which add fuel to communal rivalries and so make the integration of the federated nationalities more rather than less difficult. With the on-going change of values, individuals cease to be bound to inherited positions and roles within a hierarchical order and try to emulate their more successful neighbours and aspire to a higher social status, in which wealth and level of income acquire primary importance. Achievement in this respect, however, depends on the stage of economic development which, in Yugoslavia, varies from region to region; the *per capita* national income in the richest, Slovenia, was in 1971 6·6 times higher than in the poorest, the region of Kosovo, mainly inhabited by Albanians. As the economic level is in inverse ratio to the natural increase of population, which in Kosovo is almost six times higher than in Slovenia, the task of providing jobs in poorer areas requires a transfer of funds for new investment on an immense scale. This can only be done as a result of a highly developed altruism among the richer nationalities, or enforced by power strongly concentrated at the top. Neither, however, is the case. Nor is the transfer of labour force from poorer to richer areas a sufficient means for equalising the economic level of individual regions. Moreover, there are many Yugoslav workers who look for employment abroad; in the early 1970s there were almost 600,000. Further problems arise with the assimilation of people from areas with a different cultural level and background.

So, the Yugoslav strategy is menaced by the danger that the weakening of religious elements in national consciousness will be substituted by secular outlooks based on more pragmatic lines of economic interests, social status and prestige. Yet all tensions resulting from centrifugal tendencies are to a considerable extent counterbalanced by the centripetal tendency which is being sustained as a response to the challenge of the outside menace. Yugoslav defiance of Soviet aspirations for uncontestable leadership in the 'Socialist' bloc is her most unifying factor. In spite of all the growing economic overtones, the future of Yugoslavia depends mainly on the relative strength of her two respective nationalisms: federal and local. The former is a unifying nationalism crystallised in opposition to the aspirations of a 'Big Brother', whilst the latter is a divisive plurality of nationalisms born of individual traditional communities, which, if respective loyalties are pushed too far, may disrupt the federal unity of Yugoslavia.

Czechoslovakia has been lucky to solve her main ethnic problems, although at a high cost to her aspirations for democracy and individual liberties. The problems of the German minority disappeared not through the cession of territory but through their eviction. Yet the plan for the exchange of the Hungarian minority in Slovakia for the Slovak minority in Hungary had only a limited success. Also the attempt to 'reslovakise' Hungarians in Czechoslovakia, characteristic of the short post-war period, when the Communists tried to outbid the 'bourgeois' parties by fervid nationalism, could not fully make good the encroachment of the Hungarian language in the Slovak territories during the last hundred years of Slovak association with the Hungarian kingdom. Since about 1948 a more tolerant policy towards the Hungarian minority set in.

The only serious ethnic problem which survived until 1968 was the Czech–Slovak relationship.[30] In the atmosphere of a general reform, the Czechoslovak Socialist Republic (this label is used since 1960) has been transformed into a federation of two republics with equal rights: the Czech Socialist Republic and the Slovak Socialist Republic. Although a federation in a totalitarian regime need not necessarily be meaningful, the ability of the Slovak Communist leaders (their top man eventually became the leader both of the party and of the federation of the two states) to maintain a better relationship with Moscow than the Czech Communists (whose ranks were more depleted by heresy) could achieve became an efficient safeguard of Slovak equality with the Czechs.

The Belgian bi-nationalism, like the Czechoslovak, seems to have been resolved satisfactorily. From the foundation of the kingdom of the Belgians in 1830, the French language enjoyed higher prestige and wider usage than the Flemish. The Flemish struggle for assertion of their language on a national level in general and in the bilingual territory of Brussels in particular has been supported by a considerably higher birth rate among the Flemings than the Walloons. Whereas towards the end of the nineteenth century both ethnic groups were approximately equally represented in the Belgian population as a whole, Walloons are now outnumbered by Flemings. Consequently, it is the Walloons who became afraid of being subject to the majority on the other side. This made them more willing to draw a fixed demarcation line between the respective linguistic areas, a policy which had earlier been in the Flemish interest. In 1962/3, the whole country was divided into four linguistic areas, which on 31 December 1973 had the following proportions of the total population of Belgium: Flemish area 56·4 per cent, French area 32·1 per cent, German area 0·6 per cent (this tiny minority in the East has also been respected), bilingual (Brussels) 10·9 per cent.

On both sides of the linguistic barrier there are people whose aim is to turn Belgium into a loose confederation in which the Flemish-speaking Flanders and French-speaking Wallonia would be virtually independent. This concept is propagated by the so-called 'linguistic parties' (on both sides) which so far have, however, been unable to win more than a quarter of the seats in the Chamber of Representatives between them. The main parties (Socialists, Social Christians and Liberals) are bilingual and support the present constitutional arrangement.

Another potential source of disturbance (societal dysfunction) concerns the fragmented ethnic groups. By fragmented ethnic groups we understand cases where sections of nations living compactly on a certain territory were without their consent or even against their explicit desire, detached from their main ethnic body and incorporated into other nation-states. Ethnic fragments which constitute multi-national federations such as Switzerland or states where two nationalities have equal rights (constitute the state) such as Belgium (see above), are not understood as belonging to this category.

Whilst the groups in the category of fragmented nationalities were still quite numerous after the First World War, they were considerably diminished by changes of boundaries and mass transfers of population resulting from the Second World War. If scattered national fragments (diaspora) are not taken into account, there remain only a few sizeable ethnic minorities in this category. First of all, there are about 2·8 million ethnic Hungarians in countries adjacent to Hungary, of which more than half live in a compact territory close to the Hungarian border. Most of them are in Romania (1·7 million), partly in the north-western borderland, partly as an ethnic enclave almost in the centre of Romania (in East Transylvania). Until 1956 the latter had an autonomous region of a similar type to those in the USSR. Yet the Hungarian uprising in that year and its echo among the Hungarian minority scared the Romanian Communist leadership to such an extent that the Hungarian autonomous region was disbanded. The cultural activity of the Hungarian minority as a whole became more closely supervised and Romanian authorities started to combine the Hungarian establishments of higher education, until then independent, with the Romanian ones by introducing parallel classes for both nationalities. Although the Hungarian minority in Romania may appreciate the independent stand of Romania *vis-à-vis* the Soviet Union in international matters, as far as internal policy is concerned there are many reasons, in addition to ethnic ones, why they would prefer the less totalitarian regime in Hungary.

A more advantageous position is that of the Hungarian minority in Yugoslavia where less than half a million Hungarians enjoy a fair amount of cultural autonomy within the autonomous region of Vojvodina of which they constitute about a quarter of the population. Hungarian minorities in Czechoslovakia and the USSR fare less well. Although they enjoy facilities for cultural development, including school education in their language, the scope for self-assertion is limited by a higher degree of power concentration in the respective countries.

Other sizeable detached fragments live scattered in mixed terri-tories and/or compactly in small enclaves. They are Poles in the USSR, Germans in Poland, Romania and a few still in Czechoslo-vakia; Turks in Bulgaria, Greece and Yugoslavia. The Polish government has recently allowed 280,000 ethnic Germans to emigrate to West Germany in exchange for economic help. Emigration of small numbers of ethnic Germans has also been allowed from Czechoslovakia (their numbers had dwindled to 77,000 in 1974) and recently from the USSR where, according to the census in 1970 there were 1·8 million ethnic Germans. Romanian Germans (almost 400,000) enjoy a certain cultural self-assertion and a comparatively high social status within the Romanian population; nevertheless many of them too seem to be interested in emigrating.

The desire to emigrate was also voiced by the Turkish minority in Bulgaria. But as Turkey had nothing to offer in exchange, the Bulgarian government has not given them the necessary permission. The Turkish minority in Greece and similarly the Greek minority in Turkey are, after the exchange of population in 1922–3, of less importance. The main area of ethnic struggle between these two ethnic groups is now Cyprus. There the attempt to found a two-nation state (virtually a state of two ethnic fragments, with equal rights for unequal numbers) foundered, and the partition of the island now seems most likely. Yet, as usual in similar cases, partition becomes reality not on the basis of a just division according to the number of the respective populations but on the basis of the superior military strength of Turkey which neither the United Nations peace-keeping force in that area nor allied NATO powers were able or willing to check adequately.

A similar development has produced the contemporary protracted tension in Northern Ireland. There too the boundary between the two Irelands was not drawn according to the numerical proportions of the two ethno-religious groups (for which the respective parts of Ireland had to be their nation-states) but according to the will of the partner backed by stronger military power. Unlike in Cyprus how-ever, co-nationals of the weaker partner were not evicted and could as individuals enjoy the rights of a liberal, pluralistic regime. This, however, did not prove to be a satisfactory substitute for national self-determination. Yet because both of these ethno-religious groups

155

speak the same language and because in Western Europe the current understanding of 'nation' is by country rather than by people, there is a growing tendency to overcome the dichotomy by shifting the emphasis on to the political and socio-economic aspect of the divided society. This virtually amounts to substitution of a more or less cosmopolitan world view for communal loyalties. As has been said earlier, however, these loyalties have a particular tenacity when ethnic and religious affiliations have been merged.

As already mentioned, cosmopolitan feelings are regarded with disapproval by Marxists-Leninists, who stand for an internationalism within which they can draw distinctions between nations led by progressive forces and nations led by reactionary forces. If, however, an issue arises between two nations both dominated by Marxists-Leninists then their stand depends on the conflicting ideological positions of the contestants. Moreover, the ethnic issue itself becomes a means, a pretext rather than a problem in its own right, in the competition between two alternatives within the Marxist-Leninist fold.

A good example of these attitudes is the case of the Macedonians. These Slavs, who in the sixth century A.D. settled in ancient Macedonia, were successively ruled by Bulgarians, Byzantines, Serbs and Ottomans. The two Balkan and the two world wars divided and solidified the partition of Macedonia between Serbia (which later became part of Yugoslavia), Greece and Bulgaria. At the beginning all contestants tried to integrate Macedonians, speaking Slavonic dialects, into their respective nations. After the Second World War, however, when Yugoslavia was transformed into a multi-national federation, Macedonians there were recognised as a separate nationality and their dialect began to be fostered as a literary language. This was a blow to the Bulgarians who, for mainly linguistic but also historical reasons, claimed the whole of Macedonia for themselves. Now irredentist movements are possible in both directions; for greater Macedonia on the Yugoslav side, and for greater Bulgaria on the other. In reality, however, only the Bulgarian claims have been put forward so far: from time to time, Bulgarians are encouraged to launch nationalistic propaganda. On the other hand Yugoslavs, knowing that they are dealing not with Bulgarians themselves but with the USSR behind them, have not yet exploited their, from the ethnic point of view, more advantageous position. Meanwhile Macedonians in Greece have been subject to the process of assimilation into the Greek ethnic body.[31]

In the post-war period, the most vociferous detached minority (there were even some terrorist activities) were the Austro–Germans in southern Tirol annexed by Italy in 1919. After the Second World War, Austria reclaimed a part of this territory but without success.

In 1948 the whole region, which is predominantly Italian, was granted autonomous status with a regional parliament and government. To appease the German-speaking minority of that area, the region has been divided into two semi-autonomous provinces – Trentino (wholly Italian) and Alto Adige (261,000 German, 138,000 Italian and 16,000 Ladin-speaking population in 1971). So at least, on a lower level, the Austro-German group has obtained a territory in whose self-government it can be decisive.

The French-speaking population in Aosta Valley, the Sicilians and Sardinians whose regions also obtained autonomy in 1948, are not outnumbered by other nationals in their domains. In Sardinia however, a politico-cultural movement, claiming Sardinians to be a separate nation with their own language, considers the island's autonomy inadequate, providing better opportunities for Italians from the mainland than for native Sardinians. In 1963 a similar autonomous status was granted to the north-eastern region, Friuli-Venezia Giulia, inhabited partly by Furlanians (speaking a Raeto-Romance language or dialect), partly by Italians and to a lesser extent by Slovenes. Neither arrangement seems satisfactory.

There are still two or three more grievances expressed by the minor detached fragments of ethnic groups in Europe. In France, there are not only the detached fragments of Catalans and Basques whose problems were discussed in relation to their main bodies in Spain, but also Alsatians and Corsicans who in a way can be considered as detached fragments of the German and Italian nations respectively. In addition, in the utmost northern corner of France, there are approximately 150,000 Flemings, who have so far succeeded in preserving their national identity.

Surprisingly, a particular case of ethnic detachment became a problem in multi-national Switzerland. The issue came alive with regard to the French-speaking minority of the predominantly German canton, Bern. Since 1945 the inhabitants of the mountainous territory in the north-west (Jura), which by sheer historical accident has been incorporated into the large and rich canton of Bern and not into the poorer, wholly French-speaking, neighbouring canton of Neufchatel, have been agitating for a separate canton of their own. Supporters of this idea were mainly the Catholic members of the predominantly rural districts of the French-speaking Jura. French-speaking Protestants living in the more industrialised districts were in favour of retaining the union with the canton Bern. When the federal government eventually yielded and arranged a plebiscite in the area (in 1959) the votes against a separate canton won a slight majority. This outcome exacerbated the radicals and that part of Switzerland suffered some terrorist activity, directed against property rather than people. Another plebiscite, in June 1974, brought victory for the separatists (37,000 against 34,000 votes). However, their majority was confined to their three remotest, rural, districts whereas the other three French-speaking districts declared themselves for union with Bern. Thus the situation is still pending and awaits a final constitutional solution. Eventually, the Swiss electorate as a whole will have to decide whether or not to ratify the creation of the confederations's 23rd canton.

The last focus of some unrest happened recently among the tiny Slovene minority in Austrian Carinthia. The precise number of Slovenes in this area has not been ascertained recently, but it was steadily declining as a result of cultural and economic pressure or attraction of the German-speaking part of the province. The issue arose in connection with the creation of Yugoslavia after the First World War. The southern part of Carinthia was then a mixed territory, and a plebiscite organised in 1920 had to decide which country it should join: 59 per cent of the votes were cast for Austria and 41 per cent for Yugoslavia; but in the two districts south of the river Drau, the pro-Yugoslav vote was more than 50 per cent. However, since the plebiscite was devised for the area as a whole, these two districts with a Yugoslav majority remained with Austria. Towards the end of the Second World War, Yugoslav partisans operated in that area and after the war Yugoslavia yet again raised the claim for cession of the territory in question. Meanwhile, the number of the Slovene-speaking population diminished further; many of them also became apprehensive of the Communist regime in Yugoslavia. The presence of Yugoslav soldiers in the territory aroused nationalistic pro-Austrian feelings amongst the German-speaking population who, living in mixed areas and challenged again by renewed territorial claims, displayed less tolerance towards Slovenes than German-speaking inhabitants of other parts of Austria. The situation was eventually settled on the basis of the status quo and the Austrian government reiterated its previous obligation to grant full linguistic and cultural rights to its Slovene and also Croat minorities in another area (Burgenland). Yet, the Austrian measures to preserve minority rights were resented by nationalistic elements among the German-speaking Carinthians who then, as they were always prone to do, tried by petty means to eliminate the apparent vestiges of Slovenian language in this area. The Yugoslav government over-reacted to this in order to divert attention from its own internal ethnic problems. However, the whole issue affects too few people to become a sufficiently major issue for strengthening pan-Yugoslav nationalism. The power aspirations of the Soviet Union are incomparably more important in that respect.

A potential rather than actual source of disturbance are Albanians living in Yugoslavia. As they were allowed a considerable degree of cultural self-determination, have a comfortable majority in the autonomous region of Kosovo, and, last but not least, seem to enjoy the Yugoslav liberal Communism more than that of their kin in Albania, which is the toughest of all its brands in Europe, their claims for more self-assertion in Yugoslavia are rarely linked with secessionist aspirations. Neither are Albanian authorities too fervent in fostering irredentist feelings amongst their co-nationals in Yugoslavia. As long as the Communist leaderships in Albania and Yugoslavia see themselves as more threatened by the aspirations of the USSR, the division of the .Albanian nation into two states is unlikely to become a major issue.

Unfortunately, nothing is known about the fate of small ethnic minorities in Albania itself. However, in view of the fact that in that part of Europe nationality has been closely linked with religious affiliation, and bearing in mind the harsh treatment of religious organisations by the Albanian authorities, the position of the numerically weak Greek and Serbian minorities seems to be rather bleak.

Two ethnic groups which are not only distinct in terms of their language and culture but also by their life-style, such as the Gypsies scattered all over Europe and Lapps living in the most northerly parts of Finland, Sweden and Norway, constitute special cases. The problems connected with them are more complex than with other nationalities, but on the whole their existence is less disturbing because neither of them claim changes in boundaries or self-government for a certain area. On the whole the Lapps are better off because they are living in welfare states with very high living standards. Moreover the governments of the three Nordic countries seriously attempt to give Lapps adequate education in their native language and offer them facilities to integrate with the settled communities of the dominant nationality.

The situation of the Gypsies is much more difficult because they are too dedicated to their nomadic way of life. Even the concentrated attempts of the Communist states could not completel bring them to a settled way of life. Czechoslovakia in particula provided them with a good opportunity for a sedentary way of li but with little success. The Czechoslovak authorities consider approximately 300,000 Gypsies as a socio-economic anomaly rat than as an ethnic group; they try to disperse and assimilate t rather than acknowledge them as an ethnic minority. Howeve the late 1960s Gypsies in Czechoslovakia revealed a certain nat consciousness of their own and, led by a newly emerging i gentsia, claimed a greater opportunity for using their 'Ro language. As they have the highest birth rate in many of the e ments they inhabit and as they are difficult to assimila relevance of the Gypsy problem is likely to increase rather than decrease in the future.

Other ethnic minorities do not seem to constitute special problems in contemporary Europe. The 350,000 Swedes in Finland enjoy full cultural autonomy and full participation within the democratic institutions of that country. The case is similar with smaller groups elsewhere, such as Germans in Belgium and Denmark, and Danes in West Germany. Also in the Communist-dominated states the linguistic requirements of detached ethnic groups (fragments) are more or less respected with the aforementioned qualifications. Even the almost extinct Sorbs in East Germany (a Slavonic nationality with two ancient versions of a literary language) have, after a prolonged period of discrimination or even persecution, received helpful government attention since 1945.[32] As they (about 70,000) live in an enclave encircled by and largely mixed with the German population, the tendency to assimilate remains strong even though the ethnic group has now some scope for educating its children in the native language.

A new category of ethnic problems has been created by large-scale migration of individuals who left their homelands for political or economic reasons. Mass emigration for economic reasons is a time-onoured phenomenon in Europe. In the late middle ages there was big migratory wave of Germanic peoples to East Central Europe beyond the scope of military conquest; this migration resulted in extensive shift of ethnic boundaries between the Slavs and ans and in addition created German enclaves within the c nations. After the discovery of the Americas a large-scale rom Europe set in. The unequal pace of industrialisation in self produced further migrations such as the influx in the as of Westphalia or Upper Silesia.

n for political and ideological reasons has a long history Religious wars and the principle *cuius regio eius religio* e who did not want to change their beliefs to leave their settle elsewhere. Totalitarian ideologies of the twentieth erate on the same principle but usually without allowing to emigrate. After regimes imbued by such ideologies had wer in Russia and Germany, a large-scale exodus of dissidents or people menaced by race or class persecution establishment of the Fascist regime in Italy and especially oduced further waves of émigrés.

Second World War the emigration was mainly from the -dominated states. With the collapse of Nazi Germany, llar of Fascist regimes, their survival in Europe proved o matter of time. On the other hand the military strength so and her aspirations to preserve her type of political and mic systems in all other Communist-dominated countries, led to a continuous stream of refugees. From time to time this was increased by a large-scale exodus resulting from suppressed attempts at liberalisation or emancipation of individual satellite countries. Yet all these political emigrations have not produced any ethnic problem in the sense discussed in this paper. In most cases the émigrés assimilated well in their new surroundings. The few lucky ones who survived the hostile regimes were able to return home.

More important were the problems arising from the dissolution of colonial empires. Whenever colonial powers granted citizenship to their colonial subjects, they had to accept their immigration when political or economic reasons made life in the emancipated homelands difficult. This was especially the case with the United Kingdom and the Netherlands. So it happened that into these two countries came people who were not only of different race but, more importantly, of different socio-cultural backgrounds which had little in common with European culture. Although in both countries there has been a long tradition of racial and ideological tolerance, the assimilation of people with different customs and religious views proved less easy than cosmopolitan and secular-minded people sometimes imagine.

The Netherlands' position in this respect has been eased by her particular blend of homogeneity and communalism which, within the general federated Netherlandish culture, allows differentiation on religious or regional lines. The harmonious coexistence of distinctive sub-cultures provides a more congenial ground for integration of ethnic and religious minorities than a society which prefers the ideals of equality and homogeneity, but allows itself to be divided by class differences.

France and Portugal too had to take émigrés from their colonial empires but these, unlike those of Britain and the Netherlands, were of their own kin. Nevertheless, the return of about a million Frenchmen and a half a million Portuguese, who had to give up their higher social status in the colonies for insecure prospects in the mother country, produced problems, especially regarding those who had been born outside the mother country.

The last, more recent, wave of large-scale emigration are the so-called guest workers coming from the economically less-developed countries of the Mediterranean – Spain, Italy, Yugoslavia, Greece, Turkey and Algeria – to the richest countries of continental Europe – Sweden, Switzerland, West Germany and France.[33] Although most of these guest workers originally came for temporary employment, many of them tend to stay and even bring their families. This of course produces some problems of assimilation which again are the more difficult the more different is the socio-cultural background from which the workers come. Some of the European governments try to provide their guest workers with some scope for cultural services in their own language. Sweden goes furthest in this direction, and tends to provide, as far as possible, the basic education for all ethnic groups in their own language. Sweden also is the most out-going country for foreign workers with respect to social services, pensions etc. In general the problems encountered concerning migrant workers mainly relate to adequate housing and spending of leisure time.[34]

To conclude, one may perhaps ask the question whether all the aforementioned quests for more self-determination or longing for reunification by the detached ethnic fragments with the main ethnic bodies make sense when both Western and Eastern Europe, each in their particular way, aim at an economic, political and eventually cultural integration. In evaluating the pertinence of this proposition we have to bear in mind the scope and the relevance of the two phenomena; national self-determination on one hand and integration into supra-national associations or confederations on the other.

Solution of one of these issues does not necessarily lead to the solution of the other. If most members of an ethnic group consider their national status as unjustly inferior, they will hardly accept the merger of the ruling nationality into a scheme for wider international co-operation as a substitute. The surrender of some national sovereignty by the leading nation cannot appease the dissatisfied minority. At best it could provide it with some help in its national struggle.

Sometimes it is believed that ethnic tensions can be solved by a shift of concern or interests. This, however, would involve ideological re-education. Although this may, in principle, be possible, the experience of the last fifty years indicates how difficult it is. If Marxist–Leninists, pursuing this policy with all the strength of their unitary constellation of power and formidable coercive apparatus, have not yet succeeded, how could a liberal government, limited in its power by the constraints of a pluralistic system achieve it? This is especially difficult where, as is the case with highly developed communalism, all education is completely in the hands of the rival groups. The lesson of experience so far is that no country can escape its unsolved ethnic problems by trying to transfer the issue to another plane. However many may think it possible, the recent revival of ethnic issues points to the opposite conclusion.

Notes

1 A classic example are the Swiss Germans who, although using literary German and sharing with other Germans substantial elements of their culture, have nevertheless developed cultural features of their own and above all acquired a separate consciousness.

2 In this sense there is a certain similarity with the concept of class. Class is a sociologically relevant category only when it consists of members conscious of their identity as a class.

3 P. M. Milyukov, *Nationality, its Origin and Development* (Czech translation from Russian), Prague, Orbis, 1930, p. 69. The importance of communication for building national consciousness was discovered long before the American scholars began to apply 'communication theory' to the study of nationalism.

4 The Tatar sovereignty over Muscovite Russia, unlike that over Kievan Russia, is not considered an interruption because it was basically a matter of tribute.

5 For the understanding but also misunderstanding of this issue, Kedourie's book on *Nationalism* (London, Hutchinson, 1966) and its treatment by others can be mentioned as a good example. Although he has fully realised what kind of human needs nationalism aims to satisfy (to belong together in a coherent and stable community) and why (erosion of the family, neighbourhood and religious community) and says it quite unequivocally on p. 101 (1966 edn), most of the book is filled by utterances (based on incoherent empirical references) which made the following impression on one student of theories of nationalism:

> Kedourie regards nationalism as one of the most pernicious
> doctrines to have been inflicted on a long-suffering humanity.
> He holds that it is an antiquarian irrelevance, a baneful invention
> of some misguided German philosophers supported by the
> frustrations of obscure middle-class writers, low-born sons of
> artisans, farmers and pastors. True, there was the example of the
> French revolutionaries at hand; but the real doctrine of national
> self-determination was elaborated in the first decades of the
> nineteenth century by Fichte and his followers, in their egoist
> and idealist emendations of Kant's notion of autonomy (Anthony
> D. Smith, *Theories of Nationalism*, London, Duckworth, 1971,
> pp. 9–10).

6 Of the famous fourteen points drawn up by Woodrow Wilson, President of the United States of America, as the basis for the peace settlement, after the first World War, five are casuistic applications of the aforementioned principle. (For further details see, e.g. L. W. Doob, *Patriotism and Nationalism*, New Haven, Yale University Press, 1964, pp. 211–12.)

7 Lenin's ideas were exposed most fully in his short treatise *On the National Question and Proletarian Internationalism*; however, the main architect and 'theoretician' of the Soviet solution was Stalin. For his approach see further on.

8 Otto Bauer, *Die Nationalitätenfrage und die Sozialdemokratie*, Vienna, 1907.

9 Calculated on the basis of statistics in different issues of the *Statesman Yearbook* and national *Statistical Yearbooks*.

10 Of these, 36 million were ceded by the Austro–Hungarian empire, 26·5 million by Russia (if Finland, which before the war enjoyed a considerable autonomy, is included, then to that figure a further 3

million should be added), 6·5 million by Germany, about 6 million by Turkey and 3 million by the UK (Irish Free State).

11 North Sleswig as to between Denmark and Germany; Masurenland and Upper Silesia as to between Poland and Germany, South Carinthia as to between Austria and Yugoslavia and the City of Odenburg (Sopron) as to between Austria and Hungary.

12 The USSR annexed territories belonging to Finland, Germany, Romania, Czechoslovakia and above all, Poland. Territory annexed from Finland for strategic reasons was inhabited by a Finnish ethnic group, the Karelians. They voluntarily abandoned their homeland and settled in other areas of Finland. (Only the less numerous Karelians living from immemorial times to the east of the Finnish border stayed in their settlements. Consequently the Soviet attempt at building the Finno-Karelian republic as the sixteenth member of the Union foundered. Soviet Karelia, in which Karelians are outnumbered by Russians in the ratio 5:1, remains an autonomous republic.) For strategic reasons the USSR also annexed the northern half of East Prussia (the southern part became Polish). Similarly, as in the Finnish case, the German population of both parts of East Prussia left or were evicted and settled in other parts of Germany. The Romanian province Besarabia (between the rivers Pruth and Dniester) was annexed because it had already been a part of the Russian empire (from 1812–1918) and because a lesser part of its population were Ukrainians. Another smaller Ukrainian-speaking area, North Bukovina, was ceded by Romania to the USSR solely on ethnic grounds.

For similar reasons Czechoslovakia ceded to the USSR the so-called Ruthenia (the Czechs named it Sub-Carpathian Russia and the Soviets Transcarpathian Ukraine). Two-thirds of its population consisted of Ruthenians and Russian, Ukrainian and independent factions competed for the identification of the whole ethnic group. The will of the half-million Ruthenians, however, was not considered; similarly the will of over 100,000 Hungarians who, living alongside the Hungarian border, could easily be reunited with their own country, which meanwhile also 'slipped' into the power sphere of the USSR.

Objective ethnic considerations also played the decisive role in the cession of East Polish territories inhabited predominantly by approximately 6 million Ukrainians and Belorussians. Whereas the former had quite an articulate national consciousness, especially as far as they lived in the provinces which had belonged to the Austrian empire before the first World War, the latter were a nation in the process of building itself, i.e. in the state of transition from 'ethnographic material' to 'nationality'. Their kin to the east of the Polish border were already acknowledged as a separate nationality in 1919. The local dialect, in which some attempts at literary activity had been undertaken earlier, gave birth to the third East Slav literary language, and Belorussia became a constituent republic of the Soviet Union. The Polish population in the ceded area largely left and settled in territories annexed from Germany. Also as a result of the Second World War the incorporation of the three Baltic republics, Estonia, Latvia and Lithuania into the USSR (which had been achieved under pressure in 1940) became a sealed fact.

13 By redrawing the German–Polish and Polish–Soviet boundaries respectively, Poland returned approximately to the geographical position of a thousand years ago.

14 Italy ceded to Greece the Dodecanese (twelve Greek-inhabited islands in south-east Aegean occupied in 1911) and to Yugoslavia the territories with Slovene- and Croat-speaking populations on the north-eastern shore of the Adriatic. The city of Trieste with its environs became a neutral zone between Italy and Yugoslavia, but in 1954 an agreement was reached according to which the city itself, with the northern surroundings (the so-called Zone A), came to Italy, whereas the southern countryside (Zone B) went to Yugoslavia. On the other hand Italy was allowed to keep the whole southern part of the Tirol in spite of Austrian claims for its German-speaking districts. Another main loser of territory in the Second World War was Romania, who had not only to cede Bessarabia and North Bukovina to the USSR but also return to Bulgaria the southern Dobrudja annexed in the second Balkanic War in 1913.

15 For the shift in the attitude of the East German political leadership to this issue see J. Krejci, *Social Stratification in Divided Germany*, London, New York, Croom Helm, 1976, pp. 193-4.

16 A thorough analysis of this issue has recently been undertaken by G. L. Schwiegler, *National Consciousness in Divided Germany*, London, Sage, 1975. However, his firm conclusions that the FRG and the GDR will develop into two nation-states in their own right (i.e. with separate national consciousness) appears to be too apodictic against the background of the impressive but hardly clearcut empirical evidence which the author had collected.

17 Bessarabia, the eastern half of the Moldavian principality under the Ottoman sovereignty, was in 1812 (by the treaty of Bucharest) ceded to Russia. In 1856, by the treaty of Paris, the south-western part of Bessarabia was returned to the Ottoman sovereignty. In 1859 the Moldavian and Wallachian principalities were united into the kingdom of Romania which eventually, in 1877, emancipated itself from the Ottoman sovereignty. Nevertheless Russia, by the treaty of San Stefano and the Congress of Berlin, regained the south-west of Bessarabia. As a result of the First World War, the whole of Bessarabia was reunited with Romania. The Soviet government refrained from acknowledging this fact. Moreover, as a small Romanian ethnic minority lived to the east of Bessarabia, in the Soviet Ukraine, the Soviet leadership decided to make of this group a separate nation with its own literary language, the Moldavian one, and granted it an autonomous status. After the Second World War, Romania again had to abandon the whole of Bessarabia, the greater part of which was then merged with the Moldavian autonomous region into the Moldavian Soviet Socialist Republic.

18 The transfer, however, might have had a considerable effect on the political and economic status of individual migrants. On the whole,

German expellees and refugees from the East managed to improve both of these statuses when they settled in the West. Those who came in their stead fared better, as a rule, in the economic rather than in the political sense. For the land and other property which they received they had to accept the limitations put on their personal liberties by the newly emerging regimes.

19 A Secretary of State for Wales with a seat in the United Kingdom's cabinet cannot in itself be considered as a kind of self-government.

20 Although the extent of Occitan movement need not be exaggerated, the existence of four organisations who propagate not only the Occitan language but also autonomy (one of those organisations seems to stand for outright independence) is an indication that not all Languedoc-speakers have only French national consciousness. As there are about 10 to 14 million Frenchmen who speak one or another Occitan 'patois', the potential recruiting ground for Occitan nationality by far surpasses the size of the undisputed ethnic minorities combined.

21 English, French and Spanish are, together with Russian and up to a point Chinese, the official languages of the United Nations and its agencies.

22 Salvador de Madariaga, *Englishmen, Frenchmen and Spaniards*, London, Oxford University Press, 1937.

23 For a reassessment of the Kantian contribution to the rise of nationalism see for instance E. Kedourie, *Nationalism*, London, Hutchinson, 1960, pp. 21ff, A. D. Smith, *Theories of Nationalism*, London, Duckworth, 1971.

24 The teaching of Breton, for instance, is allowed only in secondary schools as an optional language for pupils over the age of 15; moreover it is subject to similar inconveniences as is religious education in some Communist-dominated countries. At least ten pupils in a class have to ask for the option in Breton, a suitable teacher has to be available who would be able to fit his lessons in during the breaks or after school and, last but not least, the Headmaster has to be willing to take the trouble to organise this extra work.

25 A similar divisive policy was pursued by nations who attempted to assimilate minorities in their countries. Prussian and then German governments for instance, in order to weaken the Polish minority under their rule, considered the Kashubian and Mazurian dialects as separate languages and tried to prevent their speakers from acquiring Polish national consciousness. Polish authorities in their turn, between the two world wars, sub-divided their Ukrainian and Belorussian subjects into several ethnic groups according to the local dialects and tried to foster in them a separate regional consciousness which eventually could be absorbed by Polish nationality.

26 In 1922, Lenin wrote:

We, nationals of a big nation, have nearly always been guilty, in historic practice, of an infinite number of cases of violence; furthermore, we commit violence and insult an infinite number of times without noticing it. It is sufficient to recall my Volga reminiscences of how non-Russians are treated. . . . That is why internationalism on the part of oppressors or 'great' nations, as they are called (though they are great only in their violence, only great as bullies), must consist not only in the observance of the formal equality of nations but even in an inequality of the oppressor nation, the great nation, that must make up for the inequality which obtains in actual pracüice (V. I. Lenin, *On the National Question and Proletarian Internationalism*, Moscow, 1969, pp. 142–3).

27 The practical value of the Soviet Constitution can best be appreciated by the fact that in spite of its provision that the boundaries of the autonomous regions can be changed only with their consent, between 1941 and 1944, seven ethnic groups lost their autonomy and were deported wholesale from their homelands to less hospitable regions in Central Asia and Siberia. These were four Caucasian nationalities – Balkars, Chechens, Ingushes and Karachais – and three others, Volga Germans, Kalmyks and Crimean Tatars. Also in 1949, most of the Greeks, settled at the Black Sea Coast, were deported. According to the 1939 census these ethnic groups had a 1·8 million population between them. Under Kruschev, five of these nationalities (the Caucasian ones and the Kalmyks) regained their previous status. By a decision of the Supreme Soviet in 1957 they were allowed to return to their original homes and their national autonomy was restored. The European groups of Volga Germans and Crimean Tatars however were not included in this collective 'rehabilitation'. Although individual members of these nations are apparently no longer restricted to their deportation area (they can settle elsewhere outside their original homes where they find the opportunity to earn their livelihoods), this more or less liberal attitude towards individuals is not helpful to the groups as a whole. According to the 1959 census the population of the five rehabilitated nationalities numbered 523,000; in the 1939 census they had 750,000 members between them. For a detailed account of the deportation and rehabilitation measures see especially Robert Conquest, *The Nation Killers: The Soviet Deportation of Nationalities* London, Macmillan, 1970.

28 *The Essential Stalin, Major Theoretical Writings 1905–52*, ed. Bruce Franklin, London, Croom Helm, 1973.

29 The strength of this consciousness can be seen from the fact that at the last census (1971), only 1·3 per cent of the Yugoslav population utilised the constitutional provision allowing citizens to declare themselves merely as Yugoslav.

30 From the foundation of the Czechoslovak Republic in 1918, Slovaks went through several stages of ethnic development or possible emancipation. Between 1918 and 1938 they considerably expanded their education system and the Slovak intelligentsia began to compete with the Czechs in many fields of public life. Between 1939 and 1945 they had their own formally sovereign state; although a German satellite, and with reduced territory, its existence had a positive effect on their national pride, which towards the end of the war was further bolstered by an anti-German uprising. After a short-lived period of self-government (1945–7) Slovakia again became a part of unitary

Czechoslovakia. There her main gain was economic; her productivity and living standards almost reached the level of the Czech part of the state. However, those who believed that in eliminating the socio-economic differences between two kindred nationalities, all other differences would lose significance, were disappointed. Not only did Slovaks increasingly resent the centralism of the Prague leadership, but they eventually succeeded, through making a common cause with the Czech reformists, in transforming the unitary Czechoslovak state into a federation. (For further details on Czech–Slovak relationship and on ethnic structure of Czechoslovakia as a whole, see J. Krejci, *Social Change and Stratification in Postwar Czechoslovakia*, London, Macmillan, 1972.)

31 As ethnic Greeks were always strongly represented in the area, especially in the cities and on the coast, as there was some exchange of ethnic minorities with Bulgaria and since many of the Greek expellees from Turkey in 1922–3 settled there, the Slavonic element became considerably weakened in the Greek part of Macedonia. Consisting of peasants with a limited literacy, Slavonic Macedonians became an easy object for ethnic conversion. As their spoken language is considered a mere dialect, they are supposed to use Greek as their literary language.

32 The ethnic self-assertion of Sorbs was especially difficult in that part of their country (known as Lusatia) which belonged to Prussia. Saxonian Upper Lusatia fared slightly better. Yet under the Nazi regime the discrimination changed into outright persecution everywhere. For a well-informed account of Sorbian history and analysis of their problems and language see Gerald Stone, *The Smallest Slavonic Nation, The Sorbs of Lusatia*, London, Athlone Press, 1972.

33 Sometimes we hear the argument that these people virtually help the rich countries to create their riches. This claim has to be considered cautiously. The additional labour force is needed and can be absorbed by their employer countries because these countries are already rich, i.e. they have an abundant supply of all factors of production with the exception of unskilled labour.

34 In 1974, the numeric strength of ethnic minorities created by the guest workers, was in the main host countries as follows: Federal Republic of Germany 2,490,000; France 2,263,000; Switzerland 1,065,000; Sweden 601,000, of which 240,000 became naturalised Swedish subjects. Of the foreigners in Switzerland, however, 51 per cent were Italians whose co-nationals constitute one of the federated ethnic groups there.

Bibliography

ALLWORTH, EDWARD, *Soviet Nationality Problems*, New York and London, Columbia University Press, 1971.

BANTON, M., *Racial Minorities*, London, Collins, 1972.

BARKER, T. M., *The Slovenes of Carinthia: A National Minority Problem*, New York, Washington, League of CSA, 1960.

BARTSCH, G., 'Revolution und Gegenrevolution in Osteuropa 1948–1968', *Bundeszentrale für politische Bildung*, Bonn, 1971.

BAUER, OTTO, *Die Nationalitätenfrage und die Sozialdemokratie*, Vienna, 1907.

BROCK, P., *The Slovak National Awakening*, University of Toronto Press, 1976.

BROWNE, M., *Ferment in the Ukraine*, London, Macmillan, 1971.

BRUGEL, J. W., *Tschechen und Deutsche 1939–46*, Munich, Nymphenburger, 1974.

BUTLER, D. and KAVANAGH, D., *British General Election of October 1974*, London, Macmillan, 1975.

CLAUDE, I. L., *National Minorities, an International Problem*, Cambridge, Mass., Harvard University Press, 1955.

CONQUEST, R., *The Nation Killers: the Soviet Deportation of Nationalities*, London, Macmillan, 1970.

DAVIS, H. B., *Nationalism and Socialism: Marxist and Labor Theories of Nationalism to 1917*, Monthly Review Press, New York and London, 1967.

DEUTSCH, K. W., *Nationalism and Social Communications: an Enquiry into the Founding of Nationality*, Cambridge, Mass., and London, MIT Press, 1966.

DOOB, L. W., *Patriotism and Nationalism: Their Psychological Foundations*, New Haven and London, Yale, 1964.

EHRMANN, H. W., *Politics in France*, Boston, Little Brown, 1971.

EIDHEIM, H., *Aspects of the Lappish Minority Situation*, Universitetsforlaget, Oslo, Bergen, Tromsö, 1974.

Encyclopaedia Britannica, 'World Wars'.

The Europa Year Book 1976, vol. I, London, Europa Publications, 1976.

FRANCIS, E. K., *Interethnic Relations: An Essay in Sociological Theory*, New York, Oxford and Amsterdam, Elsevier, 1976.

FRANKLIN, B. (ed.), *The Essential Stalin: Major Theoretical Writings 1905–52*, London, Croom Helm, 1973.

Grand Atlas de la France, sélection de Reader's Digest, Paris, 1969.

GWEGEN, J., 'La Langue bretonne face à ses oppresseurs', *Nature et Bretagne*, Quimper, 1973.

HAARMANN, H., *Soziologie und Politik der Sprachen Europas*, Munich, Deutscher Taschenbuch Verlag, 1975.

HERAUD, G., *L'Europe des ethnies*, Nice, Presses d'Europe, 1968.

HITCHINS, K., *The Nationality Problems in Austria–Hungary*, Leiden, E. J. Brill, 1974.

HOSTLER, C. W., *Turkism and the Soviets*, London, Allen & Unwin, 1957.

INSTITUT MARKSIZMA-LENINIZMA, *Leninism i natsional'niy vopros v sovremennikh usloviyakh*, Moscow, 1972.

JACKSON, G., *The Spanish Republic and the Civil War 1931–1939*, New Jersey, Princeton University Press, 1965.

KANN, R. A., *The Habsburg Empire: A Study in Integration and Disintegration*, New York, Octagon Books, 1973.

KEDOURIE, E., *Nationalism*, London, Hutchinson, 1960 and 1966.

KENRICK, D. and PUXON, G., *The Destiny of Europe's Gypsies*, London, Chatto-Heinemann, 1972.

KLEIN, G., 'The Role of Ethnic Politics in the Czechoslovak Crisis of 1968 and the Yugoslav Crisis of 1971', *Studies in Comparative Communism*, vol. VIII, no. 4, 1975, pp. 339–69, University of South California.

KOFOS, E., *Nationalism and Communism in Macedonia*, Thessaloniki, Institute for Balkan Studies, 1964.

KOHN, H., *Nationalism, its meaning and history*, Princeton, New Jersey, Van Nostrand, 1965.

Konstitutsiya SSSR, Moscow, 1965; *Konstitutsiya SSSR*, Moscow, 1977.

KRAUSZ, E., 'Ethnic Minorities in Britain', *Sociology and the Modern World*, London, MacGibbon, 1971.

KREJCI, J., *Social Change and Stratification in Postwar Czechoslovakia*, London, Macmillan, 1972.

KREJCI, J., *Social Structure in Divided Germany*, London, Croom Helm, 1976.

LE VINE, R. and CAMPBELL, D. T., *'Ethnocentrism: Theories of Conflict, Ethnic Attitudes and Group Behaviour'*, New York, Wiley, 1972.

LENIN, V. I., *On the National Question and Proletarian Internationalism*, Moscow, Novosti Press Agency Publishing House, 1969.

LEONHARD, W., *The Kremlin since Stalin*, London, Oxford University Press, 1962.

MADARIAGA, SALVADOR DE, *Englishmen, Frenchmen, Spaniards*, London, Oxford University Press, 1937.

MEIER, V., 'Wir leben im heutigen Rumänien', *Frankfurter Allgemeine Zeitung*, 11 September 1976.

MELGERT, W., *Foreigners in Our Community: A New European Problem to be Solved*, Amsterdam, 1972.

MILYUKOV, P. N., *Národnost, její vznik a vývoj (Nationality, its Origin and Development)*, Prague, Orbis, 1930.

MINOGUE, K. R., *Nationalism*, London, Batsford, 1967.

PHILLIPS, E., *Les Luttes linguistiques en Alsace jusqu'en 1945*, Strasbourg, Association de Culture Alsacienne, 1975.

RAUCH, GEORGE VON, *The Baltic States: Estonia, Latvia and Lithuania: The Years of Independence 1917–1940*, London, Hurst, 1970.

ROYAL INSTITUTE FOR INTERNATIONAL AFFAIRS, *Nationalism*, London, Frank Cass, 1963.

ROUGEMONT, DENIS DE, *The Idea of Europe*, New York, Macmillan, 1966.

ROUGEMONT, DENIS de, *Lettre ouverte aux Européens*, Paris, Albin Michel, 1966.

SAVEZNI ZAVOD ZA STATISTIKU (FEDERAL STATISTICAL OFFICE), *Statistički Godisnjak Jugoslavije 1976*, Belgrade 1976.

SCHWEIGLER, G. L., *National Consciousness in Divided Germany*, London, Sage, 1975.

SINGLETON, F., *Twentieth-Century Yugoslavia*, London, Macmillan, 1976.

SMITH, A. D., *Theories of Nationalism*, London, Duckworth, 1971.

SMITH, G., *Politics in Western Europe*, London, Heinemann Educational, 1975.

SNYDER, L. L., *The Meaning of Nationalism*, Westport, Conn., Greenwood Press, 1954.

STATENS OFFENTLIGA UTREDNINGAR, *Invandrar-utredningen*, vol. 3, *Invandrarna och minoriteterna*, Stockholm, 1974.

The Statesman's Yearbook, 1913, 1926, 1951, 1963, 1976, London, Macmillan.

STEPHENS, H., *Linguistic Minorities in Western Europe*, Llandysul, Gomer Press, 1976.

STONE, G., *The Smallest Slavonic Nation: The Sorbs of Lusatia*, London, Athlone Press, 1972.

Studien und Gespräche über Selbstbestimmung und Selbstbestimmungsrecht, vols I and II, Munich, Robert Lerche, 1964 and 1965.

SUGAR, P. F. and LEDERER, I. J., *Nationalism in Eastern Europe*, Seattle, University of Washington Press, 1971.

TILLY, C. (ed.), *The Formation of National States in Western Europe*, New Jersey, Princeton University Press, 1975.

TSENTRAL'NOE STATISTICHESKOE UPRAVLENIE, *Itogi vsesoyuznoy perepisi 1970 goda*, Vol. IV, Moscow, 1973.

ZESSNER, K., *Josef Seliger und die Nationale Frage in Böhmen*, Stuttgart, Seliger-Archiv, 1976.

7 The intellectuals in contemporary Europe
Michalina Vaughan

Professionals and creators

Intellectuals, according to Sorel, are those whose job it is to think and who, since it is a noble task, expect to be well paid to do so. Though apparently flippant, this definition has the merit of stressing that they make up an occupational category and claim rewards – both pecuniary and non-material – commensurate with the social prestige of the activity in which they engage. Hence they do not overlap with the wider category of those who have received an advanced education, but have not opted for any of the professions for which the learning and/or the qualifications thus acquired are prerequisites. The example of the nineteenth- and early twentieth-century Oxbridge graduates who enjoyed an independent income and never considered taking up any pursuits other than those which were deemed gentlemanly, such as the management of a family estate, highlights this distinction. Conversely, access to some of the vocations most commonly labelled intellectual is not restricted to those whose skills are the product of formal instruction and who hold appropriate degrees or diplomas. Writers who throughout the eighteenth and nineteenth centuries were singled out as intellectuals *par excellence* (the duke of Wellington's 'scribbling set') did not require then, and still tend to lack now, any qualification other than the possession of talent or a belief in their own potential which may provide a substitute for it. A similar point could be made about artists, whose relatively recent upgrading from their traditional status as craftsmen to the rank of intellectuals witnesses to a growing emphasis on creativity rather than thought *stricto sensu* as a criterion for membership of this category. The stress on occupation rather than education and on the superiority assigned to the kind of activity it entails is confirmed by this trend. Indeed, since the

172

prestige attaching to non-manual work could not be invoked by practitioners of the plastic arts as a justification for social promotion, it is only when the artistic imagination came to be valued for its own sake in an anti-rationalistic age that the artist gained recognition as an intellectual. Yet such an emphasis on creativeness stems from a controversial approach to culture.[1]

Hence intellectuals can either be defined by reference to the possession of expert knowledge, evidenced by – or rather equated with – that of a formal qualification, generally gained in a higher educational institution, and conducive to the membership of an exclusive professional group, or alternatively to that of creative skills in literature, art or science.[2] In the latter case, scientists though initially recruited from among enlightened amateurs–have become increasingly dependent on specialised tuition and corresponding qualifications, whereas literary and artistic attainment has tended to remain both compatible and frequently associated with the absence of such prerequisites. If the view prevails that intellectuals are either members of the learned professions or creators in their chosen field, it follows that education is neither a necessary nor a sufficient condition for being considered one. Yet its acquisition affects patterns of cultural consumption to such an extent that it virtually demarcates the public capable of appreciating creativeness and of consciously valuing expertise, whilst deliberately relying on the specialists' skills. The wider definition of intellectuals as 'cultural consumers' endowed with this degree of sophistication has been put forward by Lipset,[3] despite its vulnerability to criticisms derived from pattern variations in space (as illustrated by the differential availability of cultural goods in urban and rural areas) and over time (as evidenced by the uneven exposure and responsiveness to such goods at different stages in life, from adolescence to retirement). In fact, such a definition is related to the two traditional ones in so far as any cultural producers or professional experts require a clientele of 'consumers' who form a social milieu capable of bestowing sufficient commendation and of providing adequate remuneration.[4] Its endorsement implies that education will be both relatively scarce and also relevant to the appreciation of the knowledge and/or skills characteristic of the professional and creative intellectuals, i.e. that it will be broadly cultural rather than narrowly vocational. Though some dilution of meaning occurs with such a shift from expertise and creativeness to the ability to appreciate them, the category of intellectuals remains an elite, albeit with an increased and less stable membership.

The educated are no longer an elite

It was inevitable that the growth of education, especially since the end of the Second World War, should have dire consequences for elitarian approaches to the definition of what makes an intellectual. A longer period of school attendance, a more generous assistance to families whose children could not otherwise be put through lengthy courses of study, an increased output of secondary qualifications and a consequent growth in the numbers of higher education entrants and of graduates, seem to lead of necessity to a proliferation of intellectuals. Thus the Soviet practice, imitated by the developing countries, has been to so describe (at the risk of some loss of meaning) all holders of educational qualifications, whether at higher or secondary level. The range of occupations and income levels covered, if such a definition is adopted, is so wide that variations in prestige, in life-styles, in decision-making powers and in cultural consumption patterns within the category constructed must be considerable. The heterogeneity of a stratum in which not only professionals, creators and their clienteles, but all white-collar workers are included, as will necessarily be the case if a purely educational criterion – and a fairly undemanding one at that – is adopted, precludes the emergence of observable common social characteristics.[5] Thus the study of the 'Soviet Intelligentsia', the major sociological work published in the USSR in the post-Stalinist period, is predominantly devoted to an historical outline of its growth between the October Revolution and the end of the Second World War, as a result of educational expansion, rather than to any attempt at an analysis of its internal diversification. By contrast, the numerous writings produced by Polish sociologists on the same stratum in their country endeavour to draw a demarcation line between intellectuals *stricto sensu*, who make up the intelligentsia proper, and intellectual workers, with membership of a profession and/or the exercise of creativity defining the former category.[6] Hence the concept of qualification, relied on in the people's democracies to justify the persistence of social inequalities (since the occupational stratification is considered functional, while social promotion is subordinated to tested merit),[7] is relinquished as a basis for constructing a definition of the intelligentsia, in favour of the traditional Western European criteria.

Yet, even if those criteria are preferred to the concept of qualification, educational expansion remains highly significant through its social repercussions on access to the category they demarcate, as well as its intellectual repercussions on the nature of the activities they encompass. First, the faster educational intakes grow, the more likely a diversification in the social origins of entrants and, ultimately, of graduates becomes. Though cross-cultural differences refute the complacent assumption that industrialisation automatically ushers in educational democratisation, and though a privileged social background remains the most valuable of educational assets (even if the definition of privilege may differ, e.g. between Western and Eastern Europe) there is no doubt that educational qualifications have lost their former scarcity value. Since their possession is no longer primarily related to ascription, the emphasis on achievement loosens somewhat the original connection between educational attainment and social background. The Western European emphasis on tested merit, with the attendant advantages enjoyed by the 'heirs' of a traditional cultural patrimony which they are capable of 'reproducing' (to use the terminology popularised by Bourdieu)[8] may be contrasted with the systematic attempts made in Eastern Europe to offset the privilege of birth by favouring applicants of 'manual' origin, i.e. the offspring of industrial workers and peasants, through the granting of 'bonus points' or the reservation of special entrance quotas for entry to higher education. Yet the ascriptive bias of any meritocratic system is obviously very strong, since the application of such policies, e.g. in Poland, has proved relatively unsuccessful and has not undermined the entrenchment of intelligentsia children in higher education or even modified their selective preference for the so-called 'noble' courses of study, namely arts versus science subjects and theoretical versus applied courses.[9] Indeed, since intellectual merit is socially defined, it is hardly surprising that it should retain a discriminatory connotation connected with family background and emphasised by the expectations of teachers for their pupils, as well as the aspirations of parents for their children.

Thus the main feature of the educational reforms introduced in the wake of the Second World War may well be the diversification of courses and outlets rather than the democratisation of intake and output. The early leaving pattern and high failure rates characteristic of pupils and students from disadvantaged homes, as well as the socially structured occupational aspirations of students as reflected by the connection between their social origins and their educational choices, are evidence of inadequacies in implementing egalitarian policies in education. Cross-cultural variations appear to reflect differences in the degree of determination displayed in the enforcement of such policies, measured by the extent of the willingness to rely on positive discrimination, and influenced by the extent of the openness characteristic of the given academic tradition. Yet the diminishing returns reached in the 1960s when entry to Polish higher education was hedged with discriminatory prerequisites destined to offset the disadvantages of the 'culturally deprived' applicants showed that the scope for the redistribution of chances was limited.[10] The exceptionally high failure rates at the end of the first year of university studies provided additional supportive evidence. Ultimately the speed with which the offspring of manual workers may be turned into intellectuals, even loosely defined, appears to be less amenable to social engineering than the adaptation of the educational system to provide new categories of intellectuals. Access to formally available qualifications may be perceived as attainable or even as desirable only after a generation has been given a sufficient amount of instruction to develop the appropriate educational aspirations for its children. The French pattern of educational mobility under the Third Republic, when primary school teachers, mainly descended from peasant stock, saw their sons through a 'Grande Ecole', preferably 'Normale Supérieure' illustrates this generational lag.[11]

By contrast, educational reform can be immediately conducive to the production of new kinds of graduates with specific occupational outlets. The proliferation of such qualifications, facilitated by the growing complexity of the division of labour and by the increasing reliance on educational attainment rather than on previous forms of apprenticeship or of learning on the job, results in the emergence of new specialisms. The process of professionalisation, inseparable from the provision of new vocational courses and from the quest for professional status by the graduates engaging in the pursuits for which they have been trained, has led to the development of the so-called 'technical intelligentsia'. Though its members claim, like those of the traditional professions, that they could not practise their calling without the appropriate qualification and therefore that they belong to an exclusive group, they tend to enjoy a lower degree of prestige and a smaller remuneration, as a result of engaging in a more recently differentiated, hence a less socially valued form of activity. Yet this educational and occupational diversification not only results in the co-existence of different categories of experts, with varying degrees of prestige, it is also conducive to a reduction in the social esteem attaching to expertise as such. Hence the concept of profession, as it becomes more widely applicable, is somewhat devalued or at any rate is redefined in a way which, while the new professionals are more vulnerable to market fluctuations[12] than the traditional ones, detracts from the status of both.

Apart from the differentiation of graduates into a wider range of categories with different occupational and possibly professional outlets, another implication of educational growth has been the superimposition of distinct terminal levels. Since secondary tuition is no longer predominantly defined as an ante-room to universities and other establishments of higher learning, by contrast with the former tradition of public schools and grammar schools, of lycées and gymnasia, but provides terminal courses often devoid of any vocational content, the educated population – or, according to the

Soviet definition, the intelligentsia – is clearly irreducible to the pool from which professionals and creators are recruited. It might be argued that any increase in this population must affect the patterns of cultural consumption prevailing in a given society and result in an expansion of the public on which intellectuals rely to support their professional and creative activities. Yet, even on the optimistic assumption that a strong commitment to so-called cultural interests is achieved during the period of full-time exposure to formal education, secondary graduates are unlikely to r⁀tain in later life the more demanding habits they might have acquired in youth and would presumably tend to adapt to the middlebrow or even lowbrow standards prevailing in their adult environment. The emphasis in secondary schools is on the potential rather than the actual attainments of their intake, in the context of governmental plans for *éducation permanente* or at least for expanded further education, and of the modern educational philosophies from which such schemes are derived. This evolution is understandable, since the prospect of a longer lifespan entails the need to increase adaptability, so that individuals can be retrained for alternative occupations and/or trained to make a more enlightened use of increased leisure time and prolonged retirement.[13] Hence the concept of an educational continuum may be rethought to imply that secondary qualifications, though envisaged as terminal by the graduates themselves, could enable them later in life to return to full-time education either for vocational purposes ('recyclage') or in order to develop special interests. The scope for variations in patterns of cultural consumption over time would be extended accordingly. In this perspective, a secondary qualification is a token of hope in the long-run rather than a badge of achievement, so far as cultural consumption is concerned.

However, despite the powerful arguments in favour of, and the strong pressures for, an educational continuum, there is no corresponding evolution towards an occupational continuum.[14] On the contrary, there are definite cut-off points which determine the vocational opportunities available to those about to leave the educational system, even though there exists the possibility of a later return. The failure to gain access to a higher educational establishment or to graduate from one represents such a point. Moreover, differences between establishments in terms of exclusiveness and of relevance to future careers entail a hierarchy of degrees and diplomas, despite some formal equivalence. Thus the holders of qualifications issued by certain institutions are granted admittance into professions whose members are intellectuals in the traditional sense, enjoying comparatively high rewards, social prestige and, in some instances, a measure of power. Meanwhile other graduates have difficulties in

177

gaining access to, or are precluded from aspiring to, such occupational categories. They may have been channelled early on towards one of the new professions or be merely qualified to seek non-manual jobs without having gained a level of specialisation sufficient to match the entry requirements for any career. The difference between countries practising an open-door policy, such as France till 1968, where graduation at secondary level entailed a right of access to higher education, and those, like Britain, where it merely leads to eligibility and where other selection criteria are applied, used significantly to affect individual chances. It may well be receding under the sheer pressure of numbers, with a multiplication of prerequisites and an increasing reliance on examinations as a substitute for preliminary selection. However, status differentials between comparable establishments within the same system appear to be durable, whether they are formally acknowledged and reflected in sterner admission criteria, or merely a matter of common knowledge and conducive to tougher selection from among a big pool of academically strong applicants, as in the Universities of Oxford and of Leningrad, to name but two characteristic instances.

Thus educational qualifications may be limitative, and not only creative or confirmatory, of membership of the intellectual stratum. The possession of some qualifications may debar their holders from access to the courses conducive to the professions whose practictioners are considered intellectuals, while that of others either entails acceptance or at least leads up to further studies which do so. The former preclude occupational choices entailing promotion into the category of professionals, while the latter make them freely available to the academically successful. This difference is illustrated by the predicament of bureaucratic workers in the civil service and the tertiary sector at large, whose educational attainments prevent them from becoming upwardly mobile. This exclusion may not be due to the absence of an appropriate educational ladder, but to economic and social constraints hampering further study, as in the case of women burdened with family responsibilities. Qualifications which are not intrinsically terminal may become such for individuals whose disadvantages are socio-economic or cultural rather than strictly educational. However, such pressures are analytically distinct from the exclusiveness inherent in the educational system itself, within which a majority of pupils are channelled towards a type of post-primary instruction whose recipients are confined to white-collar occupations by their lack of specialisation. The very nature of the tuition dispensed to them detracts from their future potential. Goblot's famous formula 'La barrière est un niveau',[15] implying that to have reached a given educational standard entails a gain in status, can also be read in reverse, since some 'levels' amount to 'barriers', precluding the crossing of the divide which separates white-collar workers from intellectuals.[16]

The non-manuals are not intellectuals

Not only is the category of non-manual or 'white-collar' work un-specialised and uncreative (i.e. unlike that of intellectuals proper), it is not even uniformly intellectual *lato sensu*, that is consistently concerned with activities involving people rather than with operations performed on inanimate objects. Nor is the actual amount of intellectual, as distinguished from practical, tasks entailed by a particular job directly related to the formal qualifications required from applicants or actually possessed by present incumbents. Indeed requirements vary with fluctuations in the supply and demand of educated manpower, so that massive educational expansion may result in the proliferation of over-qualified intellectual workers. An instance of this imbalance is provided by France in the late 1950s and early 1960s when the excessive production of law graduates reduced many 'licenciés' to seeking administrative posts for which only secondary graduation and a 'concours' (competitive examination) at a corresponding level were prerequisites. The opposite extreme is illustrated by the people's democracies where as a result of wartime losses and of rapid bureaucratisation[17] connected both with the development of state control and with economic growth, there was an acute shortage of qualified applicants for white-collar jobs. Thus, according to the Central Statistical Office in 1960, 20 per cent of Polish intellectual workers in 1960 had only received primary instruction, 12 per cent general secondary, and 32 per cent specialised secondary, while ten years earlier the position had been even less favourable, with approximately one-third having received no schooling other than primary. The unevenness of formal quali-fications is matched by the diversity of social origins, so that this may be considered the most heterogeneous of occupational cate-gories. Access to it may signify promotion for some, e.g. for manual workers appointed to clerical posts as a reward for services rendered in the party, while it is perceived as a demotion by others, such as the pre-war officers, landlords or businessmen deprived of their former livelihood by political change, or at least as a disappointment, following upon frustrated educational expectations and difficulties in securing more congenial employment.[18] A more plentiful supply of secondary graduates from among whom non-manual workers can be recruited will undoubtedly contribute to a reduction of the re-maining differences between entrants into this occupational category in Western and Eastern Europe. Thus the third of the categories distinguished among Polish clerical workers – the adequately instructed who may well see themselves as overqualified – is bound to increase as the educated population grows.

Though the rise in non-manual employment is not attributable to educational expansion, but to sectoral reallocation and bureaucratisation, the implications of more advanced schooling for the attitudes of intellectual workers are necessarily considerable and appear to be similar under capitalism and under state socialism. The two economic systems entail discrepancies in the type of tertiary growth,[19] with a much bigger service sector in the West, yet the needs of a planned and centralised economy, the development of welfare services and the multiplication of tertiary posts in the secondary sector have led to a steady increase in the demand for administrative workers. With higher priorities attributed to the production of consumer durables and consumption goods in recent quinquennial plans, commercial staff is likely to be in much greater demand in the people's democracies, while automation will no doubt be conducive to a decrease in operative manpower and a correspondingly bigger intake of non-manual supervisory staff, regardless of the organisation of industrial ownership. Hence a degree of convergence may be diagnosed in the evolution of non-manual work. As a result, this accounts for a growing share of the active population in all industrial countries,[20] providing an occupational outlet for the steadily increasing numbers of secondary graduates. Another common trend may be found in the absence of fit between the content of the instruction dispersed in secondary establishments and the activities in which administrative and clerical workers engage. There appears to be a discontinuity between the tuition received and the work performed, much of which is composed of routine operations requiring no specialist knowledge and learnt on the job. Thus formal qualifications may be required from applicants, but prove largely irrelevant during their working lives, by contrast with the continuity which links prior training to professional practice. Job satisfaction is therefore limited both by the repetitive nature of the tasks entrusted to white-collar workers and by the restricted career prospects open to the overwhelming majority among them. Though this may be an intrinsic feature of such employment, it is one which a more highly educated labour force tends to resent more keenly. If employment is plentiful, boredom may take the form of restlessness, involving either frequent job changes or even a preference for work on a temporary basis. The rapid increase in the latter category of staff in the secretarial sector shows dissatisfaction with office work to have grown even among women, despite an enduring willingness to accept frustrating conditions and poor prospects, either because they looked forward to marriage and homemaking as their true calling, or because, having returned to paid employment in later life, they were disadvantaged by age, loss of skills and family responsibilities. It is precisely for secretarial and clerical workers, whose educational qualifications locate them, 'on a watershed between two distinct and non-overlapping parts of the occupational hierarchy',[21] that prospects of upward mobility even defined only as echelon promotion, are least favourable and have actually declined since the beginning of the century. Their plight exposes the fallacy involved in assuming that wider opportunities for gaining more advanced instruction are necessarily conducive to the increase in individual fulfilment anticipated by educational philosophers, from Condorcet onwards, as a corollary of expansion.

The vulnerability of non-manual workers to economic pressures and the widespread fear of unemployment in a sector generally singled out for early staff-reductions at times of recession, since its contribution to production is hard to assess, are intensified by a relatively low level of group cohesiveness. Unionisation has been impeded by objective factors and subjective attitudes alike. There were genuine difficulties in organising a category of workers scattered in enterprises of very different sizes and performing varied tasks – an obvious contrast with the concentration of manpower and the standardisation of jobs in factories. Related to the scale of unit and type of activity were the sense of proximity to and involvement with management, experienced, albeit to varying extents, by white-collar workers and unconducive to a policy of confrontation between competing interests, characteristic of industrial organisation.[22]

In addition to a real distance separating the working conditions of white-collar workers from those of manual labourers, there was also deliberate distancing, an assertion of middle-classness and a shrinking away from the proletariat. Status considerations largely account for the fact that resistance to unionisation was, as Bernard Shaw noted, most widespread among 'clerks and women'.[23] Undoubtedly, the high proportion of female workers for whom gainful employment was either a temporary necessity or a source of additional income were insufficiently motivated to engage in concerted action. Among others, the lack of political socialisation acted as a deterrent, while deep-seated prejudice against any forms of behaviour traditionally considered unfeminine or ungenteel died hard. However, a corresponding attitude could be detected among male white-collar workers, who equated union militancy, with its distinctly working-class overtones, with proletarianisation.[24] Even in France, where white-collar unions grew early and achieved great strength, a marked reluctance to acknowledge as similar the market situation of all wage-earners whose skills are neither scarce nor highly valued is inseparable from the interpretation of non-manual work as intrinsically superior. Such an assessment, necessary to white-collar self-esteem, was initially confirmed in the nineteenth century by the relative scarcity of educated applicants, as well as by the higher rates of remuneration for clerical than for manual jobs. Over time, these advantages have become eroded, partly by educational expansion, partly by a closing of the differential between manual and non-manual labour,[25] due to the advantages secured by the union movement on behalf of the working class in Western European industrial countries and to the official policy prevailing in the people's democracies.[26] However, the prestige ratings attributed to various occupations in the West show a definite preference for unskilled clerical over skilled manual jobs, confirming the resistance of traditional status distinctions to economic pressures. The attachment of white-collar workers to this ranking is necessarily increased by the threats to their economic position, and status considerations, whose importance was enhanced in the past by their social insecurity as members of an intermediary group, have to compensate for financial insecurity too.

It is not for the enduring centrality of the manual/non-manual dichotomy in schemas of stratification in Western Europe that an explanation is required, but for its lingering traces in the social consciousness of the people's democracies. Despite an official value system enhancing the prestige of manual workers and a hierarchy of remunerations characterised by small differentials and by a bias in favour of skilled manuals, there is some evidence that the status of 'mental' work as such has not been fully subsumed under the concept of qualification. Although this is the key concept in the allocation of prestige ratings to occupational categories, whence the higher ranking attributed to skilled industrial workers than in capitalist countries,[27] there is evidence that access to this type of job for someone previously employed in a clerical capacity is not universally perceived as a form of social promotion.[28] Furthermore, factory workers included in Sarapata's sample in his study of growing egalitarianism under state socialism were less optimistic than intellectuals and civil servants about the equalisation of the status awarded to manual and non-manual work.[29] To the extent that the former is still perceived as inferior in so far as it deals with inanimate matter and requires physical attributes such as strength or dexterity rather than mental ability, white-collar workers can still experience a sense of superiority despite low rewards. It is as specialists possessing appropriate educational qualifications that skilled manuals are rated more favourably than them, not as members of the official ruling class or as privileged earners. Since the main divide between Eastern and Western interpretations of their respective social hierarchies consists in the degree of reliance on formal qualifications for awarding prestige, the manual/non-manual dichotomy is transcended in many instances, but is not eradicated altogether.

Whether under capitalism or state socialism, it is significant that intellectual workers should consistently strive to avoid being mistaken for manual labourers rather than to be taken for intellectuals. Their psycho-social dependence on their hierarchical superiors or on their employers, on whom promotion prospects depend, and their desire to identify with the hierarchy or with management rather than with fellow-workers, certainly contrast with the collectivist traditions of the working class. However, they are no less distinct from the independence enjoyed by intellectuals, whether secured through membership of an exclusive professional body or through the practice of a creative skill. Indeed the difference between the two categories could certainly not be interpreted as one of degree rather than kind.[30] It is middle-classness rather than intellectuality that white-collar workers have asserted over time, through the life-styles they have adopted and the political affiliations towards which they have been drawn, as well, of course, as through their resistance to unionisation. Their degree of participation in cultural life and their preferred forms of cultural consumption differ markedly from those of intellectuals, as their lower educational attainments would lead one to expect. In this respect they show an affinity of taste with the petty bourgeoisie, whose preferences they tend to espouse not only in their choice of reading material and entertainment, but in the furnishing of their dwellings and the organisation of their domestic life. This similarity is all the more striking since it is not only noted in Western bourgeois societies, but in people's democracies[31] where petty bourgeois values are constantly derided by official circles and described as doomed. That their attraction should remain strong for non-manual workers, despite the prevailing ideology, witnesses to the deep-rootedness of status aspirations which planned social change appears to have left virtually unaltered.

White-collar workers share with the petty bourgeoisie a fear of downward mobility, linked with their economic insecurity and their social rootlessness, since the category to which they belong is an ante-room for both upwardly and downwardly mobile individuals. Hence a similar commitment to the preservation of their own position, despite the difference in ownership status and a consequent susceptibility to political extremism, in an attempt to resist proletarianisation. The milieux which constituted recruitment grounds for Fascist movements in the 1930s rallied again to the cail of *poujadism* under the Fourth French Republic and have failed to respond to appeals for support from the labour movement in Western European democracies. However, in terms of political affiliations, a distinction has emerged between clerical workers displaying these characteristic attitudes of unenlightened self-interest, and the growing number of technical and scientific workers,[32] whose work situation often entails an association with manual workers and who, though still a minority, indicate by their existence the possibility of a redefinition in the allegiances of non-manuals. This group, whose educational qualifications are comparatively high, is more akin to intellectuals proper in making political choices on ideological grounds rather than being guided by a concern for the conservation of social assets. In other words, its members do not tend to perceive the divide between manual and non-manual work as a demarcation between classes with divergent interests, but as a distinction between categories of wage-earners.[33] It is a distinct possibility that the growing concentration of clerical workers in larger units and the attendant changes in their working conditions will ultimately undermine traditional attitudes and induce a sense of solidarity which has been conspicuously absent to date. To the extent that *embourgeoisement* theories hold, the gulf in life-styles and educational attainments between manual and non-manual workers might also be bridged over time, though the dependence of such an evolution on the continuation or restoration of affluence induces some scepticism towards such a prospect. At any rate no indication of a *rapprochement* between intellectuals and intellectual workers can be detected and educational expansion, by multiplying and consequently devaluing the formal qualifications held by the latter, appears in fact to be widening the socio-economic distance between them. This is even more true of Eastern Europe, where the growing prestige of skilled manuals, favoured by economic and ideological considerations alike, is ultimately conducive to a downgrading of white-collar work, despite some entrenched preconceptions.[34] Since intellectuals have replaced the former privileged classes at the top of the hierarchies of material and non-material rewards and of power, their social position is in sharp contrast with the low ranking of white-collar workers on all three dimensions of stratification.

The possibility that intellectual workers are becoming alienated under state socialism has been given serious consideration by Polish sociologists and has been related to the precarious and dwindling status rating which does not offset their economic disadvantages or their power deprivation. Excluded from the official ruling class by the non-manual character of their activity, they are left out of the recruiting ground for the actual rulers by the nature of their educational attainments which act as a barrier to their admission into the intelligentsia. The source of their frustration is thus located in the social structure itself,[35] a diagnosis which confirms the Durkheimian-Mertonian conception of anomie. To the extent that state policy emphasises the need for making all forms of reward commensurate with the work accomplished, a trend towards status crystallisation can be predicted and a consequent decrease in the remnants of prestige enjoyed by non-manuals will ensue. It is difficult to conceive, however, of such a development leading to a closer identification with the working class, especially as the educational background of white-collar workers is steadily rising and their attachment to a middle-class life-style is unlikely to decline.

The intellectuals are no longer 'notables'

By contrast with the indeterminacy of the non-manual workers' social position, intellectuals have enjoyed comparatively high rewards in terms of financial gains and of prestige ratings ever since the onset of modernisation in their respective societies. Access to the professions represented one of the main avenues of social mobility in seventeenth-century England, whether through the Church, the law or the practice of medicine,[36] while the example of the French nobility of the robe, referring to a less open society, is even more illuminating.[37] The advent of meritocratic ideals, whether on ideological grounds in the wake of the French Revolution or on utilitarian grounds in the aftermath of the Industrial Revolution, furthered the claims of the professions to social status, since they were no longer perceived as stepping stones, but as culminating stages. The professional man became the embodiment of the 'notable', of the individual whose educational qualifications had sufficient scarcity to amount to a virtual monopoly in the local community and hence to a special claim on the trust of the less privileged. The democratic process favoured those whose access to positions of notability could be attributed to tested merit rather than to mere ascription. Hence the increasing share of intellectuals in the exercise of power in the parliamentary democracies, both at central and local level. The concentration of lawyers and teachers in the Parliament of the Third Republic was characteristic of this trend,[38] which was certainly not limited to France, though the alliance between landed aristocracy and entrepreneurial bourgeoisie prevented its emergence in England. Knowledge paved the way to power to the extent that its possession was held to be a guarantee of moral integrity, rather than of competence in the performance of political functions. The rule of the notables[39] was not founded on the cult of the expert, but on trust in the professional man. The small intellectual elite which set the standards of cultural consumption came to define those of public morality, as the influence of organised religion receded. The process of secularisation need not, however, be a corollary of modernisation and the attitude of the clergy to the nation-state determined its role after emancipation. The contrasting examples of the Roman Catholic Church in Italy and in Poland prior to their reunification illustrate this point. As a rule, the later a country gained independence, the greater was the prestige awarded to intellectuals for preserving its historical heritage, its culture and the language which perpetuated its identity.[40] Yet if the national Church had participated in this task, it shared in their prestige and could compete with their influence. The status of the notables could be interpreted as a transfer onto the national scene of the prerogatives they had enjoyed in the small community, an evolution from the local clientele of the professionals to the national audience of the intellectuals.

Thus, while history disproves the stereotype whereby industrialisation ushered in the reliance on education as a major channel of social mobility, it confirms the connection between the emergence of nation-states and the rise of the intellectuals. Yet the demand for trained personnel generated by an industrial economy was ultimately met by educational expansion, even if – as in England – the practice of training on the job had provided a lasting substitute for formal tuition and certification.[41] It could be argued that the requirements of specialisation were only fulfilled as a corollary of socio-political pressures in favour of a national system for the education of the newly enfranchised. However, even while acknowledging that democratisation weighed more heavily with the legislators than economic rationality, one can hardly deny that the establishment of such a system entailed a move away from Weber's second type of education, defined as cultivation, and towards his third type, i.e. specialised training.[42] This evolution may have been an unintended consequence, contrary to the pattern set by those countries in which educational planning was the outcome of revolutionary change (e.g. France and the Soviet Union) or of national emancipation (e.g. post-1918 Czechoslovakia and Poland), so that the training of cadres of the appropriate social or national background, and/or ideological orientation was a high priority. In either case, the outcome was the same – the multiplication of trained professionals, though the opportunities opened to them varied with the level of economic development and the form of socio-economic organisation. Education designed to satisfy state exigencies may be meant to fit in with planned industrialisation, as it was after 1917, or exclusively to serve bureaucratic rationalisation, as it did after 1789. In the latter instance, its 'pre-adaptation' to industry's needs[43] – which convergence theorists fail adequately to explain – actually implies that the civil service and the liberal professions are staffed with graduates sharing the same intellectual background for which the lower levels of instruction impart a proper regard among the general public. An educational common denominator for the ruling elite and a widespread acceptance of the cultural and moral superiority of the educated – it is on these foundations that the ascendancy of the notables rested.

The contrast between delayed educational provision to catch up with industrialisation and educational development in the context of an agrarian society helps explain the difference between the status of professional men within the small English community and the national role of French intellectuals. The rate of economic advance, from which the promotion of an entrepreneurial class is inseparable, and that of educational retardation, to which the endurance of both traditionalism and anti-intellectualism can be related, may account for the difficulty involved in translating the concept of 'notables' into English and for the English professionals' reluctance to accept the label of intellectuals. Hence the complex re-ordering of the occupational structure entailed by the transformation of a pre-industrial society into an industrial one had a different impact on the small, but influential, group of English clerics, lawyers, physicians and academics, and the French intellectuals. The former provided a pattern for other occupational groups seeking status mobility through the setting up of associations which produced codes of practice and designed rules governing access to the new professions. Thus training schemes and terminal qualifications conditioning entry into these exclusive bodies were internally defined in the course of an expansion which raised the membership of such associations by over 100 per cent between 1841 and 1881 and by 50 per cent between 1881 and 1911.[44] Therefore professionalisation predated the existence of an integrated educational system and embodied the ideals of private initiative, social exclusiveness and moral righteousness characteristic of the middle class.

By contrast, the reliance on formal qualifications defined by state regulations and issued by state establishments characteristic of Napoleonic organisations linked professional status with academic performance. The intellectualism of such a system was as pervasive as its state-centredness. It entailed an earlier acceptance of ascriptive criteria, as well as of centrally defined national standards. Consequently, the prestige of the educational system was the cornerstone on which claims of the notables to possess a special aptitude for political representation and leadership, in addition to their professional tasks, rested. They were thus particularly vulnerable to fluctuations in the esteem awarded to the qualifications they held. Hence criticisms aimed at the concept of excellence which underpinned the educational philosophy inherited not only by the French Third Republic, but by all those European countries in which Napoleon's reforms exercised a lasting influence, proved damaging to notables as intellectuals. It was not until the 1960s that the academic definition of culture was challenged as self-perpetuating, inward-looking and socially biased, while earlier critics had concentrated on inadequacies of provision and biases in selection. The meritocratic recruitment by which elitarianism had been justified was shown to be intellectually conservative and therefore to contradict the qualitative exigencies, as well as the egalitarian preoccupations from which it stemmed. The sociology of knowledge, exemplified by Bourdieu's work,[45] which discloses the societal constraints shaping intellectual traditions and educational curricula, undermined the confidence which the educational system had inspired among its graduates. It was both a symptom and a cause of the loss of faith which the events of 1968 brought out in the open.

Educational expansion in the post- Second World War period was a contributory factor in this disenchantment. By overstretching available facilities, it reduced the effectiveness of the tuition offered (a decrease measured not only by rising failure rates, but also by imperfect socialisation) and, by multiplying graduates, it devalued the qualifications dispensed. Increased enrolment, especially at the higher level, meant that the former scarcity of intellectuals and the social distance which separated them from the people were replaced by a proliferation of degrees and diplomas illustrating the fallacy of any dichotomisation in terms of knowledge. The zero-sum theory of academic culture, on which the notables thrived, gave way to a gradation of educational experience in terms of sophistication and vocational relevance. Law and medicine, which had accounted for 65 per cent of the student population in the 1930s, shrank to 45 per cent in the 1950s.[46] Greater diversity of courses was matched by occupational diversification, as the division of labour became more complex and new opportunities for tertiary employment appeared in an expanding economy. Therefore the traditional connection between graduation and membership of the old-established professions has been forcibly disrupted. 'The coming of the mass university signifies first of all that students can no longer find places in those professions that are quite limited and are also for the most part on the margin of the economic system: medicine, law, teaching – the three professions that formerly absorbed the great majority of students.'[47] This evolution has been analysed, in the wake of the 1968 events, as a stimulus of student unrest,[48] as a constraint on academic curricula and as a source of social change.[49] It can also be interpreted as a stage in the downgrading of professionalism, formerly dissociated from the pressures of business and surrounded by an aura of moral disinterestedness, as well as of intellectual purity. The new professions – technology-or science-based, concerned with the provision of welfare services or with mass communications – can make no such claims, since their practitioners are engaging in activities which cannot be dissociated from the organisation of production, the stimulation of consumption or the management of consensus. They are therefore involved in capitalist society and responsible for its functioning without necessarily having either much trust in its basic philosophy or much influence on its evolution. Hence a double contradiction arises – between the ideas inculcated by the educational system and the tenets on which the socio-economic structure rests, on the one hand; and between the aspirations stimulated by the possession of qualifications and the scope offered to graduates in practical life, on the other. The radicalism of the new professionals, whom Touraine calls 'technologists', is bred by these tensions.[50] It is in sharp contradistinction with the notables' ready acceptance of their own economic privileges, cultural superiority and political representativeness.

The alienation of the new professionals – and, more widely, the sense of unrest experienced by intellectuals – is not unrelated to the loss of prestige attendant upon the multiplication of degrees and diplomas, formerly valued for their very scarcity. Not only have numbers increased, but the social background of graduates has changed and the composition of the professional group reflects this trend. This phenomenon, experienced in all European countries, has only been deliberately engineered in the Soviet Union and the popular democracies. In the West, it has tended to be justified on meritocratic grounds – a form of legitimation particularly vulnerable to the critique of educational definitions of merit. By an apparent paradox, it is precisely at the time when intellectuals are recruited from among wider sections of society (despite the persistent under-representation of the manual classes) that doubts are cast on the principle – rather than merely on the methods – of selection. Hence the insecurity of the upwardly mobile is increased by philosophical uncertainties which can culminate in a sense of guilt instead of achievement. The adoption of a militant stance may then represent a form of atonement for privileges felt to be undeserved – the polar opposite of the notables' smugness. Self-doubts tend to be echoed and amplified by a widespread loss of confidence among the general public, no longer prepared to equate knowledge with wisdom or expertise with dependability. This evolution is inseparable from the crisis of higher education but is also closely related to such changes in the structure of advanced societies as urban growth, with the attendant depersonalisation of status ratings in the large metropolitan community,[51] and bureaucratisation, with the consequent reduction of economic independence for professionals. The relative importance of these structural factors may be greater in those societies, such as Britain and, to a certain extent, the Scandinavian countries, in which professional training was envisaged as distinct from academic pursuits. However, they are operative throughout Western Europe.

The disappearance of the notables can therefore be explained both by reference to the so-called education explosion of the post-war period and to a treble loss, of status within the community, of economic security and of monopoly on cultural consumption. Lower status, linked with the multiplication of graduates and the proliferation of new professions whose social importance is not always widely recognised or immediately obvious, can also be accounted for by the dissociation between place of residence and locus of work common in urbanised societies. The prestige formerly enjoyed by small-town lawyers or family doctors is necessarily reduced as opportunities for interpersonal knowledge decline in large connurbations and as intermediary occupational categories, for instance in the paramedical sector, bridge the gap between specialist and layman. Furthermore, the increase of employment by business corporations or state bureaucracies and the gradual move away from individual to group practices have undermined the actual independence of professionals, as well as the enhanced status derived from it. Economic security was no doubt reduced thereby, though variations are bound to occur for conjunctural as well as for ideological reasons. The old professions might be less vulnerable than the new to fluctuations in demand, since their services tend to be less easily expendable in times of scarcity. It would, however, be hazardous to generalise since needs are culturally determined and notoriously elastic. At any rate, the relative scarcity of professional qualifications ensures greater independence from the market for stability of employment than that enjoyed by white-collar workers, despite a reduction of the security characteristic of the notables. The example of Eastern Europe, where political change entailed the bureaucratisation of the professions under state auspices, has shown that the disappearance of self-employment cannot be equated with the loss of intellectual independence. The abundance of political and social criticisms made by intellectuals in the employ of the state can be compared with the outspokenness and unconventionality of those – especially writers and creative artists – who used to depend on private patrons in pre-industrial societies. Both instances show that the sense of cultural superiority, derived from the possession of knowledge or skills, outweighs material considerations.

Educational expansion can be held to account for the existence of multiple patterns of cultural consumption, encouraged by the new professions concerned with the dissemination rather than the production of cultural goods. Although it would be an oversimplification to contrast creators with communicators, since there is in fact a continuum of popularisers, performers, artists, authors and educators among whom the divide between the creative skills and the new professions is blurred, there is certainly a departure from the simple dichotomy between a cultivated minority and a respectfully indifferent mass. Anti-intellectualism, widespread even

– or perhaps especially – among the highly educated section of the population,[52] has undermined the elitarian sense of cultural and moral superiority which enabled this section confidently to equate its own standards with the dictates of good taste and the prerequisites of civilisation. The certainty that educational qualifications give a special right to assume responsibilities commensurate with the privilege they represent is of necessity proportional to their scarcity. This appears to have hastened the fall of Western notables, yet – although it was such scarcity which accounted for the rise of the intelligentsia in Eastern Europe – egalitarian educational policies do not appear to have proved detrimental either to its prestige or to its trust in its ability to lead.

Is there still an intelligentsia?

Although contemporary definitions tend to emphasise occupational distinctions, the concept of intelligentsia focuses on a social function performed by a group conscious of its responsibilities and acknow-ledged by others to be uniquely qualified for its performance.[53] Historically, this approach can be traced back to mid-nineteenth-century Poland, where the defence of the national culture against the occupying powers was the mission of the intelligentsia[54] and to Tsarist Russia in the 1860s, where 'a classless group of dedicated men' espoused the cause of economic modernisation and social emancipation.[55] Thus there can be considerable variations in the nature of the task undertaken by such a stratum; its mainspring may be patriotism, revolutionary zeal or the desire 'to accumulate, preserve, reformulate and disseminate the intellectual heritage of the group'.[56] However, a common commitment to this single end, whatever it may be, is a necessary attribute of the intelligentsia, binding its members together despite the diversity of their social origins. Thus it would be inaccurate to describe them as 'conscience-stricken noblemen' in Tsarist Russia, since some were descended from Orthodox priests, while many could be termed *raznochintsy* or of no estate.[57] For such a heterogeneous category to emerge as a social force, the scarcity of educational facilities, enhancing the prestige of intellectuals (in the loose sense of persons endowed with some knowledge, though not necessarily with any qualifications), was a precondition. An additional prerequisite was a degree of economic retardation which limited the occupational outlets available and precluded the formation of an entrepreneurial bourgeoisie, such as that which was instrumental in promoting capitalist organisa-tion and reformist policies in the countries of Western and Northern Europe. To this extent,

191

the intelligentsia as a social stratum is a local phenomenon, and an exceptional one, the product of the belated disintegration of the aristocratic estate and the passage of its members into the ranks of the bourgeoisie in an environment lacking in the traditional embryos of urban strata.[58]

The influence of foreign capitalists on Russian industrialisation and the absence of national states in the countries ruled from Moscow and Vienna meant that neither business nor the bureaucracy offered adequate channels for social mobility and for pursuing the Western-inspired ideal of modernisation. Frustration led to the advocacy of revolutionary means – a phenomenon which recurred in colonial territories and could therefore be correlated with a conjunction of economic underdevelopment and political powerlessness, due either to foreign domination or to autocratic rule.

The part played by the intelligentsia in the early phase of the Soviet revolution and the new regime's desperate need for trained cadres assured the acceptance of its members in the new society, despite the official proclamation of the manual class as ruling class and the egalitarian ideology, reflected in the forcible equalisation of incomes. However, the conflicting requirements of industrialisation and of political consistency resulted in 'the ambiguous [treatment] of a social category which is both negated and pampered, put back in its place in the service of the working class while tribute is being paid to its age-old virtues'.[59] Thus, incomes policy fluctuated from the austerity of the early Bolshevik phase to the emphasis on differentials under Stalin and, since the 20th Party Congress, to the systematic reduction of inequalities in remuneration.[60] The same trend has been witnessed in the 1960s in the people's democracies, though variations in the rewards allocated to different occupational categories appear to have been less pronounced than in the Soviet Union.[61] To assess whether the intelligentsia may be termed privileged, material advantages cannot be considered in isolation, but opportunities for access to positions entailing the possession of authority, as well as high prestige awards must also be taken into account. Formal qualifications being the criterion by reference to which posts in the upper echelons of the bureaucratic and managerial hierarchies are filled, especially since the cult of the individual leader was denounced in the post-Stalinist era and replaced by the quest for specialists, educational inequalities may well be the most significant source of differentiation under state socialism. They are also the most acceptable as the high prestige ratings of professionals show.[62] Yet the openness of higher education to applicants originating from the working class or the peasantry certainly exceeds the levels achieved in the Western democracies, as 50 to 60 per cent of the intake are from such backgrounds, according to research results from the Soviet Union and the more advanced peoples' democracies. However, there are clear signs of intelligentsia entrenchment[63] both in the most renowned institutions and in the theoretically oriented subjects. The transmission of educational advantages to the next generation might result in the structuration of a 'new class', as Djilas called it, gaining domination over the Communist Party[64] and controlling the economic resources available by manipulating the state machinery. While opportunities for social mobility from the skilled manual working class appear to ensure that its composition would be frequently renewed, such a stratum would, by its very existence, challenge the egalitarianism which has been erected into an official philosophy.

Theorists of industrial convergence would see in the redefinition of the intelligentsia as an occupational category a symptom of the evolution they anticipate towards a system of stratification common to advanced societies, regardless of political regime. Yet not only is the mode of recruitment into it affected by economic organisation, its heterogeneity – evidenced by the inclusion of all non-manual workers – allows for the persistence of group characteristics in some of its sections whose origins can be found in the pre-revolutionary period. While to most intellectuals the value of education is instrumental, since qualifications are means to occupational ends, a minority among the 'creators' in literature, the arts and the sciences, consider themselves the heirs of the intelligentsia in the traditional sense and feel bound to assert their attachment to the values which they regard as essential for the development of their society. Whether in defence of national independence and/or of democratic rights, the assertion of special responsibilities by members of the intelligentsia has been a feature of every crisis in Eastern Europe, the Czechoslovak experiment in liberalisation being perhaps the best-known example, and provides the only evidence for the existence of political dissent in the Soviet Union. The strength of historical precedents in support of such commitment to the pursuit of non-material ends for the general good and despite threatened or actual persecution has in fact been invoked by the Russian protesters. Underlying this appeal to the pre-revolutionary intelligentsia tradition is an implicit statement of the complementarity between cultural superiority – expressed by literary or artistic, scientific or educational attainments – and moral responsibility above and beyond the ordinary claims of citizenship.

Ultimately this conception of the intelligentsia's role is grounded in an elitarian interpretation of culture, since special duties, which, although they are onerous, may be regarded as privileges, are deduced from the status of producer rather than consumer of

193

cultural goods. Such an approach, understandable in the context of inadequate educational provision in the nineteenth century, assumes the existence of a gap between the political awareness of the enlightened few and the apathy or lack of discrimination of the mass. Therefore it is an attitude fully compatible with the contempt for mass culture characteristic of many Western intellectuals, as well as with their sense of outrage at some political decisions, for instance on issues of colonisation or of nuclear warfare. It is hardly surprising that what amounts to intelligentsia protest should have become commonplace in France during the Algerian war or indeed in the West as a whole during the more dramatic phases of the Vietnam war. However, in contrast to Eastern Europe, the plurality of political parties and movements provides outlets for the expression of dissent which prevent intellectuals from experiencing either the sense of isolation or the sentiment of moral superiority their lack generates in one-party systems. The rejection of these channels and the adoption of revolutionary means for the implementation of ideals held by some intellectuals, particularly students, to be socially desirable, has been shown during the events of 1968 in France to be a genuine alternative to participation in the polity. Therefore an intelligentsia – in the sense of a stratum whose members are prompted by the conviction that they alone can embody the conscience of a community – could have been said to exist. However, the cohesiveness of such a group and its durability may be undermined by the integrative power of the society its members want to change, particularly by the economic advantages available to them. In a sweeping generalisation, which the history of Eastern Europe confirms all too aptly, Toynbee once wrote that 'an intelligentsia is born to be unhappy'.[65] It may be too early to judge whether Western societies currently generate sufficient unhappiness among their intellectuals to turn some into an intelligentsia.

Notes

1 T. S. Eliot, *Notes towards the Definition of Culture*, London, 1948, p. 24.
2 L. Bodin and J. Touchard, 'Les Intellectuels dans la société française contemporaine', *Revue Française de Science Politique*, vol. IX, no. 4, December, 1959.
3 M. S. Lipset and R. B. Dobson, 'The Intellectual as Critic and Rebel', *Daedalus*, Summer 1972.
4 J. Chalasinski, *Spoleczna Genealogia Inteligencji Polskiej* (Social Genealogy of the Polish Intelligentsia), Warsaw, 1946, p. 20.
5 J. Szczepański, 'Inteligencja a Pracownicy Umylowi' (Intelligentsia and Mental Workers), in *Przeglad Socjologiczny*, vol. XII, no. 2, Lodz, 1959.
6 J. Szczepański, *Inteligencja i Społeczeństwo*, Warsaw, 1957, pp. 19f.

7 J. Lagneau, *Stratification et égalitarisme*, Paris, pp. 210f.
8 P. Bourdieu and J. C. Passeron, *La Reproduction*, Paris, 1970.
9 *Rocznik statystyczny* (Statistical Yearbook), Warsaw, 1965, p. 421.
10 M. Vaughan, 'Poland', in M. S. Archer (ed.), *Students, University and Society*, London, 1972, pp. 57ff.
11 M. Vaughan, 'The Grandes Ecoles of France', in R. Wilkinson (ed.), *Governing Elites*, New York, 1969, pp. 85f.
12 T. H. Marshall, 'The recent history of professionalism in relation to social structure and social policy', in *Class, Citizenship and Social Development*, London, 1963, pp. 160f.
13 J. Dumazedier, *The Sociology of Leisure*, The Hague, 1974.
14 A. Carr-Saunders, *Professions: their organization and place in society*, Oxford, 1928.
15 E. Goblot, *La Barrière et le Niveau*, Paris, 1930.
16 M. S. Archer and S. Giner, 'Social Stratification in Europe', in R. Bendix and S. M. Lipset (eds), *Class, Status and Power*, London, 1967, p. 23.
17 Polska Akademia Nauk (Polish Academy of Science), *Wyksztalcenie a Pozycja Spoleczna Inteligencji*, (Education and the Social Position of the Intelligentsia), Lodz, 1959, pp. 468f.
18 K. Lutyńska, 'Typologia Spoleczna i Drogi Kariery Urzedników Lodzkich' (Social Typology and Career Patterns of Employees in Lodz), *Przeglad Socjologiczny*, vol. 19, no. 2, 1966, pp. 65f.
19 D. Bell, *The Coming of Post-Industrial Society*, London, 1974, p. 103.
20 D. Lockwood, *The Blackcoated Worker*, London, 1966; R. Dahrendorf, 'Recent Changes in the Class Structures of European Societies', *Daedalus*, vol. 93, no. 1, 1. Winter 1964.
21 Archer and Giner, op. cit., p. 51.
22 Lockwood, op. cit., p. 137.
23 Ibid., p. 151.
24 M. Crozier, *The World of the Office Worker*, Chicago, 1971, pp. 13f.
25 A. Giddens, *The Class Structure of Advanced Societies*, London, 1973, p. 190.
26 A. Sarapata, *Studia nad uwarstwieniem i ruchliwoscia spoleczna* (Studies of stratification and social mobility), Warsaw, 1965, p. 139.
   A. Sarapata and W. Wesolowski, 'The Evaluation of Occupations by Warsaw Inhabitants', *American Journal of Sociology*, vol. 66, May 1961.
27 Sarapata, op. cit., p. 402.
28 Lagneau, op. cit., pp. 72f.
29 Sarapata, op. cit., p. 404.
30 Crozier, op. cit., p. 37.
31 Szczepański, 1959, op. cit.
32 A. Touraine, *The Post-Industrial Society*, New York, 1971, pp. 49f.
33 S. Mallet, *La Nouvelle Classe ouvrière*, Paris, 1963.
34 Giddens, op. cit., p. 233.
35 W. Wesolowski, 'Strata and Strata Interest in Socialist Society', in C. S. Heller (ed.), *Structured Social Inequality*, New York, 1969, pp. 465f.

36 L. Stone, 'Social Mobility in England, 1500–1700', *Past and Present*, vol. 33, London, 1966.
37 R. Pernoud, *Histoire de la bourgeoisie en France*, Paris, 1962, vol. 2, pp. 77f.
38 A. Thibaudet, *La République des professeurs*, Paris, 1927.
39 C. Morazé, *Les bourgeois conquérants*, Paris, 1957.
40 E. Gellner, *Thought and Change*, London, 1964, pp. 157f.
41 J. Ben-David, 'The growth of the Professions and the Class system', in R. Bendix and M. S. Lipset (eds), *Class, Status and Power*, London, 1966 (2nd edn), p. 471.
42 H. H. Gerth and C. W. Mills, *From Max Weber*, London, 1967, pp. 240f., 426f.
43 M. Vaughan and M. S. Archer, *Social Conflict and Educational Change*, Cambridge, 1971, pp. 7f.
44 W. J. Reader, *Professional Men*, London, 1966, p. 211.
45 P. Bourdieu, 'Systems of Education and Systems of Thought', in E. Hopper (ed.), *Readings in the Theory of Educational Systems*, London, 1971.
46 Ben-David, op. cit., p. 465.
47 Touraine, op. cit., p. 97.
48 A. Touraine, *The May Movement*, New York, 1968.
49 A. Gorz, *Stratègie ouvrière et néocapitalisme*, Paris, 1964.
50 Bell, op. cit., p. 465.
51 P. K. Hatt and A. J. Reiss, *Cities and Society*, New York, 1951, p. 394.
52 J. Benda, *La Trahison des clercs*, Paris, 1928.
53 J. Blaha, 'Socjologia Inteligencji', *Przeglad Socjologiczny*, vol. X, 1948, Lodz, 1949.
54 Chalasinski, op. cit., pp. 28f.
55 G. Fischer, *Russian Liberalism, From Gentry to Intelligentsia*, Harvard, 1958, p. 152.
56 L. Wirth, Introduction to K. Mannheim, *Ideology and Utopia*, London, 1968, p. xxxi.
57 N. Malia, 'What is the Intelligentsia?', in R. Pipes (ed.), *The Russian Intelligentsia*, New York, 1961, pp. 5f.
58 S. Rychlinski, 'Zaleznosc procesow demokratyzacju kultury od dynamiki spolecznej', *Przeglad Socjologiczny*, vol. XIII, no. 1, Lodz, 1959, p. 17.
59 Lagneau, op. cit., p. 71.
60 D. Lane, *The End of Inequality?* London, 1971.
61 Giddens, op. cit., p. 229.
62 W. Wesolowski, *Klasy, warstwy i wladza*, Warsaw, 1966, pp. 159f.
63 Bell, op. cit., pp. 103f.
64 F. Parkin, *Class Inequality and Political Order*, London, 1971, pp. 150f.
65 A. Toynbee, *A Study of History*, abridged by D. C. Somervell, London, 1946, p. 394.

8 Changes in social structure and changes in the demand for education

Pierre Bourdieu and Luc Boltanski

The increase in the number of holders of academic qualifications has most frequently been interpreted, either by simple reference to changes in the supply of education, the raising of the school leaving age and the increase in the number of educational institutions, etc., or by simple reference to changes in the demand for education.[1] In the latter case, analyses are generally divided according to the traditional dichotomies in the field of sociology: either, adopting a 'functionalist' approach, the increased demand for education is seen as a simple reflection of the increased social demand for qualifications brought about by technological changes, or, in the language of conflict, this growth is seen as the outcome of the struggle between groups to monopolise the key positions in the job market. Our aim here is to break away from these unilateral and partial aspects to analyse the dialectical relations between change in the structure of social classes and change in the structure of the educational system. It is a question of defining the practical mediators through which the laws of transformation of the machinery of production and of the machinery of reproduction operate and are articulated, bearing in mind that the adjustment (postulated by the 'functionalist' approach, whose theories are often nothing more than simple inversion) is only *one particular case* in the series of possible states characterising the relations between these two systems.

In practice it is via analysis of the *strategies of reproduction* that links are established between, on the one hand, the changes in the structure of the distribution of the different types of capital (economic, cultural and social capital) between the classes (which constitutes a strict definition of change in the structure of classes) and on the other hand, changes in the structure of the educational system which are linked to transformation of the function which it is made to perform by the different social classes. The strategies of reproduction, by which members of capital-owning classes or class fractions tend, consciously or unconsciously, to maintain or improve their position in the structure of class relations by safeguarding or increasing their capital, constitute a system. They depend on the state of the system of means of reproduction (the state of custom and the laws of inheritance, the labour market, the educational system, etc.), and on the volume and structure of the capital to be reproduced: it follows that any change in one or other of these factors brings about a *restructuring* of the system of strategies of reproduction which, due to the reconversion of the types of capital held into other, more accessible, more lucrative and/or more legitimate forms (within a given state of the means of reproduction), tends to cause a change in the inheritance structure.

Following the logic of this model, the education explosion (which is generally attributed *directly* to technological change and the consequent growth in the demand for qualified manpower) appears as the result of an overall transformation of the functions of the educational institution, i.e. of the structure of relations between the educational system and the structure of class relations, whose principle, or at least whose trigger, lies in a transformation of the system of strategies of reproduction employed by those fractions of the upper and middle classes which are richest in economic capital. It can in fact be established that the combined transformation of the system of the means of reproduction (and in particular of the system of inheritance) and of the method of appropriation of economic profit is the source of the intensified use made of the education system by those sections of the ruling and middle classes who previously assured the perpetuation of their position by the direct transmission of economic capital. Consequently it is also the origin of the steady inflation of academic qualifications, a process triggered off and continually maintained by their correlative devaluation. This is such as to impose on all classes and class fractions, beginning with the greatest users of the school, a continued intensification of their use of the school.

Changes in the field of enterprises

The ruling class, and in particular its dominant section, whose power is exerted on industrial and commercial undertakings, has undergone a series of systematic changes, of which the transformation of its relations with the educational system is an important aspect. These are correlates of changes in the structure of the economic field and of general business organisation, or, more precisely, of the relation between the domestic enterprise (the family) and industrial and commercial enterprises. Within this series of changes, which have been widely observed, several points need stressing: on the one hand the diversification of economic units which results from the diminution of the proportion of individual enterprises and from the appearance of 'legal persons' of a new type, or again the multiplication of companies situated on the border between the private and public sectors; and on the other hand the setting up of more diversified and complex relations between the basic economic units. To the competitive market relations between independent enterprises in the economic field as traditionally defined are added the administrative relations between enterprises making up a single firm, the relations of domination between enterprises formally distinct but attached by complex financial links, the 'personal links' between firms integrated by inter-locking directorships, or again the domination of the market which allows a large integrated enterprise to guarantee itself virtual bureaucratic control over the small enterprises from which it buys. These changes in the structure of the economic field, which are correlates of changes in the structure of enterprises, tend to increase the *de facto* interdependence between firms, thus substituting for the old *mechanical solidarity* between enterprises (and entrepreneurs) of a 'common type' as Durkheim puts it, an *organic solidarity*, based on complementary interests and on the (at least relative) apportioning of power that the setting up of complex (and sometimes circular) networks of domination engenders.

The process of restructuring of the economic field has been accompanied by an increased *bureaucratisation* of economic relations and of the operation of enterprises. In the past the head of family enterprises, who maintained no financial link with other enterprises or received no aid from the state, found himself freed from all control and as a result at liberty to confound company finances with the family holding. In this mode of organisation, where power resides in individuals rather than in positions, the delegation of institutionalised authority is almost totally absent; the arbitrariness and instability of the hierarchies within the controlling group are delimited only by a sort of customary law embodied in the 'spirit of the firm' and in the image of the 'boss'; and the search for rational and abstract criteria of recruitment (such as a degree) is almost unknown. The new mode of organisation rests, on the contrary, on the distinction between, on the one hand, institutionalised positions, which constitute the structure of the enterprise, and on the other hand, the individual agents who, often for a limited time, occupy relatively specialised positions associated with specific mandates. These positions are hierarchically organised, united by a system of formally defined relations and communicate through the intermediary of standardised channels of communication and according to

199

rationalised procedures (written regulations and orders) which make possible a functional division of responsibilities, a delimitation and hierarchy of functions, and a rationalisation of decisions. Thus, the changes in the economic field are accompanied by changes in the structure of enterprises which in turn govern changes in the characteristics of the personnel occupying the controlling positions and of the functions they fulfil, and therefore of the structures of authority in the enterprise.

The bureaucratisation of enterprises and the rationalisation of the characteristics of each position and of the associated functions have resulted in the establishment of depersonalised and rationalised procedures of training, recruitment and promotion which depend at least as much on the examination of official qualifications as on the syncretic and intuitive, or quasi-rationalised, appreciation of personal characteristics and individual qualities as a whole. The family firm run at least partially by its owners could dispense with formal criteria in the recruitment of management because the possession of title deeds to the business and/or membership of the owning family guaranteed the possession of attributes and qualities considered socially necessary (for example 'sobriety' or a 'sense of authority') and of the symbolic capital (particularly personal relations) necessary in the management of the business. In ensuring its own reproduction, the family ensured at the same time the production of personnel with the social competence (and often also the technical competence) necessary to manage the business. The tendential transformation of *individual possessory holdings* into *power systems*[2] renders inoperative the tools by which business formerly provided controlling personnel for itself, endowed with the characteristics and particularly the class habits required. Everything takes place as if the possession of an academic qualification and particularly a degree from a 'grande école', which tends to become a necessary (but not sufficient) condition of access to positions of economic power, constituted a sort of syncretic index guaranteeing possession of most of the characteristics and qualities with which the directors of large integrated firms must be endowed in order to occupy positions of power in the structures of business as did the possession of title deeds in earlier phases of the system. Doubtless, the training given in the 'grandes écoles' at least constitutes a means of acquiring the technical competence required in the administrative management of firms, if only in that it gives the agents a collection of intellectual dispositions transferable to areas which were not directly the object of instruction.

But the selection and inculcation organised by the 'grandes écoles' for cadres, doubtless conform more to the expectations of the managements of modern firms than did the products of traditional family inculcation. On the one hand, through the social selection which they operate, the 'écoles de pouvoir' tend to recruit a significant proportion of their pupils from the dominant fractions of the ruling class (proprietors, cadres of the private sector and senior civil servants); on the other hand, inasmuch as they give them an extensive network of connections which contributes to their integration into the ruling class (and correlatively to the integration of the ruling class), a certain knowledge of the rules and laws which govern the operation of the economic field, or, dispositions such as a sense of hierarchy, they tend to redouble and reinforce the class competence transmitted in a diffuse way by the family whilst adapting it to the administration of modern firms, and to legitimise it by integrating it into a scientific or technical competence (or, in other cases, to serve as a substitute for technical competence).

The change in positions of power and their occupants

Doubtless one must take care not to fall prey to the most typical error of most research on 'elites'. If one fails to distinguish between the properties which a position objectively requires of its possible occupants and which are a product of the structure of the field, and the sociologically constructed properties of the agents competing to occupy it, one thereby substitutes for the analysis of the structure of economic positions and its changes a typological description of the occupants of these positions and the changes in their characteristics. One is thereby condemned to reduce the change in the mode of appropriation of firms simply to the substitution of *managers* for *owners* who are transformed into mere stock- and bond-owners. The fact remains that changes in the social and academic characteristics of these agents can be treated as indices – but merely as ones which statistically are more easily constructed than others – of the changes in the structure of positions. But the growing *de facto* and *de jure* interdependence between enterprises, and the corresponding bureaucratisation, are accompanied by a change in the *mode of reproduction* of enterprises; in other words, changes in the structure of the economic field and in the method of appropriation of profit are reflected in, among other things, the fact that selection and promotion tend to depend more and more on academic qualifications and on co-option of fellow graduates.[3]

Change in the *mode of remuneration* of agents occupying the dominant positions in the economic field seems to constitute one of the principal agencies of mediation between the change in the structure of the economic field and change in the strategies of reproduction of the families belonging to the dominant fractions of the dominant class. Everything takes place as if the growth in size of the business unit, the direct effect of which is to bring about a growth in the number of high-salaried cadres, were accompanied by a lowering of the return on economic capital received directly in the form of profits or rents by the owners of business and, indirectly, by a change in the means of appropriation of the profits of economic capital. The bureaucratisation of firms tends in fact to increase the proportion of capital profits extracted in the form of salaries by the cadres who control the business mechanism (and inform the owners of capital as to its functioning). To account for this process, which the concept of bureaucratisation does no more than point to, one would have to analyse in each case the structure of the environment of the enterprise as the site where the strategies developed on the one hand by the holders of title deeds and on the other hand by the cadres confront one another. The interests of the cadres may coincide with the expansion of the firm, inasmuch as this no doubt constitutes the best justification they can give the holders of capital for the increase in their remuneration and the reinforcement of their power. It can be seen, on this hypothesis, that the expansion of the firm, which increases the number of managers in a position to draw their salary from the profits of the enterprise and led by the logic of their group interests to increase the size of the enterprise and thus to extend the dimensions of its administrative machinery (hence the number of cadres), tends to take the form of a self-perpetuating process involving the substitution of salary (and of direct profits obtained in monetary form)[4] for rent as the major method of remuneration of the dominant fraction of the ruling class.[5] This new method of remuneration of capital, whose *power of dissimulation* – the joint product of the inertia of the old categories (rent, salary, profits, etc.) inherited from classical economics and the technico-meritocratic ideology of 'public service' associated with the academic mode of legitimation – is one of the most significant advantages, tends to substitute academic qualification for property-holding qualification as the means of appropriating the profits of economic capital. It is in such terms that one must understand the increased profitability of certified cultural capital. This is *the most apparent effect* of a change in the method of remuneration of capital occurring alongside a change in the mode of economic appropriation by the ruling class; the growing weight of academic qualifications in the recruitment criteria for managers tends to make them the principal mediators between the social classes and economic institutions.

The structural mode of domination

Thus the principle which lies behind all the changes which can be observed in the characteristics of agents occupying the dominant positions in the economic field consists in a *restructuring* of the economic field. From change in the mode of appropriation of capital profits comes a restructuring of the system of relations between the economic field and the instruments of reproduction, and in particular of the educational institution, giving rise to a profound change in the functions of the field of institutions specifically charged with the reproduction of the controlling class and, by corollary, a change in the structure of that field. The distinction drawn between owners and managers[6] has the effect of mystifying the change in the methods of appropriating the profits of economic capital which is linked to a reorganisation of the economic field and, more precisely, to the transition from a personal mode of domination – in which the appropriation of the enterprise by the family was the foundation of the opposition between the owner and the salaried director – *to a structural mode of domination.* In actual fact, the change in the mode of domination of the economy is accompanied by a change in the mode of appropriation of profits which surpasses and invalidates the former distinction between inheritance rights and authority over the enterprise, to which some seek to reduce the transformation which has taken place in economic structures.[7]

Instead the enterprise tends more and more to function as a field on its own, that is, as a system of differentiated positions which are united by objective relations of complementarity, competition and/or conflict and which can be occupied by relatively interchangeable agents who, in the strategies which put them in opposition to those who hold different positions, are obliged to take account of the objective relations between the positions. The behaviour of the enterprise, considered as an institutionally constituted collective body endowed with the power of acting and reacting to the actions and reactions of other enterprises and other interest groups (fund raisers, producers, consumers, trade unions, the state, etc.), is itself the product of interactions (whether of co-operation, competition or even conflict) between the individual or collective agents with convergent or divergent interests who occupy positions of power in the field of the enterprise (with titles like shareholders, presidents, directors, etc.).[8] What might be termed, by analogy with individual psychology, the personality structure of an enterprise, which determines its 'behaviour' (for example 'timorous' or 'bold') and the totality of the strategies it employs, is a function of the structure of the field which the enterprise forms, and which is itself a product of the particular history of the enterprise in its relation with the collective history of the economic field. The enterprise owes an ever-increasing proportion of its properties to the position it occupies in the economic field, as the relations between enterprises (and other collectivities, like the state) multiply, diversify and intensify. It can be presumed that this general evolutionary tendency in the economic field is bound to reinforce a particular category of positions within the power relations constituting the firm, i.e. those situated at the centres of the network of relationships; and that this in turn helps to attract a new type of agent.

The tendency to substitute the economico-political culture supplied by the *Institut d'Etudes Politiques* or the *Ecole Nationale d'Administration* for the old cultural capital, with its scientific and technical bias, transmitted in the scientific 'grandes écoles', whose house rules were sometimes modelled on those of a military academy, seems to correspond to a change in the *habitus* now required of managers.[9] This change is without doubt the effect of the internal restructuring of the ruling class and also of a transformation of the means by which the domination of the controlling class over other classes operates. In fact, corresponding with the change in the characteristics of the controlling personnel (which accompanies changed relations between enterprises in the economic field and between the economic field and other fields) there is also a change in the nature of authority which may be interpreted as a relative relaxation of hierarchical relations, if not within the whole enterprise at least within the management section, which perhaps expresses a more profound change in the mode of domination of the controlling class. This redefinition of the strategies of interaction between classes or between hierarchical positions is one aspect of the fundamental modification of the social definition of authority or rather, of competence, in the technical and legal sense of the word, which is doubtless itself inseparable from a change in the collective representations of the acceptable and the unacceptable, the tolerable and the intolerable.

The personal method of domination preponderant in a previous state of the economic field (characterised by the mechanical division of labour between family businesses) required agents who had strongly internalised the traditional (in extreme cases, military) models of authority and who were sufficiently acquainted with the technical procedures used in the enterprise to be able to mediate between the owner and the subordinate personnel (technicians, foremen, etc.). By contrast, the *structural mode of domination* requires agents capable of conducting *external public relations* (with other businesses, the state administration, etc.) necessary to the operation of the large integrated firm and to the maintenance of its control over the market, and also the *internal public relations* by which, in normal times, the internal order of the business is maintained. Less and less often equipped with institutional insignia (such an honours) or natural insignia (such as grey hair and portliness) of authority, the new managers – 'young directors' and 'modern' bosses – must, in order to indicate the hierarchical position they occupy and the new principles by which it is legitimated, elaborate a new *symbolism of excellence*. Their outstanding qualities become an aptitude for discussion and negotiation, a knowledge of foreign languages and, perhaps especially, civilised and subtle manners which are the antithesis of the forceful and surly roughness which characterised the traditional owner, at least in his archetypal form. The high-level official (a modern form of the 'diplomat') is substituted for the officer in the arsenal of social models from which the managers can draw their inspiration in building up the new style of sociability objectively required by the changes in the economic field. One could expatiate at length on the changes associated with this, which concern all aspects of existence of the new managers, from their consumer habits to their day-to-day ethics or even their physical appearance, a sign of a new relation to the body. And the new life-style which is glorified in the glossy magazines and articles in the fashionable weekly papers, imposes itself as legitimate all the more easily because the rise of the new 'masters of the economy', originating from the dominated fractions of the middle classes or, most often, from the traditional fractions of the ruling class itself, by means of a reconversion of their capital and a conversion of their *habitus*, coincides with the decline in the traditional sections (officers, owners of family enterprises, etc.), the old guardians of the temperate asceticism of the civilisation of thrift.

The change in the mode of reproduction

These changes in the economic field have had the effect of enabling the dominant fractions of the ruling class to proceed to the full utilisation of the specific powers of the educational system as an instrument of reproduction. In the past the direct transmission of power from person to person, and most frequently, from father to son, a power moreover intended to be exercised personally by its holder and thus guaranteed by that individual alone, meant that the traditional owners had no use for an institution which seeks to interpose its anonymous mediation and impose its impersonal legitimacy. The new reproduction effected by the mediation of the school, as an independent agency, is to direct reproduction by the family what the structural mode of domination is to the personal mode. Instead of the *direct* transmission of social positions between the holder and the heir designated by the holder himself (with or without the approval of custom or law: whether officially or legally acknowledged or not), the transmission effected by the intermediary of the school rests on the *statistical* aggregation of the lone actions of individual or collective agents who are subject to the same laws, those of the educational market. The transition from the mode of reproduction based on the direct transmission of the economic patrimony in which the school fulfilled at the very most a legitimising function, to a more diversified mode of reproduction, which confers an important function on the transmission of the cultural patrimony, is a correlate of the school's assumption of the power, held until then by families, to make decisions about reproduction. That is to say that the school now selects from the whole group of children of the same age and the same social class those who are intended to reproduce the class in all its characteristics or to be excluded from that class.[10] More generally, the new mode of reproduction limits the powers of the family which, in the former mode of reproduction, controlled all the mechanisms of reproduction, from fertility and marriage to inheritance – through which was accomplished the transmission of social positions to which the patrimony gave access – and also, at least to a large extent, controlled education. But it does so only to restore those powers in another form, through the better hidden mechanisms of social statistics, which, because they rest on a logic of probability, are capable of conferring on the class as a whole properties which individual members, considered separately, may be denied.[11]

It is because it functions statistically that the school can contribute to the reproduction of the ruling class only by sacrificing individuals who would be spared by a mode of reproduction which left power over transmission in the hands of the family: it follows that the opposition between the interests of individuals or families which the school sacrifices and the interests of the class which it *statistically* serves constitutes the specific contradiction of this mode of reproduction. The victims of this blind instrument of random reproduction can oppose it either by *compensatory* strategies of an individual kind (like the utilisation of social capital, to make good the deficiencies of educational capital) or by collective strategies which are aimed (like the revolt against examinations and qualifications) at the class itself, through threatening the mechanisms capable of reproducing it.[12] But the statistical mode of reproduction would inevitably lead to a redistribution of chances in each generation if it were not able to rely on the effects of another form of direct transmission, from family to children, but one that is hidden and ignored by the laws of inheritance, namely the transmission of cultural capital.[13]

Like electoral results which aggregate the totality of votes cast in the solitude of a multitude of polling-booths, the anonymous national examination, the heart of the Jacobin ideology, possesses the innocence and the impartiality of a slanted drawing of lots, that is to say, one that is soundly based, because it is grounded in nature.

It is opposed to recruitment through connections, through nepotism and through all the mechanisms of co-option based on networks of acquaintanceship, just as to arranged marriages there is opposed the free 'discovery', amid the random encounters of a faculty, of a spouse endowed with socially adjusted and thus statistically predictable characteristics. In short, the new strategies and mechanisms are in opposition to the former ones, but only as so many new *modes* of fulfilling the former functions. The equivalent of the error which leads one to oppose owners and managers would consist here in mechanically opposing the family and the school, without seeing that it is a question of describing the transition from one mode of reproduction to another, or in the other case, from one mode of appropriation to another, the two kinds of transformation being moreover correlated and structurally homologous. It is thus that the mechanisms of selection which tend to produce educational groups (by faculty, school, discipline, etc.) which socially are very homogeneous, tend to ensure class homogamy no less effectively, but in a quite different mode, than did the interventionism of families with all their former techniques (garden parties, balls, etc.) of directly controlling opportunities for social intercourse.[14] Likewise, being educated at a 'grande école' confers, under the title of 'old boy', a sort of certificate of credit-worthiness or letter of credit giving the right to all sorts of material and symbolic advantages in the eyes of all agents endowed with the same characteristics. It follows that the mechanisms of transmission are, in this case, doubly hidden, the dissimulation perpetrated by statistical aggregation being reinforced by the dissimulation of the direct transmission of cultural capital which slants the statistics. And here there enters the most specific and doubtless the best hidden effect of this mode of reproduction, which is bound to appear inefficacious – at any rate, less efficient than former methods – when measured – as it is in practice – in terms of the *family*, because its effects, inasmuch as they can only operate through the intermediary of *statistical actions*, are all situated at the level of the class as a whole. It is as if lower practical efficiency in the work of reproduction at the individual level were the exact price to be paid for greater efficiency in the work of dissimulating the work of reproduction.[15]

But the complexity of the relations between school, family and enterprise is further increased by the fact that the dissociation of the economic enterprise from the family does not prevent the family from continuing to concentrate, albeit in another form and by other means, the capital which each member holds for himself. It is as if the new mode of appropriation of capital rendered possible (and even desirable) the founding of a truly *organic solidarity* between the members of the family. In contrast to the holders of an economic patrimony who are divided as much as united by their common claim to appropriation of the inheritance, which is continually threatened, moreoever, by division and dispersion, subject to the risk of wills, testaments and misalliances, the owners of diversified capital, with a strong cultural component, have everything to gain by maintaining the family ties which allow them to pool the capital possessed by each of their members. Thus, the network of family relations can be the locus of an unofficial or even clandestine circulation of capital which may either function to support the official networks of circulation or to oppose their effects when these are contrary to the family interests: the dialectical relationship between the official and the unofficial, between the family network and the economic network of capital circulation, allows, here as elsewhere, the maximisation of profits of apparently incompatible systems of requirements. For example, it allows the profits procured by prestigious academic qualifications to be compounded with the devices which protect these returns, and allows the advantages of links between firms to be supplemented with the secondary benefits derived from matrimonial exchanges between the managers. Thus the 'integrated' family owes its cohesion to a specific principle, namely to 'family spirit' and affection as transfigured forms of the interest specifically attached to membership in a family group, i.e. a share in its capital, the integrity of which is restored by the integration of the family. In fact, by this sort of magical accountancy, membership of an integrated family assured each individual not only the profits corresponding to his personal contribution or even to the collective contributions of all the members of the group, but the profits which are the product of the multiplication of each one's contribution by everyone's contribution. Thus, the case in which the shareholders belonging to one family delegate to one of their members the right to manage the family portfolio is only a specific example (in which the profits of integration are limited by the particular properties of the type of capital considered) of all the relations of participation where the capital accumulated by each of the members of the group by virtue of the positions he occupies in different institutions and fields – and in particular his capital of social relations – is pooled in such a way that each one has his part of it and all have the whole of it. In short, if *social capital* is relatively irreducible to the different types of capital and in particular to economic and cultural capital (whose profitability it can multiply) without, however, being completely independent of it, it is because the volume of social capital possessed by an individual agent (and thus the group of which he is a part) depends on the volume of capital held by each of its members multiplied by the degree of integration of the group.

The change in strategies

Such changes in the structure of the system of means and mechanisms of reproduction are retranslated into changes in individual strategies which help to strengthen or accelerate the former. The holders of individual or family wealth tend to reconvert certain parts of their property, which can be transmitted by inheritance, into educational investments in such a way as to leave their children a part of their patrimony in the form of certified cultural capital favouring access to dominant positions in the machinery of enterprises. It is known that the conversion of economic capital into certified cultural capital and the transition from the status of independent entrepreneur or owner to that of salaried manager can constitute a strategy which allows families who occupy the dominant positions in the ruling class to maintain their control over the field of business whilst ensuring for their children, through the intermediary of the school, the qualifications which authorise them to appropriate a part of the economic benefit of companies in the form of salaries, a better concealed (and also perhaps surer) method of appropriating profits than rent. It is by this logic that the enormous differences which often exist between income obtained in the form of salary by different holders of the same qualification are explained. For those who come from class fractions which lack economic and/or social capital and whose inherited patrimony is made up almost entirely of cultural capital, salary represents remuneration solely for the embodied cultural capital which, by their activity, qualification-holders invest in the enterprise. In this case salaries tend to be measured against an academic qualification which functions as a standard (comparable in this respect to money) allowing the cultural capital invested to be evaluated and, in consequence, its conversion rate to economic capital to be determined. On the other hand, when the diploma is the product of the reconversion of personal property into certified cultural capital and the holder of the diploma also possesses economic and/or social capital giving access to positions of power in companies, the level of salary is relatively independent of the academic qualification held and of the mass of certified cultural capital (so that it may be subject to very wide fluctuations)[16] and thus salary tends to constitute only a dissimulated form of appropriation of profit.[17]

The salary-earning bourgeoisie

The inherent duality in the salary of academically qualified cadres which can be a means of appropriation of economic profits or a remuneration of invested cultural capital, would suffice to confer a fundamentally ambiguous character on the whole category. In addition, the characteristics which distinguish cultural capital from economic capital and the academic qualification from the property-holding qualification, tend to trap the salary-earning bourgeoisie, whose development follows the growth of certified cultural capital and the progress of bureaucratisation of enterprises, in contradictions specific to the mode of reproduction which has an academic component. Cultural capital is characterised by the fact that it can only reproduce and increase if it is *incorporated* in agents. Objectified cultural capital – the product of the materialisation, in objects such as tools, monuments or art works, of the cultural capital embodied in the agents who have produced it (the cultivated *habitus*) – can only contribute to its own simple or enlarged *reproduction* by being reincorporated in particular individuals (through reading, use or perception, which are all activities organised by the school). Furthermore, it can only become materially productive (as a means for the appropriation of material capital in the form of objectified cultural capital), in integrated enterprises devoted to cultural production and possessing the economic capital necessary to bring together the cultural producers. In consequence, the holders of this type of capital, i.e. the whole of the salaried bourgeoisie (engineers, research workers, teachers) are placed in an ambiguous position in the class structure. If they do not make their cultural capital produce, by refusing to work, they can no longer draw profit from it (or, anyway, more and more rarely) except within enterprises endowed with economic capital, and thus able to provide facilities and salaries. This is what distinguishes them from the *liberal professions* who, being self-employed, can use their incorporated cultural capital without the contribution of external capital (or, at least, are only dependent on a restricted accumulation of capital). The ambiguity which is the principle of the existence and social practice of the salaried bourgeoisie, holders of capital the use of which is subordinated to the possession of economic capital and which can only make a profit by being sold as labour power, also underpins the ambiguity of their consciousness and political practice, hesitating between 'participation' and 'revolt'. It is as if the position they occupy in the distribution of capital and the advantages they benefit from, as holders of cultural capital, in relation to the middle and working classes, oriented them towards the ruling class, whilst the position they occupy in the distribution of the different types of capital and, by the same token, of power separates them from the dominant fractions of the ruling class which hold the economic capital and/or occupy the positions from which its utilisation is controlled, without necessarily bringing them nearer to the dominated classes. This holds particularly for those among the intellectual fraction of the new bourgeoisie, for whom the change in the structure of intellectual enterprise, (itself brought about by change in the nature of industrial undertakings), the progress of science, and the growing complexity of technology, leads to a loss of status as cultural producers free of all attachments or as small independent inventors, and a new status as salaried cultural producers, integrated in research teams supplied with costly equipment and engaged in long-term projects.[18]

In short, it is as if the growth in the quantity of cultural capital which is objectified in machines, tools or instruments like computers, and thus the amount of cultural capital which needs to be incorporated in order to reproduce this machinery and make it produce, tended to bring about the transition from direct sale by the producer of products which each independent producer could make from his own capital to the sale of skilled labour-power to large foundations of cultural production. This process, which first occurred in the realm of the exact sciences, where it leads to a very high concentration of mental workers in large public or private enterprises, has reached the realm of the human sciences where a series of technological changes, brought about by the use of the computer and by the development of the demand for applied research to serve the large public and private bureaucracies, force the craftsmen of mental production towards the most traditional university disciplines such as the humanities and philosophy.

The crisis of small businesses

The complex economic changes discussed above are commonly held to involve the decline and disappearance of a great number of small industrial and commercial enterprises. Generally such observations are confined to consciously apocalyptic descriptions of this process, and do not analyse its underlying mechanisms or discuss its specific effects. In fact, under the guise of the pure and simple disappearance of populations or categories, is hidden a work of reconversion (variably successful, variably radical) which is undertaken by individual agents in accordance with the logic of their particular situations and is objectified in a change in the structure of relations defining the specific function of the middle classes in the class structure and the positions of the different fractions within the middle classes. When all the indicators are taken into account, from the development of the number of active persons to the development of the age-distribution, they combine to demonstrate a crisis in the mode of reproduction of the self-employed, the small entrepreneurs living from the direct exploitation of their patrimony. Between 1954 and 1968 the population of the various categories of self-employed saw a decrease which was greatest among small farmers and least among large traders and industrialists; small traders and the artisans occupying an intermediary position. These morphological changes affect not only the size of the different groups but also, and linked to this, most of their essential characteristics.[19]

The relative morphological stability of a particular occupational group can hide a change in its structure, especially a change in the relative weight of the economic and cultural capital which its agents must possess in order to keep themselves in that category. In consequence, the resilience of the group is, in this case, the product of the group working on itself, by means of *on the spot reconversion* by the agents present in the group (or their children) at the start of the period in question and/or their replacement by agents from other groups. Thus, for example, the relatively small drop in the overall size of the category of tradesmen, mostly made up of holders of small individual enterprises (93 per cent), whose resistance to crisis can partly be imputed to growing household consumption, conceals an internal transformation of the structure of this profession. The stagnation or diminution of food businesses (especially those in general foods) which are particularly hard hit by the competition of the large supermarkets[20] or clothing businesses, is almost compensated for by a growth in businesses dealing in cars, domestic equipment (furniture, interior decorating, etc.) and especially those dealing in equipment for sports, leisure and culture (book and record shops), and chemists. These changes in the nature of commercial enterprises – which are correlates of simultaneous transformations in the consumption of households, in turn related to the growth of incomes and especially, no doubt, to the increase in cultural capital brought about by the expansion of educational opportunities – have in common the fact that they demand, in different degrees, possession of a certain amount of cultural capital by their owners or managers.

In fact it is tempting to extend this hypothesis and to argue that the category of craftsmen has undergone internal changes very similar to that of the tradesmen, with luxury and artistic crafts, which demand an economic patrimony but also some cultural capital, tending to take the place of the traditional crafts. On this hypothesis (which is impossible to verify given the present statistics available) it is understandable that the drop in the size of the middle categories should be accompanied by a rise in the level of cultural capital as measured by level of education. At all events, it is as if the expansion of the market for symbolic goods (such as books, records or reproductions of works of art) or of goods with a symbolic component (such as ornaments or clothes), and the establishment of a very large market for symbolic services,[21] favoured individual enterprises based predominantly on the possession of cultural capital rather than individual enterprises based predominantly on the possession of economic capital, and, because of this, more vulnerable to the growth of the internal competition engendered by the growth of external competition.

Craftsmen or traders in luxury, cultural or artistic goods, managers of fashionable women's 'boutiques', retailers of 'remaindered' clothes, sellers of 'genuine' exotic clothes or jewellery or rustic objects, record sellers, antique dealers, decorators, designers, photographers or even restaurateurs or owners of fashionable 'bistros', country 'potters' and avant-garde booksellers, all seek to prolong the lack of distinction between leisure and work, between militancy and dilettantism, characteristic of the student condition, long after their student days are past. These sellers of symbolic products find in such ideally ambiguous occupations – in which success among a clientele recruited especially from the upper classes depends at least as much on the 'presentable appearance' of the seller and the display of his products, as on the nature and quality of the merchandise – a means of obtaining the best yield from their cultural capital, for here technical competence counts less than familiarity with the culture of the upper classes and mastery of the signs and emblems of distinction and taste. This new type of craftsmanship and trade, with its high cultural input, makes it possible to realise the income potential of the class inheritance directly transmitted by the family, without other academic legitimation, even when it is simply a matter of good manners or even physical appearance (in so far as this results from the internalisation of the body norms current in the ruling class). These trades provide a refuge for the children of the ruling class who have been eliminated by the school. They thus represent new possibilities in the *compensatory strategies* in the reproduction of the ruling class which, in an earlier state of the system of the means of reproduction, worked above all through the transmission of the patrimony (the purchase of land, apartments, partnerships, etc.).

One must refrain here too from describing the collection of changes leading to the restructuring of the middle classes as an aspect of 'mobility', that is to say as a simple displacement of population, for these are in fact correlates of broader changes in the position of these classes *vis-à-vis* the distribution of types of capital, the division of labour of symbolic manipulation, and the maintenance of the established order. Besides the traditional petty bourgeoisie to whom the tasks of physical and ethical control fell (policemen, foremen, teachers, etc.) there now develops the new petty bourgeoisie made up of the occupations devoted to *presentation and representation*, retail and cut-price sellers of advice and imitation symbolic goods who try to minimise everything which separates them from the legitimate sellers of the same goods and services (e.g. physiotherapists

v. doctors, etc.). The new fractions of the middle classes, in their role as intermediaries between the classes – which they share with the other fractions[22] – apply new means of symbolic manipulation corresponding to a new form of domination. To the traditional type of manipulation which is openly ethical and directly oriented towards domestication are added all the forms of subtle manipulation which, substituting seduction for repression, public relations for public force, publicity for authority, aim to produce social integration, which the inculcation of norms had not been able to bring about, by the *imposition of needs*.

Demoralisation and the strategies of reconversion

The tendency of members of a class fraction to reproduce themselves with all their properties, that is to say to reproduce in their children their own condition and position or, conversely, to effect a *reconversion*, i.e. a change in the strategies and means of reproduction intended to reproduce or raise their position whilst abandoning their condition, is determined by their evaluation of the chances of maintaining their position, or to put it another way, by their perception of the present and future position of their class in the social structure and of their own present and future position in that class. This evaluation of the chances of maintaining their position is itself the joint product of subjective estimates about the conditions necessary for maintaining their position (itself determined, with some time-lag, by changes in objective chances) and subjective evaluations of the chances of meeting these conditions. In its turn this estimate controls their strategies of reproduction and thereby, the objective chances of their being maintained in the class.

The choices made with regard to the education of their children (and in particular the choice of a profession) involve speculation which is very similar to the management of a share portfolio, and as a *long-term* speculation is one which expresses all the hopes and estimates of the future of the class. The educational strategies of the threatened categories are only one of many manifestations of the demoralisation of these classes (sometimes explicitly encouraged by the pessimistic forecasts of economists and the self-interested prophecies of politicians and technocrats). Traditionally oriented towards the search for security (as witnessed, for example, by low birth rate) and thus particularly sensitive to the least fluctuation in the indices of insecurity, the artisans and tradesmen seem to have lost all confidence in their economic capacity and particularly in their ability to perpetuate and reproduce themselves. This sort of deep-seated anxiety, which exists relatively independently of the economic situation, affects the long-term aims of the agents and contributes to the policy orientation of entrepreneurs in matters such as investments, stocks and prices, thus ultimately determining the objectives chances of survival of the class. Hence the perception of the future of the class or, perhaps the 'morale' of the class, is related dialectically to the development of economic and commercial activity and, of course, to the strategies of reproduction.[23]

The demoralising effect of a pessimistic portrayal of class future contributes to the class decline which underlies it. It follows that the economic and political competition between classes also operates at the level and through the intermediary of the *symbolic manipulation of the future*; the forecast, that rational form of *prophecy*, helps the coming of the future it prophecies. There is no doubt that economic news reporting, which is content to bring to light and publicise the laws of the market economy which condemn small farmers, craftsmen and tradesmen to decline, objectively serves the interests of those who are economically dominant, since it contributes, through the dialectic of the subjective and the objective, to the realisation of the phenomena it describes. Demoralisation is never anything but a self-fulfilling prophecy.

What is at stake in the conflict between rival prophecies is nothing other than the attitude of the declining classes *vis-à-vis* this decline; either one of demoralisation, which leads to the *rout* of the group, through the sum of individual flights, or one of *mobilisation*, which leads to the collective search for a collective solution to the crisis. What separates rout from mobilisation is fundamentally the possession of symbolic means allowing the group to master the crisis and to organise themselves to put up a collective counter-attack instead of fleeing from the loss, real or imagined, of social status into reactionary resentment and the portrayal of history as a conspiracy. The economic alienation which leads to Fascist despotism is at the same time a logico-political alienation (and not, or not only, a psychological one as Neuman believes). The declining classes and class fractions turn towards racism or, more generally towards the false concretisation of a scapegoat group (Jesuits, free-masons, Jews, Communists, etc.), as the cause of their actual and potential difficulties, because they do not command schemes of explanation which would enable them to understand the situation and to mobilise themselves collectively in order to modify it.

The self-destructive behaviour of the peasants

The peasantry represents a limiting case where the relation between objective determinism and anticipation of its effects is clearly observable. It is because they have internalised their class future, that is to say the image which the urban bourgeoisie has of their future and the

215

destiny which it arranges for them, that the peasants act in ways which tend to threaten their reproduction as a class. In a system based on free enterprise and formal democracy it is impossible to suppress the peasants without their complicity; emigrating towards the towns, sending their children to secondary schools, and marrying their daughters to townsmen are the sort of actions by which the peasants conspire against the future of their own class by making themselves the accomplices of those who seek their disappearance. It is as if, having lost 'control of their own social interactions', the peasants could only undergo the laws of competition which, as Engels says, are imposed on them 'despite anarchy, in and by anarchy'. Thus the weakening of the relative autonomy left to the peasants today, in the domain of symbolic as well as economic exchanges, authorises practices which, like the exportation of girls for or by marriage, contribute to the crisis of peasant society. Statistics establish that the sons of peasants, when they do marry, marry the daughters of peasants whilst the daughters of peasants mostly marry non-peasants.

To explain this mechanism which leads to the celibacy of a significant proportion of the heads of the peasant families, thus threatening the biological and social reproduction of the group, it is not enough to invoke the decline of parental authority (itself in need of explanation) or the differential effect of schooling, as something which reinforces the girls' aversion to the peasant condition. In addition one must also explain why the group continues to expose its girls (and also a proportion of its boys) to such dangerous influences, and hence account for its educational strategies which are themselves, as we shall see, the product of the same contradictory intentions. In fact, these matrimonial strategies of boys and girls – whether they are imposed (as still frequently happens), suggested, merely approved, or unwillingly accepted by the parents – demonstrate, in their mutual antagonism, that the group does not want the same thing for its girls as it does for its boys or, worse, that it basically does not want its boys for its girls even if it wants its girls for its boys. In resorting to rigorously opposite strategies according to whether they have give or take women, peasant families betray the fact that each of them is divided against itself. Whilst endogamy bore witness to the uniqueness of the criteria of evaluation, and thus to the agreement of the group with itself, differential exogamy, and thus the duality of the matrimonial strategies, brings to light the duality of the criteria used by the group to estimate the value of an individual and thus its own value as a class of individuals.

By a logic analogous to that which governs the process of inflation (or when more intense, *panic*) each family or agent contributes to the depreciation of the group as a whole, which is itself at the root of its matrimonial strategies. It is really as if the group conspired against itself (acting as if its right hand did not know what its left hand was doing); it helps to set up the conditions of celibacy – or flight from the community – which it condemns elsewhere as a social disaster. In addition, in giving its girls (which it used to marry into a higher station) to townsmen, it reveals that consciously or unconsciously it accepts what in fact betrays it, the urban image of the present and anticipated value of the peasantry. Always present but repressed, the urban image of the peasant imposes itself on the consciousness of the peasant. The breaking down of the *certitudo sui*, which the peasants had managed to defend against all symbolic attacks, including those of the integrative school, reinforces the very challenge which initiated it. The crisis in *'peasant values'*, which may express itself through *anarchy* in matrimonial exchanges, redoubles the crisis concerning the value of the peasant, his possessions, his products and his way of life on the material and symbolic markets. The internal defeat, felt on the individual level, which is the source of these isolated betrayals each performed under cover of the anonymous solitude of the market, has as its collective unintended consequences the flight of the women and the celibacy of the men.

The same mechanism underlies the change in peasant attitudes towards the educational system, the principal means of symbolic domination by the urban world. Because the school alone appears to be capable of teaching the skills insistently demanded by the economic and symbolic markets, such as the manipulation of the language or the mastery of economic calculation, the resistance which up till then had been put up against schooling and school values fades away.[24] Submission to the values of the school reinforces and accelerates the repudiation of traditional values. The school thereby fulfils its function as a means of symbolic domination, contributing to the conquest of a new market for urban symbolic products. Even when it does not manage to provide the opportunity for appropriating the dominant culture, it can at least inculcate recognition of the legitimacy of this culture and of those who have the means of appropriating it. Symbolic domination accompanies and redoubles economic domination.

The correlation found between rates of school enrolment and rates of celibacy among farm workers (aggregated on a regional level) must not be interpreted as a causal relationship. This would be to forget that the two variables are each the product of a third factor, even if education can contribute in its turn to strengthening the mechanisms which lead to celibacy in men. The unification of the economic and symbolic markets (one aspect of which is the generalising of use of the educational system) tends to transform the system of reference groups in relation to which the peasants define their position in the social structure. The social space of the village,

217

an enclosed microcosm with its own hierarchies (distinguishing for example between 'large' and 'small' peasants), is replaced by a larger social field in which the peasants as a group occupy an inferior and subordinate position. The nature of the peasant condition and his subjective understanding of the social world, derived from the fact that the *locally based networks of acquaintance and system of interdependence* constituted the frame of reference in relation to which the peasants interpreted their social position. Their objective position in the wider social universe surrounding this field and endowed with its social hierarchies, its rulers and its ruled and its class conflicts, had no practical effect on the vision which the peasants had of their world and their position in it. Between the peasants and their objective class condition (defined by economic activity and occupational situation, both associated with a specific position in the relations of reproduction) was interposed the dense *screen* of locally based social relations traditionally associated with farming. One of the factors in the demoralisation of the peasant, which is seen equally clearly in the education of children, in emigration, or in the abandonment of local forms of speech, lies precisely in the breaking down of this screen: the peasant now grasps his condition by comparison with that of the minor civil servant or the manual worker. The comparison is not abstract and imaginary as formerly. It operates in relations of real competition, every time the peasant is obliged to measure himself against non-peasants, particular at the time of marriage. In giving preference to townsmen, women reveal (because they have the power and an interest in so doing) the changed attitude towards the peasant condition which in fact obsesses all members of the peasant community even if it cannot be expressed. They thus assert the dominant criteria of social stratification; and judged on this basis, the products of peasant education, and in particular the peasant mode of behaviour with women, have small value. By the standards prevailing on the dominant market, the peasant becomes a 'peasant' in the towndweller's derogatory sense. In the logic of racism which is also found between classes, the peasant is obliged in his practice to reckon with the image of himself which the townsmen give him; and he still recognises even in his *denials* the devaluation which the townsman makes him undergo.

The role of the educational system in accelerating this circular process of devaluation is clear. In the first place, there is no doubt that the influence of formal instruction is now strong enough to undermine the strategies of reinforcement by means of which families seek to make their children invest in the land rather than in the school – when, that is, the school itself has not been enough to discourage them by its negative sanctions. The resulting deculturalisation is exercised less by virtue of the pedagogical message itself than through the intermediary of the experience of studying and enjoying the quasi-student condition. The prolongation of compulsory education and the lengthening of the period of study turns the children of farmers into 'schoolchildren', 'students' even, cut off by all their experience, their life-style and, in particular, their temporal rhythms from the rest of peasant society.[25] This new experience tends in practice to destroy the values transmitted by the family and to redirect their affective and economic investments away from the reproduction of the (family) line, towards the reproduction, by the lone individual of the line's position in the social structure. In giving them the same training as the children of salary- and wage-earners (workers and office-workers) who are themselves future salary- and wage-earners, the school makes them feel that it is possible and even probable that they will gain access to wage-earning status and thus have the chance of enjoying in adolescence the status of an adult endowed with a *personal income* and the rights linked to this status.

Besides having the effect of cutting the farmers off from their means of biological reproduction (through celibacy) and social reproduction (through the contradiction between the family's values and the values transmitted by the educational system) these mechanisms combine to produce a catastrophic picture of the future of the class. The technocratic prophecy about the decline of the peasantry reinforced this view by giving meaning and coherence to the various disparate indices of doom encountered in daily life. Thus, by a kind of circular process, the very experience of the agents can only confirm the experts' most pessimistic views of the future. Without succumbing to conspiracy theory the objective effects of the academic process can be seen to be too directly adjusted to the technocratic view of the demise of the peasant class for the almost instantaneous adaptation of the supply of education to the growth of demand to be the result of an automatic harmony. Industrial concentration and the flight from the country, often imputed to the 'natural tendencies of the economy', are also the product of an economic policy which by systematic intervention reinforces the mechanisms adapted to serve the interests of the dominant fractions of the ruling class. The greater proximity of the educational apparatus which resulted from the siting of secondary schools in small and medium-sized areas (and from the depopulation of hamlets and small rural communities to the benefit of the towns) has indisputably fulfilled a political function, consciously or unconsciously sought. It has helped to accelerate the schooling and, thus, the deculturation of the children of farmers (and also of small country traders and artisans) since instruction is no longer hinged on the boarding requirement, precipitating, at the same time, the decrease in the size of these social classes.

Doubtless it has also prevented the revolt of the uprooted by transmuting their objective bankruptcy into reconversion, their proletarisation into social promotion, and by providing adolescents excluded from traditional activities not with a job, but at least with a provisional occupation, staying on at school.

Conclusion

The reconversion strategies employed by families belonging to very different classes and sections of classes which had in common the fact that they previously secured their reproduction mainly by the transmission of economic capital, have had as their main effect the establishment of a relative consensus on the conditions of access to dominant, and thus rare, positions in the social structure. By tending to make educational qualifications at least the formal condition for the appropriation of profit and the universal yardstick of the value of economic agents, they have contributed to the unification of the markets in economic and symbolic assets. In other words the number of scarce and valued commodities has become limited whilst the number of agents and groups competing for these objects has multiplied, thus intensifying competition itself. Put another way, by intensifying their use of educational institutions and thereby increasing the number of qualifications put into the labour market, the classes and fractions who in the past made relatively little use of the school, have compelled the classes and class fractions whose reproduction was chiefly or exclusively assured by the school to increase their investments in order to maintain the relative scarcity of their qualifications and, in consequence, their position in the class structure.

The educational market thus becomes one of the most important loci of the class struggle, which, by the logic of escalation, gives rise to a general and constant growth in the demand for education or, to put it another way, an inflation of academic qualifications. Strategies of reconversion are nothing but the sum of the actions and reactions by which each group tries to maintain or change its position in the social structure or, more precisely, to maintain its position by changing. In the particular (but more common) case where the actions by which each group strives to win new advantages over other groups, and thus to *transform the structure* of objective relations between classes, are counteracted (i.e. *sequentially invalidated*) by the reactions of other groups which themselves are oriented towards the same goals, the reproduction of the class structure operates through a *translation* of the distribution of academic qualifications held by each class or section of a class. For example, this can be grasped in terms of differential chances of entry to higher education which map onto social origins and also have the effect of inducing the continued growth of accumulated cultural capital. This conversion process provides the clearest and the most specific demonstration of the academic mode of reproduction, which can conserve the *ordinal ranking* of the different classes, that is to say the *social order* in the double sense of the word, only at the price of a change in the essential properties of each of them, namely a re-conversion of economic capital into cultural capital or an increase in the cultural capital already owned.

The academic polarity between stability and change must be abandoned in order to understand that the reproduction of the class structure is not subject to the perpetuation of particular social classes as concrete groups defined by the sum of their substantive characteristics, observed at a given moment in time. The reproduction of the social structure, i.e. of the distribution of the different types of capital between groups and classes – of which a number of qualities (income, level of education, etc.) can be modified without any change in their dominant or dominated position *vis-à-vis* other groups – can be realised in and through the translation of the structure whenever the members of the dominated classes enter separately, through statistical actions and reactions, in the free play of competition, i.e. in that form of class struggle which is imposed on them by the dominant class.

Notes

1 The analyses presented here are based on a body of empirical research, the findings of which (particularly the statistical findings) have been published in detail elsewhere. See especially P. Bourdieu, 'Reproduction culturelle et reproduction sociale', *Informations sur les sciences sociales*, vol. X, no. 2, 1971, pp. 45–79; P. Bourdieu, L. Boltanski, P. Maldidier, 'La Défense du corps', *Informations sur les sciences sociales*, vol. X, no. 4, 1971; L. Boltanski, 'L'Espace positionnel. Multiplicité des positions institutionnelles et habitus de classe', *Revue française de sociologie*, vol. XIV, 1973, pp. 3–26; P. Bourdieu, L. Boltanski, M. de Saint Martin, 'Les Stratégies de reconversion', *Informations sur les sciences sociales*, vol. XII, no. 5, 1973, pp. 61–113.

2 In accordance with the antithesis introduced in 1932 by A. A. Berle and G. C. Means, *The Modern Corporation and Private Property*, New York, Macmillan, 1932.

3 Statistical analysis of the social and educational characteristics of the heads of the 300 largest French enterprises established that in 1972, the larger the enterprise, the more likely it was that its head held a degree; and that the proportion of heads without higher education qualifications decreased sharply between 1952 and 1972. (The study by W. L. Warner of managers of businesses shows as well that the proportion of sons of

owners decreases in the course of time to the advantage of degree-holders. See W. L. Warner, 'The corporation man', in E. S. Mason (ed.), *The Corporation in Modern Society*, New York, Atheneum, 1972, pp. 106–21.)

The change in the nature of enterprises has also been accompanied by a diversification of the channels of training, corresponding to the diversification of positions within the field: the decrease in the relative proportion of 'polytechniciens' (graduates of the École Polytechnique) amongst managers between 1952 and 1972 (from 36 per cent in 1952 to 33·5 per cent in 1962 and 24·5 per cent in 1972) was compensated particularly by the growth in the relative proportion of heads who had graduated from the École des Hautes Études Commerciales (HEC) on the one hand, and from the Institut d'Études Politiques (IEP) and from the law faculties on the other. Everything seems to indicate that this new type of recruitment corresponds to the growth of multi-national links and of relations between the public sector and the private sector. Possessing a body of skills of a new type, such as handling foreign languages, a practical knowledge of company operations and of marketing techniques and advertising, heads who are graduates of institutions such as HEC or the Institut Européen d'Administration des Affaires (INSEAD) are predisposed to seek positions in multi-national companies: they contrast in many ways with heads who are graduates of an engineering institution and whose interests, bound up with a specific enterprise and essentially localised, tend more towards production than marketing and distribution, towards the internal management of the enterprise rather than the assessment of market prospects. As for the growth in the proportion of managers who are graduates of law faculties or who have been trained at the Institut d'Études Politiques in Paris, it may be bound up with a growth in the interrelations between the economic field and government administration. More precisely this may be linked to the entrance into the industrial field often through the intermediary of the nationalised or semi-public sector, of agents whose academic career and whose competence in economics and political science rather than in science or technology leads them to ocupy the newest (and most risky) positions in the administrative field and to make themselves the bearers and exporters of ideological changes associated with the progress made by the École Nationale d'Administration (ENA) at the expense of the École Polytechnique as the source of reproduction of top-level public officials.

4 It appears that the bureaucratisation of enterprises is also associated with an increase in the payments in kind taken by the cadres out of the profits of the enterprise in the form of travel, official housing, cars, services, meals, etc.

5 The change in the mode of appropriation of the profits of capital and the substitution of salary for rent brings about, (via changes in the relationship to time, i.e. from an immediate to a deferred mode of taking out profits), a series of systematic changes in the modes of thought, career plans, habits of consumption and, more generally, in the whole life-cycle which will be the subject of a later analysis.

6 In fact, the change in the mode of appropriation of enterprises and the relative dissociation of the stockholders from the managers has served as a pretext for the myth, which Keynes was perhaps the first to express, of the 'tendency of the large enterprise to socialise itself' (J. M. Keynes, 'The end of laissez-faire', 1926, republished in *Essays in Persuasion*, London, Macmillan, 1931, pp. 314–15). This myth, which leads to the application of a single logic to every public or private enterprise, forms the basis of the ideology which portrays the head of an enterprise as a public official and the public official as the head of an enterprise. The significance of this antithesis between owners and managers is understood only when it is perceived that it is the mainspring of the ideology of the 'decline of the ruling class' or of the 'democratisation of elites'.

7 In addition to the fact that the managers of large firms are also in a number of cases the owners of smaller subsidiaries, so that the 'managers' also possess, for the most part, the 'rights of ownership' (which is undoubtedly the best means of getting rid of the owners), the 'salary' of the manager, made up, to a large extent, of 'bonuses' and fringe benefits, tends more and more to take a form which distinguishes it from the 'salary' of the subordinate cadres and *a fortiori* of the employees. As for the owners, they tend more and more, even when their business is small and managed in a traditional way, to allow themselves a proportion of the profit in the form of salary. When the firm achieves the status of a legal subject, to be protected for its own sake (independently of the owners), this is doubtless the key milestone in the process of dissociation between the entrepreneur holding real or personal rights and the entrepreneur with specific interests. More precisely, it signals the separation between the domestic enterprise and the economic enterprise, on which the restructuring of the economic field and the accompanying change in the mode of enterprise appropriation, as sanctioned by commercial law, tend to confer a permanent existence, shielded against the biological or social accidents which may affect the individuals or groups who make it operate.

8 Thus, for example, R. A. Gordon (*Business Leadership in the Corporation*, Washington, University of California Press, 1966) distinguishes at least eight types of agents – individual or collective – invested with power over the enterprise.

9 The inertia of the educational system and the efforts of holders of qualifications threatened with devaluation tend to limit the repercussions (visible nevertheless) in the field of the 'grandes écoles' of changes in the economic field: the struggle between 'grand corps', that is to say between former students of the rival écoles which give access to them, can only however intensify in a period when, as at the present time, the relation between the means of reproduction of the controlling class and the structure of this class undergoes transformation.

10 Every strategy of reproduction may be described as a positive or negative strategy according to whether one examines it in terms of its functions of inclusion or in terms of its functions of exclusion which combine with one another to maintain the *numerus clausus* of reproducible agents. In their negative form these strategies generally consist

either in limiting the number of biological products of the class in such a way that they do not exceed the number of positions (fertility strategies), or in excluding from the class a part of the biological products of the class by transferring them to other classes or by keeping them in an ambiguous status or one cut off at the borders of the class (examples which come to mind, in the aristocratic mode of reproduction, are those of the enforced celibacy of girls consigned to religious institutions or the departure of the youngest sons for the army or the colonies). The specific mode of reproduction now tending to become dominant in the ruling class rests above all on the fact that the negative strategies, whose functions for the class as a whole are as indispensable as those of disinheritance in former modes of reproduction, are not exercised by the family but by the school. This appears as the independent and inescapable action of an external force even when the school serves its objective and collective class interests.

11 On statistics and the axiom of *omni et nullo*, see G. Bachelard, *Le Nouvel Esprit scientifique*, Paris, Presses Universitaires de France, 1934, pp. 113–14.

12 To grasp the contradiction in all its potency, one must include in the number of victims not only those that the system condemns, 'the failures', but also the holders of qualifications normally giving right of entry to a bourgeois profession who are unable to get these qualifications honoured in the market. The overproduction of heirs with degrees has an inflationary effect which was ignored so long as the family had control over reproduction and adjusted the number of endowments to the number of positions to be reproduced.

13 The development of the mode of reproduction is clearly linked to changes in the social representation of legitimate inheritance or even of the legitimacy of inheritance, as well as in this case to an increased awareness about the arbitrary nature of the direct transmission of inheritance.

14 The same observations have been made in the United States, where the growth of education associated with an intensification of academic selection (which increases the social homogeneity of each institution or level of teaching) tends to counterbalance the greater freedom which young people enjoy in the choice of their spouse, because of the slackening of traditional family bonds (cf. B. K. Eckland, 'New mating boundaries in education', *Social Biology*, vol. 17, no. 4, December 1970, pp. 269–77).

15 Statistical action tends to give social mechanisms all the appearances of natural ones. Because they are all based on statistical aggregation, mechanisms as different as the market (economic or matrimonial), the vote or the educational means of reproduction tend to prevent agents from apprehending the sum of the actions and constituent reactions making up the processes in which they themselves are immersed. Because their patterning is at the level of aggregates and because of their dispersion in time and space these statistical effects conceal the mechanisms of social reproduction. Thus statistical action, the product of a creation which is organised without being concerted, tends to

confer on social mechanisms the universality, necessity and innocence characteristic of natural phenomena. The declining importance of the mechanisms of mutual acquaintance (and thus of mutual control) the operation of which is that much easier in smaller social units, where the different dimensions of existence tend to be merged, is perhaps the necessary condition for the establishment of depersonalised mechanisms of social reproduction. One sees that the use of statistical techniques as a means of totalling up the actions and reactions which individual agents tend to carry out or undergo separately, without themselves being able to understand them as a series, tends to reserve for specialists the monopoly of the synthetic perception of the movements generated by the action of the mechanisms of the reproduction and hence the monopoly of the manipulation and diffusion of the synthetic image of the way in which the social order works. Finally, if this statistical mode of social action is combined with ideological procedures of suppression and censorship, (and perhaps it is more effective than them, because it is more impersonal and more invisible), the dissimulation of the mechanisms of social reproduction, the ideological utilisation of the statistical data concerning phenomena which conform to a statistical logic (e.g. consumer statistics or pre-election opinion polls) can constitute a fundamental means of mystifying the mechanisms which form the mainspring of social order.

16 It follows that outside the strictly educational market, the degree is worth what its holder is worth economically and socially, the yield of educational capital (a reconverted form of cultural capital) being a function of the economic and social capital which can be devoted to exploiting it (cf. P. Bourdieu, 'Reproduction culturelle et reproduction sociale', *Informations sur les sciences sociales*, vol. X, no. 2, 1971, pp. 45–72).

17 Human capital theories could rightfully impute the relative growth of the rate of returns on certified cultural capital (in relation to the profits of economic capital) to the change in the relative scarcity of the different factors of production linked to technological changes, if and only if, the salary offered in the labour market to the holders of the specific degrees always closely corresponded to the amount of cultural capital which degree holders invest in enterprises by virtue of their employment in the company. And that is hardly ever the case, even in the most favourable market, that is to say in the educational system, where one observes differences in careers based on the same qualification between teachers of different social backgrounds.

18 Cf. J. Schmookler, 'Technological progress and the modern American corporation', in Mason (ed.) op. cit., pp. 141–65. Previously invention demanded creative aptitude rather than training, and thus constituted a risky process. This was because of the *rudimentary state of science and technology*, which were more easily mastered; and linked to the simplicity of scientific culture was a corresponding simplicity of the equipment used. Thus less well-to-do inventors could equip their own workshops without the assistance of employers or with the help of private individuals. Today, as the decline in the proportion of

independent researchers in patent statistics shows, invention depends on conditions which are hardly ever fulfilled except in large research enterprises.

19 Because the relative growth or decline in the size of a specific group, for example a socio-occupational group, is frequently accompanied by a change in its characteristics, simple comparison of the change in size of different socio-occupational categories between two dates gives only a very limited idea of the transformation of the social structure during that period. The reification of social taxonomies (for example socio-occupational taxonomies) helps to maintain an illusion (that essential characteristics are unchanged) which justifies the most cavalier and the most hazardous diachronic comparisons. The same illusion is at the root of the *morphologism* which tends either to ignore social changes in the groups studied which accompany the change in their size, or at best to view them as the mechanical results of a change in the density of the group. Morphological schemes which are valid for animal societies where ecological equilibrium is essentially a function of the relation between the size of different species and the relative scarcity of their means of sustenance, are extremely dangerous when hastily and mechanically transposed to human societies, particularly to stratified societies (which invest different groups and their material and symbolic products with a very different symbolic, and thus economic, value according to the dominant or dominated position which they occupy in the social structure).

20 Between 1962 and 1971, the number of supermarkets rose from 200 to 1800 (to which one might add 100 hypermarkets) and the number of self-service concerns, which represented 4 per cent of the food trade in 1962, represented 35 per cent of the total by 1970 (cf. M. Fauston, *L'Evolution du commerce français depuis 1962, d'après l'opinion des commercants*, Paris, Collections de l'INSEE, 13th April 1972, p. 29, Série Enterprises). 'Integrated' commercial enterprises (companies with large cut-price stores, companies with multiple branches, large specialised supermarkets, food and trade co-operatives) comprised in 1970 27·1 per cent of the total of retail commercial concerns compared with 15 per cent in 1960 and 11·1 per cent in 1950. In the food trade, as with industrial goods, one sees since 1960 a net acceleration in concentration, the size of the large commercial organisations increasing appreciably (cf. C. Quin with the assistance of J. P. Fremont, *Tableau de bord de la distribution francaise*, Paris, Groupe de recherche sur la distribution et les modes de vie, December 1971, pp. 58–9). One must also emphasise the growth in the size of the new stores; up to the present time, more than 3500 multiple-department stores or large specialised supermarkets have been recorded with sales areas of more than 400 m^2 compared with less than 1000 ten years ago (cf. Quin, op. cit. p. 7).

21 As witnessed by, for example, the growth in the size of professions devoted to the sale of advice or of professions which act as agencies, and perhaps more generally the growth in the majority of symbolic goods and services offered in the markets which supply the new

sections of the controlling class who, being holders of cultural capital, are disposed to attach a price to the goods or services in which cultural capital is incorporated.

22 Whose position and, at the same time, whose attitudes, are changed by their very existence.

23 Demonstrated by the quasi-perfect agreement between the 'development of the economic situation', observed retrospectively, and the plans of entrepreneurs in so far as they are revealed by 'periodic surveys on the economic situation'.

24 The progressive decline in the value of vernacular speech in the market of symbolic exchanges is but one particular instance of the devaluation which affects all the products of peasant education: the unification of this market has been fatal for all these products, manners, objects, clothes, dismissed as old-fashioned or vulgar or artificially conserved by local scholars in the fossilised state of folklore.

25 The longer the children of agricultural workers have been in the educational system, the more likely they are to leave agricultural work. Amongst the children of agricultural workers, those who have followed a general or technical course of study, at a secondary or higher level, are the most likely to turn away from agriculture, in contrast to those who have had only primary education or an agricultural training.

9 The religious condition of Europe
David Martin

What follows here concentrates on certain key contemporary issues of the European situation. The first of these is the relation of religion to national awareness, and also to regional, sub-cultural awareness. It attempts to provide classifications and generalisations governing religion and the national centre, religion and the regional periphery. The second area of concentration is that of power and the different types of power nexus and concatenations of conflict. This analysis of power links up with an analysis of secular elites, especially Marxist elites but also liberal ones in their pursuit of hegemony. It assumes there is a long-standing tension between elite power in the nation-state and independent structures of religious loyalty or criticism. The last section is particularly concerned to explore that tension. There are further foci of attention, notably the impact of migration and the general lineaments of continental practice.

I Religion and nationhood

Europe is a unity by virtue of having possessed one Caesar and one God, i.e. by virtue of Rome. It is a diversity by virtue of the existence of nations. The patterns of European religion derive from the tension and the partnership between Caesar and God, and from the relationship between religion and the search for national integrity and identity. The solution and dissolution of the partnership between Caesar and God, state and Church will be touched on below, but the first task for analysis concerns the relationship of religion to the nation-state. Where Caesar himself does not demand a worship complementing the worship of the deity the nation-state itself demands adulation. Christianity may be a religion which rejects the worship of Caesar or the exaltation of the ethnic group but in order to retain even the possibility of suggesting more worthy

228

objects of praise it must be positively related to the national consciousness, particularly as this is highlighted in a myth of national origins. A positive overlap with the national myth is a necessary condition for a lively and widespread attachment to religion: the majority of people cannot bear too sharp a contradiction between their universalistic faith and their group identity. Of course, other factors may affect that liveliness and that attachment in very large measure, but if national myth and religious faith are contradictory the social power of religion is restricted. The religious faith which survives such a contradiction is likely to be composed of refugees from the national myth looking for a sectarian haven capable of creating an alternative society.

In most countries of contemporary Europe it is of enormous importance that the existence of the nation and its heroic folk memory is either rooted directly in religion or positively related to it. If we consider first the northern Protestant nations this is true without exception, although in some cases the original Reformation was more a dynastic decision than a matter of national awareness, which meant that the collaboration of Protestant religion and national self-consciousness was most marked in the period of liberal nation building in the nineteenth century. In Norway and Denmark, for example, the Haugean movement and the Grundvigian movement both, in different ways, accelerated and deepened national self-awareness in the nineteenth century.[1] In England and Holland, by contrast, the events of the Reformation itself and the wars which succeeded it indelibly welded together a land and a people. Both land and people received their founding myths at this time: the defeat of the Armada, the lifting of the siege of Leyden. Sweden's national myth became coextensive with the triumphs of its Protestant conquering hero, Gustavus Adolphus. Switzerland is a little more complicated, since its founding myth of independence against Austria antedates the Reformation, but Swiss national identity was gradually assimilated to Protestantism, particularly as the active sector of Swiss life was Protestant and the active centre of Calvinist Protestantism throughout the continent was at Geneva. Much later the Protestant-Catholic war of 1847 further linked the maintenance of Swiss unity to Protestantism. The most obvious example of the coincidence of faith and nation is provided, then and now, by Scotland. The main organ of Scottish identity was and is its Church.

In Catholic societies the relationship is more complex, partly because of the continuing war over the existence of an over-arching loyalty to Rome. In certain cases the identity of faith and nationality is absolutely clear. In the Iberian peninsula, for example, the process of making Catholicism identical with nationality occurred through eight hundred years of war with the Islamic southern part of the peninsula. In Poland the Church was the focus of national unity during the political fragmentations of the twelfth to fourteenth centuries, and then coalesced with romantic nineteenth-century nationalism to forge an almost total identity of nation and religion against foreign dominance. Again, in Ireland, though the Church was not necessarily in the forefront of nationalist agitation against English dominance, it provided the focus and the symbols around which the sense of Irish unity was maintained. In Belgium Catholics and Liberals together fought against Austrian and French and then against Dutch control, so that Catholicism was very positively associated with the independence which Belgium eventually achieved in 1830. And indeed, sharing this achievement with the Liberals meant that the two forces need not initially polarise or attempt to eliminate each other from the sense of pride in national origins.

In other cases, however, the relationship of Catholicism to national consciousness is more ambiguous: in France, Czechoslovakia and Italy the Catholic Church had to contend with the myths of liberal, secular nationalism; in Czechoslovakia (strictly in Czech Lands) and in Hungary it had to contend with national roots in Protestantism. In the French case the opposition between the nation as integrated by Catholicism under the old regime and the liberal nationalism proclaimed by the Republic divided the myth between irreconcilable opponents. Clerical and anti-clerical factions fought over the banner of the nation; an old *intégrisme* confronted the new *intégrisme*. It was fertile soil for secular religions.[2] Particularly during the period of the Third Republic from 1870 up to the separation of Church and state in 1905 the spirit of Jeanne d'Arc faced implacable opposition from prophets like Jules Ferry preaching a religion of the Fatherland.[3] Between the world wars there was a characteristically French conflict between the right-wing, Catholic, anti-papal Action Française and Republicans, whether Freemasons, Jews, Protestants or materialists.[4] In Italy the conflict of secular nationalism with the Church was even clearer. The Pope was an enemy of the Italian nation. The consequence was a secularist liberal intelligentsia and the growing influence of freemasonry and deism in the elite, including the monarchy itself. On the other hand it was inevitably a matter of national pride that Catholicism was Roman and the Pope Italian. And in any case the attitude of the Church to Italian unity had not been one with that of the Pope.

Czechoslovakia is a different sort of case.[5] The nation was born in the proto-Protestant Hussite movement and persistently in Czech history the baneful influence of Germans and of the Catholic Church were linked together. This sentiment runs all the way from Hus to the liberal Catholic 'Away from Rome' movement and the establishment of the Czech National Church. Hence the success of the

Counter-Reformation, though finally assured by the Battle of the White Mountain in 1620, rested uneasily on a base which gave it little support. Since Protestantism was largely eliminated by the Counter-Reformation, the national feeling found it difficult to root itself in loyalty to religion whether Catholic or Protestant. Catholicism was disqualified by its associations; Protestantism was largely destroyed. There is perhaps an echo of this in Hungary where the birth of nationalism and the rise of economic development were partly associated with Calvinism.

In the Balkans and in Russia Orthodoxy is plainly associated with national awareness. In the cases of Serbia, Bulgaria, Romania and Greece the Church was the vehicle of identity during the period of 'the Turkish yoke'. In Russia itself the Church was the soul of nationhood during the early period of domination by invaders from the East. To this day part of the strength of Orthodoxy lies in a feeling that being Russian and being Orthodox amounts to the same thing. The identity of other nations now in the Soviet Union is likewise nourished by Churches: the Armenian and Georgian Orthodox Churches, the Uniate Church of the Ukraine, the Catholic Church in Lithuania, the Lutheranism of the Volga Germans.

Germany itself is a complex case. There is on the one hand the fact that it is the country of Luther's Reformation and there is the important relationship of Luther's Bible to the German language. But the splitting up of Germany into Catholic and Protestant princedoms, respectively concentrated in south and west, and north and east (Protestant Württemburg and Catholic Silesia excepted) refracted any direct connection between religion and the overarching myth of the nation. However, when national unification came it was under the aegis and dominance of a Protestant power, Prussia, in a situation where Catholicism retained some identification with the national feeling of Southern Germans. The 'secular' religion of German nationalism under Hitler and its war against both Catholicism and the 'Confessing' Lutherans further complicates the picture. So does the fact that a victorious atheist Russia has ever since threatened Germany and divided its territory, thus encouraging a religious counter-definition amongst West Germans.

Cases where it is very difficult for the national myth to coalesce with religion arise where there are several highly distinctive religions within a national border, each with major followings. In this situation no religion can carry the national identity and indeed each religion works divisively against it. In Yugoslavia, Catholic Croatia and Orthodox Serbia both represent unions of religion and nationhood, while Bosnia is largely Muslim. The new state must suppress the divisive element without going so far as to revive aspirations to

231

nationhood by sheer repression, which would in any case be interpreted as favouring one or other of the rival 'nations'. Alongside
this cat-and-mouse policy there has to be built up an overarching
secular myth based on the heroic activities of the partisans, socialist
reconstruction and national independence and unity, especially against
Russia and other unfriendly nations. Albania's situation is similar,
since neither of its three religions, Catholic, Orthodox and Muslim,
can conceivably carry the national identity. Catholicism is in any
case compromised by association with Italian Fascist colonialism.
However, while Yugoslavia defends its independence against
Russian hegemony by openings to the West, Albania does so by
association with China—at least until recently.

In the paragraphs above two factors have been mentioned which
bear on the question of the efficacy of the association between nation
and religion and they ought now to be discussed. One factor is the
relationship to Russian hegemony, now and in the past, and the
other is the extent to which religion in a given country can plausibly
be associated with an antecedent right-wing or Fascist regime. In the
case of Bulgaria Russia is the 'elder brother' both historically and
now, and the Orthodox Church can be seen as compromised by
association with the pre-war regime. Hence the pattern of Russian
atheism and severity towards religion is likely to be faithfully followed.
Eastern Germany also follows the Russian pattern, partly because its
leadership was established to do so. Any connection with the Fascist
taint was to be rigidly eschewed and this meant a break with *all*
previous continuities, including the Church. The break was the
more necessary because the Church was continuous with the culture
of a single Germany. Those who could not make the break fled to
the West, thereby further weakening any ideological resistance
within the DDR. The spirit of the new state had to be remade anew
and this meant a severe control of the socialisation process and the
elimination of its religious element. German Communist youth was
to worship sport. In short, the old nationalism was unusable and its
associations tainted. In the case of Poland, both historically and
now, Russia is a source of fear and domination, and the Catholic
Church, repressed by Russians and Germans, heroically resisted
both. One Polish priest in five died in Nazi camps. Hence the association of religion and nation is reinforced and the Russian pattern
seen as unacceptable. Romania conforms more to the Polish situation, particularly since it is sandwiched militantly between Russia
itself and pro-Russian Bulgaria. It needs to assert its independence,
which partly accounts for its pro-Chinese policy. The Church,
furthermore, represents a Latin culture inserted between Slav
cultures, and pride in this Latin character assists identification with
the Church. Again, though the Church had some association with

the pre-war, right-wing regime and with the 'Iron Guard', the Patriarch Justinian established cordial relationships with Communists during and after the war, thus lessening the plausibility of any compromising identification with Fascism.

Czechoslovakia, Hungary, Yugoslavia and Finland provide intermediate cases. Czechoslovakia's proto-Protestant myth can be reinterpreted as a religious anticipation of a class revolution, especially as regards its radical wing. This myth holds no danger for the regime since the body of practising Protestants in Czechoslovakia is small. Furthermore, when the West acquiesced in the dissection of Czechoslovakia, Communism (and hence Russia) was the only possible source of national recovery for many Czechs. On the other hand Czechoslovakia had been exposed to secular liberalism for which Russia also represented a threat, and this threat was finally realised in 1968. Indeed there was at this time some revival of interest in religion and it is significant that the martyrdom which made the deepest impression was that of a Protestant theological student, Jan Palach. In Hungary there was also a fear of Russian domination, realised in 1956, but the position of the Church, though aligned with Hungarian nationalism, was weakened by association with pre-war, right-wing regimes and its feudal character and property. Yugoslavia's fears of invasion were never realised; and the Ustacha regime in Croatia, established in the war, was not only right-wing but deeply compromised by the slaughter of large numbers of Serbs.[6] Nevertheless the Church itself was only partly involved in these nationalist excesses, and still remains the one guardian of Croatian national self-awareness. As the regime itself is atheist, Croatian self-consciousness has to rely on its historic religion. Finland was invaded by Russia in 1939 but eventually retained its independence. The Lutheran Church is strengthened by its association with the heroic war of independence, yet weakened by the fact that it had previously largely aligned itself with the right in Finnish politics.[7]

The relationships between nationship and religious identification so far discussed all bear on the present situation, some directly and closely, some in a more implicit manner. For example, in nations like Britain or Holland where the myth of origins is some four centuries old, where the external threats once associated with it have long since receded and where nationhood is not experiencing any other contemporary threat, the sense of linkage between nation and religion lies dormant. In nations like Poland there has never been a time when the myth is irrelevant; and very similar threats are posed at the present time to those of the past. So the myth is as green and necessary and explicit as ever it was. This is worth underlining since some elements in the above analysis are more plainly of direct relevance to the present; none however have no relevance to the present. The candles burn before Palach's grave in Prague; the audience at the final London Promenade concert sings 'And did those feet in ancient time, Walk upon England's mountains green'. Religion maintains itself by songs and candles. As Ireland illustrates, King William's defeat of the Irish at the Boyne is part of contemporary reality. Like the candles it still burns.

Certain conclusions follow from this analysis and these are worth explicit statement. First, an indissoluble union of Church and nation arises in those situations where the Church has been the sole available vehicle of nationality against foreign domination: Greece, Cyprus, Poland, Belgium, Ireland, Croatia. In such countries bishops have spoken for nations and in Cyprus actually led one in the independence struggle as well as after it. If the struggle for independence becomes self-conscious at the time of romantic nationalism then the union is a peculiarly potent one, with overtones of a suffering Messianic role. Such one finds in Poland. As will be seen later, all the countries mentioned remain areas of high practice and belief: the symbols must not only exist but be seen to be visibly tended. The Greeks must celebrate the Resurrection, the Irish climb St Patrick's Mountain, and hundreds of thousands of Poles make a pilgrimage to our Lady of Czestochowa. In religion these are present facts. The myth of identity is strengthened further wherever the dominated group have been at the border with another faith: Spain, Austria, Malta, Greece and Poland (at different times) with Islam, Poland with Protestantism and Orthodoxy, Ireland with Protestantism. These are the unions of religion and nation based on suffering and threat. Indeed wherever there is a threat and a border situation the nation is pushed towards its historic faith, even sometimes when it is officially atheist but faced nevertheless with a threat from an atheistic country: this is the contemporary situation of Romania and Poland, and to a much lesser extent of Hungary and Czechoslovakia. Germany and Austria are also the defeated located at a border with atheistic victors. And just as there are unions of faith and nation based on suffering so there are unions, *less potent*, based on glory: notably the empires of Holland, Spain, Sweden, Austria and England. These unions are, *ceteris paribus*, much more relaxed; the symbols are less in need of being visibly tended. The most potent unions of all combine past glory and present suffering; once again, Poland.

Ambiguous or negative cases arise under the following circumstances. First, there is an ambiguity where domination restores a religion, as the Counter-Reformation restored Catholicism in Hungary and in Czech Lands, yet has to leave the myth in the hands of a beaten minority. Second, there is ambiguity where a revolution forces the nation to split into two and an old 'intégrisme' confronts a new 'intégrisme'. This is most likely to happen in Catholic countries since Catholicism is inherently an 'intégriste' and organicist system. Third, there is ambiguity where the myths cannot be shared by the whole nation since different areas are dominated by differing religions. This situation is exacerbated where delayed or historically 'late' unification finds these differences a nuisance, irrelevant or positively divisive: examples are Germany, Albania and Yugoslavia. Fourth, there is ambiguity if the ecclesiastical authority explicitly opposes national unification, as in Italy.

II Ideal types of relation between power and countervailing power

Thus far this analysis has concentrated on religion and nationhood as complementary or antagonistic guardians of overall group identity and of the master symbols of belonging. It is now necessary to introduce a second element: power and countervailing power as they relate to patterns of norms. A general discussion of the basic types of relation between power and countervailing power is a prerequisite for elaborating a fundamental categorisation of sorts of religious culture. The relationship of religion to power arises because it is not only the bearer of identities but a source of legitimacy and of philosophies supporting legitimacy.

Power and alternative power exist in varying relationships: a skewed balance set within agreed limits of tolerable diversity, a confrontation of irreconcilables attempting to skew the balance very heavily one way or the other, an overwhelming monopoly of power. The first comprises a long-term sediment of tolerance, so institutionalised over a long period of time as to seem normatively necessary. It generally derives from past situations where each side had to recognise that total victory was impossible and opted for limited tolerances which were susceptible to slow enlargement. The apparently necessary nature of the norm of tolerance acts so as to constrict the exercise of power, and each successful constriction adds to the likelihood of future constraint. Stability thus achieved permits a widening of agreed limits and as limits are widened stability is increased, thereby allowing a further extension of limits. Such a breadth of tolerance, though it must stop short and sharp before the possibility of total freedom, makes extreme opposition or violence appear perverse. If however tolerance presses against these very wide limits it questions legitimacy itself and initiates the anarchic dissolution of society.

The second type of power relationship, which comprises the confrontation of irreconcilables, is composed of rival forces which have had a taste of total authority and desire to taste it yet again. For them the aim is not tolerance and compromise but victory. This

235

unifies both sides and disciplines them amongst themselves because the prospect of a lost battle involves the likelihood of total and permanent defeat. Such an anticipation increases violence and bitterness and creates a tendency to spirals of escalating bitterness. At any point where one side might feel in favour of accommodation it is unlikely that the other side feels similarly; and neither side dare rely on such reciprocity of anticipation. These embattled situations lead each side to elaborate philosophies which commit the soul of the nation into its keeping and define opponents as traitors. Moreover, the aspiration to a philosophy expressing one's viewpoint holistically leads to doctrines whereby each side regards the happy future of humanity as coextensive with its own victory, thereby increasing the likelihood of inhumanity and legitimising it. The two principles of keeping the nations's soul and anticipating the future of humanity may be yoked together, thereby making tolerance of those who resist equivalent to condoning treason and colluding with crimes against humanity's future. Prior to victory opponents are conceived as moral criminals; after victory the law confirms the deliverances of morality.

The third type of power relationship arises after victory, either for those who affirm older principles of 'intégrisme' sometimes under the banner of a nationalised Catholic ideology, or for those who affirm new forms of 'intégrisme', normally within a Marxist framework. Confining comment to the latter it is clear that any system which proclaims the end of ontological *laissez-faire* must find the tolerance of error morally offensive and see error and evil as complementary. It may declare an initial confidence in their elimination through natural social processes, but faced with the malignant virulence of 'superstition' it will find that these processes need assistance from administrative fiat. Alternatively it may eschew tolerance from the beginning since the toleration of error and evil allows them too great a degree of destructive scope. Hence the struggle must continue to be sharp and bitter. In actual practice policy moves between these two options. Total power aims at producing total peace. Given absolute control of socialisation and communication total power will cease to be necessary, since the people will act automatically as the rulers desire, and the desires of the rulers are legitimated as the people's will. All contrary wills inhere in the enemies of the people. Legitimacy, like power, will be total and when both are total both are otiose. Thus the 'sacred canopy' of ideological monopoly is restored.

Now, the above three types, rooted respectively in stable tolerance limits, unstable massive conflict and the stable, massive exercise of power are obviously logical constructs. The first two are based on spirals of stability or instability and the third outlines the logic of total power without such restraints as may arise in practice. Clearly in practice there are often limits to total power just as in practice the stability of systems based on tolerance limits is broken by all kinds of sectional conflicts. What one is pointing to are tendencies either to eliminate dissent, or to institutionalise severe, overlapping conflicts between dichotomous groupings, or to institutionalise conflicts which are merely sectional and usually unconnected. These three possibilities are in fact four since there are two varieties of total power ('Catholic' intégrisme and Marxist totalitarian societies), and for that matter there are also three varieites of systems based on tolerance limits. Thus a fundamental classification will incorporate six categories in all, of which only five are really operative since the sixth is represented by Europe overseas, i.e. the United States.

III Fundamental categories

The fundamental categories can now be formulated and in so doing a whole series of empirical and logical relationships will be implied. From the following analysis it will be clear why the principles of classification should be based on whether or not a culture is Protestant and whether or not it is pluralistic, the two principles being in fact very closely linked to each other.

The first category consists of cultures where Protestantism is dominant, either because they lack Catholic minorities (as in Scandinavia) or because Catholic minorities largely arrived after the pattern had been set in periods of total Protestant dominance (as in England and the United States). For the sake of completeness it is worth indicating the sub-varieties of this pattern. The Scandinavian countries are cultures with inclusive state Churches largely without Protestant dissent. England is a culture with a less inclusive state Church and a very important sector of Protestant dissent. The USA is a culture where the principle of dissent has been universalised; competing denominations exist within an overall umbrella of general religiosity. *Within* these three sub-varieties of Protestantism it is notable that the degree of anti-clericalism and the extent of practice vary with the amount of dissent. The United States contains the highest amount of dissent and therefore has little anti-clericalism and 40 per cent weekly practice. Everything combines to prevent anti-clericalism. There is no association of any specific religion with the state. The Catholics, by arriving later and taking up lower status positions, have been on the progressive side of politics. Religion has been the *sole* source of migrant identity. And each denomination has moved in flexible symbiosis with various currents of sub-cultural change so that no log-jam associated with religion *per se* has built

237

up across the movement of social development. On the other hand state Churches, by their continuing association with elite culture, cannot vary their style with sub-cultural change, and tend to link up with major blocks lying athwart change in general.[8]

All the cultures concerned illustrate the varied operation of two principles fundamental to Protestantism. The first principle is the notion of the religio-political individual conscience operating outside all ecclesiastical policies. This conscience finds a varied expression according to where the individual is located in the social structure, but is most pervasive in those strata penetrated by nineteenth-century liberalism. It is therefore most pervasive in the USA and Britain where it serves to define politics in terms of morality, and somewhat less pervasive in Scandinavia. The second principle is that of the withdrawal of the Church as an institution from any attempt at the independent domination of society. In one sense this may appear to make the Church even more conservative than in Catholic countries, but the result is that integrist philosophies propounded by the Church as an institution do not become a major area of political tension. The conservatism of Protestant state Churches arises because they eliminate ecclesiastical independence and make the Church isomorphic with extant social structure. The avenues of social mobility through the Church are closed up and the clergy become more closely linked to the elite both in style and in recruitment, and sometimes in their marked indifference to religion. It is this situation which makes the *cultural* gap yawn widely when the industrial revolution breaks up paternalist relations between upper and lower cultural segments. However, although the Lutheran state Churches were initially opposed to Social Democracy, and although today their active members still tend to cast a conservative vote, nevertheless they accepted the fact that the Social Democratic parties might achieve hegemonic power. In Norway and in Britain there were significant variations on this acceptance, which further lessened tension. In the Norwegian case the 'old left' was originally associated with the religiosity of the Bergen area poised against the Swedish domination emanating from semi-secular Oslo. Thus both democratic and nationalist impulses were channelled through a religious party, and religion was explicitly dissociated from a conservatism which was both secular and inadequately nationalist.[9] In the British case the whole democratic impulse was initially channelled through an alliance of dissent and Liberalism, but to the extent that this included capitalists was well as craftsmen and the petty bourgeoisie, the Conservative party was able to appeal to even lower strata on the basis of a reform of Liberal abuses, notably in the sphere of factory legislation. At the same time the 'integralist' element in the Anglican Church tried to turn the Liberal and dissenting flank by stressing the analogies between medieval organic-ism and working class solidarity. The result was a form of Anglo-Catholic Socialism in the state Church which could not and did not appear in Scandinavia. Hence not only were all the religious out-groups (Jews, Catholics and dissenting free-churchmen) spread out among the parties of democracy and equity, but in so far as Liberalism and Protestant dissent were successful a section of the state Church joined forces with those to left of the Liberals and the dissenters. Anti-clericalism cannot gain ground where the Liberals have a strong free-church support, where Jews and Catholics offer considerable support to Labour, and where the Labour party itself draws strength from a radical section of the free churches and a medievalist segment of the state Church. The net consequence is a working class separated off less by political opposition or by political solidarity (which in any case it does not possess) than by a cultural distinctiveness which alienates it both from the aristocratic style of the state Church and the liberal styles of the free churches. Something further is said about this pattern below, by way of comparison with Holland.

The second category comprises cultures with a Protestant majority but a very substantial Catholic minority: Holland, Germany, Switzer-land.[10] As a matter of fact in all such countries at the present time the Catholics are the largest bloc of practising Christians, but the pattern itself derives from a historic ratio of 60:40 associated with a status skew in favour of Protestants, which is in turn associated with greater social dynamism in the Protestant sector. Each culture is subdivided into Catholic regions and Protestant regions, very broadly south and north respectively. Such societies have developed a *cultural* rather than a purely political bi-polarity and political life has partly turned around the issue of the emancipation and rights of the Catholic sector. Thus the aspirations of relatively depressed groups have been expressed in Catholic organisations, or in parties greatly influenced by Catholics, rather than through parties simply expressing the differences of status and class. The existence of a powerful, if somewhat deprived, bloc, made tolerance and political compromise the most obvious option, more particularly in Holland and Switzerland, with extensive traditions of political co-operation. Since Catholics are not motivated to support the conservative parties of the elite, the exclusive association of religion with the right cannot occur. Furthermore, when political polarisation is weak some members of both religions are able to take up positions on the left without adopting a schizophrenic stance. In all cases the relatively deprived Catholic sector has been more 'organic' and better organised than the Protestant sector. The long-term complexities and indeed the pathology of the German case from 1933–45 cannot be gone into here, but they derive broadly from the special circumstances

239

of a late national unification and the consequences of defeat in 1918, linked to the inability of the middle class to push its industrial achievement through into the political and cultural sector. Hence the deposit of subservience activated by national disaster.

The Dutch case is particularly interesting in that it offers a useful comparison with both England and Belgium. The comparison with England arises because the English system involves a flexible elite, somewhat open to liberal influences yet basically conservative, facing a counter-culture composed of a partial conjunction of dissenting religion and liberals of various kinds, the latter resting on the base provided in the provinces by the former. The dichotomous basic pattern remains undisturbed even by the advent of Labour, since a section of the dissenters crossed over the into the Labour party on finding that the Liberal party was sometimes dominated by Whiggery and in any case was losing the mass appeal which gave it access to power. But in any case dissenters and other liberals with a 'social' orientation passed over to the Labour party and gave it an imprint, which in alliance with other ideologies incoherently held together, made it an acceptable replacement to the Liberals as the vehicle of a counter-culture *vis-à-vis* elite culture. In the Dutch case both orthodox Calvinists and Catholics were excluded from the Liberal centre, the initial reliance of Catholics on the liberalism of Liberals broke down over the issue of education, while the orthodox Calvinists were forced to recognise that their national myth was not safely in Liberal keeping.[11] They were therefore forced into an appeal to the people, which constituted a form of mobilisation parallel to the mobilisation of the Catholics.[12] The two dissident sectors each mobilised in systems of social isolation and then talked to each other at the elite level over the walls of their respective ghettos. This then set a pattern which is coextensive anyway with a long-term Dutch tradition of decentralisation and of tolerant accommodation between flexible local elites. The Socialists, when they arrived on the scene, were forced into a parallel form of protective ghetto and realised that they could only attract the lower echelons within the other ghettos if they ameliorated their rhetoric so as not to prejudice religious loyalties. (This exactly parallels the Norwegian situation in that the extremist tendencies of the new left after the First World War had to be ameliorated to accommodate the regional religious bloc represented by the 'old left' parties, thus laying the foundations of Norwegian political democracy.) Eventually, the Catholic party moved somewhat to the left, recognising the internal pressure of the lower echelons within it, and engaged in a series of coalitions based on a system of proportional representation which exactly reflected a culture based on a spectrum of positions encapsulated in 'ghettos' (or pillars) rather than on dichotomous alternatives as in the English model.

Thus the 60:40 situation breeds sub-cultural segregation, especially in education, whereby religion is not fully identified with a particular point on the political axis, and whereby the Catholics in particular, who form the largest religious body, move towards the centre-left. The further comparison with Belgium turns on the difference between a cultural discrimination defined in purely religious terms, and a cultural discrimination defined in both religious and linguistic terms. Either way, however, elements of 'pillarisation' (*verzuiling*) follow: the Catholic Church achieves an identity separate from the elite, and the politics of status are criss-crossed and stabilised by the politics of cultural defence. Only differentiation eventually weakens the religious-political tie, as is now evident in Holland, Switzerland and Germany.

Whether the advent of higher mobility, geographical, social and in terms of the media, together with elements of secularisation in the large cities is weakening the Catholic 'pillar' in Holland is an issue of current debate. Certainly the system has experienced strain as social mixing has increased in the large cities and as very rapid social development has dislocated all kinds of secure definitions. Indeed, the very internal integration of the Catholic pillar has made the conflict between old and new radical middle classes, between administrators and progressive theologians, doubly resonant and violent. And it may be that equality is so close as to render cultural defence more a constriction than an advantage. Certainly the vote for the Catholic party has been very much reduced since 1967. Where Catholic confessional voting ceases there is first of all apathy and then voting to the left. But so far the system stands and is a direct expression of the 60:40 proportion between the religious.[13]

This is partially reflected in its essentials both in Germany and Switzerland. In Switzerland, of course, the Catholic Church is not associated with the politics of the conservative elite. The political stance of Catholicism in Germany has been central rather than right wing, even though there was an intimate honeymoon with the CDU immediately after the Second World War.[14] In both countries Catholics have suffered some partial exclusion from the military, administrative, educational and commercial elites and have responded accordingly through the politics of the centre and some degree of sub-cultural integration.

The analytic principles underlying social development in these two main categories are worth further explanation. Where dissent is extensive or universal, i.e. where inclusive Churches identified with the state, the status quo and the elite are weak, as in Britain, or non-existent

241

as in the USA, the varieties of relatively deprived groupings (amongst which Catholics are included) are strung out along the political spectrum in such a way that conflict is not exacerbated by religion *as such* constituting the major differentiating symbol as between left and right. And since religion can be located to the left as well as the right, even if less strongly so, it can ameliorate and constrain the fissiparousness of the left. Common symbols, including those of religion, can continue to unite the society above the secondary symbols of conflict. Paradoxically this is achieved in the USA by the total break between an institutional Church and the state, allowing religious symbols to remain a major part of the common vocabulary of legitimation, while in Britain the Church can remain established because religion itself has not been at the core of conflicts, and is thereby capable of providing some of the symbols of social unity.[15] In Norway the existence of a provincial dissent, albeit formally within the state Church, and the association of that dissent with the 'centre' parties of what is called the 'old left' operates in a similar manner. In Sweden the rather limited extent of Protestant dissent, and of the liberalism associated with it, is too minor to affect the situation in this way. Indeed in Sweden, Finland and Denmark there have been fissions between Social Democratic parties and the established Churches, and distinct elements of anti-clericalism. But the fact that these state Churches are Protestant and believe both in a withdrawal of the Church from active political interventions *and* in the principle of the independent religio-political conscience prevents the fission widening into the confrontation of rival blocs. The state Churches, by ceasing to be active parts of the operative power structure, can remain part of the common symbolism of the states concerned, along with their respective monarchies. It is significant that, with the exception of Belgium, monarchies only remain in Protestant countries, and for exactly the same reasons that established Churches have survived. State Churches are not disestablished except in some Protestant cantons in Switzerland; indeed in Sweden it is currently suggested that *all* Churches be established. In Switzerland, Holland and Germany the position is slightly different in that the relatively deprived sectors are disproportionately Catholic, and this focuses an extensive area of egalitarian concern on the emancipation of groups whose self-definition is largely in terms of religion not status. The 'intégrisme' of the Catholic sector thus stands aside from the nexus of Church, state, *status quo* and elite dominance. So once again religion *per se* as embodied in one inclusive institution is not located too exclusively at one point on the political spectrum, and politics are in any case criss-crossed by issues of cultural defence expressed in religious terms. The federalism of all three societies corresponds somewhat to this religious variety, and further breaks down tendencies to dichotomous confrontations in which religion sides too exclusively with one of the polar opposites.

The crucial element in the above argument has been whether or not religion becomes too closely associated with the right wing in politics, thereby explicitly alienating sectors of the population and jeopardising its place among the master symbols of social consensus and legitimacy. The other element discussed, pluralism, deserves equal stress. As already pointed out it takes various forms:

(i) The competition of all denominations with each other in which they are spread out amongst all major parties and are severally associated with most status positions.

(ii) The competition between a state Church allied to an elite culture and dissenting groups in various locations, but found particularly amongst the 'respectable' working class and petty bourgeoisie.

(iii) 'Competition' within the state Church itself, whereby internal movements succeed in ameliorating the elite elements in its culture so as to accommodate democratic or petty bourgeois aspirations.

(iv) Competition between rival blocks, Protestant and Catholic, in which liberal Protestants ally with latitudinarian and agnostic sectors.

This results in a kind of 'consolidated' competition between rival oligopolists. Types (i), (ii), (iii), are represented by the USA, the UK, Scandinavia respectively, and (iv) by Germany, Holland and Switzerland. The consequences for practice are clear. Type (i) results in an element of overall 'civic religion', complemented by a vast variety of 'vulgarisations' of religion at every status level. Practice is therefore high. Type (ii) results in very partial vulgarisations associated with the liberal segments of the population, and it cannot achieve the universal vulgarisations appropriate to the whole range of status groups. The state church remains allied to elite culture. Thus both the liberal, petty bourgeois, and elite social sectors are within reach of institutional Christianity, but the working class is largely outside it. Practice is fairly low, but civic religion can be retained at the overall societal level and an implicit, cultural Christianity is widespread within the working class. The workers' withdrawal is only from the institutional 'style' of the religious sectors. Type (iii) results in very low practice because the state Church, which is the principal body, retains elite style and connections. But there is a great deal of associational, sub-ecclesiastical religious activity and the broad cultural identifications with 'Christianity' in a loose sense are not broken. Type (iv) is peculiar in that the elite culture becomes explicitly liberal, and latitudinarian, even more so perhaps than in Type

243

(iii), and Catholic and (sometimes) orthodox Protestant sectors may organise against it. Religion becomes associated with the politics of regional and cultural defence, and included within the sector covered by that defence there subsists deprived and working class elements. The result is high practice within the organised sub-sectors, and to the extent that these are *highly* organised as in Holland, rather explicit *dis*sociation from institutional religion amongst those not so organised. This type of pattern delays the consequences of social differentiation evident in the other types. But once near parity of status is achieved, cultural defence ceases to overlie the process of social differentiation. The Church then retires from *explicit* involvement in the political sphere to concentrate on the cultural sphere. Thus the connection with the CDU in Germany is relaxed and the Catholic vote in Switzerland and Holland slumps.

The third category concerns Catholicism in its historic heartlands. The argument as outlined above emphasises the stabilising effect of Catholicism where it is a dispersed and fairly small minority, and where it is a large minority settled in a territorial redoubt. However, the effect of Catholicism in its historic heartlands has been quite different, precisely because it has been numerically almost coextensive with the whole society and has grown with the whole structure of status and elite power and culture. Where Catholicism dominates it leads to large political and social fissures, organic oppositions and secularist dogmas of various kinds. This kind of fissure can be charted in Portugal after 1910, in Spain in the 1930s, in France, more especially from 1870 to 1905, and in Italy from the mid-nineteenth century onwards. There are certain partial exceptions such as Belgium and (perhaps) Austria which repay further exploration. In characterising the third category one draws both on the model of polarising spirals previously suggested and on the comments made about the organic nature of Catholicism, which at the overall societal level is embodied in national 'intégrisme'. The Catholic Church itself is an organic society, dedicated to the notion of unity, and when the Church weds itself to a society any social split threatens its organic character. As a minority, clearly the Church creates for itself an organic sub-culture, a 'column' as the Dutch and Belgians describe it, but as a majority any social division breaks the column in the middle. This makes the issue of the Church a central one, and 'religion' is identified with the Church since religion has been already defined as coterminous with the ecclesiastical institution and with its regulating norms. Thus in societies with Catholic majorities social divisions are coloured and sharply defined by such issues as clericalism, and ecclesiastical rules relating to marriage, and above all by the issue of education, which includes the educational role of the secular priesthood and the regular orders. In 1974 for example, divorce was a major issue in Italian politics; in Belgium since 1968 the question of the revision of the Pacte Scolaire of 1959 (whereby a system of parallel schooling was set up) has been an important issue.[16] The issue of education was of course an endemic crux of conflict in France, with the Second Empire favouring the Catholics and the Third Republic favouring the anti-clericals and expelling the religious orders. Conflicts of this type have persistently converged on the issue of Church and state: in France the struggle culminated in 1905 with the separation of Church and state. For the same reason there is controversy over the role of religious symbols in expressing the national unity. Whereas in Protestant societies the secular symbols of *res publica* and the religious symbols converge, in Catholic societies the symbols of Church and republic diverge.

Certain other comparisons with Protestant societies underline the nature of the Catholic case: for Protestant societies the issue of divorce in its religious aspect gradually settles into a matter of the *internal* regulation of ecclesiastical bodies and of cultural definitions of the marital bond. The point of Protestant issue with the state, particularly among dissenting groups, has turned either on matters of the regulation of individual morals with regard to (say) alcoholic consumption or the rights of the individual conscience with respect to military service. Occasionally such questions of conscience are also part of the politics of cultural defence as in the symbolic crusades over prohibition and anti-pornography campaigns. In Catholic societies, historically and now, the question of individual conscience is rarely raised, being understood neither by Catholics nor secularists. Objections to central authority are, however, understood and also objections to bureaucracy, since Catholics and republican governments have a plenitude of both, each reflecting the other. But the individual conscience is a different matter. Pacifist and protest movements in Protestant societies have a high component of religious individualism; in Catholic societies they have a high component of organised politics. By the same token student revolt and intellectual dissent in Anglo-Saxon countries easily take on various religious and quasi-religious colourings, whereas in Catholic countries it easily flows into dogmatic positions and highly organised political cells.

But such spirals of polar opposition do not necessarily pursue their logic to the end, though the difference in 1968 between France and Britain was highly indicative. No British government fell by virtue of fires sparked off in London University. The model presented earlier must remain a model *ceteris paribus*, and external threat brings together erstwhile opponents. The First World War provided an initial break in the polarities of French politics, and the Second War both discredited the collaborating right and allowed a

Catholic reforming centre to emerge.[17] Indeed the dislocations of the war gave a reforming social Catholicism a chance to emerge, throughout Western Europe, in France, Belgium, Austria and Germany. Catholicism moved towards the creation of a stabilising centre and could include openings to the left. This shift was initiated by those Catholics who contributed most to the reconstruction of post-war Europe: Adenauer, Schumann. This was a tradition continued in his own way by de Gaulle. If, however, the war is not external but civil then the logic of polarisation is pursued *à l'outrance*, and the Spanish and Portuguese reversion to integral Catholicism follows. Should the 'civil war' occur after the overall shift in Vatican politics has partly shifted the Catholic Church away from the right and after the local Catholic Church has itself been partly disengaged and marginally differentiated then religion may well view 'liberal' revolution with benevolent neutrality. This is now the case in contemporary Spain and – perhaps – Portugal.

When the spirals are weakened then the issue of anti-clericalism weakens likewise. If the definition of religion as exclusively on the right is eroded then the left will be glad to be augmented by believing Catholics. If believing Catholics are seen on the left then the definitions in terms of ecclesiastical right and secularist left are gradually relegated to the folk memory. If Catholic education no longer need be viewed as part of the socialisation of an anti-republican sector then there is less motive to oppose it. Thus in France the issue of education now barely raises the bogeys of clericalism; and the Pacte Scolaire in Belgium, though once again an issue, was nevertheless indicative of a spirit of accommodation which still exists.

This is the point at which to mention divisions *within* the Church corresponding to the relatively greater spread it now achieves along the political spectrum, including the extreme left as distinct from the Communist left. If there is to be religious 'dissent' in Catholic societies it works by parties within the Catholic Church itself and these, like the Catholic Church, tend to have an explicitly political content. (By contrast the parties within Lutheran Churches, such as the Inner Mission, work by the percolation of a slow cultural stain.) These parties actually strain at the institutional character of Catholicism, and at the margins they initiate a free religiosity sitting light to institutional loyalties. This in turn breeds reassertions of institutional discipline, and the resulting struggle is complicated by very general reactions to the institutional constraints of all modern bureaucracy. The spread of the free radical religiosity of Dissenso in Italy was one such movement and it not merely sparked off attempts at ecclesiastical discipline but was complemented by popular archaic movements of a superstitious and eschatological kind. Of course the fate of Dissenso indicates how free radical religiosity can flow eventually in channels dug by the more directly political left. Some Catholics are now standing as independents in the Communist lists. The general post-war shift was recognised by the Vatican and then given a further acceleration by the Council, which both legitimated the opening to the left and provided a context for movements to the right, either stranded elements of pre-war Catholic conservatism or free-floating expressions of archaic and popular religiosity. The former are more prevalent in France, the latter in Italy. One should perhaps note that the possibility of Communist hegemony in Italy from 1974 on has revived Catholic-Communist antagonism: the Vatican strongly inhibited a Communist vote in the 1976 elections.

The French example provides the richest illustration of the shifts and counter-moves which have occurred, and it also merits further discussion of the most important case of the Protestant majority-Catholic minority situation in reverse. As has been said, the old right was discredited by Vichy and along with it the collaborationist bishops of the old Action Française. The liberals grew in influence; the Mission de France embarked on the worker-priest experiment. The partial absorption of worker priests into a militant working class milieu led to the suspension of the experiment and temporary disarray, but in its place there appeared a new kind of militant Christian social action. This has been complemented by less stress on retreats, rosaries and ritual. The result has been a notable collaboration between militant laity and clergy in social relief and reform, sometimes in company with Marxists, and certainly for a while in dialogue with them. The most obvious instance of lay Catholic action is the Jeunesse Agricole Chrétienne. It began between the wars in rural France and under priestly tutelage. During and after the war it became a form of self-help both in the world of general culture and in the world of farming techniques and organisation, and then evolved into a radical instrument of the younger generation and became a modernising influence. (With regard to economic innovation it parallels both Haugean dissent in Norway and Orthodox Calvinist dissent in Holland.) Movements and activities of this kind have linked up both with the left and the technocracy. Most extreme have been the manifestations of a new monasticism in the *communautés de base* (small communes), some of which are led by married priests. This, of course, parallels movements towards radical communitarianism in Italy, and in Holland, such as the semi-secularised group 'Shalom'.[18] This new emphasis on activism at the expense of contemplation and the new clerical, or ex-clerical militancy and politicisation aroused various reactions. Even a liberal, such as the Cardinal-Archbishop of Paris appointed in the 1960s, felt it right to use what authority remained. The Church had at least to repudiate the left wing of the Jeunesse Etudiante Chrétienne in so far as there was any suggestion that the Church was corporately implicated in its policies. 'Les Silencieux' form a puzzled centre, perhaps a majority, worried and confused by the new trends. Meanwhile the old 'intégrisme' remains, in areas like the Brittany hinterland or Hérault: it objects to those changes in the liturgy which express a more horizontal sense of community and it has even threatened secession.[19] It now has a rallying point: Eccône.

So far as the Protestant minority (3 per cent) is concerned, its link with the kind of social and cultural action just mentioned is through the revival of monasticism in association with ecumenical activity at Taizé. The Protestants have traditionally been on the 'left', partly because the Republic consolidated their position in French society, partly because in the late nineteenth century they were influential in the Third Republic.[20] The 'intégrisme' of the Catholics defined them, along with freemasons and Jews, as amongst the alien elements in France and they accepted this role *vis-à-vis* the Catholics. Their contribution in the 'progressive' sector of French life was not only political but scientific and professional: the 'bar Protestant' is a phrase indicative of their influence. They were tightly knit in familial dynasties, largely in response to their isolation – a factor contributing to a relatively high degree of practice for Protestants. This interlinked character has never disappeared. Nor has their sense of history and martyrdom. It is the memory of the persecutions after the Revocation of the Edict of Nantes in 1685, and the memory of the 'intégriste' reaction to them which keeps them to the left. Indeed in the Cévennes, where they form a regional majority and where the memory of the old martyrdoms is fiercest they vote Communist. Their left-wing stance complements the labour or progressive sympathies of the Catholic minorities in Anglo-Saxon countries. Both cases are interesting instances of the structural position of a religious community refracting the impact of status: middle-class Protestants in France and middle-class Catholics in England cast a disproportionately large radical vote.

In Italy there is a somewhat different version of the spirals found in the French pattern. One has to remember that Italy experienced unification rather than revolution and that this unification was one imposed by a Liberal anti-clerical and anti-papal leadership. This leadership worked a system of patronage and shifting mutations of cabinet personnel: it was able to assume a high degree of consensus over socio-economic questions, since the Catholics had left politics at papal bidding and the lower classes had not arrived. When the latter did arrive, and socialism with them, the liberals decided to compound with the Catholic Church over such issues as divorce, the orders and education. By 1919 the Catholics had achieved massive representation through the Popular party, a reformist and democratic body, and the Socialists were in Parliament as the largest single party. As in Spain, France and Holland, socialism had important anarchist roots and support from landless agricultural labourers. The Catholics were internally divided, though their dislike of the Liberal state derived more from the temporal politics of the Vatican than any alienation of Catholics as such. At any rate the mutual suspicions of Catholics, Liberals and Socialists made possible the Fascist take-over. After the war all the old symbols of legitimacy were compromised except the Church. The Lateran Treaties of 1929 had formalised a reconciliation between the Church and Fascism and gave some legitimacy to Fascism, but thereafter Church and party came increasingly into conflict. The other survivor into the post-war period was the Communist party, which received even more credit for the resistance than it deserved, and reaped a reward in terms of dominant positions in unions and local government. The Christian Democrats now unified all those afraid of communist revolution and eventually became the ruling party to such an extent that it has been possible until the mid-70s to identify Christian Democracy with government and administration. The Christian Democrats attract those of every category who are marginally better off than others in the same category and they draw disproportionately on the practising Catholics; the Communists are the reverse in both respects. Both parties exploit face-to-face groups, including the family, and insert themselves in the social fabric, often using ideology more as a weapon in intra-party disputes than as a basic resource with the electorate at large. The Catholics have their stronghold in the Venetias and Trentino, the Communists in the central belt of Emilia, Tuscany and Umbria, and both beliefs achieve some degree of closure in their respective social systems: ideological at the top, recreational at grass-roots level. The Socialists, for their part, draw on the non-practising Catholics, whereas the Communist party appeals to a sector part of which is explicitly opposed to the Church.[21] Two things are crucial: a marked decline of general hostility towards the Communist party and decreased deference towards clergy amongst the young.

The system is one which is split in terms of a set of criteria amongst which the Church is very important. Thus far it resembles France. But the Church has not been burdened with the advocacy of a monarchist right: on the contrary, it fought the liberal monarchy and when it emerged in politics it adopted a position near the moderate centre. After the war it was associated with a form of Christian Democracy which covered a large range of positions, including the centre-left. Moreover, by the 1960s both the Church and the Communist party had made moves away from total intransigence, some of these moves being pragmatic and some ideological.

The Church ceased to be wholly identified with the Christian Demo-arats, the Communists espoused the 'Italian' way of Communism, cnd a brand of Christian politics emerged highly critical of current social arrangements and unwilling to endorse automatically the Church's position on such controversial matters as divorce. The Catholic labour organisations became more independent of the Church; and the Church itself entered the realm of social criticism. Thus some of the spirals which unwound in France also unwound in Italy.[22] And it was no longer possible to impose Catholic marriage discipline on the whole society; in 1974 divorce was accepted. Perhaps the really indicative paradox is here: 61 per cent of practising Catholics still support Democrazia Christiana; and 51 per cent of practising Catholic women voted for divorce.

Two exceptions to the polarities found in cultures characterised by Catholic dominance have been mentioned. They are Belgium and Austria, though the latter only deviates marginally from the classic model. The Belgian case is very instructive. It illustrates first the fact that Catholics are less polarised against 'progressives' if they are fighting a common enemy, in this case foreign control by Austrians, French and more especially the Dutch. The relative unities forged in this struggle for independence set the crucial parameters of later development. The 'set' at a nation's birth has *enormous* constraining force for the future.[23] Furthermore, this set was confirmed and strengthened by the external threat or actuality of German occupa-tions in the two world wars. Indeed, it was this set which not only provided the restrictions on polarisations in Belgian society but made possible a stable monarchy. The monarchy was born with the struggle for independence and was identified both with the struggle against the Germans in the Great War and the conciliatory social policy immediately following it.[24]

Belgian Catholicism can be described as sub-dominant in spite of its numerical dominance. This is because dominance or sub-domin-ance is not merely a matter of numbers or even of political power but of cultural evaluation. The critical symbol of cultural devalua-tion in Belgium has been the official attitude to the Flemish language. Until recently Flanders was economically depressed compared with Wallonia; Catholicism is associated with the small towns and countryside of Flanders and with the Flemish tongue against French and industrial Wallonia. This deprivation expressed itself in religious and linguistic terms, thus providing a cross-cutting criterion for the expression of differences. Since Wallonia is in the French sphere and French is associated with secularism Flanders is forced back on a sharper identification with Catholicism.

Nevertheless, the classic polarities did appear in the late nineteenth century and notably over the question of Church-state relations, which dominated Belgian politics at the expense of social and economic issues. The crucial issue, as in France, was over education and over the setting up of 'public schools', though in Belgium the net result was more favourable to the Catholics than in France. In Belgium the Catholics retained a larger sector of the education system just as they held a larger share of political support, especially from 1884 to 1914. Being pushed less hard they were in their turn less extreme. Ultra-right Catholics emerged to criticise a Catholic parliamentarianism which tolerated error along with truth. But they did not attack the system as such or hopelessly pursue an outworn system as did those French Catholics who devoted themselves to a royal restoration. As in France, the rationalist societies and free-masons sought to make the Church and state independent, to laïcise education, welfare and even burial. Furthermore, the two contestants were the sources of each other's discipline. Yet the constitutional frame held, but within a pattern of discrete, disciplined sub-cultures. When the socialist party appeared it fitted rapidly into both, the party eschewed ideology, but became sectarian in its opposition to sectarianism and in its creation of a third sub-culture, consisting of unions, friendly societies and co-operatives. So doing, it in turn set a pattern for Catholic organisations. Like Holland, Belgium is marked by segregated columns on behalf of which their respective elites meet and negotiate; as with Holland, Belgium represents a relatively stable system of sub-cultures which have some tendency to relaxation at their frontiers. If the nation is split it is not so much by the politics of interest as by the politics of culture and language, of which political Catholicism is the living expression. At the same time, of course, the Catholic political party has itself been split since 1968 by the language issue: the Christian Socials operate with separate Flemish and Wallonian wings.

Austria is also an instance of *verzuiling* or *Lagermentälitat*, and the 'columns' retain their perspectives on each other in spite of increasing erosion of status difference and diminution of ideological oppositions. Cultural definitions can not only precede and canalise the oppositions and philosophies of class, but can outlast them. In between the wars the two poles were organised as alternative societies, a Black Austria and a Red Austria centred on Vienna, each with para-military wings. The crunch came with the occupation of Red Vienna in 1934, followed by a brief period of Catholic corporatism until Austria was incorporated by Germany in 1938. Thus far the historical situation conforms to the polarisation model. But two factors are important in diminishing the polarity. Austria emerged late as a democratic entity, and the strife of the First Republic from 1918 to 1934 was a relatively short episode. When the Second Republic was formed after the Second World War the shift in Catholicism itself had occurred, and the Catholic Church in Austria withdrew from the kind of explicit involvement in Austrian politics which had characterised the pre-war Christian Social Party. Perhaps a third influence is the fact that the party which retains *cultural* links with Catholicism, the People's Party (OUP), is an organisation not only of self-defined 'state-bearing' elements but of peasants, shopkeepers and white-collar workers. This divides the class vote. Hence there is a continuing need for coalition and compromise which exists alongside a continuing tension and supsicion.[25]

There are one or two analytic points to be made concerning the pattern in societies where Catholicism is, or has been, the religion of the vast majority of the inhabitants. Obviously, all of them have been afflicted by dichotomous polarisations in which the Church has provided a major focus of contention. The greater the initial friction, the greater the subsequent conflict is likely to be, because where oppositions become fundamental, the role of education grows more crucial. Catholics want the right to bring up the next generation as Catholics; Republicans do not want the next generation reared as monarchists. This is the French situation formed in the crucible of Revolution and Restoration, and in the hopes of repeating both which were retained on either side of the fissure.

The French situation has been continually exported via the influence and attraction of French culture and the orientation of its intelligentsia. Nevertheless, most other societies provide some important and ameliorating variation on the French pattern. One type of variation relates to the different kinds of relationship of centre to periphery. The French relationship is clearly rooted in the dominance of Paris, and Paris is the capital of a vast devastated basin so far as Catholicism is concerned. But Belgium and Austria are made up of eastern and western blocs, with the capital in the western bloc. Of course, that is a gross oversimplification but the crucial point relates to the relative balance of forces. Each side came to recognise the irreducibility of the other and the danger to the nation as a whole should conflict be pushed to the furthest limit.[26] Even in Spain there was a measure of balance between the Castilian centre and the massive peripheries of Galicia, the Basque country and Catalonia. In Portugal the 'tone' of Lisbon looked towards the more secularist south but the bulk of the population was in the Catholic north. Indeed, looking at Portugal a further factor is evident and that is the ambiguous relation of the Church to the liberal elite which ran the country from 1910–26. Both in the nineteenth and the twentieth centuries the Portuguese liberals were severe on the Church, and between 1910 and 1926 the Church and the nascent socialist movements suffered together. This hardly united the causes of socialism and Catholicism, but it provided a modicum of empathy which persisted even through the time of the corporate state 1926–74. When the revolution came its leaders were moderate in their ecclesiastical policy and the bishops responded with similar moderation. The impact of the ambiguous relation between Portuguese Catholics and liberals is, in a way, the obverse of the situation which obtained in Belgium. As has been pointed out above, the liberals and the Catholics were involved together in the struggle to found the nation. This ameliorated their subsequent conflict to quite a significant degree.

In all the societies concerned war had an important effect on the dynamics of unity and disunity. In France after 1870 and in Spain after 1898 the Church was blamed for defeat. Yet the First World War brought even French Catholics and French secularists together to defend the Republic. Similarly in Belgium the fissures closed under external pressure. Indeed, the history of the Christian Social Party reflects precisely the unities forged in the First and Second World War, and the linguistic divisions which grew in the 1930s and 1960s. In Austria the Second War gave an opportunity for the spirals of hostility to unwind. The old pattern was disrupted just at the point where the Church had come to realise the danger which explicit political involvement engendered for its structural mission.

Italy is a complex case because of the initial Catholic withdrawal from politics following unification, but it is important that the Catholic Church first stood apart from a modernising but rather corrupt liberal centre and then refused total identification with the Fascist regime. It was thus able to emerge as a political rallying point for the moderate centre and uncorrupted section of the right, as it did in France.

In general one can say that the Catholic Church, in response to social processes of differentiation and by way of bitter experience, 'saw' the futility of spirals of conflict and the danger of explicit involvement in the politics of a political party, including the politics of the Spanish government. This danger arises because such involvement alienates those whose politics are different from the basic mission of the Church. Since the existence of varied self-conscious social sectors is itself an aspect of differentiation, so too the Catholic Church's relative withdrawal from explicit politics, especially those of a restorationist right, is equally an *aspect of differentiation*. This is a case of differentiation initiating further differentiation. The war itself assisted the realignments necessary, first producing an alliance of the Church with the centre and centre right, and then a partial withdrawal from all alliances. This fact, combined with the recognition of irreducibility on both sides, reduces the tendency to total conflict and allows some free outriders to appear in both camps, crossing the old lines of conflict. The 'outriders' are likely to be 'free' Marxists, not the Party itself, and 'free' Catholics. The one area where the Catholic Church cannot easily withdraw is where it provides the focus of a regional nationalism, since that nationalism is the *only* significant 'sector' in its own area, or where the system of *verzuiling* has built up so tight a Catholic organisation that its inertias, including political involvement, cannot easily be broken.

The fourth category comprises those societies where the polarisations endemic in a Catholic culture issued in a return to 'integralist' society. This return often involves an appeal to the military, who in Spain, for example, have historically seen the preservation of the true, Catholic Spain as reverting into their hands after periods of democratic corruption. The importance of the ecclesiastical issue is seen by its key role in the First Republic 1868–74 and in the Second Republic 1931–6. It was Article 26 of the 1931 Constitution, separating Church and state, confiscating some Church property, restricting the Orders and excluding them from education, which first really focused and hardened opinions against the Republic.[27] Spain, Portugal and Orthodox Greece belong to or have 'participated' in this category, as did Austria from 1934 to 1938; outside Europe Chile provides a contemporary example. Such societies normally adopt a corporatist ideology and schemes of 'vertical integration'. It is interesting that in Greece the Colonels explicitly defined themselves as the defenders of Greece's Orthodox heritage. Such regimes attempt to achieve modernisation and economic development without cultural radicalisation or the political and personal fragmentations of liberalism. In Spain, 'Opus Dei' is, or was, a major vehicle of this: an ascetic lay order of elite personnel which has played a considerable role in government and is dedicated both to modernisation and tradition.[28] And indeed in Spain the economic transformations achieved have been remarkable.

Such regimes are obviously authoritarian: their hierarchical principles complement those of the Catholic Church. Again, like the Catholic Church they condone moderate cultural deviance and repress explicit opposition. They allow intellectual dissent provided it does not organise; and Protestantism has had to exist against some legal restriction and cultural constraint. In any case Protestantism consists of tiny minorities dating mainly from the nineteenth century.[29] Authoritarian regimes of the right are less all-embracing in their control than communist societies, since for the latter cultural deviance is as dangerous as organised opposition. Catholicism is defined as the source of the national tradition and is supported in that specific role; as with the absolutist rulers of the eighteenth century there is no tolerance of ecclesiastical independence. The principal technique is the control of the higher appointments, which usually ensures a compliant official voice. The manipulation of the appointment of the sometime Archbishop of Athens by the Colonels was one important example.[30] However, the very recognition of the Church and of its traditions allows those traditions to be used as vehicles of opposition. The Church can become a funnel for opposition once it is freed from the overwhelming fear of being crushed and persecuted from the left. Thus the Spanish Church from about 1960 onwards has proved a source of opposition to the regime, particularly where this opposition is linked to the historic Spanish aspirations towards regional autonomy in Catalonia and in the Basque country. In the Basque country Catholicism is a major carrier of a radical separatism; in Catalonia the separatism is expressed more in cultural and linguistic terms. Both areas have moved to the left: Catalonia before the Civil War, partly because the Republic granted some autonomy, the Basque country after the war because the new regime denied it.

In any case, the Spanish Church is open to influences from international Catholicism, either the Second Vatican Council or the French Church, which reflect developments in the Church as a whole and its partial *rapprochement* (*aggiornamento*) with the situation in Europe and the world at large.[31] Nationalism cannot convert a Church into a pure expression of the nation. Nevertheless, there are obviously a variety of elements in the Spanish Church.[32] There is a layer of local superstition pre-dating Christianity itself. There is the kind of Catholicism that believes Spain more Catholic than the Pope and rejects outside or modernising influences, whether derived from him or elsewhere. Then there is a generation affected by the Council and by the ferments of the 1960s which finds the 'intégrisme', authoritarianism, the psychic constriction and role-bound character of the older Catholicism not easily tolerable. Thus there arises a generation gap, particularly with those whose priestly formation took place in the conformist period from 1940 to 1960. Young priests have been shown to nourish surprisingly radical opinions; they also sometimes work with local Communists. This gap in itself leads to tensions, fewer vocations and defections. Indeed, it is characteristic of this 'liberated' Catholicism, in Spain as in Holland, that once the conservative dykes are breached after a long period of holding back the waters of modernity, then there is a tendency to react to extremes, politically and existentially. Hence the suspicion with which the regime views the Church from time to time, hence maybe the 1970 proposals for a state monopoly of education, and the tension with the Vatican even under the very moderate policy of consolidation inaugurated by Pope Paul. (A parallel opposition to the authoritarianism of the state exists in the Brazilian Catholic Church.)

On the other hand, the role of the Church in relation to the regime is symbolically represented in the building of enormous edifices and the mausoleums created for General Franco and the fallen in the Civil War. At the level of state symbolism Church and state are forced to be one; organisationally the Church can and must be controlled; culturally it can funnel opposition, including opposition which has (or had) no other legitimate outlet. In this last respect it plays the role of the Church in authoritarian societies of the left. The church building has time and again been chosen as the best venue for radical demonstrations.

A short note is appropriate on Portugal since the revolution of 1974. Prior to that time the upper clergy had been quiescent and their appointments controlled by the regime. Protest and political dissidence came largely from Portuguese Catholic missionaries in the overseas territories. The Church inherited a tradition of anticlericalism and middle-class indifference on the one side and support from the smaller proprietors of the north and centre on the other. There were exceptions to the record of quiescence, notably the Bishop of Oporto, who protested from a liberal viewpoint. Being a non-theological body, the Portuguese Church found the winds of change from Rome not entirely to its liking: it stood rather by the Pilgrimage to Fatima and the mystique of Empire. The movement of dissident priests back from Africa to Portugal imported revolution, just as happened in the case of the military.

With the coup the bishops published a pastoral praising democracy, but the increasing leftward trend alerted ecclesiastical uncertainties, especially with respect to the control of Catholic radio. The Catholic population itself is spread along the political spectrum, less so in the Communist party, but everywhere else including the close ally of the Communist party, the MDP. Perhaps there are proportionately more Christians in the non-Marxist Social Democratic Centre and the MPD than in the Socialist Party of Mario Soares. The Social Democratic Centre has a member of Opus Dei as its secretary; and there are also Christian Democrats who have been banned from elections. Based on Braga and more traditional Catholic areas, the CDS used explicit Christian symbolism and ecclesiastical connections, partly to the embarrassment of the Church. The banning of the CDS was probably advantageous. Clearly the Church laity have been coexisting with the new Portugal, even, to some extent, enthusiastically, but that coexistence, particularly so far as the hierarchy are concerned, is threatened by Communist attempts at hegemony and the atheistic philosophy inevitably associated with it. Since then democratic forces and the Church have been in practical alliance: the freedom of Catholic radio and of the official Socialist newspaper have turned out to be the same cause. (This material is taken from various sources, but particularly *The Times* and Adrian Hastings, *The Tablet*, 12 and 19 April 1975.) There is little doubt that the influence of the priests and parish weeklies, more especially in the Catholic north, prepared the way for the defeat of left extremism in November 1975.

The Greek situation exemplifies a clear pattern with local variations of truly Byzantine complexity. Basically the Colonels violated the laws of the Church (and of Byzantium) by trying to retire any democratic or non-compliant bishops and leaning on the sometime liberal but now reactionary Archbishop of Athens, Hieronymos. They even had in mind the use of the Church as a mini-Vatican of the eastern Mediterranean, fostering pan-Hellenic ambitions in that area. The resultant tensions and the eventual overt conflict with Makarios plus the mainland unrest signalled by the 'polytechnic events' in Athens led directly to the desperate throws preceding the Cyprus débâcle and to the division of the island. Once the Colonels were deposed the hierarchy was again in part retired, but not before the image of the Church had been seriously damaged amongst the young. What remained, however, was the union of the Church and the Greek spirit, and the pattern of rural rite and festival intertwining the Church and the café as twin foci of social existence.

Authoritarian societies of the left provide our fifth category, one in which the immanent possibilities of societies are overprinted by the fact of Russian hegemony and the imposition of Communist governments. History is full of contingencies of this kind from the Battle of the White Mountain to the Battle of Stalingrad. As has just been remarked, the Church must be controlled organisationally, by the manipulation of appointments, the infiltration of government agents and by subventions of money which are dependent on compliant behaviour. In authoritarian societies of the right the Church must act as it does because it is forcibly united to the state; in authoritarian societies of the left it is often forcibly separated from the state.[33] Churches are reduced to the level of private associations for religious deviants, who are usually allowed no more scope than is required for the bare performance of worship, and often less than that. Freedom of cultic behaviour is frequently interpreted to mean that active evangelisation amounts to interference with the rights of others while atheistic propaganda is part of the liberation of the backward and psychically deviant. In Russia, indeed, religious socialisation under the age of eighteen is forbidden. As evangelisation is forbidden so too is political comment. The public voice of the church can be raised no higher than a request for its rights under codes of 'socialist legality', in itself often a dangerous operation. It is also allowed and encouraged to support the 'peace' conferences of the Eastern bloc and to perform certain political roles

257

through ecumenical organisations.[34] Participation in such organisations is conditional on obedience to governmental policies, and on a reciprocal silence from other churches in the West who desire such participation. The overall impact of this is threefold. First, the Church is totally excluded from the official symbolism of the nation. Second, its public voice and symbolic presence can only be deployed in total obedience to national policy. Third, it must accept complete privatisation in that it cannot explicitly form a sub-culture or contribute to debate on public issues. As an association of private persons it operates under a Ministry of Cults, with which it must be registered, and which, in the Soviet Union at least, defines the minimum local numbers necessary for registration and the opening of a church.[35]

All the above follows from the fact of the end of ideological *laissez-faire*. Error cannot be allowed open competition with truth, and truth requires active administrative action. This administrative action operates through total control of the media and means of socialisation, which means that there is an inverse relationship between the number of believers in a given milieu and exposure to media and the socialisation processes. Since the administrators must themselves be untainted they are necessarily part of the Communist party, which is the vanguard of truth. And since administrative power is the chief focus of power and status it follows that the elite are almost entirely non-religious. Given that this is the situation in the power elite and given the differential impact of media and socialisation, it follows that believers are concentrated amongst the relatively powerless, the relatively uneducated and those least integrated into the social and economic process. Whether they are least integrated because they are believers or vice versa varies from case to case. In this way the relationship of practice to education and status is the reverse of that obtaining in Western societies. Religion is pushed to margins, geographical and social.

Since the aim of Communist societies is to exorcise culture of all contrary or recalcitrant elements, it cannot afford even the cultural deviance found in authoritarian societies of the right. A Solzhenitsyn is a peculiar offence, particularly when his opposition is twofold: to the mistakes and the theory of the regime and to the subservience of the Church. But just because the thrust of Communist policy is comprehensive control of culture as well as of structure this means that churches and sects are symbols of opposition without needing to do more than actually exist. Since politics are proscribed, except in the form of inner-party pressures, political opposition is pushed down to the level of culture, either literature or religion, particularly as passed from hand to hand in *samizdat* form, i.e. as underground literature.

Restriction to the private sphere makes religion merely an aspect of the individual life-cycle, and this cannot be covered by the formulations of officially certified truth. Nevertheless it must be discouraged and displaced by functional equivalents in the form of socialist rituals for birth, confirmation, marriage and death. These rites, more especially baptism, are the most tenacious aspects of religion in Communist as in Western societies, since they touch the person most nearly. They set him in cosmic space, carry forward the subterranean continuities and nostalgias of culture, and focus familial pressures for the symbolic expression of those continuities.[36] Hence the need to refurbish all the non-religious elements of folklore in order to cover up the discontinuity which could be left by the demise of religion. In Russia at least this policy has been partly successful, especially in relation to the marriage rite.

Policy is in fact variable, moving between periods of relative tolerance and vigorous repression, but the aim is unchanging. This is because a scientific prediction has been made about the demise of religion and about the triumph of 'science' by administrators who are self-defined as the only philosophic guardians of social science. If the facts do not 'naturally' conform to their prediction then the reality must be forcibly manipulated, else science and its priesthood are discredited. On their own premises they have no option but to persecute.

Under these kinds of pressure the Churches themselves remain conservative in their ethos: to adjust theologically is to concede the last bastions of independence. On the whole dialogue does not ensue between Marxists and Christians, except in Catholic Poland and Yugoslavia, merely because Marxist truth can gain nothing by commerce with error. The relationship is an endurance test, not a discussion. Even Churches must repeat the public rhetoric of Communism, since he who is not publicly with Communism must be against it. This is not to say that the rhetoric is entirely believed either within Churches or outside them. An acceptance of the 'sacred canopy' of Marxist dogma in the population at large is accompanied by a very widespread pragmatic scepticism. Yet this is not the same as disbelief, but runs parallel to the distinction made in Western societies between 'real' Christianity and the extant institutional Church. It allows dissidents to hanker after the 'real' Marxism of a libertarian or Trotskyist left. 'Marxism has not failed; it has never been tried' – to adapt the defence of Christian apologists.

The aim of all such systems is unity and ideological monopoly, and it is even possible to use the old state Churches as interim vehicles for suppressing deviance. Orthodoxy in Russia and in Romania is used to suppress Uniate and other deviants. Religious nationalism such as exists in Catholic Lithuania and the western Ukraine can be suppressed as mere 'bourgeois nationalism', whereas Russian nationalism is 'loyalty to the socialist fatherland'. Philosophical annihilation goes hand in hand with repression. Yet unity is not achieved because total control even of Orthodoxy itself or the Baptist Churches breeds vigorous schisms within both, and the schismatics accuse the official leadership of being state puppets. Thus the puppets sometimes need and ask to be allowed some marginal leeway in order to prevent breakaway movements of untraceable, uncontrollable, unregistered schismatics. In certain cases, notably the Jews, language and culture have to be suppressed along with religion in order to prevent sub-cultural diversification. Where even this fails the state may eventually prefer migration, since this weakens the resistance of those left behind. Even so, migration which was used freely by Russian sects under Tsarism is not now a right but an occasional privilege.

In fact the only major instance of religious independence exists in Poland, where the Catholic Church is so strong as to constitute an element of semi-recognised political opposition, even indeed of limited criticism.[37] Each side warily watches and treats the other within agreed norms and uses the fact of rivalry to discipline deviants within its own ranks. Only here, in the most Catholic land in Europe, does the central issue for Catholicism – education – recur as a major question within the Eastern bloc. The Communist concessions in Poland are purely pragmatic and display the usual alternations between strong pressure and relative relief, especially in the crucial fields of education and socialisation. The Catholic Church, for its part, tries to escape from the consequences of a Vatican policy geared to the situation in Eastern Europe as a whole – since this gives too much away. The Church also minimises the impact of the Vatican Council because this could create divisions for the government to exploit.[38]

Something more must be said about the relationship of ideological monopoly and of the newly revived 'sacred canopy' to Baptists, eschatological sectarians, groups like the Old Believers, and communitarians like the Molokans. Molokans, by virtue of forming separate communities, economically and socially, were clearly offensive to social unity, and were further endangered by their very rationalism and progressivism. They were so close to Communism; therefore they were otiose and should be disbanded.[39] Many of them turned to the Baptists, who were representative of the classic Protestant ethic, and who asked only for the right to be good, sober, disciplined workers on some other basis than the imperatives of 'socialist morality'. They were allowed to exist narrowly within these confines and they form a 'constituency' (as distinct from membership) of about 1 per cent of the Russian population. Most Baptists are in the interstitial, moderately educated sectors of urban life, whereas Orthodoxy is concentrated in the lowest (and largest) sector of the peasantry. Nevertheless, the subservience which is the price of Baptist survival has led to the appearance of the 'Initiative Group', itself comprising the best-educated and younger Baptists, and those most fully integrated into the Soviet economy.[40] The Old Believers, who were themselves at one time the functional equivalent of representatives of the Protestant Ethic are in relatively tolerated decay. The Witnesses usually define the regime as anti-Christ, and they are repressed with rigour because they are clear channels both of alienation and religious fantasy, as well as contaminated by a capitalist organisational style and American origins. The Pentecostals suffer only slightly less and for the same reasons. Such sects become visible by virtue of their dogged attempts to socialise their children in their beliefs. An index of repression and fear is provided by the desuetude of sectarian pacificism: military service is defined by socialism as central to loyalty, and opposition to it carries enormous costs in visibility and vulnerability. So much for the utopianism of Tolstoy or of the Doukhokors. (It is one of the paradoxes of liberty that self-defined progressive states treat military service as *the* obligation. Switzerland is just such an instance of 'democratic' intolerance, and so in some degree is the United States.)

It is worth noting that the sectarians and traditional Protestant denominations are present in any numbers only in Russia. The other religious minorities in Eastern Europe are 'Churches' such as Catholicism in East Germany (8 per cent), Calvinism in Hungary (20 per cent), and Islam in Yugoslavia (12 per cent) and Bulgaria (8 per cent). Given the antagonism between Catholicism and the regime in Hungary, relationships between the Calvinist Church and the regime have been less acerbic. Catholicism in East Germany is heavily pressured and also more lively and resistant than the Lutheran Church.

Jewry is repressed as a source of deviant culture, religiously and ethnically defined,[41] though it can also be repressed by relatively liberal Communists as in Poland because Jews who escaped to Russia returned as a key element in the post-war Stalinist elite. The same criteria for repression apply to any religion which has an ethnic base potentially at odds with the imperatives of overall Russian unity. Any such fissiparous union of autonomous national sentiment and religion is labelled as 'bourgeois nationalism' by contrast with the true nationalism of the 'socialist fatherland'. Catholic Lithuania, and to a lesser extent, semi-Catholic Latvia and Lutheran Estonia are each countries where religion has some association with nationality, particularly so in the case of Lithuania.[42] Hence the severe and partially successful pressure to which the Catholic Church in Lithuania is currently subjected. The resistance of the one-time established

Lutheranism in Estonia has been quite weak; the Church does not provide a very effective focus of national feeling. Interestingly enough both Lutheranism and the Mennonite faith provide vigorous foci of ethnic identity amongst those Germans scattered in various parts of Russia.

IV Religion and regional identity and autonomy

At this point the discussion of the five basic categorie, can be concluded, and a subject taken up which from time to time has arisen during the course of analysis: the question of regional sub-culture. It is never quite clear of course where a genuine nation exists as distinct from a regional tone and sense of belonging. La Vendée is a region, Brittany and Catalonia are somewhat more than regions, Lithuania and Croatia are nations incorporated in other nations. The discussion of regions must necessarily overlap with what has previously been said about national myths and the attitudes towards cultural diversity which vary according to our five different categories. Regionalism introduces a particular aspect of power; the power of the centre versus the periphery. The centre may dominate politically and/or numerically; or the situation may be bi-polar. Regionalism also introduces a particular aspect of identity: the problem of the shading off of one identity into another, and the overlapping and subsumption of identities at margins and borders. Some general principles arise with respect to the specific questions of periphery and centre, however much these overlap with other issues of status difference or economic deprivation, both actual and perceived. Furthermore, there can even arise some overlap between a regional religiosity, geographically defined, and the kind of dispersed sub-cultural sector normally represented by Protestant nonconformity: Wales is the obvious example. I mean that Protestant dissenting denominationalism, normally dispersed in a wider society at rather specific status levels *can* constitute a regional religiosity.

If regions and areas with a specific religious tone attached to them are listed they are plainly of various kinds, though often at the border with another country or pressed against the border of the sea. Examples are: Lappland, the Bergen hinterland, the Göteborg and Jönköping regions, North Jutland, Friesland, Wales, Scotland, the Western Isles, Northern Ireland, Cornwall, North Lancashire (the Fylde), Flanders, Brittany, La Vendée, Alsace, the Jura, the Cévennes, the Basque country, Catalonia, Malta, Croatia, Serbia, Bosnia, Cyprus, the Calvinist and Lutheran regions of Hungary, Muslim Southern Bulgaria, Lithuania, Estonia, Georgia, Armenia. These variously involve:

(1) areas where the religious frontier is marginally different from the national border; hence presumably the 1 per cent of Orthodox Christians in Finland whose national affiliation lies athwart their religious affiliation.

(2) Relatively remote and usually rural peripheries which retain and then emphasise orthodoxies once dominant at the centre: hence Friesland with its orthodox Calvinists split off from the liberalised Dutch Reformed Church, and North Jutland, characterised by a kind of piety now practically extinct in Copenhagen.

(3) Alternative poles to the official centre, where the centre can be defined as relatively secularist: the area of Bergen poised against the ambience of Oslo, or Slovakia set against Czech Lands and Moravia.

(4) An area of different language or dialect where religion supports identity, contrasted with a relatively secular capital: Flanders *vis-à-vis* Brussels, Brittany *vis-à-vis* Paris.

(5) An area where language is a *relatively* weak defining element, thus thrusting the onus of definition on to religion: the Basque country and to some extent Wales.

(6) An area where a language has died out making religion the *only* possible source of renewed identity: Cornwall.

(7) An area originally defined by conversion to a different religion which must retain that religion if it is to have any contemporary source of identity: the 'island' of Catholic, 'Italianate' culture in Bulgaria.

(8) Islands, like Malta and Cyprus, for whom religion has both provided the sense of internal belonging *and* a sense of external affiliation, plus on occasions the role of buffer or strategic point *vis-à-vis* different and hostile religions.

(9) A Protestant island or peninsula in a Catholic sea or vice versa: Württemburg, the Cévennes, Silesia, the Jura, the areas of Upper Austria to which Protestants retreated at the Counter-Reformation. This is quite close to (7).

(10) Areas retaining the old religion after the new religion has taken over the heartlands of a culture: the Fylde and some of the Western Isles which escaped the Reformation.

(11) Areas which have acquired a specific religio-ethnic character by virtue of the clustering of migrants: semi-Catholic Preston, Liverpool.

(12) A 'plantation' defined and sustained by the hostility of the relatively dispossessed: Protestant Ulster.

(13) An area where the national Church or a free Church acquires relatively greater strength and achieves some self-consciousness because of it: the Göteborg hinterland with its Lutheran awareness, Jönköping with its noticeable colouring of free-church adherents.

(14) Ex-nations or proto-nations for whom a major (or the major) source of identity is religion: Scotland, Estonia, Croatia, Lithuania, Armenia.

(15) Areas with national sentiments which are principally defined by culture, language and politics but which also need religion to be congruent with that definition, especially as regards clerical personnel and language: Catalonia.

(16) An area of mixed religion placed at a linguistic junction, which paradoxically gains some self-awareness and increased religious self-consciousness by virtue of internal rivalry and being alternately in one cultural sphere and then another: Alsace, partly Protestant and partly Catholic, and using two languages.

(17) An area of weak ethnic consciousness and a depressed and dispersed mode of life for whom expressions of identity can only occur in some minor variant of the metropolitan religion. The influence of Laestadianism among the Finnish and Swedish Lapps is an instance of this, the principal symbol of identity being a difference in clerical dress. [43]

Certain characteristics of these several different types of identity are worth underlining. Many are remote or in some way cut off: this makes both for distinctiveness and definition as well as preventing the latest waves of culture from corroding the local way of life too quickly. If they are also rural then this makes for dispersed communication and weakens impulses from the metropolitan centre. Some are placed at borders and either draw strength from the presence of co-religionists across the border, or from the fact that they are the last outpost of one religion before the territory of the infidel begins.

One of the kinds of special area and region listed above is based on migration, i.e. the movement of people from a regional or national culture to another national or cultural context. This has varied implications for religious practice and identity according to whether or not certain conditions are fulfilled. As is well known, foreign migrants tend to cluster at the cultural centre rather than the periphery, and so may increase the alienation of periphery from centre.

The conditions which bear on the maintenance of religious identity and practice with respect to migration can be rapidly stated. They are: whether or not the migration is seasonal; whether or not whole families are involved; whether or not the roles available in the host culture allow clustering in given urban sectors; whether or not the religion of the host culture is significantly different from that of the migrants; whether or not there are historic mutual perceptions as between members of the two cultures which are hostile or involve superiority and/or inferiority; whether or not religion has been a major focus of such perceptions; whether or not adequate numbers move to form a supporting environment; whether or not other foci of identity like language have to be dropped; whether or not the group achieves forms of social mobility which break down endogamy, whether or not historic 'peculiarities' (like the role of women or the wearing of turbans) are defined as *jointly* crucial for the identity of the religion and of the culture.

If one considers some of the varieties of movement from national cultures into migrant areas one can see how these conditions apply. West Indians, with Anglican, Catholic or Methodist backgrounds have moved to Britain; so have Catholic Poles, Maltese, Italians and Hungarians, and Orthodox Armenians, Russians, Cypriots and Greeks; so also have Muslim Pakistanis, and Bangladeshis, Sikhs and Hindus. Algerian Muslims and North African Jews and Russians have moved to France; Spaniards have moved to France and Switzerland; Italians have moved to Switzerland and Germany; Turks have moved to Germany, Portuguese have moved to Germany and France. Two of these are classic cases of diaspora where there is no indubitable region to which they may return: Jews and Armenians. Jews may, of course 'return' to Israel, but that is not where they come from.

We may take those cases which illustrate the application of the conditions outlined above. The West Indians come from a practising culture to a non-practising culture; they are of the same religion as the inhabitants; they are defined by themselves and others as inferior; their religious 'style' is different, i.e. enthusiastic. The result is a tendency to form groups belonging to an enthusiastic variant of the Christian religion, Pentecostalism, which can provide a sense of protective enclosure and catharsis for migrants. The Scots and Welsh came from practising cultures to a non-practising culture; they are not self-defined as respectively so superior and so inferior that there is a sense of important difference. The result is an accommodation to the English levels of practice and eventual loss of identity. The Irish came from a practising to a non-practising culture; there is a historic perception of England in which religion is the major focus of difference; the religious difference is considerable; the Irish feel they are regarded as inferior; they achieve relatively little social mobility, at least until very recently. The result is that they retain a fairly high level of practice and religious identity. The Poles came from a practising to a non-practising culture; they concentrated overwhelmingly in London and were involved in little geographical mobility; they mostly came together and in wartime conditions of crisis requiring mutual support; they came from a culture where religion was defined as the source of hope in difficulty. They therefore maintained a high level of practice. The Pakistanis came from a 'practising' to a non-practising culture; their religion was very different and defined as indissolubly wedded to their culture; they felt themselves regarded as inferior and different and were easily discernible as different; they had specific customs regarded as essential to their identity which clashed with the customs of the host culture, such as the place of girls in schools. The result was the setting up of institutions of cultural defence and demands for special treatment. Jews came (largely) from Eastern and then from Central Europe; they achieved social mobility, but geographically they shifted in a regular sequence from certain specific areas of a particular status to other specific areas of a higher status, thus retaining some cohesion. They were defined by themselves and others as different; they had specific customs which defined that difference and they tended to hold that some minimum adherence to their customs was essential to the retention of identity; *but* their mobility within the education system made endogamy difficult to apply and a relatively friendly environment corroded symbolic acts designed to distinguish and mark Jews off. Hence, on the one hand, Jews retained a high proportion of adherence in terms of synagogue affiliation, but on the other, let peripheral customs go and achieved a lower level of practice.

These processes, illustrated from British examples, can be applied to continental examples. The practising Breton moving to secular Paris sinks to the level of practice amongst those in his new group; the Italian in France does likewise and then returns to whatever was his original practice on going home; the Italian in Britain, in a Protestant environment, is likely to practise. The Italian in Switzerland is in a relatively practising environment. He is likely to practise. And incidentally he succeeds in altering the religious and linguistic balance of the country. The Russians and Ukrainians in Paris, as in London, are likely to practise and lay stress on the Church as the resonating memory of their culture, because their diaspora includes specifically religious reasons for flight. But with the next generation one cannot be sure. The Protestants who fled from Eastern Europe to Austria and Western Germany are likely to find in the Church a spiritual home which is also a cultural one, especially perhaps where surrounded by Catholics, as in Austria, the Palatinate, etc. Flemish people going to Brussels do as the Bruxellois do. The operation of some of these same principles has been common observation concerning all those Europeans who migrated to America: deprived to the possibility of retaining culture through language they carried their past forward through religion.

We must now examine certain key examples of regional cultures, notably where religion is related to proto-nationalism, but also where a strong regional sense is mediated by religion. Croatia and

Flanders have already been discussed, and so too has the Bergen hinterland.

At this point I want to take three examples of regional sentiment which are right wing, two which were to the right and have now moved to the left, one which has been persistently left, and one which remains to the right but has a left wing. I will discuss Slovakia, Brittany and La Vendée; the Basque country and Catalonia; Wales and Ireland.

Slovakia may be regarded as an instance of bi-polarity; it includes about a third of the population of Czechoslovakia and is much the most practising area of that country. It has always been on the wrong 'foot' and that foot a right one. This has come about by a mutual process of definitions by Slovak nationalists and by those for whom Slovak nationalism was dangerous. The first step in the 'wrong' direction was taken because Slovakia was a satellite of Hungary, which in turn was a satellite of Austria. When the Hungarian liberals rose against Austria in 1848 the Slovaks rose against the Hungarians, hoping to gain favour with Austria. They did not. And with the liberal state of 1918 they became part of one Czechoslovakia. National awareness fed on three sources. The first was the belief that they were economically exploited so that their pattern of industrialisation was distorted to provide feeders for eventual processing by Hungarian and later by Czech industry. The second was that their intelligentsia and white-collar workers were relatively unrepresented in the administrative elites, most conspicuously the Czech army. This exclusion ran parallel to a relative devaluation of the Slovak language. The third source of national awareness was religion: Slovaks distrusted the Hussite and atheist traditions of the Czechs. So when the Slovak People's party was founded in 1913 it was led by a priest Hlinka and it expressed religious and status and economic devaluations. It declared itself 'For God and People' and advanced the slogan 'In Slovakia speak Slovak'.

During the liberal republic the government coalitions always had a majority in Czech Lands and were a minority in Slovakia, where the Slovak nationalists constituted the largest single party. The next wrong step occurred in 1938 and 1939. Hitler leaned in the Slovak direction as part of his overall plan to destroy Czechoslovakia and in 1939 an independent Slovakia emerged under his protection and under the aegis of German economic pressures and dynamisms. The new Slovakia became a one-party 'clerico-Fascist' state with a Catholic priest, Tiso, as President. One has to remember that Slovakia was strongly Catholic, though there was a small autonomist Protestant party, and that the priesthood was a widely available channel of advancement for every level of society. The new regime developed *pari passu* with the Ustacha regime in Catholic Croatia.

In this situation the Communist party (together with Russia) had come to be regarded as the champion of Czech democracy against Hitler. After various tactical tries and turns in the war the Communists eventually returned to this position, adopting their pre-war anti-Munich, patriotic policy. In the National Coalition governments after the war the Communists were strongest in Czech Lands, where they secured 41 per cent of the vote in 1946, and only a minority in Slovakia where they received 30·4 per cent of the vote, as compared with a vote of 62 per cent for the Slovak Democratic party. This pushed them towards a centralist policy. They had to undermine the Slovak party as a nucleus of reaction and successor to 'clerico-Fascism' and simultaneously claim that Slovakia had 'nothing to fear from the Czech working class'. After February 1948 the Communist take-over was complete – the Stalinist leaders of the 1950s regarded autonomism as a purely Slovak affair and purged the Slovak intelligentsia accordingly. At the same time a combination of economic development and repression of Catholicism made nationalism more overt and self-conscious, particularly over the issue of Slovak migration to Czech Lands. The Prague Spring proposed some degree of devolution in every sphere towards local economic decision, workers' participation, and Slovak autonomy. The re-opening of churches and recovery of religious life at this time was most obvious in Slovakia. The Russians invaded, but Slovak autonomy was retained, and Husak, who had been imprisoned as a Slovak patriot, now presided over the new state.

Brittany and La Vendée have in the past clung to a militant Catholicism, and have seen their regional identity and faith mutually threatened by a secularist Paris. In the case of Brittany the language has been downgraded and the use of Breton names discouraged. So, for various mutually supporting reasons, Brittany and La Vendée are areas of devout practice and right-wing voting. The Basque sentiment began similarly. The desire for autonomy looked back to medieval popular forms of forum democracy. The language was in decline, throwing the onus of identity on to religion. Yet at the same time the Castilian Spanish, which made inroads in the Basque tongue, was defined as the tongue of a neglectful centre associated with liberal secularists. So Basque nationalism was fiercely Catholic and right wing. But given a situation in which Madrid was taken over by right-wing exponents of centralism it moved to the left, taking its fervent Catholicism with it. So there appeared the phenomenon of the guerilla priest. Catalonian sentiment began partly in a symbiosis of republican and federalist sentiment and partly in a conservative movement of linguistic and cultural revival which was successful.[44] There was less need of a religious vehicle of identity; and in any case Catalonia was the emporium of refugee radicalism and European political influence. During the dictatorship of Primo de Rivera the achievements and aspirations of its autonomous regional and middle-class culture were slighted. It moved further to the left, and, when a measure of autonomy was granted by the Republic in 1931 the move to the left was sealed. The sociological generalisations which follow are simply stated: if the language and culture of the periphery can carry identity alone and if the centre is not perceived as religiously very different then religion is not likely to be the focus of regional sentiment. If language is less viable as a source of identity and if the centre is perceived as different, whether it is secularist or of another religion, then religious nationalism is the likely outcome. It depends on who is responsible for trying to curb the urge to autonomy: whoever it is one adopts the opposing political stance. The Irish case can be understood in the same way. Ireland was subject to perceived and actual neglect and expropriation; it was dominated by a small Protestant elite; it was a geographical unity but suffered from the 'wedge' made by Ulster Plantations of the late sixteenth and seventeenth centuries; the language gradually gave way to English, in spite of its retention in certain western areas of the Gaeltacht; it relied first on the Liberals and then on the Labour party for support in the British Parliament. Overall, the national sentiment belongs to a predominantly rural society, with only one important urban cultural centre, Dublin, and it is therefore conservative in tone; but given the historic role of the Conservative party in relation to Ulster Unionism, and the complex fissions following the Irish civil war, its militant segment includes very left-wing elements. These left-wing elements include the specifically Marxist IRA which has been under heavy Catholic displeasure for twenty-five years.

Wales has been the obverse of Slovakia: always on the left foot. In the eighteenth century much of Wales embraced a localised, democratic religion, the Calvinistic variant of Methodism. The new faith appealed to those slightly removed from the system of social pressures and sanctions: the yeomen, artisans and shopkeepers. The gentry and to a lesser degree the Established Church were isolated by these changes and faced a vigorous, independent movement based on the chapels promoting land reform and political and civil liberties. Democratic religious organisation and rhetoric and democratic choral singing came to provide the dominant ethos; and the chapels were in explicit alliance with Liberalism. At the same time the educated man took precedence within an overall egalitarian system: he was the major influence in the chapel and became the manager in the colliery. Indeed, noncomformist traders and managers created a new professional class through which they dominated the schools and local politics. Its greatest triumph was when a Welsh Baptist lawyer, Lloyd-George, became Liberal Prime Minister in 1916, and its symbolic success was signalised by the disestablishment of the Church in 1911.

With the emergence of a large working class in South Wales and the advent of socialism the chapels severed their explicit Liberal connection. Chapel-goers now mostly voted Labour, and there appeared a strong trade union–chapel axis. Depression, unemployment and migration deepened the Welsh attachment to Labour and produced Communist enclaves. At the same time erosion occurred; the effects of mobility and new centres of entertainment diminished the life of the chapels. English began to replace Welsh and an English middle class took many important industrial positions, not to mention Welsh country cottages. The cultural penetration alerted the guardians of Welsh language and identity, more especially in the noncomformist, Welsh-speaking, professional middle class. A Welsh nationalism emerged to challenge the dominance of Socialism and Liberalism, as well as the dominance of England. Its roots were religious and linguistic, the politics of cultural defence. Nevertheless, nationalist politics could not be conservative: that remained part of the definition of English economic and cultural hegemony. Wales continued to counter-distinguish herself from England by egalitarianism rather than deference, Welsh rather than English, chapel rather than church, even though both chapel and language were on the decline. Indeed, the fact of decline was the stimulus of renewed identification. England, taken on its own, possessed an in-built conservative majority, bolstered by the unionism of the Ulster Protestants; Scotland and Wales provided the possibility of a Socialist government and fragments of Liberal opposition. The mutually antagonistic political and religious definitions of the English centre and the Welsh or Scots peripheries were reactivated by the very process of homogenisation.

Since the discussion has turned on issues of centre and periphery, the special position of Ireland can be used to illustrate just how complex and important the questions of centre and periphery are. After all peripheries can be centres, or represent and stand for centres, while centres can be peripheries. Ireland is peripheral to England, but England is peripheral to Europe and to Rome. The Roman centre, at its moment of weakness before the barbarians, was strengthened on its distant Irish periphery, from which the faith returned to Scotland and England, moving first from peripheral island to peripheral island: Iona to Lindisfarne. So Ireland, like Poland, is the hard circumference of the Roman centre of the circle. Since Ireland is indeed peripheral to England and England defines its marginality in relation to Europe through Protestantism, Ireland is strengthened in her Catholicism and in her relation to England's historic enemies, Catholic Spain and France. This in turn strengthens the fear and prejudice of Englishmen with regard to Popery, and justifies repression. Indeed it justifies the 'planting' of a Protestant people from another periphery, Scotland, on the north-east periphery of Ireland. Once there the plantation dominates and needs the local population. And when this situation leads to partition, as in 1922, the local Catholics in Northern Ireland find themselves a people of the centre still pushed to the social periphery of a periphery. The historical scene is set for violence, intransigence, fear and religious bigotry. In Southern Ireland, where Catholicism and the state are one, the historical enmity no longer obtains. The Protestant cause is defeated without any doubt; but the Protestants remain in positions of relatively high status and constitute a declining 5 per cent of the population concentrated in the Dublin area and the south-west coast. Five per cents are rarely dangerous, ratios of 60–40 often are, and especially so when set in a wider pan-Irish context of 75–25 which makes a minority of the local northern Protestant majority.

Just one isolated query remains over from the analysis so far provided before we proceed to a discussion of the consequences of industrialisation and modernisation in the context of the five basic categories outlined. This query concerns the relationship between the incidence of free churches dispersed through the wider culture and the incidence of regional sentiment relying on religion as a vehicle. Religious dissent of the free-church type is largely a Protestant phenomenon, except for its efflorescence in Russia since the revolution, and latterly in Brazil and Chile. It is at its maximum in the USA; it is powerful in Britain; it is of a minor importance in Sweden and Germany; and in so far as it exists in Scotland and Holland it consists of movements towards a restatement of Calvinist orthodoxy.[45] The free-church principle overlaps regional sentiment only in Wales, Cornwall and Friesland, unless one includes internal parties within Lutheranism, in which case it also overlaps regional sentiment also in the Bergen hinterland. Clearly, the free-church principle is largely characteristic of Protestant cultures and then only under highly specific conditions which cannot be enumerated here; and it has a very limited association with regional awareness.

V Correlates and consequences

This chapter has been concerned with power at the level of the state, with power through the agency of systems of meaning, and with their interrelationship. It is now necessary to turn to the contours of practice and belief as observed on the ground, exercising power and having power exercised upon them.

The European map of religious practice consists of a dark heartland at the European centre of which the hub is Switzerland. An arm moves down towards Venice and a thick tongue stretches along the Rhine up to southern Holland, with a fork downwards into Flanders. Isolated blocks lie like dark continents separated by some movement of the continental plates. Slovakia, Poland, Brittany, the Massif Central, Ireland, Northern Iberia, Greece. England and Russia are shaded lightly: England greys somewhat to north and west, Russia lightens as the eye travels east. Scandinavia is the area least tinged by religious practice, constituting a region of off-white across the north of the continent, which also stretches down deep into Lutheran Germany and especially Protestant East Germany. Along the underside of the continent below the Tagus and through the marches of south-west Spain there is another area scarcely darker, cutting patchily across southern Italy, into Albania, Serbia, Montenegro and Bulgaria. Most of these southern areas have been regions of disaffection for a long time, and indeed their borders correspond curiously to the rim of Islam's advance into Christendom.

Perhaps some figures may indicate what levels of intensity underlie the relativities just indicated. I would estimate that on any given Sunday those present in church constitute about one person in four of those over seven and able to attend; perhaps the figure should be a little higher. The figure for East Europe is about the same, but it represents a sharper recent decline from higher levels existing prior to the advent of Communist governments. In Russia perhaps about 5 per cent are regularly in church (where the buildings are available) with may be somewhat higher proportions at the margins, as for example the Ukraine and Armenia in the south and Lithuania and Latvia in the north-west. In Scandinavia the percentages vary between 2 and 4 per cent, and this is repeated for the Protestant state Churches taken *on their own* in Holland, Germany and England. If the overall proportion rises (as it does in the UK, to some 12 per cent) this either derives from a Catholic diaspora or the existence of substantial dissent, e.g. the nonconformists in England and the neo-orthodox schisms in Holland, or both. In dissenting Wales and (sociologically) dissenting Scotland and Northern Ireland, Protestant weekly practice rises to about 25 per cent; and a mild reflection of this is seen in Norway in the religious form that regionalism takes in the Bergen hinterland. Protestant practice also rises to the 25 per cent level or higher where it is a minority, as in France, or is at the border with Catholicism, as in Switzerland. But in general Protestant practice on any given Sunday is about 5 per cent and Catholic practice (overall) about 35–40 per cent. However, this varies from the 95 per cent of Eire, and the 75 per cent of northern Spain and Poland, Bavaria, western Austria and southern and central Switzerland, to the 10 per cent of southern Spain, southern Portugal and the Paris basin,[46] areas of large-scale industry with industrial proletariat, or of latifundia with rural proletariat.

Catholic weekly practice is at its optimum where it is the expression of a repressed nationalism (Poland) or of a repressed regional nationalism (the Basque country) and in these circumstances it achieves majority practice: Eire 95 per cent, Poland 75 per cent, the Basque country 80 per cent, Brittany 75 per cent. Then it achieves good levels of practice where it is either a moderately sized minority of (say) 10 per cent as in the UK or 20 per cent as in the USA or a very large minority as in Germany, Switzerland and Holland. In these latter it is assisted by heavy regional concentrations, and whereas in the UK and the USA Catholicism creates a purely cultural integration, in Holland, Germany and Switzerland it builds up 'pillars' covering most aspects of life. The consequence is practice of 40 per cent and over. However recent data do indicate falls in the US, UK, Holland, Germany, Australia and elsewhere from the mid-1960s on. Poor conditions exist for Catholicism in those whole societies where it is the official majority faith and where this has given rise to dichotomous splits in the society such that Catholicism is largely identified with one side of the split. This has been the case in France, Italy and Spain and leads to an overall weekly practice of 20 per cent, 30 per cent and 35 per cent respectively. The weekly figures for France show a drop even between 1971 and 1975: 21 per cent to 17 per cent. Spain and France are also marked by steep gradients of practice in relation to status.

Protestant practice has special characteristics which should be noted. It involves a quite substantial amount of seasonal and occasional conformity, so that between a third and a half of Protestants have contact with the church from time to time: this type of practice is relatively low in Sweden but quite substantial in England.[47] Second, the penumbra of belief is high (60 per cent believe in God in Sweden, 70–80 per cent in England, 90 per cent in Germany) and the practice of prayer is very widespread. Private prayer is a practice of at least half the population in most Protestant countries; and there is in addition a web of religiously toned associations which generally covers about one person in three. Confirmed indifference in Protestant societies generally affects only about a third of the population, while confirmed piety is characteristic of only about one-sixth.[48]

In Orthodox societies the resistance to secularisation is weaker, so that Serbia, Bulgaria and Russia probably achieve little above 5 per cent practice, and that more sharply concentrated in older groups than elsewhere. The variations occur where Orthodoxy can retain a positive relation to nationalism, as it does in Greece (40 per cent plus?), and in Romania (25 per cent plus?). Romania uses the Church as one element in the national counter-definition of an isolated Latin culture. Catholic societies in East Europe are probably in the range 20–30 per cent, with the exception of Poland; Catholic

273

enclaves are in any case always stronger than the surrounding Orthodox or Protestant areas whether in Croatia and Slovenia or in the
DDR. Firm practice in the youngest generation rarely characterises
more than 10 per cent, again Poland excepted.

But the relevant category here is Communist government, and this
has certain general consequences. The first is that the area of explicit
atheism is very much larger than in western Protestant societies and
considerably larger even than in those Catholic societies of the West
where large Communist parties exist. Grass-roots Communism in
the West is mainly non-ideological, but in the East ideological
conformity is officially propagated within the state education system
and the media. It generally claims about one-third of the population,
though in Orthodox Bulgaria, Russia and the Czech Lands it may
amount to two-thirds. Furthermore, the intermediate third, between
believers and non-believers, possesses a vague inchoate belief, often
hesitant, which is supplemented by occasional conformity to the
rites of the Church. Specifically ecclesiastical religion, where religious
and priestly authority is fully accepted, is pushed back so that it
accounts for about a third of the believers.[49] It seems that the rite
has a continued power which is analogous to the continued appeal of
prayer in the Protestant West.

The social location of religiosity in Communist countries is very
well illustrated by recent surveys conducted in Slovenia. Nine peasants
out of ten are 'religious' and five workers out of ten are accounted so.
By contrast with the West, the white-collar stratum is less religious than
the workers. Both migration to the towns and increased education
diminish religiosity. The younger workers are *more* religious than
the older since they are of a peasant origin: this conforms to the
Polish pattern rather than (say) the Bulgarian pattern and the pattern
of other Eastern European states where religion declines among the
younger working-class groups. It is interesting that these surveys
mention the danger of Christianity becoming the ideology of the
lower, deprived strata, a position to which the younger clergy are
already moving. (One may perhaps recollect that Slovenia is one of
the few areas with a pre-war tradition of Christian Socialism.) In
other words, Christianity in the East returns to the sociological
condition originally noted by St Paul: 'not many wise, not many
mighty, but the offscourings of the earth'. Other researchers note the
possibility of a hardening core of Christian witness centred on faith
in Jesus Christ.[50]

The most tenacious aspect of religion, East and West, is the rite of
Baptism: it is relatively weak in Russia (45 per cent), Bulgaria, East
Germany and England (60 per cent) but it is normally practised by
at least 90 per cent of the population in the West, including those
countries with large Communist sectors. And it is a majority practice

in most East European countries. Ecclesiastical marriage is much less universal, especially in countries where there has been a tradition of laïcist militancy. In countries like West Germany it is perhaps seen as an aspect of administration, and is widely practised on that account. In Eastern Europe ecclesiastical marriage is sometimes a minority practice, particularly in view of the fact that it makes the participants visible to the authorities in a way baptism need not. Confirmation tends to be a majority practice where it is associated with initiation into adulthood, so that in Scandinavia over 90 per cent of the population is confirmed.

Various important changes underlie these static figures. First, practice is generally in decline. Second, it is tilted towards the older generation, but much more sharply so in Eastern Europe than in the West. Poland is quite exceptional in this since the state cannot deprive the Church of institutional access to the young. Third, where practice is poor in Catholic countries there is a greater degree of participation and personal communion among those who *do* practise. Fourth, where Christianity is under pressure there emerges a core, of which perhaps faith in Christ is the key element, and this becomes relatively irreducible and perhaps more coherent as the vague and uncertain elements are shorn away. Religion also acquires, where this is allowed, some capacity for social and political criticism. Fifth, ecclesiastical religion in terms of priestly authority and the regulation of familial morality is everywhere diminishing. Sixth, superstition is probably in decline but remains as a substantial free-floating element in most Protestant societies (supplemented by suggestions of reincarnation and spiritualism); and it also remains as an element embedded in the life of the Church and outside it in undeveloped rural areas, e.g. in parts of Spain, Portugal and Greece. Indeed in these areas there is a very substantial extra-ecclesial religiosity. Seventh, alongside superstitution there lies a very widespread folk religion based on decency, limited reciprocity, and belief in 'something' which is often accompanied by a respect for the ritual forms of religion in Church and in state but without any great understanding of their meaning. This folk religion and this civic religion are particularly widespread in Protestant societies and they are not eroded by the recoil of ecclesiastical religion and institutional practice. It is perhaps most significant that in the orthodox East the core of resistance is the rite, in the Protestant West private prayer.

This leads to a consideration of the internal condition of the Church. In this connection one must be aware of cultural layers which are encapsulated in Catholicism: para-Christian and pre-Christian manipulative magic, semi-Christianised systems of mediation, expressing local loyalties and providing sources of personal consolation and assistance, the religion of the Council of Trent, the religion of the Second Vatican Council. The last-mentioned makes more progress where the Catholic Church is decreasingly isomorphic with the social order, where the level of literacy is increasing, and where the incidence of the new middle class is high enough for them to regard authoritarianism and priestly prestige as a constraint. It makes much less progress where there is an external threat against which unity is essential, as in Poland, or where the majority of Catholics are of low status or peasants or of the old middle class.

The changes of the last decade or so which have occurred in conjunction with the Council have been most dramatic in the USA, Holland, Spain, and, in lesser degree, Germany. They include a devolution of authority expressed in schemes of participation: lay consultation, episcopal collegiality, democratic procedures in monasteries and priestly associations. Ecclesiastical roles have become more specialised, they demand more expertise and are less programmed by rigid socialisation. Priests are organised in groups in relation to larger areas. Liturgy is a dialogue of priest and people based on joint celebration, with a premium on clear communication and personal encounter rather than the invocation of the numinous. In all this one sees the triple operation of rationalisation, specialisation and the urge to personal contact which is bred by large-scale bureaucratic structures. Private confession declines as corporate communion increases. Thus the new 'personalism' is corporate in its emphasis rather than individualistic. The Cursillos de Christian dad of the early 1960s exemplify just such a personal religion: a corporate 'Protestant' feeling resembling the Wesleyan class meeting. Indeed, in its most radical manifestations it results in a free communitarianism, where the participants translate the gospel into communal anticipations, sometimes with a direct political content. These openings to the communitarian left are paralleled by associations of traditionalists, as well as archaic folk movements, to the rural right. The majority in the middle are often confused and disoriented. Hence in part the decline in practice and hence, in particular, the defections of clergy and falling numbers of vocations.

The process of differentiation which dissolves the all-round role of the clergy also separates the Church off from other spheres. In the East it becomes simply a private and privatised association, though there are exceptions: Poland where it provides the soul of the culture, and Romania where Church and state still collaborate. Nevertheless, in most East-European states, Church and state have been separated, and since there are no parties, the Church is similarly separated from politics. This separation from politics can be seen operating in many contexts. In Spain the Church edges out of the system of legitimacy. In France and Italy it moves from right to centre, loosens the spirals of mutual antagonism and therefore of anti-clericalism, and gradually disentangles itself from direct support of a political party. The same is true of Germany. More Catholics appear on the left, the traditionalists and integrists become a minority wing, and the Church itself becomes a vehicle of political and social criticism. Bishops move to the centre-left.

At the same time the mechanisms of sub-cultural integration also weaken, particularly where Catholics come very close to overall parity with Protestant majorities. This again is more likely to occur where there is a large new middle class able to use the electronic media to spread its viewpoint, as in Holland. Nevertheless, though there are moves to universal schooling within state systems, the Catholic Church retains a heavy commitment to separate schools, since these are the sole key to distinctive socialisation. The socialisation provided by Catholic schools in countries once dominated by anti-clericalism and by struggle over education often becomes less rigid, so lessening the fear of the state that such schools train up the next generation of the right. Certainly this is the case in France. Protestants, on the other hand, are happier to accept the highly general religious 'instruction' usually provided in state schools, unless they belong to neo-orthodox breakaways. And in one or two Protestant countries, Sweden for example, the religious element is largely deprived of any tincture of commitment. Britain seems to be moving in a similar direction. Indeed, such education often simply initiates people into the folklore or the minimal morality or the basic classics of Christian civilisation. In so far as religious education is provided by the media it becomes less static, less dominated by ritual or Church sources, more open to the dramatisation of basic existential situations and political and social debate. In the interesting phrase of the recent report (1976) on religious education in Britain, it 'explores life stances'.

As has already been remarked, official Catholic social morality concerning the family is often disregarded, especially by educated and student Catholics, and this is congruent with widespread moves to separate the norms of Christianity or the Church from the legal norms governing family life. This again makes familial life a matter of Christian conscience not external regulation. Broad ideas of personal fulfilment partially replace rigid legal and social categories and prohibitions. Indeed, in Eastern countries there is even an attempt to replace wholesale the religious element in the celebration of the family life-cycle: birth, adulthood, marriage and death.

The final section of this brief summary must be concerned with the impact of industrialisation and modernisation on the churches, and the best focus for this is a review of practice in relation to occupation. Certain categories of work may be listed which lead to low practice. First, there are steel workers, metal workers, and people in all large

277

and highly mechanised industrial complexes, especially when these are located on their own and with no admixture of other categories. Second, there are large-scale farming enterprises, employing seasonal hired labour, or in Eastern Europe state farms. These categories are marked by size, impersonality and the pervasiveness of the mechanical. They subject men rigidly to process in the case of industry, and to uncertainty in the case of large-scale capitalist farming. Then there are groups which vary. In Catholic societies the extractive industries and fishing are often likely to be dechristianised, while in Protestant societies they are more likely to be influenced by dissent.

In all cases the intelligentsia is likely to be more explicit against or for religion.

In Catholic societies they generally have a lay secularist viewpoint which also extends to the health and perhaps legal professions. In Protestant societies they are either humanistic or they have a free personal religiosity, often tinged by medievalism, anarchism and communitarian nostalgias. In Communist societies intellectuals barely exist, except as a sector of administration and ideological control – hence their rigid atheism, except where humanistic and Christian traditions have some partial resonance, as in Czechoslovakia, Poland and Catholic Yugoslavia. This is where some dialogue has occurred, now largely silenced by increasing state pressures on the Churches.

Workers in administration necessarily vary according to the basic ideological leaning of the state: in Spain highly practising, in Protestant countries moderately so, and in Communist countries barely practising at all. 'Independents' are largely confined to Western societies and tend to practise at whatever is the local level of church attendance. Technicians are rather similar to administrative workers: indeed they also are an aspect of control. In Eastern societies they are relatively uninterested in ideological questions, and where there is a strong Catholic Church, as in Poland, they are not as markedly non-Christian as philosophers, literary men and other heirs to humanism. In the West they also have a tendency to be non-ideological or to exhibit a naïve acceptance of some world view, such as fundamentalist Protestantism which they conceive of as an 'explanation' analogous on the religious level to their own scientific explanations. This religiosity links with a greater conservatism than is found in the humanist intelligentsia. Indeed, the humanist intelligentsia, aided by the new middle class in the media, education and the expressive arts, has become partially radicalised by a rivalry with, and a distaste for, the technicist mentality, which they associate with the concept of pollution and exploitation of the world. Everywhere in Catholic or Protestant societies the new middle class is less practising than the old.

This brings us to groups prone to high practice. First, there are the Western administrative and business elites, who are in any case always disproportionately Protestant, except of course in southern Europe. Second, there are the white-collar workers and lower echelons of the personnel manning the education system. Third, there are the petty bourgeois sectors: shopkeepers, small-business men. Fourth, there are small farmers in traditional areas impregnated by deference and hierarchy, medium-sized farmers owning their own land under settled agricultural conditions, the gentry themselves and (within the limits set by large distances and isolation) those engaged in herding and shepherding. In so far as both the growth of industry and the industrialisation of the countryside tend to draw people from country to the towns this has implications for the proportion of those practising in a given society.

Indeed, in general the disorientations of industrial society in terms of conceptual, geographical and social mobility, all militate against the roots and the sense of the familiar and familial which support Christian images of the world. But alongside this general mobility certain fundamental facts stand out. In so far as work takes place in a personal setting where people own their homes, or their farms, or their own individual skills and professional abilities, in contexts which are familiar and on a human scale they are more likely to practise Christianity and be sensitive to it. In so far as they are submerged in a mass, dominated by vast enterprises and large-scale private or state undertakings, subjected to a soulless process based on mechanism, they are less likely to practise Christianity or to be aware of its meaning. The intelligentsia varies. If sensitised to forms of control inimical to its own expressionist sensitivity it may revert to highly personal religiosity, in particular either a free, unbounded mysticism or aesthetic ritualism. But if the intelligentsia is converted into the agent of technical exploitation carried out under the aegis of state power it succumbs to a materialistic ideology.

So long as these conditions outlined above continue so long does religious practice decline. It is possible to sum up the rival ecologies of practice and non-practice with two contrasting models. Imagine first Dimitrovgrad in the East or Bilonsville in the West: towns recently invented and rapidly developed around a huge complex based solely on heavy industry. They lie within the general area of a vast city and are surrounded more immediately by an agricultural region of either capitalistic or state farms. The labourers recruited from the capitalist farms come from an anomic, rootless rural proletariat, used to one agricultural crisis after another. Imagine, second, Marcester and Marislava: towns dating from Roman or early medieval times, expanding slowly around the employment provided by small light industries or services, or shops and provincial administration.

The tone is civic: the building materials are organic, the shapes rounded and human in scale. People mostly own their homes and the size of the houses varies only slightly according to income. There is little unemployment; families rarely break up in divorce or separation. No great roads slash through or over the old streets; bells sound through tree-lined avenues. People stay put; relationships of dependence, when they exist, are personal; different professions and avocations mix; long-established craftsmen consort with the members of old firms of solicitors and family businessmen. Round about are moderate-sized farms, personally owned by those who run them, and there is a long tradition of modest, steady, agricultural prosperity. Other things being equal according to the given political culture and its history, Marislava and Marcester practise and believe, Bilonsville does not practise, Dimitrovgrad neither practises nor believes.

Postscript

A postscript is necessary in view of certain salient facts: the total manipulation of culture in Eastern Europe in the interests of power and of intellectual theory, and the concomitant reversal of the relation of religion to status obtaining in Western Europe. This forms the essential frontier of the contemporary world and the most crucial element in the situation of religious belief. It requires summary comment.

Western Europe exhibits partial conformities under varying degrees of strain; Eastern Europe exhibits residual impulses to nonconformity under immense pressures toward total conformity. The stepping up of restrictions on the churches are expressions of this pressure. Western Europe is a system illustrating tendencies to a limited pluralism; Eastern Europe is a system illustrating a tendency to a total monism. Why? How? Why should the 'sacred canopy' retain a secularist guise and with 'scientific' pretensions?

The ruling ideology of Eastern Europe is an intellectualist formation originally expressing the position of intellectuals, especially of those who possessed ethnic or religious marginality in a state of partial disintegration. This ideology served the power interests of these intellectuals in the course of confronting the old administrative elites and it also helped to mobilise and solidify the hitherto untheoretical sector of the deprived in so far as these had already achieved positions of *relative* power and affluence within the current system. Whether intellectuals were able to achieve their ends depended on a variety of factors, among them the speed of industrialisation and resultant disorientation of meaning systems, the relative prestige of intellectuals, and the existence of situations where society had *already* split into warring poles. In some cases the power impulses of certain sectional oligarchies in the leading sectors of the proletariat were also subserved by this intellectualist ideology, although it was grasped in a vulgarised and rigidified form.

Once in control, for a variety of reasons which require no elaboration here, the intellectuals and the sectional working-class oligarchies found themselves confronted by the remorseless imperatives of power, made doubly remorseless by their own ideology, which disallowed conflict and claimed a monopoly of power and ontological rectitude. Thus armed and constricted they set about total control in terms familiar to them: the manipulation of culture through socialisation, education and the rejection of all verbal dissidence. Creatures of the word, they feared the word more than the rite. As happened with Puritans in the past, the metaphysical aura of the ideology served to cover the impulses to power, economic in the Puritan case, but political and cultural as well in the intellectual case. The twin aspects of this power were exploitation of the population in the interests of domination, and exploitation of the natural resources and of technique to provide enough rewards for selected sectors to make the domination secure. Power did not need to be shared, but rewards needed to be meted out to key sectors. Trapped in the technicist requirements of statism they needed to reorientate education in modes antagonistic to the expressionistic and traditionalist elements in humanism, and this had the double pay-off of limiting access to the past and diminishing the range of persons open to notions of intellectual dissidence. Intellectual dissidence in its turn had to fight to hold on to these traditions, and included in the traditions was some access to older concepts of freedom embodied in the religious past. Older style humanists were doubly inclined to this in cases where they belonged to those sectors of the older elite now persecuted by the new elite. At the same time the technicist mentality had its usual consequence of ideological indifferentism, in so far as socialisation was incomplete; but mere indifference could not generate a charge of ideological resistance on a large scale. One element of syncretism between old and new had a paradoxical consequence: the older 'intégrisme' had created the marginality of part of the radical intelligentsia, notably a *déraciné* Jewry, but it now passed on identical tendencies to the new intégrisme, so that after the first period of power the same marginal sectors of the intelligentsia came under pressure, and were thrust out or pushed towards dissidence *vis-à-vis* the new regime. Another element, equally paradoxical, is not due merely to syncretism with the older systems of integration but to the logic of monistic systems: schisms between doctrinal elites controlling different territories, heresies within territories defined by overt verbal dissidence or variation, reference to sacred scriptures, a class of committed ideologians, and rites of ideological reinforcement. The only limits on the logic of total power are temporary and pragmatic: where the old 'intégrisme' was extremely powerful as in Poland, where rival 'intégrismes' might diverge and disintegrate the state, as in Yugoslavia, where the old 'intégrisme' might be *used* against marginal groups as in Romania, and where external threat suggested the utility of a temporary union of old and new 'intégrismes' as in the Russian patriotic war against the Germans.

In the West, as has been suggested, all power is partial and socialisation is fragmented somewhat by religious and linguistic sub-cultures and sub-cultures based on status. Certain points are salient. The humanist intelligentsia still has interests in confronting the old administrative elites, especially when these ally themselves with the rising group of manipulative technocrats. But now it fears most of all the logic of total control. Its expressionist ideology pushes it towards the sources of power in the communication system where it spreads discontent with the old legal-military-clerical elites, but largely in the name of expressionist ideologies deriving from extreme liberalism rather than in the name of disciplined revolution. The liberal option is strengthened in those countries with Protestant traditions which also lack disciplined revolutionary forces. The technical elite itself is largely subordinate to the administrative elite by virtue of specialisation since it has no special ideological axe to grind and few sources from which to construct one. It simply conforms to the religious tone of the immediate elite, often indeed in a naïve form. In West and East it conforms: its indices of belief *and* unbelief are those of its immediate milieu. The imperatives of industrialisation and the need to satisfy popular aspirations in the interests of stability force the old administrative elite and technocratic sector forward in courses which disorientate and weaken the traditional meaning systems of Europe. This disorientation and the extension of pluralism can create the conditions under which either the older forms of integration will try to reestablish themselves in control, or the pluralistic tendency will be pushed dangerously close to anarchy and atomism, or the monism of the Eastern European system will come to seem attractive by virtue of the ideological vacua and disintegrations which have been created. Indeed, the first two of these options *can* combine to assist the progress of the third. Which of these options, singly or in combination, will be taken up is not clear; what is clear is that the alternative Eastern form of integration cannot loosen without massive internal contradiction.

Notes

1 D. Breistein, *Hans Nielsen Hauge, Merchant of Bergen, Christian Belief and Economic Activity*, Bergen, Grieg, 1955.

2 D. G. Charlton, *Secular Religions in France, 1815–1870*, London, Oxford University Press, 1963.

3 A. Dansette, *Religious History of Modern France*, vol. II. New York, Herder & Herder, 1962.

4 E. Weber, *Action Française*, Stanford University Press, 1962.

5 Cf. E. Steiner, *The Slovak Dilemma*, Cambridge University Press, 1973, on which I have drawn extensively. I am also grateful for conversations with E. Gellner on these topics.

6 Stella Alexander, an unpublished MS on Yugoslavia, Chapter 1, Section B.

7 E. Allardt, 'Patterns of Class Conflict and Working Class Consciousness in Finnish Politics', in E. Allardt and Y. Littunen (eds) *Cleavages, Ideologies and Party Systems*, Transactions of the Westermarck Society vol. X, Helsinki, 1964.

8 From this derives the relative status of clergy in the different types of Protestant pattern: high in Sweden, considerably lower in the United States. Other related consequences are to be located in the prestige of humanistic life-styles, the slower pace of popularisation in education and so on. S. M. Lipset brings out such differences in his comparison between the USA and Canada in *Revolution and Counterrevolution*, London, Heinemann, 1969. The distinction he outlines between the USA and Canada marks an intermediate point between the American and British sub-variants of the Protestant pattern.

9 S. Rokkan and H. Valen, 'Regional Contrasts in Norwegian Politics', in Allardt and Littunen, op. cit.

10 Cf. M. P. Fogarty, *Christian Democracy in Western Europe 1820–1953*, Indiana, University Press, Notre Dame, 1957. This provides a particularly useful analysis of the religious organisations, unions and parties in countries of mixed religions.

11 H. Daalder, 'The Netherlands: Opposition in a Segmented Society', in R. A. Dahl, *Political Oppositions in Western Democracies*, New Haven and London, Yale University Press, 1966.

12 L. Brunt, 'The "Kleine Luyden" as a Disturbing Factor in the Emancipation of the Orthodox Calvinists (Gereformeerden) in the Netherlands', *Sociologica Neerlandica*, vol. VIII, no. II, 1972.

13 J. M. G. Thurlings, 'The case of Dutch Catholicism: a Contribution to the Theory of a Pluralistic Society', *Sociologia Neerlandica*, vol. VII, no. II, 1971. Cf. also G. Larkin, 'Isolation, Integration and Secularisation', *Sociological Review*, 1974. It is interesting that where Catholic voters cease to vote confessionally their left voting reflects degree of previous Church attachment.

14 W. Kreiterling, 'Les Catholiques allemands et la social-démocratie', *Projet*, November 1966.

15 Cf. R. Bocock, *Ritual in Industrial Society. A sociological analysis of ritualism in modern England*, London, Allen & Unwin, 1974.

16 J. Billiet, 'Changement religieux et système scolaire en Belgique', in *Actes de le 12ième Conference de Sociologie Religieuse*, Lille, CISR, 1973.

17 H. W. Paul, *The Second Ralliement: The Rapprochement between Church and State in France in the Twentieth Century*, Washington, Catholic University of America Press, 1967.

18 G. Van Tillo, 'Redefinition of Religion in the Shalom Movement' and D. Hervien, 'Protestation religieuse, protestation sociale: le cas des communautés de jeunes en France', in *Actes*, op. cit.

19 J. Ardagh, *The New France. A Society in Transition, 1945–1973*, Harmondsworth, Penguin, 1973.

20 S. R. Schram, *Protestantism and Politics in France*, Alençon, 1954.

21 G. Galli and A. Prandi, *Patterns of Political Participation in Italy*, New Haven, Yale University Press, 1970; and L. Hazelrigg, 'Occupation and Religious Practice in Italy: the Thesis of "Working Class Alienation"', in *Journal for the Scientific Study of Religion*, vol. 11, no. 4, December 1972.

22 S. H. Barnes, 'Italy: Oppositions on Left, Right and Center', in Dahl, op. cit. Cf. T. T. Mackie, 'Generational Change in Italian Politics: the Democrazia Christiana', Workshop on Language, Religion and Politics, LSE, April 1975.

23 For an exposition of this notion which is assumed throughout the present chapter cf. Lipset, op. cit.

24 V. R. Lorwin, 'Belgium: Religion, Class and Language in National Politics', in Dahl, op. cit. Cf. also R. Verdoot and D. Rayside, 'The Splitting of the Belgian Social Christian Party along Language Lines', Workshop on Language, Religion and Politics, LSE, April 1975.

25 F. C. Engelmann, 'Austria: The Pooling of Opposition', in Dahl, op. cit.

26 H. Bogensberger, 'Austria', and F. Houtart, 'Belgium', in H. Mol (ed.), *Western Religion*, The Hague and Paris, Mouton, 1972.

27 Cf. R. Carr, *Spain 1808 – 1939*, Oxford, Clarendon Press, 1966.

28 Opus Dei is currently (January 1974) not powerful in the Spanish government. Cf. D. Artigues, *El Opus Dei en España*, Paris, 1971.

29 P. Almerich, 'Spain' in Mol, op. cit.

30 'Shadow over the Greek Church', in *Greek Report*, April 1969.

31 R. Doucastella, 'Géographie de la practique religieuse en Espagne', in *Social Compass*, vol. XII, nos 4–5, 1965.

32 J. Marcos Alonso, 'A Social and Psychological Typology of Religious Identification in Spanish Catholicism', *Social Compass*, vol. XII, nos 4–5, 1965.

33 B. Bociurkiw, 'Church-State Relations in Communist Eastern Europe', *Religion in Communist Lands*, vol. 1, nos 4–5, July–October 1973: and C. Cviic, 'Recent Developments in Church-State Relations in Yugoslavia', *Religion in Communist Lands*, vol. 1, no. 2, March–April 1973.

34 One should study in this connection W. C. Fletcher's contribution to the Carleton Conference (1971), 'Religion and Soviet Foreign Policy', now published as *Religion and Atheism in the U.S.S.R. and Eastern Europe* edited by B. Bociurkiw and J. W. Strang, London, Macmillan, 1975. One has to remember that the World Council of Churches takes two pressures particularly into account. It defers to the third world,

including Arab states where Israel is concerned; and it desires to retain the participation of the Orthodox, partly to widen its ecumenical front *vis-à-vis* Rome. The first pressure leads it to emphasise the racialist issue and the second pressure leads it to play down offences against liberty (including religious liberty) in the East, and emphasise the colonialism of the West. To some extent it carries forward the position of the Christian Peace Conference centred on Prague. Since Peace descended on Prague in 1968 this particular organisation has become useless for the purposes of Russian foreign policy. However, the CPC was very active in the condemnation of American foreign policy. What was involved for a pro-Russian Christian of goodwill is best illustrated from the autobiography of the Czech Protestant theologian, J. Hromadka. One may say that the Russian episcopate is totally responsive to the Soviet government; over Czechoslovakia for example, and recently in its attitude to Solzhenitsyn.

35 For a general survey, cf. M. L. Stackhouse, 'Christianity and the New Exodus', in D. Cutler (ed.), *The Religious Situation*, Boston, Beacon, 1968. One should consult in particular the work of A. I. Klibanov on the Russian side and the writings of Ethel and Stephen Dunn (e.g. *Slavic Review*, no. 1, 1967). The most succinct general survey of the Russian situation in particular is B. Bociurkiw's contribution to R. H. Marshall, *Aspects of Religion in the Soviet Union, 1917–1967*, University of Chicago Press, 1971.

36 D. M. Aptekman, 'Causes of the Vitality of the Ceremony of Baptism under Modern Conditions', *Soviet Sociology*, vol. IV, no. 2; and I. V. Krianev and P. S. Popov, 'The Emotional Effect of Religious Ritual and the Process of Overcoming It', *Soviet Sociology*, vol. II, no. 4.

37 'Znak', the lay organisation of Catholic intellectuals, is of some importance here, cf. the article by A. Swiecicki in *Actes*, op. cit.

38 S. Staron, 'State-Church Relations in Poland. An Examination of Power Configuration in a Noncompetitive Political System', *World Politics*, vol. 21, no. 4, 1969. Something of the danger of divisions between older and younger Catholics can be seen in Croatia. The hierarchy feel that 'openness' and participation are easily misunderstood by the uneducated, while younger priests support greater specialisation of function, lay involvement and the optional character of celibacy. This division now takes place, of course, in a situation of increased pressure on the Church following accusations that it is involved in Croatian nationalist propaganda. Cf. *Absees*, April 1973, p. 275; and M. Hickling, 'Worse Church-State relations feared in Yugoslavia', *British Weekly*, 27 April 1973.

39 A. I. Klibanov, 'Sectarianism and the Socialist Reconstruction of the Countryside', *Soviet Sociology*, vol. VIII, nos 3–4, Winter-Spring 1970.

40 I am grateful to Mrs Christel Lane for information about the 'Initiative Group' in a paper read at the LSE Seminar on the sociology of religion. Her paper 'Some Explanations for the Persistence of Christian Religion in Soviet Society' has been most useful, together with brief summaries of the contents of Russian theses and surveys in J. R. Millar (ed.), *The Soviet Rural Community*, University of Illinois Press, 1971.

41 It is interesting that the only Jewish community to survive the Nazi period more or less intact was in Bulgaria, which has no important anti-semitic tradition. Jews mostly left for Israel in the early years of the Communist regime: some 150,000 Muslims similarly left for Turkey. Polish Jews have from time to time left for Israel, no doubt encouraged by the anti-semitism which the post-war left shares with the pre-war right.

42 Marshall (ed.), op. cit.

43 For highly interesting material on geographical sub-cultures in Britain, France, Belgium, etc., cf. J. D. Gay, *The Geography of Religion in England*, London, Duckworth, 1971; and F. Boulard, *An Introduction to Religious Sociology*, London, Darton, Longman & Todd, 1960. An important aspect of both studies is their emphasis on the extra ordinary persistence of patterns over centuries. In 1978 there will appear the most detailed of productions in this field: I. A. Isambert's atlas of religious practice in France.

44 For the symbiosis of republicanism, refugee sentiment and federalism cf. J. E. Fagg, 'Republican Politics in the Reign of Isabel II,' *Mediterranean II*, Malta, June 1976; and for the centralising pressure of eighteenth-century absolutism cf. W. N. Hargreaves-Maudsley, 'Centralism and Regionalism in the Eighteenth Century', ibid. There is an interesting study to be done of the role of radical choirs in regional sentiment, for which cf. W. Weber, *Music and the Middle Class*, London, Croom Helm, 1975, and H. Raynor, *Music and Society since 1815*, London, Barrie & Jenkins, 1976.

45 Northern Ireland is not made up of dissenters but of three semi-territorial churches: Roman Catholic, Church of Ireland and Presbyterian, corresponding to the Irish, and to the English and Scots founding communities. Cf. R. Rose, *Governing Without Consensus*, London, Faber, 1971.

46 For all such materials one should consult the relevant chapters in Mol (ed.) op. cit. There is a fair amount of evidence bearing on the decline of Catholic participation since the mid-1960s, which though – or because – it starts from a higher base line is more noticeable than Protestant declines over the same period. The decline from 21 per cent to 17 per cent per Sunday in France 1971–5 is noted in the text and derives from polls of French public opinion quoted in *The Times*. In this poll carried out by Sofres for the first French TV channel 26 per cent said they went to church once or twice a month or occasionally, and 68 per cent, said they prayed from time to time. The average practising Catholic is aged 65 or over, lives in towns of 2,000–20,000 inhabitants, is or has been a senior manager, an important shopkeeper, an industrialist, a doctor or a lawyer. *Doxa* (Nos 17 and 18, 7/9, 1973) shows Italians divided into about one-third regularly practising, one-third occasionally and one-third non-practising, the proportion of practising dropping sharply amongst males and somewhat among young people (30 per cent in the age group 16–34). This lower level was concentrated among those aged 25–34. Some 45 per cent of Italians received communion in the course of a year. Australian Gallup shows

an overall decline of churchgoing per Sunday 1961–72 from 44 to 31 per cent, to which Catholics contribute disproportionately. The dip in American churchgoing over this period was largely Catholic. In the UK A.E.C.W. Spencer writing in *The Month* for April 1975 describes a Catholic recession from about 34 per cent per Sunday in 1965 to about 25 per cent in 1973. If we take these varied indices, including declines noted elsewhere for Holland and Germany, their import seems to be that there is a general decline in regular Catholic participation, which is particularly noticeable in Protestant cultures where hitherto practice has run at a high level.

One further point of particular interest may be mentioned and it is that Catholic conversions in the UK have been noted by R. Currie and A. Gilbert as running parallel to the vitality of Protestant churches and that these in turn run parallel to very broad indices of confidence and 'vitality' in the society as a whole. The confidence of the early 1950s and the decline from 1960 onward is clearly noticeable in the data. Such findings clearly have relevance to the general European situation and the loss of morale since the high points of the 1950s. The same authors also document the variations in free-church and Anglican vitality in relation to the fortunes of the Liberal and Conservative parties, at least up to the First World War. The direct impact of political confidence, societal or sectional, and the negative effect of wars are factors that all need transferring to the European context. For example, 1968 saw a universal trembling of the indices. Cf. R. Currie and A. Gilbert, *Churches and Churchgoers*, Oxford University Press, 1978.

47 R. F. Tomasson, 'Religion is Irrelevant in Sweden', in J. K. Hadden (ed.), *Religion in Radical Transition*, New Brunswick, Transaction Books, 1971; and *Religion in Britain and Northern Ireland*, London, Independent Television Authority, 1970.

48 Cf. P. Salomonsen, 'Contemporary Religious Attitudes in Denmark', in *Actes* op. cit.

49 Cf. Z. Roter, 'Nature et structure de la religiosité en Slovenie' in *Actes de la 11iéme Conference de Sociologie Religieuse*, Lille, 1971; and E. Cimic, 'Structures de la conscience religieuse dans les milieux ruraux et urbains', as above in *Actes 11*. The English Summary of H. Kubiak's *Religiosity and Social Milieu*, Warsaw, 1972, is useful in showing the decline in specifically ecclesiastical religion in a Polish steelworks. M. Jaroszewski makes similar points in 'Practiques et conceptions religieuses en Pologne' in *Recherches internationales à la lumière du Marxisme*, 1965. These Marxist views need to be set against the work of such scholars as V. C. Chrypinski and J. Majka. It is helpful to consult Majka's 'The Character of Polish Catholicism', *Social Compass*, vol. 15, nos 3–4, 1968.

50 *Absees*, April 1973, p. 270, for material on Slovenia. For the possibility of a 'hard core' emerging, cf. E. Kadlecova's article on Czechoslovakia in H. Mol, op. cit.

10 Armed forces and European society

Gwyn Harries-Jenkins

Although ideological opposition to the sociological analysis of armed forces is now less marked than hitherto, studies of the relationship between the military and society are still relatively few in number. The idea of 'conflict' has increasingly preoccupied sociologists and anthropologists in recent years on both the theoretical and empirical level (Rex, 1961), yet comparatively little attention has been paid in these studies to the role of the military. The concept of conflict has been carefully studied. Analytical distinctions have been drawn between those conflicts which, 'do not contradict the basic assumptions upon which the relationship is founded', and those 'in which the contending parties no longer share the basic values upon which the legitimacy of the social system rests' (Coser, 1958, p. 151).The applicability of this analysis to the position of armed forces, however, is not clear. The contention that ours is a society born out of war and largely devoted to it is often either overlooked or rejected. The identification of conflict with social change is rarely extended to consider the links between military institutions, war and socio-political change.

What is clear is that during the development of European society, man has made war in every climate and at every degree of latitude, sometimes within a single ethnic or social group, sometimes among different communities. War, and the preparations for war, have moulded social organisations and have determined technical and industrial progress in this and earlier centuries. The foundations of many of our institutions, in thought, technique and organisation have been evolved in armies or during wars. Correlli Barnett sums this up very clearly (1967, p. 15), 'The Schlieffen Plan preceded the Marshall Plan. Staff Colleges preceded business schools. The first schools of engineering and technology were military.' In the contemporary scene, discussions about the role of the military in politics, the relationship between the institutional patterns of armed forces and social processes, and the profound impact of the nuclear arms race on social structure and international relations are indicative of the continuing importance of the military within society.

The military system

To meet the needs of their national policy and to implement their sense of national purpose, European nation-states have evolved incredibly complex military institutions. These, despite the search for a military detente, continue to employ some 10 per cent of the economically active population. From a total European population of some 725 million people, almost 9 million are military personnel on active duty. Only in Luxembourg and Ireland are fewer than 5 per cent of the population in the armed forces. In Portugal and Bulgaria, to take two contrasting examples, one person in every five is a serviceman. The economic cost of this continues to be very high. In the countries of the North Atlantic Treaty Organisation, as is shown in Table 10.1, more than 4 per cent of the Gross National Product at factor cost is spent on defence. Expenditure on the military frequently constitutes the most important single item of central government expenditure. In the Federal Republic of Germany and in Portugal, for instance, defence spending is more than 30 per cent of the government's budget. Even in those countries where this is not the most important single item, as in the United Kingdom where defence spending is no longer the major item of government expenditure, this share of total expenditure may be as high as 20 per cent.

But the significance of the military may be measured in a different way. Armed forces are the largest organisations in contemporary Europe and the most technically developed. Established for the explicit purpose of achieving certain goals, the military is a purposive instrument which draws much of its strength from its formal status structure with clearly defined lines of communication and authority. The thoroughness with which it regulates and controls the life of its members has served as a model for the development of other organisations. Management theory, in particular, with its emphasis on goals, strategic and tactical plans, targets and objectives, consistently echoes in its language and techniques the characteristics of the military organisation. Henri Fayol's Universalist functional theory of management, first published in 1916 under the title *Administration industrielle et générale*, owes a considerable debt to well-established military practices.

Armed forces, however, are also systems of interdependent human beings. Under the impact of complex technology, the military has increasingly moved toward the recruitment, often in competition

289

TABLE 10.1   Defence expenditure of NATO countries, 1964–1973, as a percentage of GNP factor cost, based on current prices

	1964	1965	1966	1967	1968	1969	1970	1971	1972	1973
Belgium	3·8	3·5	3·5	3·5	3·5	3·3	3·2	3·2	3·2	3·1
Canada	4·2	3·5	3·3	3·4	3·1	2·8	2·8	2·7	2·5	2·3
Denmark	3·2	3·2	3·1	3·1	3·3	2·9	2·8	2·9	2·8	2·5
France	6·3	6·1	5·9	5·9	5·5	5·0	4·6	4·4	4·2	4·2
Federal Republic Germany	5·9	5·5	5·3	5·6	4·7	4·7	4·3	4·5	4·8	4·7
Greece	4·1	4·0	4·2	5·1	5·6	5·8	5·8	5·6	5·3	4·8
Italy	3·7	3·7	3·8	3·5	3·3	3·0	3·0	3·3	3·5	3·4
Luxembourg	1·6	1·5	1·5	1·3	1·0	1·0	0·9	0·9	1·0	1·0
Netherlands	4·7	4·3	4·1	4·3	4·0	3·9	3·8	3·8	3·8	3·7
Norway	3·9	4·2	4·0	3·9	4·0	4·0	4·0	3·9	3·7	3·7
Portugal	7·3	6·8	6·9	8·0	8·2	7·6	7·9	8·3	8·4	7·5
Turkey	5·6	5·8	5·4	5·5	5·2	5·2	5·2	5·4	5·0	4·5
United Kingdom	6·8	6·6	6·5	6·5	6·3	5·8	5·7	5·8	6·2	5·6
United States	8·8	8·2	9·1	10·2	10·1	9·5	8·7	7·8	7·3	6·8

Source: NATO document ISM (73) 7, 16 July, 1973.

with other organisations, of highly skilled and educated individuals. National officer corps have become a group of professionals who as a result of prolonged training acquire a skill which enables them to render specialised service. Many are concerned with the management and carrying out of violence, but the increasing concentration in armed forces of technical specialists has produced a considerable narrowing in many areas of the skill differential between officers and civilian professionals. In the same way that these officers have developed more of the skill and orientations common to civilian administrators and civilian leaders, the enlisted ranks have evolved as a type of craft group in which the diversity of skills and expertise mirror and rival those of the parent society. The development of these new fields of specialisation which differ radically from the traditional military skills has, in turn, had considerable repercussions on the old norms of military authority and behaviour. One effect of this, as Janowitz (1960) has shown, has been a shift within the military establishment from authoritarian domination to greater reliance on manipulation, persuasion and group consensus. Here, the organisational revolution which has affected civilian society, has equally modified the traditional relationship within the armed forces between professionals and the employing organisation (Harries–Jenkins, 1970).

At the same time, these changes in military organisation and professionalism are balanced by the perpetuation of the unique goals of armed forces. While the military institution has come more and more to typify the accepted characteristics of large-scale organisations, the primary goal of the military establishment continues to create its own special environment. Armed forces are thus much more than an organisation or an association of professionals. They form a community which encompasses and controls the life and work of its members much more than do most other formal or social organisations. In many ways, the military professional is the archetype of Whyte's organisation man (1956). The apparent need to conform to the needs and standards of the establishment produces a sense of corporateness which is reinforced by the pervasiveness of the military community. Traditionally this has been a closed community, sharply segregated from civilian life. Separation between place of work and place of residence, a characteristic of most civil occupations, has been largely absent. Instead, professional, residential and social life completely intermingled – to the extent that the military was often considered to be truly representative of what Goffman calls 'The Total Institution'.

The retention of this sense of community has a number of functional advantages. It may help in the integration of new members into military life. Conflicts between family and career obligations can be minimised. It contributes to the development of a powerful *esprit de corps*. Most importantly, when the realities of the professional life invade family and social life, the resulting sense of community, with its overtones of what Burgess calls the 'companionate' family, meets the needs of an organisation which insists on its members being completely mobile. But the organisational and professional revolution in armed forces, particularly the move towards 'civilianisation', has greatly lessened this sense of community. There is increasing evidence of a demand within the armed forces of Western European industrialised societies for those political, social and economic rights which are enjoyed by other citizens. No longer are members of the armed forces content to be marginal men living in geographic and social isolation. A growing demand for the right of group representation (Harries-Jenkins, 1976), and the right of political participation are symptomatic of changing attitudes towards a traditional definition of military community. Equally, an increased sense of relative deprivation has encouraged amongst military men the critical analysis of the claimed advantages of membership of the military community (Werner, 1976). No longer can it be presumed that the inculcated ideology of this community will be accepted without question. A spirit of utilitarianism has frequently replaced that sense of normative commitment which was traditionally associated with its existence. Calculative rather than moral attitudes often characterise a situation in which armed forces are identified not as a community but as a dynamic organisation offering chances of promotion, interesting work and a level of salary which should compare favourably with conditions in civilian institutions. Nor has this trend been unsupported by national governments.

The social and political isolation of the military has marked dysfunctional tendencies. Of these, one of the most important is the way in which the maintenance of military boundaries and a corporate identity weakens the integration of armed forces into the larger society. The perpetuation of a rigid boundary between the military and civilian sector contradicts attempts to ensure that armed forces are an intrinsic part of a democratic society. Consequently, the importance placed on the functional advantages of the military community, even though this continues to be a fundamental characteristic of service life, is now less than it has been hitherto. Indeed an awareness of the dysfunctional features of the traditional military community may lead a national government to take positive steps to break down a sense of isolation. The implementation of such a policy is thus an explicit feature of governmental action in West Germany. The Basic Law and the Services Act (*Grundgesetz und Soldatengesetz*), for example, guarantee to the soldier the right to participate in political life and to assume political responsibility.

Servicemen are consequently elected to the Bundestag, Länder parliaments, district and municipal councils. Through this and their membership of other organisations, 'servicemen and their families are fully accepted and integrated in the life of the community' (1973/ 74 *White Paper, The Security of The Federal Republic of Germany and The Development of the Federal Armed Forces (Zur Sicherheit der Bundesrepublik Deutschland und zur Entwicklung der Bundeswehr)*, p. 133). All of this is a response to the belief that the *Bundeswehr* has to be an intrinsic part of the democratic society. As the 1975/76 *White Paper* on the same subject points out (p. 148): 'The guiding image of the citizen in uniform forms the bridge which links the Bundeswehr to society and firmly roots our armed forces in state and social order.'

The breakdown of the isolation of the military community has thus considerably changed traditional relations between the military and the rest of society. Armed forces, however, continue to display over civilian institutions massive political advantages such as the marked superiority of organisation, a highly internalised symbolic status and a monopoly of arms noted by Finer (1972, p. 6). The potential effect of this upon the remainder of society has generated long-standing issues of civilian control over the military. In the United States, notions such as C. Wright Mills's 'power elite' or Harold Lasswell's 'garrison state' were concepts designed to highlight the persistent dangers which existed. In many respects, the European position is more complex. On the one hand, armed forces in some countries have already become the strongest political force, thereby establishing governments and controlling the formation of foreign and domestic policy. In others politicisation of the military has ensured that armed forces have been integrated into the political superstructure as part of the legitimate order. For yet others, the trend away from conscription towards the all-volunteer army raises new questions about the potential within armed forces for internal rigidity and political isolation (Janowitz, 1973).

The issue of the potential political power of armed forces is thus far from settled, but this power is only one of the four characteristics of the military – their organisation, professionalism, sense of community and power – which delineates the specific institution. These are, moreover, universal characteristics. Despite the position of any armed force as a symbol of particularistic national ideology, the military in all European countries displays considerably similar characteristics. They tend, as van Doorn (1974) points out, to have the same values and norms of behaviour. They resemble each other in their organisational pattern and rank structure, in their technology and training programmes, and in their ritual and ceremony. Consistently, the similarity of their function and life-style has produced a universal model of the military institution which, after it was developed in Europe, was exported throughout the world. In short, armed forces are an international type of social institution in which comparative studies illustrate not only their universality but also the importance of their contribution to the development of the parent society.

The military organisation

In a comparative study of six military regimes, Feit (1973) stresses that soldiers are, both literally and metaphorically, 'armed bureaucrats'. The view that armed forces can be closely identified with the concept of bureaucracy is particularly noticeable in studies of military organisation. Indeed, as Moskos (1971) points out, this has been a *leitmotiv* of most studies. This identification of the military as a bureaucracy, however, is neither a new conclusion nor is it unexpected. Weber, in discussing the concept of bureaucracy, particularly the way in which the bureaucratic structure is associated with the concentration of the means of administration, argues that only the bureaucratic army structure allowed for the development of the professional standing armies (1946). His comment is still valid today: 'Specifically, military discipline and technical training can be normally and fully developed, at least to its modern high level, only in the bureaucratic army.' More importantly, his eight propositions about the structuring of legal authority systems and his eight defining characteristics of the bureaucratic administration staff, appear to reflect very clearly what Friedrich (1952, p. 31) has called the Prussian enthusiasm for the military type of organisation.

Armed forces thus seem to have characteristics which fit very closely with what Hall (1963) has described as the generally recognised elements of bureaucracy: hierarchy of authority, division of labour, technically competent participants, procedural devices for work situations, rules governing the behaviour of positional incumbents, limited authority of office and differential rewards by office. Consequently, many of the general criticisms of Weber's theory can be equally applied in a study of the military as a bureaucracy. One such criticism is that a structure which is rational in Weber's sense can easily generate consequences which are both unexpected and detrimental to the attainment of the organisation's goals. Michalik (1976), in discussing the problems of professional ethics in the Polish military, stresses that internal conditions in the army may also make for excessive control, self-assertion, authoritativeness, and meddling into the private lives of individuals. In turn, this may produce attitudes of passiveness, non-independent thinking, lack of initiative and the expectation of ready solutions from others.

The emphasis which is placed here on the possible dysfunctional consequences of bureaucracy within the military, is echoed in a number of other studies. One of the most interesting questions in this area is the extent to which the hierarchy of authority itself is dysfunctional. While the structure of power and authority in the military resembles that in other large-scale organisations, there are marked differences of degree. The structure in theory gives a rational, impersonal and legitimate authority to the office-holder. A strictly defined rank relationship attempts to ensure, with the aid of legally based organisational regulations, that obedience is due not to the person who holds authority but to the impersonal order which has confirmed his rank. At the same time, however, the division of military tasks into functionally distinct spheres, each furnished with the requisite authority and sanctions, creates an authority according to function. In many cases, these two sources of authority – rank and function – coincide. Sometimes, however, they are distinct. The ensuing potential conflict which may occur because any superior can give an order to a subordinate even if it contradicts the functional division of labour, then tends to generate dysfunctional consequences for the military organisation.

These tendencies are more pronounced where the power base within armed forces continues to be authoritarian in form. This retention of the traditional form of power despite peripheral shifts towards a leadership based on supportive or collegial management is perhaps an inevitable characteristic of the military bureaucracy. The specific organisational forms of armed forces with their emphasis on efficiency, co-ordination and subordination seemingly produce an inevitable preference within the military for authoritarian rather than democratic attitudes (Abrahamsson, 1972). It is perhaps not unreasonable to expect, as Korpi (1964) has suggested, that people choosing a military career would tend to be relatively authoritarian. In a study of the Swedish armed forces, he shows that recruitment to the army tends to over-represent individuals with authoritarian tendencies and outlooks. From this, it can be inferred that the emphasis placed on the importance to the military of rational legal authority may well have self-defeating consequences. Rules, designed as means to ends, may well become ends in themselves. Discipline may discourage innovation. The authority structure in the formal organisation may produce differences in outlook among those engaged at different levels of the organisation in their particular specialisms. Many 'traditional' officers may thus feel themselves threatened by specialists whose attitudes to the structure differ from their own. More importantly, attitudes derived from the emphasis placed on authority may, in turn, condition political orientations. In a different context, this is confirmed by Busquets (1974) in his analysis of the crisis of legitimacy in Latin Europe. Here, the conversion of the armed forces into an internal security force has created a military which feels more confident ideologically if it possesses dogmatic, exclusive, aggressive and authoritarian attitudes. In a contrary sense, an awareness of the possible effect of these attitudes upon military ideology is reflected in the efforts made by the Federal Republic of Germany to guarantee the economic and social interests of the serviceman by allowing him to join the Bundeswehr Servicemen's Association and the Public Service, Transport and Traffic Union.

Similar attempts can also be noted in a number of European states where governments, by allowing or encouraging the creation of a system of group representation, have either consciously or unconsciously imposed checks on these authoritarian tendencies. The examples of the Dutch 'Union for Conscripts' (VVDM) and 'Union for Volunteers and Conscripts' (BVVV DM), the Belgian 'Syndicat Belge des Officiers' (SBO) and the Danish 'Association of Regular Army and Naval A-Branch Officers' are thus indicative of attempts made to guarantee the rights of individuals within the military organisation. In contrast, one of the persistent complaints made by the unofficial 'Comités des Soldats' in France is that authoritarianism continues to flourish (Pelletier and Ravet, 1976, p. 85): 'le règlement militaire permet en fait à n'importe quel gradé de donner les ordres les plus fantaisistes, et par conséquent de punir quand il le veut n'importe quel subordonné pour "refus d'obeissance".'

The emphasis which is placed on the possibly dysfunctional consequences of authority as it was envisaged by Weber, consequences which will be discussed more fully in a subsequent consideration of the relationship between this authority and professional expertise, should not, however, overshadow the other criticisms which have been made of the alleged bureaucratic characteristics of armed forces. One of the critical comments echoes Simon's (1945) attack on those theorists who attempt to offer 'timeless' principles of organisational efficiency. Thus Segal and Segal (1971, pp. 282–4) have suggested three phases of organisational development. In the first of these, *the pre-bureaucratic model*, ascriptive, traditionalistic and affective bases of recruitment to the military were prevalent. This contrasts with Weber's contention that officials of a bureaucracy in its most rational form are selected on the basis of a professional qualification, ideally substantiated by a diploma gained through examination. Thus in the second phase of development, *the bureaucratic model*, there is a broadened base of recruitment which stresses achievement rather than ascriptive criteria of selection. A major difficulty here is that of relating any selected criterion of achievement to the role and function of the individual servicemen. This is a problem which in the context of contemporary society suggests that a more pertinent model may be that of a *post-bureaucratic* military organisation. Here recruitment and promotion are based on organisational and administrative ability rather than on the primary combat skill which hitherto had been more closely identified as the relevant expertise within a military organisation.

The validity of a model which stresses the sequence of bureaucratic development in the military by reference to changes in the pattern of officer recruitment is confirmed by the quantitative data which is available. Traditionally membership of the officer corps in European society was reserved for an aristocracy. *Das Portepee adelt,* is an expression which sums up the common practice in the past. In the United Kingdom, for example, the existence until 1871 of the Purchase System – an example of Weber's decentralised patrimonial authority – ensured that a high proportion of officers came from the aristocracy and landed gentry. In 1830, one-fifth of officers came from the aristocracy, while in the military elite 248 generals from a total of 507 were either title-holders or the sons of title holders (Harries–Jenkins, 1977). In the Prussian military establishment of 1824, the military elite was almost wholly noble in origin, while in the whole of the officer corps, as in Britain, fewer than half of the officers could be described as coming from the middle class.

A number of studies have clearly demonstrated the considerable broadening of social recruitment to the military profession which has taken place in the nineteenth and twentieth centuries (Janowitz, 1960; Razzell, 1963; van Doorn, 1965; Kjellberg, 1965; Kourvetaris and Dobratz, 1973). But this shift from 'ascription' to 'achievement' has not been uniform. Abrahamsson (1972, pp. 44–54) suggests that in contemporary society four patterns of officer recruitment can be identified. In the first (elitist) as represented by Great Britain and Spain, there is still a very pronounced elite domination even though the source of this differs. In Great Britain the prevalence of the elite can be explained as the combination of officers coming from the landed gentry and professional middle class with those whose fathers were in the army. In Spain, in contrast, a very high proportion – almost one-half – of officer candidates come from military families. The second pattern of recruitment (upper-class domination with some lower-class representation) is indicative of the situation in the Netherlands, Ireland, West Germany and France. Here there is a tendency towards greater social representativeness, although the representation of the lower, particularly lower rural classes is offset by a continuing military occupational inheritance. In the third pattern (mixed), as in Norway and Sweden, there is a much lower proportion of the elite categories,and in both countries the military is one of the most broadly socially representative of all occupational groups. Finally, the fourth pattern (working-class dominance) typifies the situation in Poland and Czechoslovakia where the representation of the working class is indicative of the massive proletarisation of the officer corps in response to an imperative demand to promote various forms of the social advancement of the lower classes (Wiatr, 1968, p. 234).

Yet in accepting that the armies of the nineteenth century were ascriptive-based or that contemporary armed forces are more socially representative, it would be injudicious to conclude that Weber's ideal type of bureaucracy is satisfied in one case and not in the other. What is more relevant is the conclusion that the characteristics of the ideal type may be regarded as separate variables. Thus, the British army in the nineteenth century may have been ascriptive-based but the hierarchy of authority had been long established. Over time, changes in the parent society may affect one dimension of the bureaucracy more than another, in the way in which there has been in a number of European armies a marked shift in the pattern of organisational authority. This shift from authoritarian domination to greater reliance on management may or may not be accompanied by changes in the pattern of recruitment. In this context, it is significant that in the United Kingdom where, since the decision taken in 1957 to phase out conscription, the structure of the military has been based on that of the all-volunteer army, recruitment to the military continues to be highly selective. Whilst recruiting advertisements have stressed the shift in the pattern of internal authority, the source of recruitment, particularly that of officers, continues to reflect an elitist domination. This is particularly noticeable in the recruitment of regular officers to the army where, despite intermittent variations, there is evidence of a continuing tendency to select candidates whose education and socialisation is associated with the privileged lifestyle of a minority within society. This mode of selection is rational in that it reflects the exercise of a form of social control, but it is still significant that we are now witnessing in European armed forces modifications to the style and format of internal bureaucratisation rather than radical changes to the fundamental base of the military bureaucracy.

The professional soldier

Comparable developments have also affected military professionalism. Traditionally, the 'profession of arms' was identified with the exercise of combat skills, the professional soldier developing from his feudal, mercenary and militia antecedents into an expert in the management of violence. His professional norms of behaviour were well defined. He enjoyed the monopoly of a well-integrated body of knowledge and skill which in most European armies was imparted through a formal training process. He was a member of an exclusive professional group with a strong sense of corporate identity which had evolved a complex set of ethics and code of military conduct. Within the constraints of this code with its neo-feudal undertones, the professional enjoyed the capacity to apply his specific knowledge and skill. Despite the claims made from time to time by bodies of amateur volunteers that citizens under arms could carry out these military functions, the traditional military in Europe was founded upon the concept of an exclusive craft embodying specific values and norms.

The heroic military leader was the ideal-type exemplar of this professional. His virtues – bravery, self-sacrifice, patriotism, sense of service and so on – appeared to differentiate him from lesser men. 'The career of arms', argued Salazar (1938, pp. 118–22), 'requires from those who seek or are called on to pursue it, certain specific qualities which we call the military virtues: valour, fidelity, patriotism.' But increasingly, this self-image was confronted with challenges from several directions. Consequently the development of military professionalism can be described as Janowitz (1960, p. 21) has suggested, as a struggle between heroic leaders, who embody traditionalism and glory, and 'military managers', who are concerned with the scientific and rational conduct of war. There is a fundamental distinction. In the nineteenth century, it was the contrast between British or French attitudes towards planning and administration and those of Prussian officers with their advanced training in the areas of staff methods and organisation. In this century, it is the difference between the leader who is primarily a charismatic personality, and the more realistic, conservative and management-oriented commander. Both types have an important part to play in the contemporary military, but now technological developments in armed forces have been so comprehensive that increasingly the role of the heroic leader in the European military has been subordinated in importance to that of the military manager.

Contemporary armed forces, however, require specialists of an additional type. Neither the heroic leader nor the military manager is able to cope with all the complex functions of civil society which are combined within the single total institution of the armed forces. To support the operations of combat units, armed forces must cater not only for the functional, social and physical needs of the soldier but also for those of his family. Accordingly, the military is forced to employ a large number of specialists whose diverse skills ensure that armed forces can operate as a self-sufficient institution. The activities of this third group thus complement those of the other two, the combination of skill creating the modern military establishment.

299

The pattern of professionalism in the armed forces, can, however, be viewed from another standpoint. Some of the employed professionals work on the periphery of military activities. These are the marginal men whose function duplicates almost exactly that of their civilian counterparts. As doctors, dentists, teachers, lawyers, and so on, they retain close links with professionals in the parent society. For many of them, these civilian colleagues become their reference group. They belong to the same professional associations. They are bound by a common non-military code of ethics which influences their social and political perspectives. Indeed, the continuing growth of their skill specialisation forces them into an increasingly close relationship with these colleagues to the extent that many of this group of military professionals are in the armed forces, but not of it.

The second group, in contrast, are more closely identified with military goals. These are the officers and men who work in such secondary-level functions as those of engineering, logistics and administration. Their distance from the centre of military activities varies. In the past they may have been at the periphery of the military system, their inferior status reflected in such areas as lower pay, lower rank or fewer privileges. But one result of technological change has been growth in the number of these men who owe their rank not to the number of men they command but to their technical skills. Concomitantly, they have moved closer to the centre of the system. In some formations they form an integral part of the combat unit. In others, while they remain geographically and functionally isolated, they are no longer seen to be at the periphery of the organisation.

A feature common to both groups is indicated by the evidence which suggests that these professionals typify a military which is moving towards a convergence with the structures and values of civilian society (Moskos, 1971). They are part of a continuously expanding military bureaucracy which faces management and professional problems comparable with those to be found in other large organisations. But this is not to suggest that the third group of professionals, who are essentially specialists in violence, are free from these problems. This is the group at the centre of the system who are directly involved in the primary combat functions of armed forces. They are the heirs of the heroic leader, but many of them find that they have to concern themselves more and more with management issues. This concern, however, does not always lessen the preference of these servicemen for the retention of ideals of physical courage, group loyalty and personal leadership. It is at this centre of the military system that membership of the small primary (face to face) group becomes an important characteristic of military life. Identification with a small membership group modifies the concept of commitment to the armed forces as a whole. Professionalism, here, tends to be decentralised, for the organisation has to be flexible to respond to external challenges. A monolithic professionalised organisation would be mechanistic in this situation, particularly in the armed forces where there has been a possibly unique fusion of profession and organisation (van Doorn, 1965). Accordingly, in an attempt to avoid the possible dysfunctional consequences of professionalism, considerable emphasis is placed on the functional advantages of small group relationships among these combat forces. At the same time, members of these groups tend to be generalists rather than specialists. Rotation policies mean that they move from base to base, and often from function to function, at specific time intervals. The emphasis which is placed within the military system on mobility of personnel thus encourages a generalist attitude which forms an important component of the military mind.

This attitude is developed further by the recruitment and professional socialisation policies which are commonly adopted by European armed forces. The specialist who works at the periphery of the military establishment can be rightly categorised as an 'achievement professional'. He is initially trained outside the armed forces. His competence to exercise his acquired skill is tested either by the professional association which he wishes to join or by some other impersonal rational examining body. A complex socialisation programme, usually carried out in an institutionalised setting, inculcates in him the norms of behaviour which are common to all members of the occupational group irrespective of their future employment. In short, the characteristics of his primary professionalism emphasise the importance of such elements as his monopoly of a well-integrated body of knowledge and skill, his ability to apply this as a social service and his sense of commitment to the professional body.

While the specialist in violence shares some of these characteristics as indicators of his professionalism, he is primarily a bureaucratic professional. He is wholly trained within the armed forces. It is the latter which delineates his area of activity, determines his role and evaluates his ability. Unlike the achievement professional, he rarely possesses a transferable primary skill which can be utilised in the parent society. His claim to a distinct professional status is inextricably bound up with his continuing membership of the military.

In this context, professionals who work in the area of secondary-level functions occupy an intermediate position. Some of them will have been trained as specialists outside the organisation. Engineers and accountants, for example, are frequently members of their relevant professional associations who have been trained in an institutionalised setting in common with their civilian counterparts.

Concomitantly, others of their military colleagues will have been trained wholly within the military. Within the armed forces, both types of professionals carry out similar and often identical functions. In itself, this need not be a source of stress. This, however, may arise if the achievement professional continues to regard his civilian colleagues as a reference group. This can create a situation which reflects the difference between the cosmopolitan and locally oriented professional. Here, the civilian trained specialist tends to be more outward looking; his military colleague in contrast, may be more inward looking. For the latter, the source of his expertise is the military organisation which, having trained him, designated and confirmed him as a professional. For the former, it is the professional socialisation that preceded his entry into the military which continues to be the primary source of his status and designation.

These internal differences are indicative of an important characteristic of professionalism in the armed forces. They suggest that the military is an organisation in which the pattern of occupational development differs from that which is common in other areas of activity. The unique goals of armed forces, their professional development in Europe before the nineteenth-century demand for the regulation of other socially important occupations in such fields as medicine and commerce, and their particularistic ethos are elements of their unique situation. This situation is reflected in a number of areas. It can be seen, for example, in the way in which professional authority is exercised within the organisation. Here armed forces have had to adjust to the existence of two essentially different types of authority. Weber, as Parsons points out, started from the basic premise of the organisation of authority within the corporate group (Weber, 1964, pp. 59–60). Essentially, this was derived from the legal powers which, in armed forces, are associated with a sanctions mechanism that is recognised and regularised by a complex set of official rules. This form of authority has been legitimised by allocating to office-holders specific powers of command which vary in accordance with their rank. It is not essential that those in command should have either a superior knowledge or superior skill to that of their subordinates. They may possess these attributes. They may be senior to those whom they command but these properties are neither logically nor legally essential to their exercise of bureaucratic authority.

At the same time, servicemen enjoy 'professional' authority. This is based on what Weber termed 'technical competence' or 'control by means of knowledge'. This suggests the existence of an analytically distinct form of power which is a type of sapiential authority. It may be, but need not be, related to the rank held within the military organisation, for it is derived from the specialist expertise of the individual. Its very existence suggests that the hierarchical structure within armed forces is modified by the existence of a distinctive collegial pattern of relationships. These in their operations may ignore the rules prescribed by the formal superior-subordinate pattern of authority. They encourage, for example, the growth of an informal organisation in which prestige and status are closely associated with the accepted sapiential authority of an individual. In short, they are indicative of social and functional networks whose characteristics contrast very sharply with such bureaucratic symbols of formal authority as rank, ceremony and rule observance.

The presence of these two types of authority is not a uniquely military phenomenon. They similarly exist in a large number of other organisations. In armed forces, however, the considerable emphasis placed on the importance of rank, in combination with the need to recognise the importance of sapiential authority, does produce a singular situation. The two sources of authority, for example, may give rise to conflict when men are forced to accept orders which contradict their perception of what is professionally and functionally deemed to be a suitable course of action. Members of armed forces in this situation are given very little opportunity to reject those commands which apparently contradict conclusions derived from their own expertise. Here, 'an order is an order'. Similar problems may arise when attempts are made to evaluate the performance of those men whose authority within the organisation is primarily derived from their expertise. A degree of strain is perhaps inevitable when the evaluation is carried out not by a professional peer but by a superior within the bureaucratic hierarchy. The established regulations may, however, insist upon this, for the rank structure incorporates the right to carry out such an evaluation as one of its salient characteristics.

In accommodating the existence of these two types of authority the armed forces of European countries differ in their adopted practice. As a general statement, it can be argued that complex military organisations tend to stress the importance of sapiential authority. Less complex ones emphasise the significance of the rank structure. In some countries, a high degree of formal organisation can be combined with a mass enthusiasm for an ideological ideal (van Doorn, 1974). This can affect the organisation in the sense that clanning may be negligible (Nagy, 1976). Where a party structure exists within the armed forces at all levels, the authority of political functionaries may considerably modify the importance within the organisation of both bureaucratic and sapiential authority. Another way of adjusting to these two forms of authority is to try and unite them into a single form of the military ethic. At one level, this implies the increased professionalisation of members of the armed

303

forces. It suggests indications of a greater identity with civilian professional standards. Military skills become less exclusively specialist. 'A civilian qualification for every military professional, or at least skills saleable in civil life is the ideal.' (Hackett, 1962, p. 63).

At another level, the development of the military ethic presupposes the creation of a collective political, professional and social consciousness of kind (Huntington, 1957). For most European armed forces this is primarily the task of military training schools. These schools, however, encounter a number of problems in their attempts to ensure that entrants to armed forces are socialised into the professional, social and cultural values of the military and the parent society. Peripheral experts who are initially trained outside the organisation still undergo only a short military socialisation programme. This may not modify their internalised professional attitudes. The need for armed forces to adapt to new technological developments may encourage the adoption of a policy of civilian rather than military training. While this may develop effective professionalism, it can also have dysfunctional consequences for the encouragement of a specific military ethic (von Baudissin, 1973). The widening of the social base of recruitment should encourage the entry into the armed forces of entrants of a higher intellectual calibre, but they may be no longer as committed as hitherto to the acceptance of the normative standards of the organisation. Alternatively, where armed forces continue to rely on their traditional sources of recruitment, it may be difficult for the military to shift from the emphasis which has in the past been placed on the bureaucratic rather than sapiential components of professional authority. Here, the innate conservatism of the soldier, his traditional preference for an ordered life and his mistrust of civilian norms make it difficult for the military to alter entrenched attitudes.

The military community

These military training schools thus have a key role in the professionalisation of armed forces. In trying to integrate a heterogeneous group of specialists into the military establishment, they seek above all to develop a strong sense of community. Their objective, as Indisow (1971) has pointed out in a study of the sociology of the profession of medical officer in the Polish armed forces, is to create a feeling of professionalism in which the essence of the profession is a specific complex of highly specialised professional, professional and military, and general military skills. These, due to their integral characteristics, designate the military as the exclusive place for the exercise of the activity. In this context, the sense of community places less emphasis on the means whereby professional socialisation is carried out than upon the ends themselves. Such an approach stresses the common interests, activities and goals of the military professional and the intricate informal social networks which reinforce the feeling of group solidarity.

This enculturation, however, is only one aspect of the military community. It is important in that as a learning process and training programme it seeks to ensure that the serviceman acquires specific norms, values and relevant roles. But there is a broader view of the military community. The fusion of profession and organisation, in combination with the particularistic goals of the military, encourage the formation of an almost unique type of environment. In part this uniqueness is derived from the identification of the community with the territorial factor, the place, the locality. Additionally, however, it involves specific items other than area, so that common ties and social interaction are component characteristics of the military community. The community can then be said to exist when the interaction between members of the armed forces is designed to meet individual needs and to further group goals, when there are institutions established for the gratification of physical, social and psychological needs and when this takes place within the limited geographical area of the military base.

The geographical isolation of these bases is noticeable in most European countries. Historical, strategic and economic reasons frequently ensure that garrisons are located outside industrial agglomeration areas. The difficult problem of land acquisition for military purposes is, as the West German Ministry of Defence points out in the *White Paper* 1973/74, still somewhat easier to solve in the less densely populated areas which are used mainly for agriculture. This spatial isolation may therefore be a reason for the growth in these garrisons of a self-sufficiency. Yet even where garrisons are located in a major city, the use of the base as the location for the carrying out of the greatest share of daily military activities encourages a similar growth. This suggests that self-sufficiency is not only dependent on geographical factors but also arises from the functional needs of the armed forces. These generate a wide range of activities. Not only must the specific needs of the servicemen be met, but the assumption by the organisation of a degree of responsibility for military dependants, increases the scope of these activities. As a result, the military base, in its provision of social services, recreational and shopping facilities, accommodation and so on, mirrors the characteristics of a small town.

Yet in many ways, the military community, despite its urban facilities, retains features which are reminiscent of Redfield's 'folk society' (1947, p. 293). It is small, isolated and homogeneous. There is a strong sense of group solidarity. The ways of living are conventionalised into the coherent system of a culture. Social interaction is traditional, spontaneous, uncritical and personal. The sacred prevails over the secular; the economy is one of status rather than the market. It differs, however, in that the military community is literate rather than non-literate, that there is legislation and that kinship is not an important feature of social relationships. But it is still nearer to Redfield's ideal type in its characteristics than it is to an urbanised society based on association.

These definitional characteristics of the military community are also, however, a commentary on the demand for social change in this area. Other parts of military life have become post-industrial in form. Social networks, for example, are not dependent upon the territorial base or face-to-face contact. Migration is transilient, for the mobility of armed forces, in association with a planned policy of rotation, ensures that the composition of the community is dynamic rather than static. Most importantly, behaviour, to use Richmond's words (1969, p. 272), 'is governed by a constant feed-back from highly efficient information storage and retrieval processes based upon diffuse networks of independent communications systems.'

It is this amalgam of the traditional and the modern, and the intermingling of the folk-society with the post-industrial society that creates to a large extent the specific characteristics of the military community. At one level, armed forces are a social system that not only tends to regulate the total lives of the inmates but which also sets barriers to social interaction with the outside world. In this respect the military is a total institution. The suggestion that the community is 'a collectivity of actors sharing in a limited territorial area as the base for carrying out the greatest share of their daily activities' (Sjoberg, 1965, p. 115), is developed further. The total institution is thus a different kind of entity, whose characteristics underpin the wider concept of the military community. Its defining characteristics are the primacy of organisation and the emphasis placed on goal attainment. Here communal ties have become increasingly dependent upon the centralised authority, upon the sophisticated communications network which controls behaviour and upon organisational membership. The organisation can seek to break down the barriers of social isolation. Servicemen can be encouraged to participate in political life, as in West Germany. Their skills can be used in the civilian field. They can be seconded to civilian organisation and training institutions. They can move off the base so that the positive separation between place of work and place of residence weakens the parameters of the total institution. Yet the communality of life and the consciousness of kind still persist, and at this second level the military community exists, irrespective of whether its structure continues to be that of a total institution or not. The major part of social interaction is still oriented towards meeting individual needs and obtaining group goals. Members of the community consistently evidence their dependence on the possession of common ends, norms and means. They are not only able to, but frequently do, act together in the common concern of life in areas which are wider than their military function alone.

It is, however, possible to delineate within this community a number of sub-groups. The perceived homogeneity which is a characteristic of armed forces in this context is modified in some countries by the existence of complementary and often competing sub-cultures. On the one hand, officers continue to enjoy a life-style which is characterised to some extent by a ceremonialism that is reminiscent of the culture of the landed interest in the eighteenth and nineteenth centuries. In comparison with much of civilian life, this style is anachronistic. Whilst this style may have the functional use of facilitating the integration of officers into a community despite their geographical and social mobility, it contrasts very forcefully with the community life of the enlisted men. Here, the existence of a distinctive sub-culture is recognised in the images of enlisted life which stress the total institutional and continuing qualities of the community. It is a cross-national culture which is shaped by peculiar demographic and social stratification features (Moskos, 1970). Essentially, it is the culture of the proletariat of the military establishment, in which norms and values derived from the early socialisation of the soldier are modified by the realities of the social organisation of armed forces.

Armed forces and politics

The existence of these sub-cultures weakens the absolute homogeneity of the military community. Not only is the corporate sense modified by the vertical separation of armed forces into specific functional units, each of which retains and develops its own traditions, and by the creation of geographically isolated institutional centres, but it is also affected by the social divisions within military life. One effect of this has been noted by Finer (1968, p. 19). In discussing the capacity and propensity of the armed forces to intervene in politics, he stresses that the power advantages of the military over all civilian organisations are qualified by its heterogeneity. 'No military force is a perfectly hierarchical and solitary organisation.' Similarly, van Doorn (1974) stresses, in recognising that the military inevitably acquire some degree of political power even when a country's laws and constitution emphasise the dominance of the civil authority, that the relation between the officer corps and society completely differs in character from that between enlisted man and society. Consequently, it can be argued that the internal differentiation of armed forces creates within the military specific interest groups whose attitudes towards the civil power are far from homogeneous.

Overt military intervention in politics is, however, only one part of the complex pattern of civil–military relationships which is a feature of contemporary European society. The militarisation of politics, in the sense that military regimes come into power, is a far from universal phenomenon. Concomitantly, no simple monocausal theory can explain the presence or absence of military intervention in politics. It can be attributed to the degree of professionalism among armed forces. Huntington (1957), for example, has argued that this is the decisive factor in keeping the military out of politics. In his view, a highly professional officer corps, motivated by military ideals, will be politically sterile and neutral. It is, however, noticeable that a number of highly professional officer corps as in Germany during the 1930s or as in France in 1958 and 1961 were far from neutral. In contrast, the examples of Switzerland, Sweden and the United Kingdom in the West would, *inter alia*, appear to support the hypothesis that Huntington has put forward.

In seeking alternative explanations for this variation, Finer (1968) has suggested that the internal level of political culture may be a significant variable. Thus in countries of *mature political culture*, the need for governments to rely on the support of the armed forces to maintain themselves is at a minimal level. Conversely, in a country of a *developed political culture*, a general uncertainty about the legitimacy of institutions may encourage the intervention of the military when overt political crises arise, as in the Kapp *putsch* in Germany in 1920 or in the 'Four Generals' coup of 1961 in France. Finally, in countries of a *low political culture*, the government is strongly dependent upon the support of armed forces, so that, here, as in Greece, Turkey and Portugal, for example, a chronic political crisis may encourage military intervention. In this instance, armed forces may either impose an indirect military regime by varying their support for one political party or another, or they may more actively take steps to supplant the civil regime.

The methodological problem of evaluating a given level of political culture illustrates, however, the complex nature of the factors which may affect the potential political power of armed forces. The notion of political culture is closely linked to the level of military intervention. The extent to which armed forces are prepared to influence, pressurise, displace or supplant the civil regime, may be determined by the internal level of the national political culture. But the latter is not the only factor which may affect the parameters of the level of intervention. To some observers, a more critical and limiting factor is the existence of a military industrial complex. The convergence of interests which this complex suggests, indicates that the potential dominance of the military is reflected in a diverse range of areas from strategic dimensions to issues of domestic economic priorities (Sarkesian, 1972, p. vii). It can be argued that the military has become so persuasive in European political systems that it has distorted the generally accepted pattern of representation and democratic political life. This suggests that armed forces, while they constitute a pressure group which is similar in its form and objectives to other interests such as industry, public administration and education, are nevertheless in a specially recognised position. Certainly the military differs from these other interest groups to the extent that servicemen with very few exceptions are not allowed to participate directly in elections or political canvassing. But the privileged position of the armed forces may counter-balance this. The general issue of the rise of the military-industrial complex is thus the extent to which this has become a dysfunctional element in domestic and international politics because of the rapid growth of armed forces to a position of dominance within national economic systems.

An awareness of the way in which armed forces because of this dominance can impose constraints upon decision-making in European nation-states, is reflected in the wider debate about the perceived legitimacy of these armed forces. The problem of military legitimacy is no new issue in European society. Critics of the military establishment have persistently argued that these are self-recruiting and self-defining institutions which do not receive general approbation. Armed forces, by this argument, are not legitimate by virtue of affectual attitudes. There is no general belief in their absolute validity by virtue of a rational acceptance of a 'natural law'. It is questionable whether a belief in their legality is either generally accepted or imposed by a universally approved procedure. In practice, reaction to this problem is exemplified in a number of ways. It can be seen in an opposition to the growth of armed forces. It is apparent in a diffuse but persistent reluctance to serve in the military (Teitler, 1975). It is noticeable in an awareness of the need to preserve a delicate balance between the military's special sense of inner group loyalty and their participation in the larger society (Janowitz, 1973). In short, the relationship between the military and the contemporary parent society is considerably affected by the continuing existence of this problem of legitimacy.

Conclusion

It is an awareness of possible military reaction to this perceived problem which draws attention again to the whole question of the place of armed forces in contemporary European society. The issue of direct military intervention in the provenance of the civil regime is but one facet of a much more complex pattern of civil-military relations. In this area, the apparent advantages of armed forces are overwhelming. The superior organisation of the military, their professional attributes, their sense of community and their monopoly of arms encourage a re-examination of the assumption that it is somehow 'natural' for armed forces to obey the civil power. But the pervasiveness of the military goes much further than this. Consistently, armed forces have served as a model for the subsequent development of other social institutions. They continue to employ a disproportionate percentage of a country's economically active male population. Military expenditure is still a large part of many national budgets. Their social and economic importance, added to their direct or indirect political influence, consistently elevates them to a position of significance within European society.

This, however, may still be the expression of a pluralistic structure in which armed forces are assigned a specialised role as managers of violence. But the decreasing use of warfare among great powers, the decline of the mass army and an increasing aversion to violence, raise new questions about the future of armed forces. A radically broadened conception of their role negates the present tendency to equate military functions solely with the ability to wage war. It gives more explicit recognition to the dependence of society upon the military for carrying out many civil functions (Biderman, 1971). This, in turn, raises fresh issues. In the last decade, the debate has centred around the civilianisation and professionalisation of the military. Now, there are indications of an increasing awareness of the problem of the dominance of the military within society. This is not to suggest that European nations are becoming more bellicose. Indeed, a considerable body of evidence points to different trends. This awareness is more pragmatic; it recognises that as armed forces become more and more a body of professional specialists and managers carrying out their task in close co-operation with political leaders, the importance of their domestic functions increases. To some critics of the military, this suggests that armed forces are becoming increasingly involved in areas of activity which were traditionally divorced from their primary function. Now they are near to being an essential part of the political order. In summary, they are no longer thought to be an isolated institution on the periphery of society. Instead, armed forces are seen to be an integral and dominant feature of European society, their pervasiveness affecting whole areas of activity.

Yet paradoxically, this changing perception of the role of armed forces in contemporary society is taking place at a time when there is increasing evidence of the decline of the mass army. In the past, the mass armed force ensured through popular participation in military service that the military, particularly the army, was 'known' to the individual citizen. Where there was an absence of a conscript tradition, as in the United Kingdom, then the military continued to be an alien institution to the great majority of the public. But in continental Europe, the obligations of compulsory military service, irrespective of the attitudes towards the military which this produced, did ensure that armed forces were seen as a pervasive and accepted social institution. The contention that the right of the citizen to bear arms was a fundamental characteristic of citizenship legitimated the existence of these forces and the identification of the military as the *Schule der Nation* contributed considerably to the recognition of its function.

The contemporary decline of the mass army in the industrialised societies of Western Europe changes considerably this traditional perception of the link between armed forces and society. At the same time, a reluctance to accept without question the unquestioned legitimacy of armed forces reflects the wish of the public to pass judgment upon those institutions of the state which affect their lives, and as part of this challenge, the contemporary military which is less visible, less known and less understood is a primary target for criticism. We are thus faced with a complex situation in which armed forces are on the one hand increasingly converging with civilian organisations in terms of military structure, technology, management and function. This transformation of the military organisation and the military professional is, on the other hand, balanced by a trend towards selective recruitment into the armed force. This is a trend which is particularly significant where the military system as in the United Kingdom is based on an all-volunteer force. It is, however, also noticeable in other European armed forces where the transition from the mass army to the volunteer intensive conscript force is similarly associated with a recruitment based on highly selective criteria.

The fundamental dilemma, therefore, is that the more professional the armed force, the more it corresponds closely to other large-scale civilian organisations, the less it is representative of the society as a whole. In this situation, the legitimacy of armed force is subject to challenge. The identified class interests of the military are thought to differ from those of the majority within the parent society. Carried to an extreme, criticism of the military identifies armed forces as symbols of oppression which inhibit individual and social freedom. Whether criticisms of this kind are justified, whether they are evidenced by empirical data is largely immaterial. What is important in contemporary European society is the extent to which an increasingly uniform perception of the military as an organisation, as a profession, as a community and as a political force forms the basis of ongoing civil-military relationships. These have always represented an uneasy alliance and a contemporary fear that trends within Europe threaten to separate the military from the larger society and transform it into a more isolated institution with selective linkages to other civilian organisations, does little to solve long-standing issues and remove long-standing doubts.

Bibliography

ABRAHAMSSON, B. (1972), *Military Professionalization and Political Power*, London, Sage.

ALBROW, MARTIN (1970), *Bureaucracy*, London, Macmillan.

BARNETT, CORELLI (1967), 'The Education of Military Elites', *Journal of Contemporary History*, vol. 2, no. 3.

BIDERMAN, ALBERT D. (1971), 'Toward Redefining the Military', *Teachers College Record*, vol. 73, no. 1.

BUSQUETS, JULIO (1974), 'The Legitimacy Crisis in Latin Europe', paper presented to the Research Committee on Armed Forces and Society of the International Sociological Association, Toronto.

COSER, L. (1958), *The Functions of Social Conflict*, London, Routledge & Kegan Paul.

FEIT, EDWARD (1973), *The Armed Bureaucrats*, Boston, Houghton Mifflin.

FINER, S. E. (1972), *The Man on Horseback. The Role of the Military in Politics*, London, Pall Mall.

FINER, S. E. (1968), 'Armed Forces and the Political Process', in Julius Gould (ed.), *Penguin Social Sciences Survey, 1968*, Harmondsworth, Penguin.

FRIEDRICH, CARL J. (1952), 'Some Observations on Weber's Analysis of Bureaucracy', in R. K. Merton *et al.* (eds), *Reader in Bureaucracy*, Chicago, Free Press.

HALL, R. H. (1963), 'Concepts of Bureaucracy – An Empirical Assessment', *American Journal of Sociology*, vol. 69.

HACKETT, GENERAL SIR JOHN (1962), *The Profession of Arms*, London, Times.

HARRIES–JENKINS, GWYN (1970), 'Professionals in Organizations', in J. A. Jackson (ed.), *Professions and Professionalization*, Cambridge University Press.

HARRIES–JENKINS, GWYN (1976), *Trade Unions in Armed Forces*, Hull, Department of Adult Education.

HARRIES–JENKINS, GWYN (1977), *The Army in Victorian Society*, London, Routledge & Kegan Paul.

HUNTINGTON, SAMUEL P. (1957), *The Soldier and the State: The Theory and Politics of Civil-Military Relations*, Cambridge, Mass., Harvard University Press.

INDISOW, LONGIN (1971), 'Sociology of the Profession of Medical Officer', in M. Janowitz and J. van Doorn (eds), *On Military Ideology*, Rotterdam University Press.

JANOWITZ, MORRIS (1960), *The Professional Soldier. A Social and Political Portrait*. Chicago, Free Press.

JANOWITZ, MORRIS (1973), *The U.S. Forces and the Zero Draft*, London, IISS, Adelphi Paper, 94.

KJELLBERG, F. (1965), 'Some Cultural Aspects of the Military Profession', *European Journal of Sociology*, vol. VI, no. 2.

KORPI, W. (1964), *Social Pressures and Attitudes in Military Training*, Stockholm, Almquist & Wiskell.

KOURVETARIS, GEORGE A. and BETTY DOBRATZ (1973), *Social Origins and Political Orientations of Officer Corps in a World Perspective*, University of Denver, The Social Science Foundation and Graduate School of International Studies.

MICHALIK, M. (1976), 'Normative Linkages between Civilian and Military Sectors of Polish Society', in G. Harries–Jenkins and Jacques van Doorn (eds), *The Military and the Problem of Legitimacy*, London, Sage.

MOSKOS, CHARLES (1970), *The American Enlisted Man*, New York, Russell Sage Foundation.

MOSKOS, CHARLES (1971), 'Armed Forces and American Society: Convergence or Divergence?', in Moskos (ed.), *Public Opinion and the Military Establishment*, Beverly Hills, Sage Publications.

NAGY, EMIL (1976), 'The Role of Mass Communication in the Political Socialization of the Hungarian Armed Forces', in G. Harries–Jenkins and Jacques van Doorn (eds), *The Military and the Problem of Legitimacy*, London, Sage.

PELLETIER, ROBERT and RAVET, SERGE (1976), *Le Mouvement des soldats*, Paris, François Maspero.

RAZZELL, P. E. (1963), 'Social Origins of Officers in the Indian and British Home Army; 1758–1962', *British Journal of Sociology*, vol. XIV.

REDFIELD, ROBERT (1947), 'The Folk Society', *American Journal of Sociology*, vol. 52.

REX, JOHN (1961), *Key Problems of Sociological Theory*, London, Routledge & Kegan Paul.

RICHMOND, ANTHONY (1969), 'Migration in Industrial Societies', in J. A. Jackson (ed.), *Migration*, Cambridge University Press.

SARKESIAN, SAM C. (1972), *The Military-Industrial Complex, A Reassessment*, Beverly Hills, Sage.

SALAZAR, OLIVEIRA (1938), *El Pensamiento de la Revolucion Nacional*, Buenos Aires.

SEGAL D. R. and M. W. (1971), 'Models of Civil-Military Relationships at the Elite Level', in M. R. van Gils (ed.), *The Perceived Role of the Military*, University of Rotterdam Press.

SIMON H. A. (1945), *Administrative Behaviour*, New York, Macmillan.

SJOBERG, GIDEON (1965), 'Community', in J. Gould and W. L. Kolb, *Dictionary of Sociology*, London, Tavistock.

TEITLER, G. (1975), 'Conscript Unionism in the Dutch Army', in G. Harries–Jenkins and J. van Doorn (eds), *The Military and the Problem of Legitimacy*, London, Sage.

VAN DOORN, JACQUES (1965), 'The Officer Corps: A Fusion of Profession and Organisation', *European Journal of Sociology*, vol. VI, no. 2.

VAN DOORN, JACQUES (1974), 'Armed Forces', *Encyclopaedia Britannica*.

VON BAUDISSIN, LIEUTENANT-GENERAL WOLF GRAF (1973), *Officer Education and the Officers' Career*, London, IISS, Adelphi Papers, 103.

WEBER, MAX (1946), *Essays in Sociology*, (ed. and trans. by H. H. Gerth and C. Wright Mills), Oxford University Press.

WEBER, MAX (1964), *The Theory of Social and Economic Organization*, (ed. Talcott Parsons), New York, Free Press.

WERNER, VICTOR (1976), 'Syndicalism in Belgian Armed Forces', (trans. G. Harries–Jenkins), in *Armed Forces and Society*, vol. 3, no. 4.

White Paper (1973/74), *The Security of the Federal Republic of Germany and the Development of the Federal Armed Forces (Zur Sicherheit der Bundesrepublik Deutschland und zur Entwicklung der Bundeswehr)*.

WHYTE, WILLIAM H. (1956), *The Organization Man*, New York, Simon & Schuster.

WIATR, J. J. (1968), 'Military Professionalism and Transformations of Class Structure in Poland', in J. van Doorn (ed.), *Armed Forces and Society*, The Hague, Mouton.

Index

Abrahamsson, B., 295, 297
activism, religious, 247–8
agrarians, 33–4
Albanians: ethnic groups, 133, 141, 152, 158–9;
religion, 232, 235
Algeria, emigrants, 100, 145, 265
alienation, 85
Alsatians, 130, 144, 157
Althusser, L., 9–10, 13
America *see* United States
Anderson, P., 15, 16n
anticlericalism, 246–7
Archer, M., 1, 30n, 179n, 181n, 186n
Ardagh, J., 31n, 248n
Armenia, 264–5, 272
assimilation, migrant, 111–15
Austria: ethnic groups, 142n, 158; immigrants, 98–9, 132, 266; politics, 267; religion, 234, 244, 246, 263
Austro-Germans, 156
authoritarianism: military, 291, 295–8, 302–4; religious, 257–62
automation, 61–2

Bain, G., 96n, 122
baptism, 274–5
Barnett, C., 288
Bashkirs, 134
Basques: ethnic groups, 130, 138, 141, 144, 146;
religion, 255, 263, 268, 272
Bauer, O., 140n, 169
Bavarians, 132n
Bédaux system, 58
Belgium: ethnic groups, 132, 136, 153–4, 157; immigrants, 98–100; military, 296; religion, 230, 234, 244–5, 250–3, 263; state, 138
Bell, D., 180n, 189n, 193n
Belorussians, 134, 142n, 147, 149
Bendix, R., 59, 67, 186n
Bergmann, J., 30n, 33n, 42n
Biderman, A., 310
Blau, P., 2n, 16–17, 47n
Böhning, W., 109, 122
Boltanski, L., 19–21, 197
Bottomore, T., 16
Bourdieu, P., 19–21, 175, 188, 197, 209n
bourgeoisie, 209–14
Braunthal, G., 29n, 30n, 33n, 36n, 38n
Bretons: ethnic groups, 129–30, 138, 141, 144–6n; religion, 263, 266, 268, 272
Britain: class, 80–91; education, 178, 186–7; ethnic groups, 129–30, 138, 141, 144–7;

315

immigrants, 98, 100–1, 105, 112, 161, 265–6;
industry, 30–2, 35, 41, 75–9;
labour, 32–3, 37, 42–3, 70, 74–91;
military, 289–90, 297–8, 308, 311;
nationalism, 140;
politics, 144, 269–71;
religion, 35, 229, 233, 237–40, 243, 245, 262–6, 272–4, 277;
see also Ireland, Scotland, Wales
Brittany *see* Bretons
Buckley, W., 8n, 16
Bulgaria: ethnic groups, 133, 141, 155–6;
military, 289;
religion, 232, 261–3, 274;
state, 142
bureaucratisation, 199–202, 294–7, 300
business *see* industry
Busquets, J., 295
Butler, D., 41n, 169

capital: class, 197–8;
cultural, 209–10, 213;
industry, 28–48;
power, 23, 37–9;
private, 20, 28–48
capitalism: class, 86–91;
state, 28–48;
systems, 74–5;
see also industry
Castles, S., 95n–6n, 102n, 106, 122
Catalans: ethnic groups, 130, 138, 141, 144, 146;
religion, 255, 263, 268–9, 272
Catholics: dissent, 246–7;
ethnic groups, 130, 151;
majority, 244–54;
minority, 239–44, 261–4, 273;
nationalism, 229–37;
and Protestants, 245;
societies, 229–54, 261–4, 273
Causer, G., 19–20, 28
Chuvashs, 134
celibacy, and education, 217–20
change: education, 197–221;
industry, 67–9, 198–210;
military, 309–12;

power, 201–7;
religious, 246–7, 275–7;
reproduction, 199–202, 205–9, 214;
social, 8, 10, 197–221
Channel Islands, 130
church: attendance, 272–6;
see also religion
class: Britain, 75–91;
capitalism, 86–91, 197–8;
education, 179–85, 197–8, 214–21;
identity, 125n;
immigrant, 95, 102, 111, 113;
industry, 199–202, 205–6, 213–15;
migrants, 95, 102, 111, 113;
middle, 209–14;
military, 297–8; peasants, 215–20;
religious, 274, 280–1;
social, 207–8;
Sweden, 75–91
clergy, role, 276
collectivism, 2
colonialism, 161
Communism: Czechoslovakia, 153;
education, 174, 191–3;
intellectuals, 278;
migrants, 106, 114, 117;
nationalism, 139;
religion, 247–50, 254, 258–60, 272, 274;
USSR, 148–50;
Yugoslavia, 150–2, 159
community, military, 291–2, 304–7
competition, religious, 243
conflict: migrants, 112–15;
religious, 245–7;
theory, 3;
workers, 62–4
Conquest, R., 167–8
consciousness, national *see* nationalism
conscription, 298, 311
Corsicans, 130, 144–5, 157
Coser, L., 3, 288
craftsmen, 211–13

Croats, 133, 138, 141
culture: capital, 209–10, 213;
    intellectuals, 173–5;
    nation, 125–35
Cyprus, 155, 234, 262–3, 265
Czechoslovakia: ethnic groups, 133,
    141–2, 149, 153–5, 159;
    military, 298;
    politics, 153, 193, 267–8;
    religion, 230–1, 233, 263, 278

Dahlström, E., 78–9n
Davis, L., 63n, 66n, 71n
democracy, 41–3, 84–91
demography see population
demoralisation, 214–15
Denmark: ethnic groups, 131;
    immigrants, 98;
    religion, 229, 262–3, 271–2
Denton, G., 30n–1n, 39n, 41n
deportation, 149n;
    see also migration
determinism, 4, 6–7, 11, 14
diaspora, 265–6, 272;
    see also migration
dirigisme, 45
disease, mental, 116n
divorce, 245, 250
Djilas, 193
Dobratz, B., 297
domination, mode, 202–5
Doob, L., 140n, 169
Drewe, P., 108n, 123
Drucker, P., 61
Durkheim, E., 3, 125, 184, 199
Dutch see Netherlands

economism, 6, 9, 13–14
education: celibacy, 217–20;
    class, 179–85, 197–8, 214–21;
    communist, 174, 191–3;
    elite, 173–9, 191, 198–201;
    expansion, 188–91, 198;
    industry, 199–207;
    intellectual, 173–9;
    military, 304;
    occupation, 172–3, 177–87;
    reform 89;
    religious, 245, 251, 277;
    role, 192–4

egalitarianism, 87
Ehrmann, H., 30n–1n, 33n, 37n,
    169
Eisenstatt, S., 5–6
elites: changes, 201–7;
    education, 173–9, 191, 198–201;
    industrial, 29;
    integration, 36–7;
    military, 34, 297–8;
    national focus, 126;
    pre-capitalist, 34–6;
    religious, 228, 243, 254;
    see also power
employment   see   industry,
    occupation
enterprises: changes, 198–210;
    small, 211–12;
    see also industry
Estonians, 134, 141, 142n, 261–2,
    264
ethnic groups: autonomous, 160;
    characteristics, 124–39;
    fragmented, 154–9;
    history, 139–43;
    migrated, 160–2;
    nomadic, 159–60;
    non-governing, 143–53;
    numbers, 162n;
    problems, 21–2;
    see also nationalism
European Economic Community,
    33, 44–5, 103–7
expenditure, military, 289–90, 310

family: industry, 198–209, 214;
    military, 292;
    religious, 248
farmers, 33–4
Faroese, 131
Fascism, 249, 253
Fayol, H., 289
federation, state, 137–8, 148–9, 151,
    156
Feit, E., 294
finance see capital, expenditure,
    salary
Finer, S., 29n, 30n, 32n, 37, 293,
    307–8

Finland: ethnic groups, 131, 141, 142n, 159–60;
religion, 233, 242, 263–4
Flemish, 132, 136, 153–4, 157, 250, 266
forces *see* military
Fordism, 56, 59–60, 70
France: education, 176–8, 185, 187;
ethnic groups, 130, 136, 142, 144, 146, 157;
immigrants, 98–101, 104–7, 112–16, 119, 161–2n, 265;
industry, 30–1, 36, 38, 41, 58;
labour, 33, 37, 70, 181;
military, 290, 296–7, 308;
nationalism, 140;
politics, 9, 35, 144, 276;
religion, 35, 230, 244–8, 251–3, 262–4, 268, 272–3, 277;
xenophobia, 116n
Franco, General, 31, 121–2, 146, 256
Friedmann, G., 56, 58
Friedrich, C., 294
Frisians, 132
functionalism, 2–27
Furlanians, 132, 136, 157

Gallicians, 144
Gaudemar, J. de, 97n, 122
Germany: ethnic groups, 125n, 132–3, 136, 142–3, 153, 155, 157, 162n;
immigrants, 97–9, 101, 105, 103, 107–8, 160, 265–6;
industry, 30–1, 41;
labour, 32–3, 42–3;
military, 289, 293, 296–7, 305, 308;
nationalism, 139–40, 142;
politics, 277;
religion, 231, 234–5, 239–43, 246, 263–4, 271–6;
xenophobia, 116n
Germany, East: religion, 232, 261, 274

Giddens, A., 28, 182n, 184n, 192n
Giner, S., 19, 22, 30n, 94, 179n, 181n
Goblot, E., 178
Gorz, A., 113, 115, 122
Gouldner, A., 2, 7–12
government: migrants, 103–5;
self, 143–53;
see also politics
Gramsci, A., 6, 50, 59
Greece: emigrants, 100, 108;
ethnic groups, 132, 136, 141–2, 155–6;
industry, 30, 39, 41;
military, 35, 290;
religion, 234, 254, 257, 262, 264–5, 273;
state, 142
Gypsies, 133, 136–7, 159–60

Hackett, General, 304
Hall, R., 294
Harries-Jenkins, G., 19, 288, 291–2, 297
Hayward, J., 30n–1n, 38n–9n, 41n
hegemony, 70–1
Hirsch, F., 39
history, and nation, 125–35, 139–43
Hobsbawm, E., 6
Holland *see* Netherlands
Hoxie enquiry, 59
Hungary: emigrants, 265;
ethnic groups, 133, 142, 149, 152–5;
politics, 267;
religion, 230–1, 233–4, 261–2
Huntington, S., 304, 308

Icelanders, 131
immigration *see* migration
Indisow, L., 304
industry: capital, 28–48;
craft, 211–13;
education, 199–207;
migrants, 101;
military, 309;
organisation, 29–32;
religion, 277–80;

see also enterprises, labour, trade unions
Ingham, G., 29n, 32–3n, 42n
innovation *see* change
institutions: interdependence, 7–15, 19–24;
  military, 291–4, 304–7;
  state, 9–24
insubordination, migrant, 112–14
integration: migrant, 111–15;
  military, 292–3;
  religious, 254–7
intellectuals: communism, 278;
  culture, 173–5;
  education, 173–9;
  as notables, 185–91;
  occupation, 172–3, 177–85;
  role, 192–4
intelligentsia, 22, 191–4, 278–82
interactionism, symbolic, 3
interdependence, institutions, 7–15, 19–24
internationalism, 23, 150, 156, 255
Ireland: emigrants, 104;
  ethnic groups, 130, 138, 141;
  military, 289, 297;
  politics, 269–71;
  religion, 230, 234, 262–3, 272;
  see also Britain
Islam *see* Muslims
Italy: emigrants, 265–6;
  ethnic groups, 132, 136, 138, 142, 157, 162n;
  industry, 38–9, 320–1;
  labour, 33–4, 63, 65, 70;
  migrants, 97–100, 104, 160;
  politics, 6, 276;
  military, 290;
  religion, 35, 185, 230, 244–9, 253, 273

Jackson, J., 94n, 122
Janowitz, M., 291, 293, 297, 299, 309
Jews: Britain, 265–6;
  intelligentsia, 281;
  ethnic group, 133–4, 137;
  USSR, 261
job-design, 64–7

Karelians, 134, 142n, 160
Kavanagh, D., 44n, 169
Kedourie, E., 140n, 145n, 169
Kjellberg, F., 297
Kogan, N., 31n., 33n, 40n, 41n
Komi, 134
Korpi, W., 295
Kosack, G., 95n–6n, 102n, 106
Kourvetaris, G., 297
Krejci, J., 18, 21, 124, 142n, 153n, 170

La Palombara, 33n, 36n, 40n
labour: free, 103; movements, 29, 32–3, 42–3; *see also* trade
Ladins, 132n
Lagneau, J., 174n, 182n, 192n
land, military, 305
language: nation, 125–36, 138, 144–5, 148, 151;
  religion, 268
Lansing, J., 94n, 123
Lapps, 131, 159, 262, 264
Latvians, 134, 141–2n, 261, 272
Le Monde, 119
Lenin, 9n, 10n, 140n, 148–9, 170
Lipset, M. S., 173, 186, 238n, 250n
Lithuanians: ethnic groups, 134, 141, 142n;
  religion, 259, 261–2, 264, 272
Lockwood, D., 1, 74n, 112, 123, 180n–1n
Lundqvist, A., 75–84 *passim*
Luxembourg, 100, 132, 289–90

Macedonians, 133, 156
Madariaga, S., 144, 170
Maltese, 132, 234, 262–3, 268
management, scientific: automation, 61–2;
  characteristics, 55–7;
  congresses, 58–9;
  corrections, 60–1;
  crisis, 62–7;
  improvers, 77–8
Manx, 130
Mari, 134
marriage, 275

Martin, D., 19, 228
Marxism: capital, 28, 15–27;
  class, 95;
  nationalism, 139, 156;
  religion, 236–7, 259;
  social structures, 2–8, 15–27;
  USSR, 149–50;
  see also Communism
mass production, 56–60, 67–9
Mayo, 60
Merton, 4, 184
Meynaud, J., 30n–41n *passim* 47n
Michalik, M., 294
Michels, R., 88
migration; worker: ages, 109–10;
  assimilation, 111–15;
  assisted, 96;
  class, 95, 102, 111, 113;
  communists, 106, 114, 117;
  conflict, 112–15;
  economic effect, 108–9;
  employment, 98, 100–3;
  government, 103–5;
  health, 109, 116;
  illegal, 103;
  industry, 22, 101;
  insubordination, 112–14;
  integration, 111–15;
  military, 305;
  numbers, 98;
  official policies, 103–7;
  origins, 97–100;
  problems, 160–2;
  religion, 264–5;
  sex, 111;
  subordination, 112–13;
  trade unions, 95, 105–7;
  unemployment, 108–9;
  wages, 107
Miliband, R., 14, 28n, 32n–4n, 39n, 80n, 86
military forces: bureaucracy, 294–7, 300;
  changes 309–12;
  community, 304–7;
  education, 304;
  elites, 34, 297–8;
  industry, 309;
  integration, 292–3;
  organisation, 294–8;
  politics, 292–3, 307–9;
  religion, 256–7;
  soldiers, 298–304;
  system, 289–94;
  unions, 296
Milyukov, P., 126, 170
models, 7–8, 67–70
Moldavians, 134, 143, 148
monarchy, 249–50
Montenegrins, 133, 137
Moore, R., 106, 123
Mordovians, 134
Morocco, 100, 117n
Moskos, C., 294, 300, 307
Muller-Jentsch, W., 30n, 33n, 42n
multi-nationalism, 39, 43–5
Muslims: Albania, 232;
  Britain, 265–6;
  Bulgaria, 261–2;
  Spain, 229;
  Turkey, 261n;
  USSR, 148;
  Yugoslavia, 128, 133, 151, 231, 261–2

Nagy, E., 303
nation, concept, 125–6
nationalism: ethnic groups, 125, 128–50;
  communism, 139;
  industry, 43n;
  multi, 39, 43–5;
  religion, 228–35, 243–4, 255;
  state, 125–43, 151
Netherlands: ethnic groups, 132;
  immigrants, 98–100, 106, 112, 161;
  industry, 36, 38;
  military, 290, 296–7;
  religion, 35–6, 229, 233, 239–41, 243, 247, 251, 262, 271–3, 276
North Atlantic Treaty Organisation 289–90
Norway: ethnic groups, 131, 136, 159;
  military, 290, 297;

religion, 229, 238, 240, 242, 247, 263, 272;
  unions, 63, 70

Occitanians, 144
occupations: education, 172–3, 177–87;
  immigrants, 98, 100–3;
  intellectual, 172–3, 177–87;
  religion, 277–80
'Opus Dei', 35, 40, 254
organisation, 67–71
Orthodox religion, 230–2, 273–4

Paine, C., 109, 123
Paris Treaty, 45
Parkin, F., 74
Parsons, 4, 7, 11
participation, worker, 64–5
Pascual, A., 94n, 107n, 123
Payne, S., 9, 31n, 34n, 40n
peasantry, 215–20
Pelletier, R., 296
Pichierri, A., 19, 23, 55, 57n
Poland: education, 175, 179, 185, 191;
  ethnic groups, 133, 141–2, 148n–9, 155;
  emigrants, 265;
  migrants, 97;
  military, 298;
  religion, 185, 230, 232, 234, 260, 272–4, 278, 282;
  state, 142
  politics: military, 292–3, 307–9;
  religion, 228–82 *passim*;
  see also communism, Marxism, nationalism, power, state
polycentrism, 70–1
Pomacks, 133n
population, 97, 143
Portugal: emigrants, 100, 116–17, 119, 265;
  ethnic groups, 130, 161;
  immigrants, 16;
  military, 35, 289–90, 308;
  religion, 240, 244, 252–4, 256–7, 272
Poulantzas, N., 9, 13–14

power: authoritarian, 257–62;
  capital, 37–9;
  changes, 201–2;
  conditions, 16;
  economic, 38–9;
  integrated, 254–7;
  military, 294–6;
  religion, 235–9, 244–54, 280–2;
  worker, 74–91
Power, J., 96n, 103n, 123
professions, 185–9, 210–12, 294–304;
  see also occupations, workers
protest see conflict
Protestants: dominant, 237–44;
  minority, 248, 254, 260–5, 271;
  nationalism, 229–35
psychology, 60

rationalisation, industry, 56–7
Ravet, S., 296
Razzell, P., 297
Redfield, R., 305
refugees, 96–7, 143n, 145, 154;
  see also migration
regions, religious, 262–71;
  see also ethnic groups
rehabilitation see deportation
religion: authoritarian, 257–62;
  activist, 247–8;
  changes, 275–7;
  class, 274, 280–1;
  clergy, 276;
  communism, 247–50, 254, 258–60, 272, 274;
  competition, 243;
  divorce, 245, 250;
  education, 245, 251, 277;
  folk, 278;
  industry, 31, 35, 277–80;
  integration, 254–7;
  language, 268;
  marriage, 275;
  military, 256–7;
  monarchy, 249–50;
  nationalism, 228–35, 243–4, 255;
  occupation, 237–9, 244–54, 277–80;
  politics, 125–45 *passim*;

228–82 *passim*;
power, 235–7, 257–62, 280–2;
practice, 272–80;
protest, 245–7;
regions, 262–71;
see also Catholics, Muslims, Protestants
reproduction, changes, 199–202, 205–9, 214
Resler, H., 38n, 47n, 74n
retail trade, 212
Rex, J., 94n, 112n, 123, 288
Richmond, A., 306
Romania: ethnic groups, 133, 141–3, 148, 154–5;
religion, 232–4, 259, 273, 282;
state 127
Russians *see* USSR
Ruthenians, 142n

salary, 107, 201–2, 209–11
Salazar, O., 299
Salcedo, J., 19, 22, 94, 123
Sardinians, 132n, 157
Sarkesian, S., 309
Scase, R., 23, 74, 75n
Schweigler, G. L., 142n, 170
science, management, 55–71
Scotland: ethnic groups, 130, 138, 146–7;
religion, 229, 262–4, 271–2;
see also Britain
Segal, D. and M., 296
Segerstedt, T., 75–84 *passim*
Serbs, 133, 141
Sicilians, 132n, 157
Sidjanski, D., 30n, 33n, 38n, 44n–5n
Simon, H., 296
Sjoberg, G., 306
Slavs, 142, 145, 149
Slovaks, 133, 141, 153, 267–8
Slovenes, 133, 141, 157–8, 274
Smelser, N., 4
social structure, 1–27
socialism *see* communism, democracy, politics
soldiers *see* military
Smith, A., 5, 140n, 170
Soler, R., 30n–1n, 40n

Sorbs, 133, 160
Sorel, 172
Spain: emigrants, 97–8, 104, 107n, 112n, 116–17, 160, 265;
ethnic groups, 130, 138, 141, 144, 146;
industry, 31, 34, 36, 40;
labour, 37;
military, 35, 297;
politics, 144, 268, 276;
religion, 229, 234, 244, 246, 252–6, 272–3, 276–8
speech, 217n;
see also language
Stalin, 140n, 149–50, 192–3
state: abstract concepts, 6–24;
capitalism, 28–48;
federated, 137–8, 148–9, 151, 156;
nationalism, 125–43, 151
Stone, G., 160n, 170
strikes, 62–4, 105n;
see also workers
subordination, migrants, 112–13
supra-nationalism, 43–5
Sweden: class, 80–91;
ethnic groups, 131, 159–60, 162n;
industry, 41, 75–9;
labour, 23, 33, 37, 42–3, 74, 78–91;
military, 297, 308;
religion, 229, 238, 242, 264, 271–3, 277
Switzerland: ethnic groups, 125n, 132, 157–8, 162n;
immigrants, 99, 101, 103, 116, 265–6;
military, 308;
religion, 229, 239, 241–3, 272–3;
xenophobia, 116n
systems theory 7–15

Tatars, 134, 141
Taylor, J., 63n, 66n, 71n
'Taylorism', 56–60, 67–9
Teitler, G., 309
territory, 125–36
Tingsten, H., 87n–8
Touraine, A., 56, 69, 184n, 188n
Tirolese, 138

trade unions: British, 42–3;
EEC, 44–5;
influence, 23, 42–3;
management, 58–9, 62;
migrants, 95, 105–7;
military, 296;
role, 77–9;
Swedish, 42–3;
USA, 59, 63;
Tunisia, 100
Turkey: emigrants, 100, 108, 265;
ethnic groups, 132, 141–2, 155;
military, 290, 308;
nationalism, 148;
religion, 261n
Turner, J., 17

Udmurts, 134
Ukrainians: ethnic groups, 134,
138, 141–2n, 147, 149;
religion, 259, 272
unemployment, 108–9
Union of Soviet Socialist Republics
annexations, 142n;
communism, 148–50;
deportation, 149n;
education, 174, 191–2;
emigrants, 265–6;
ethnic groups, 134, 137, 141–3,
147–50, 261;
nationalism, 139–41;
religion, 148, 230, 232, 257–62,
271–4
unions see trade
United Nations, 144
United States: and Europe, 43n,
140;
hegemony, 70–1;
industry, 56, 59–60;
job design, 65–7;
military, 290, 293;
religion, 237–8, 243, 272n–3, 276;
unions, 59, 63
Van Den Berghe, P., 1
Van Doorn, J., 293, 297, 301, 303,
307
Vaughan, M., 19, 22, 172, 175n–6n

Vendée, La, 268
Vernon, R., 39n, 43n–4n

wages see salary
Walloons, 132, 136, 153–4, 250
war: church, 246, 253;
deaths, 143;
industry, 58–60;
migration, 160;
nationalism, 139–42, 154, 156;
society, 288–9, 310
Watson, M., 30n–1n, 38n, 41n
Weber, M., 294, 297–8, 302
Welsh: ethnic groups, 129–30, 141,
144–6;
religion, 269–72; see also Britain
'white-collar' workers, 179–85
Whyte, W., 291
Wiatr, J., 298
Windmuller, J., 30n, 33n, 36n
Woodward, J., 69
work: alienation 85;
conditions, 76–7;
see also labour
workers: conflict,
62–4, 112–15;
participation, 64–5;
peasants, 215–20;
power, 74–91;
'white-collar', 179–85;
see also class, labour, migration,
trade unions

xenophobia, 116n

Yannopoulos, G., 108–9, 123
Yugoslavia: communism, 150–2,
159;
emigrants, 100, 116–17;
ethnic groups, 150–2, 154–9;
Muslims, 128, 133, 151, 231,
261–2;
nationalism, 139, 149;
religion, 231, 233–5, 278, 282;
state, 138

Zariskie, R., 30n, 33n, 41n

Routledge Social Science Series

Routledge & Kegan Paul   London, Henley and Boston

39 Store Street, London WC1E 7DD
Broadway House, Newtown Road, Henley-on-Thames,
Oxon RG9 1EN
9 Park Street, Boston, Mass. 02108

Contents

International Library of Sociology 3
General Sociology 3
Foreign Classics of Sociology 4
Social Structure 4
Sociology and Politics 5
Criminology 5
Social Psychology 6
Sociology of the Family 6
Social Services 7
Sociology of Education 8
Sociology of Culture 8
Sociology of Religion 9
Sociology of Art and Literature 9
Sociology of Knowledge 9
Urban Sociology 10
Rural Sociology 10
Sociology of Industry and Distribution 10
Anthropology 11
Sociology and Philosophy 12
International Library of Anthropology 12
International Library of Social Policy 13
International Library of Welfare and Philosophy 13
Primary Socialization, Language and Education 14
Reports of the Institute of Community Studies 14
Reports of the Institute for Social Studies in Medical Care 15
Medicine, Illness and Society 15
Monographs in Social Theory 15
Routledge Social Science Journals 16
Social and Psychological Aspects of Medical Practice 16

*Authors wishing to submit manuscripts for any series in
this catalogue should send them to the Social Science Editor,
Routledge & Kegan Paul Ltd, 39 Store Street,
London WC1E 7DD*

● *Books so marked are available in paperback*
All books are in Metric Demy 8vo format (216 × 138mm approx.)

International Library of Sociology

General Editor John Rex

GENERAL SOCIOLOGY

Barnsley, J. H. The Social Reality of Ethics. *464 pp.*
Belshaw, Cyril. The Conditions of Social Performance. *An Exploratory Theory. 144 pp.*
Brown, Robert. Explanation in Social Science. *208 pp.*
● Rules and Laws in Sociology. *192 pp.*
Bruford, W. H. Chekhov and His Russia. *A Sociological Study. 244 pp.*
Cain, Maureen E. Society and the Policeman's Role. *326 pp.*
●**Fletcher, Colin.** Beneath the Surface. *An Account of Three Styles of Sociological Research. 221 pp.*
Gibson, Quentin. The Logic of Social Enquiry. *240 pp.*
Glucksmann, M. Structuralist Analysis in Contemporary Social Thought. *212 pp.*
Gurvitch, Georges. Sociology of Law. *Preface by Roscoe Pound. 264 pp.*
Hodge, H. A. Wilhelm Dilthey. *An Introduction. 184 pp.*
Homans, George C. Sentiments and Activities. *336 pp.*
Johnson, Harry M. Sociology: *a Systematic Introduction. Foreword by Robert K. Merton. 710 pp.*
●**Keat, Russell,** and **Urry, John.** Social Theory as Science. *278 pp.*
Mannheim, Karl. Essays on Sociology and Social Psychology. *Edited by Paul Kecskemeti. With Editorial Note by Adolph Lowe. 344 pp.*
Systematic Sociology: *An Introduction to the Study of Society. Edited by J. S. Erös and Professor W. A. C. Stewart. 220 pp.*
Martindale, Don. The Nature and Types of Sociological Theory. *292 pp.*
●**Maus, Heinz.** A Short History of Sociology. *234 pp.*
Mey, Harald. Field-Theory. *A Study of its Application in the Social Sciences. 352 pp.*
Myrdal, Gunnar. Value in Social Theory: *A Collection of Essays on Methodology. Edited by Paul Streeten. 332 pp.*
Ogburn, William F., and **Nimkoff, Meyer F.** A Handbook of Sociology. *Preface by Karl Mannheim. 656 pp. 46 figures. 35 tables.*
Parsons, Talcott, and **Smelser, Neil J.** Economy and Society: *A Study in the Integration of Economic and Social Theory. 362 pp.*
Podgórecki, Adam. Practical Social Sciences. *About 200 pp.*
●**Rex, John.** Key Problems of Sociological Theory. *220 pp.*
Sociology and the Demystification of the Modern World. *282 pp.*
●**Rex, John** (Ed.) Approaches to Sociology. *Contributions by Peter Abell, Frank Bechhofer, Basil Bernstein, Ronald Fletcher, David Frisby, Miriam Glucksmann, Peter Lassman, Herminio Martins, John Rex, Roland Robertson, John Westergaard and Jock Young. 302 pp.*
Rigby, A. Alternative Realities. *352 pp.*
Roche, M. Phenomenology, Language and the Social Sciences. *374 pp.*

3

Sahay, A. Sociological Analysis. *220 pp.*
Simirenko, Alex (Ed.) Soviet Sociology. *Historical Antecedents and Current Appraisals. Introduction by Alex Simirenko. 376 pp.*
Strasser, Hermann. The Normative Structure of Sociology. *Conservative and Emancipatory Themes in Social Thought. About 340 pp.*
Urry, John. Reference Groups and the Theory of Revolution. *244 pp.*
Weinberg, E. Development of Sociology in the Soviet Union. *173 pp.*

FOREIGN CLASSICS OF SOCIOLOGY

● **Durkheim, Emile.** Suicide. *A Study in Sociology. Edited and with an Introduction by George Simpson. 404 pp.*
● **Gerth, H. H.,** and **Mills, C. Wright.** From Max Weber: *Essays in Sociology. 502 pp.*
● **Tönnies, Ferdinand.** Community and Association. *(Gemeinschaft und Gesellschaft.) Translated and Supplemented by Charles P. Loomis. Foreword by Pitirim A. Sorokin. 334 pp.*

SOCIAL STRUCTURE

Andreski, Stanislav. Military Organization and Society. *Foreword by Professor A. R. Radcliffe-Brown. 226 pp. 1 folder.*
Carlton, Eric. Ideology and Social Order. *Preface by Professor Philip Abrahams. About 320 pp.*
Coontz, Sydney H. Population Theories and the Economic Interpretation. *202 pp.*
Coser, Lewis. The Functions of Social Conflict. *204 pp.*
Dickie-Clark, H. F. Marginal Situation: *A Sociological Study of a Coloured Group. 240 pp. 11 tables.*
Glaser, Barney, and **Strauss, Anselm L.** Status Passage. *A Formal Theory. 208 pp.*
Glass, D. V. (Ed.) Social Mobility in Britain. *Contributions by J. Berent, T. Bottomore, R. C. Chambers, J. Floud, D. V. Glass, J. R. Hall, H. T. Himmelweit, R. K. Kelsall, F. M. Martin, C. A. Moser, R. Mukherjee, and W. Ziegel. 420 pp.*
Johnstone, Frederick A. Class, Race and Gold. *A Study of Class Relations and Racial Discrimination in South Africa. 312 pp.*
Jones, Garth N. Planned Organizational Change: *An Exploratory Study Using an Empirical Approach. 268 pp.*
Kelsall, R. K. Higher Civil Servants in Britain: *From 1870 to the Present Day. 268 pp. 31 tables.*
König, René. The Community. *232 pp. Illustrated.*
● **Lawton, Denis.** Social Class, Language and Education. *192 pp.*
McLeish, John. The Theory of Social Change: *Four Views Considered. 128 pp.*
Marsh, David C. The Changing Social Structure of England and Wales, 1871-1961. *288 pp.*
Menzies, Ken. Talcott Parsons and the Social Image of Man. *About 208 pp.*

4

●**Mouzelis, Nicos.** Organization and Bureaucracy. *An Analysis of Modern Theories. 240 pp.*

Mulkay, M. J. Functionalism, Exchange and Theoretical Strategy. *272 pp.*

Ossowski, Stanislaw. Class Structure in the Social Consciousness. *210 pp.*

●**Podgórecki, Adam.** Law and Society. *302 pp.*

Renner, Karl. Institutions of Private Law and Their Social Functions. *Edited, with an Introduction and Notes, by O. Kahn-Freud. Translated by Agnes Schwarzschild. 316 pp.*

SOCIOLOGY AND POLITICS

Acton, T. A. Gypsy Politics and Social Change. *316 pp.*

Clegg, Stuart. Power, Rule and Domination. *A Critical and Empirical Understanding of Power in Sociological Theory and Organisational Life. About 300 pp.*

Hechter, Michael. Internal Colonialism. *The Celtic Fringe in British National Development, 1536–1966. 361 pp.*

Hertz, Frederick. Nationality in History and Politics: *A Psychology and Sociology of National Sentiment and Nationalism. 432 pp.*

Kornhauser, William. The Politics of Mass Society. *272 pp. 20 tables.*

●**Kroes, R.** Soldiers and Students. *A Study of Right- and Left-wing Students. 174 pp.*

Laidler, Harry W. History of Socialism. *Social-Economic Movements: An Historical and Comparative Survey of Socialism, Communism, Co-operation, Utopianism; and other Systems of Reform and Reconstruction. 992 pp.*

Lasswell, H. D. Analysis of Political Behaviour. *324 pp.*

Martin, David A. Pacifism: *an Historical and Sociological Study. 262 pp.*

Martin, Roderick. Sociology of Power. *About 272 pp.*

Myrdal, Gunnar. The Political Element in the Development of Economic Theory. *Translated from the German by Paul Streeten. 282 pp.*

Wilson, H. T. The American Ideology. *Science, Technology and Organization of Modes of Rationality. About 280 pp.*

Wootton, Graham. Workers, Unions and the State. *188 pp.*

CRIMINOLOGY

Ancel, Marc. Social Defence: *A Modern Approach to Criminal Problems. Foreword by Leon Radzinowicz. 240 pp.*

Cain, Maureen E. Society and the Policeman's Role. *326 pp.*

Cloward, Richard A., and **Ohlin, Lloyd E.** Delinquency and Opportunity: *A Theory of Delinquent Gangs. 248 pp.*

Downes, David M. The Delinquent Solution. *A Study in Subcultural Theory. 296 pp.*

Dunlop, A. B., and **McCabe, S.** Young Men in Detention Centres. *192 pp.*

Friedlander, Kate. The Psycho-Analytical Approach to Juvenile Delinquency: *Theory, Case Studies, Treatment. 320 pp.*

Glueck, Sheldon, and **Eleanor.** Family Environment and Delinquency. *With the statistical assistance of Rose W. Kneznek. 340 pp.*

Lopez-Rey, Manuel. Crime. *An Analytical Appraisal. 288 pp.*
Mannheim, Hermann. Comparative Criminology: *a Text Book. Two volumes. 442 pp. and 380 pp.*

Morris, Terence. The Criminal Area: *A Study in Social Ecology. Foreword by Hermann Mannheim. 232 pp. 25 tables. 4 maps.*
Rock, Paul. Making People Pay. *338 pp.*
●Taylor, Ian, Walton, Paul, and Young, Jock. The New Criminology. *For a Social Theory of Deviance. 325 pp.*
●Taylor, Ian, Walton, Paul, and Young, Jock (Eds). Critical Criminology. *268 pp.*

SOCIAL PSYCHOLOGY

Bagley, Christopher. The Social Psychology of the Epileptic Child. *320 pp.*
Barbu, Zevedei. Problems of Historical Psychology. *248 pp.*
Blackburn, Julian. Psychology and the Social Pattern. *184 pp.*
●Brittan, Arthur. Meanings and Situations. *224 pp.*
Carroll, J. Break-Out from the Crystal Palace. *200 pp.*
●Fleming, C. M. Adolescence: Its Social Psychology. *With an Introduction to recent findings from the fields of Anthropology, Physiology, Medicine, Psychometrics and Sociometry. 288 pp.*
● The Social Psychology of Education: *An Introduction and Guide to Its Study. 136 pp.*
●Homans, George C. The Human Group. *Foreword by Bernard DeVoto. Introduction by Robert K. Merton. 526 pp.*
● Social Behaviour: *its Elementary Forms. 416 pp.*
●Klein, Josephine. The Study of Groups. *226 pp. 31 figures. 5 tables.*
Linton, Ralph. The Cultural Background of Personality. *132 pp.*
●Mayo, Elton. The Social Problems of an Industrial Civilization. *With an appendix on the Political Problem. 180 pp.*
Ottaway, A. K. C. Learning Through Group Experience. *176 pp.*
Plummer, Ken. Sexual Stigma. *An Interactionist Account. 254 pp.*
●Rose, Arnold M. (Ed.) Human Behaviour and Social Processes: *an Interactionist Approach. Contributions by Arnold M. Rose, Ralph H. Turner, Anselm Strauss, Everett C. Hughes, E. Franklin Frazier, Howard S. Becker, et al. 696 pp.*
Smelser, Neil J. Theory of Collective Behaviour. *448 pp.*
Stephenson, Geoffrey M. The Development of Conscience. *128 pp.*
Young, Kimball. Handbook of Social Psychology. *658 pp. 16 figures. 10 tables.*

SOCIOLOGY OF THE FAMILY

Banks, J. A. Prosperity and Parenthood: *A Study of Family Planning among The Victorian Middle Classes. 262 pp.*
Bell, Colin R. Middle Class Families: *Social and Geographical Mobility. 224 pp.*

Burton, Lindy. Vulnerable Children. *272 pp.*

Gavron, Hannah. The Captive Wife: *Conflicts of Household Mothers.* *190 pp.*

George, Victor, and **Wilding, Paul.** Motherless Families. *248 pp.*

Klein, Josephine. Samples from English Cultures.
  1. Three Preliminary Studies and Aspects of Adult Life in England. *447 pp.*
  2. Child-Rearing Practices and Index. *247 pp.*

Klein, Viola. The Feminine Character. *History of an Ideology. 244 pp.*

McWhinnie, Alexina M. Adopted Children. *How They Grow Up. 304 pp.*

● **Morgan, D. H. J.** Social Theory and the Family. *About 320 pp.*

● **Myrdal, Alva,** and **Klein, Viola.** Women's Two Roles: *Home and Work.* *238 pp. 27 tables.*

Parsons, Talcott, and **Bales, Robert F.** Family: Socialization and Interaction Process. *In collaboration with James Olds, Morris Zelditch and Philip E. Slater. 456 pp. 50 figures and tables.*

SOCIAL SERVICES

Bastide, Roger. The Sociology of Mental Disorder. *Translated from the French by Jean McNeil. 260 pp.*

Carlebach, Julius. Caring For Children in Trouble. *266 pp.*

George, Victor. Foster Care. *Theory and Practice. 234 pp.*
  Social Security: *Beveridge and After. 258 pp.*

George, V., and **Wilding, P.** Motherless Families. *248 pp.*

● **Goetschius, George W.** Working with Community Groups. *256 pp.*

Goetschius, George W., and **Tash, Joan.** Working with Unattached Youth. *416 pp.*

Hall, M. P., and **Howes, I. V.** The Church in Social Work. *A Study of Moral Welfare Work undertaken by the Church of England. 320 pp.*

Heywood, Jean S. Children in Care: *the Development of the Service for the Deprived Child. 264 pp.*

Hoenig, J., and **Hamilton, Marian W.** The De-Segregation of the Mentally Ill. *284 pp.*

Jones, Kathleen. Mental Health and Social Policy, 1845-1959. *264 pp.*

King, Roy D., Raynes, Norma V., and **Tizard, Jack.** Patterns of Residential Care. *356 pp.*

Leigh, John. Young People and Leisure. *256 pp.*

● **Mays, John.** (Ed.) Penelope Hall's Social Services of England and Wales. *About 324 pp.*

Morris, Mary. Voluntary Work and the Welfare State. *300 pp.*

Nokes, P. L. The Professional Task in Welfare Practice. *152 pp.*

Timms, Noel. Psychiatric Social Work in Great Britain (1939-1962). *280 pp.*

● Social Casework: *Principles and Practice. 256 pp.*

Young, A. F. Social Services in British Industry. *272 pp.*

SOCIOLOGY OF EDUCATION

Banks, Olive. Parity and Prestige in English Secondary Education: a Study in Educational Sociology. *272 pp.*

Bentwich, Joseph. Education in Israel. *224 pp. 8 pp. plates.*

● **Blyth, W. A. L.** English Primary Education. *A Sociological Description.*
   1. Schools. *232 pp.*
   2. Background. *168 pp.*

Collier, K. G. The Social Purposes of Education: *Personal and Social Values in Education. 268 pp.*

Dale, R. R., and **Griffith, S.** Down Stream: *Failure in the Grammar School. 108 pp.*

Evans, K. M. Sociometry and Education. *158 pp.*

● **Ford, Julienne.** Social Class and the Comprehensive School. *192 pp.*

Foster, P. J. Education and Social Change in Ghana. *336 pp. 3 maps.*

Fraser, W. R. Education and Society in Modern France. *150 pp.*

Grace, Gerald R. Role Conflict and the Teacher. *150 pp.*

Hans, Nicholas. New Trends in Education in the Eighteenth Century. *278 pp. 19 tables.*

● Comparative Education: *A Study of Educational Factors and Traditions. 360 pp.*

● **Hargreaves, David.** Interpersonal Relations and Education. *432 pp.*

● Social Relations in a Secondary School. *240 pp.*

Holmes, Brian. Problems in Education. *A Comparative Approach. 336 pp.*

King, Ronald. Values and Involvement in a Grammar School. *164 pp.*
   School Organization and Pupil Involvement. *A Study of Secondary Schools.*

● **Mannheim, Karl,** and **Stewart, W. A. C.** An Introduction to the Sociology of Education. *206 pp.*

Morris, Raymond N. The Sixth Form and College Entrance. *231 pp.*

● **Musgrove, F.** Youth and the Social Order. *176 pp.*

● **Ottaway, A. K. C.** Education and Society: An Introduction to the Sociology of Education. *With an Introduction by W. O. Lester Smith. 212 pp.*

Peers, Robert. Adult Education: *A Comparative Study. 398 pp.*

Pritchard, D. G. Education and the Handicapped: *1760 to 1960. 258 pp.*

Stratta, Erica. The Education of Borstal Boys. *A Study of their Educational Experiences prior to, and during, Borstal Training. 256 pp.*

Taylor, P. H., Reid, W. A., and **Holley, B. J.** The English Sixth Form. *A Case Study in Curriculum Research. 200 pp.*

SOCIOLOGY OF CULTURE

Eppel, E. M., and **M.** Adolescents and Morality: *A Study of some Moral Values and Dilemmas of Working Adolescents in the Context of a changing Climate of Opinion. Foreword by W. J. H. Sprott. 268 pp. 39 tables.*

● **Fromm, Erich.** The Fear of Freedom. *286 pp.*

● The Sane Society. *400 pp.*

Mannheim, Karl. Essays on the Sociology of Culture. *Edited by Ernst Mannheim in co-operation with Paul Kecskemeti. Editorial Note by Adolph Lowe. 280 pp.*

Weber, Alfred. Farewell to European History: *or The Conquest of Nihilism. Translated from the German by R. F. C. Hull. 224 pp.*

SOCIOLOGY OF RELIGION

Argyle, Michael and **Beit-Hallahmi, Benjamin.** The Social Psychology of Religion. *About 256 pp.*

Glasner, Peter E. The Sociology of Secularisation. *A Critique of a Concept. About 180 pp.*

Nelson, G. K. Spiritualism and Society. *313 pp.*

Stark, Werner. The Sociology of Religion. *A Study of Christendom.*
  Volume I. *Established Religion. 248 pp.*
  Volume II. *Sectarian Religion. 368 pp.*
  Volume III. *The Universal Church. 464 pp.*
  Volume IV. *Types of Religious Man. 352 pp.*
  Volume V. *Types of Religious Culture. 464 pp.*

Turner, B. S. Weber and Islam. *216 pp.*

Watt, W. Montgomery. Islam and the Integration of Society. *320 pp.*

SOCIOLOGY OF ART AND LITERATURE

Jarvie, Ian C. Towards a Sociology of the Cinema. *A Comparative Essay on the Structure and Functioning of a Major Entertainment Industry. 405 pp.*

Rust, Frances S. Dance in Society. *An Analysis of the Relationships between the Social Dance and Society in England from the Middle Ages to the Present Day. 256 pp. 8 pp. of plates.*

Schücking, L. L. The Sociology of Literary Taste. *112 pp.*

Wolff, Janet. Hermeneutic Philosophy and the Sociology of Art. *150 pp.*

SOCIOLOGY OF KNOWLEDGE

Diesing, P. Patterns of Discovery in the Social Sciences. *262 pp.*

● **Douglas, J. D.** (Ed.) Understanding Everyday Life. *370 pp.*

● **Hamilton, P.** Knowledge and Social Structure. *174 pp.*

Jarvie, I. C. Concepts and Society. *232 pp.*

Mannheim, Karl. Essays on the Sociology of Knowledge. *Edited by Paul Kecskemeti. Editorial Note by Adolph Lowe. 353 pp.*

Remmling, Gunter W. The Sociology cf Karl Mannheim. *With a Bibliographical Guide to the Sociology of Knowledge, Ideological Analysis, and Social Planning. 255 pp.*

Remmling, Gunter W. (Ed.) Towards the Sociology of Knowledge. *Origin and Development of a Sociological Thought Style. 463 pp.*

Stark, Werner. The Sociology of Knowledge: *An Essay in Aid of a Deeper Understanding of the History of Ideas. 384 pp.*

URBAN SOCIOLOGY

Ashworth, William. The Genesis of Modern British Town Planning: *A Study in Economic and Social History of the Nineteenth and Twentieth Centuries. 288 pp.*

Cullingworth, J. B. Housing Needs and Planning Policy: *A Restatement of the Problems of Housing Need and 'Overspill' in England and Wales. 232 pp. 44 tables. 8 maps.*

Dickinson, Robert E. City and Region: *A Geographical Interpretation 608 pp. 125 figures.*

The West European City: *A Geographical Interpretation. 600 pp. 129 maps. 29 plates.*

● The City Region in Western Europe. *320 pp. Maps.*

Humphreys, Alexander J. New Dubliners: *Urbanization and the Irish Family. Foreword by George C. Homans. 304 pp.*

Jackson, Brian. Working Class Community: *Some General Notions raised by a Series of Studies in Northern England. 192 pp.*

Jennings, Hilda. Societies in the Making: *a Study of Development and Re-development within a County Borough. Foreword by D. A. Clark. 286 pp.*

●**Mann, P. H.** An Approach to Urban Sociology. *240 pp.*

Morris, R. N., and **Mogey, J.** The Sociology of Housing. *Studies at Berins-field. 232 pp. 4 pp. plates.*

Rosser, C., and **Harris, C.** The Family and Social Change. *A Study of Family and Kinship in a South Wales Town. 352 pp. 8 maps.*

●**Stacey, Margaret, Batsone, Eric, Bell, Colin,** and **Thurcott, Anne.** Power, Persistence and Change. *A Second Study of Banbury. 196 pp.*

RURAL SOCIOLOGY

Haswell, M. R. The Economics of Development in Village India. *120 pp.*

Littlejohn, James. Westrigg: *the Sociology of a Cheviot Parish. 172 pp. 5 figures.*

Mayer, Adrian C. Peasants in the Pacific. *A Study of Fiji Indian Rural Society. 248 pp. 20 plates.*

Williams, W. M. The Sociology of an English Village: *Gosforth. 272 pp. 12 figures. 13 tables.*

SOCIOLOGY OF INDUSTRY AND DISTRIBUTION

Anderson, Nels. Work and Leisure. *280 pp.*

●**Blau, Peter M.,** and **Scott, W. Richard.** Formal Organizations: *a Comparative approach. Introduction and Additional Bibliography by J. H. Smith. 326 pp.*

Dunkerley, David. The Foreman. *Aspects of Task and Structure. 192 pp.*

Eldridge, J. E. T. Industrial Disputes. *Essays in the Sociology of Industrial Relations. 288 pp.*

Hetzler, Stanley. Applied Measures for Promoting Technological Growth. *352 pp.*

Technological Growth and Social Change. *Achieving Modernization. 269 pp.*

Hollowell, Peter G. The Lorry Driver. *272 pp.*

●**Oxaal, I., Barnett, T.,** and **Booth, D.** (Eds). Beyond the Sociology of Development. *Economy and Society in Latin America and Africa. 295 pp.*

Smelser, Neil J. Social Change in the Industrial Revolution: *An Application of Theory to the Lancashire Cotton Industry, 1770–1840. 468 pp. 12 figures. 14 tables.*

ANTHROPOLOGY

Ammar, Hamed. Growing up in an Egyptian Village: *Silwa, Province of Aswan. 336 pp.*

Brandel-Syrier, Mia. Reeftown Elite. *A Study of Social Mobility in a Modern African Community on the Reef. 376 pp.*

Dickie-Clark, H. F. The Marginal Situation. *A Sociological Study of a Coloured Group. 236 pp.*

Dube, S. C. Indian Village. *Foreword by Morris Edward Opler. 276 pp. 4 plates.*

India's Changing Villages: *Human Factors in Community Development. 260 pp. 8 plates. 1 map.*

Firth, Raymond. Malay Fishermen. *Their Peasant Economy. 420 pp. 17 pp. plates.*

Gulliver, P. H. Social Control in an African Society: a Study of the Arusha, Agricultural Masai of Northern Tanganyika. *320 pp. 8 plates. 10 figures.*

Family Herds. *288 pp.*

Ishwaran, K. Tradition and Economy in Village India: *An Interactionist Approach.*

Foreword by Conrad Arensburg. 176 pp.

Jarvie, Ian C. The Revolution in Anthropology. *268 pp.*

Little, Kenneth L. Mende of Sierra Leone. *308 pp. and folder.*

Negroes in Britain. *With a New Introduction and Contemporary Study by Leonard Bloom. 320 pp.*

Lowie, Robert H. Social Organization. *494 pp.*

Mayer, A. C. Peasants in the Pacific. *A Study of Fiji Indian Rural Society. 248 pp.*

Meer, Fatima. Race and Suicide in South Africa. *325 pp.*

Smith, Raymond T. The Negro Family in British Guiana: *Family Structure and Social Status in the Villages. With a Foreword by Meyer Fortes. 314 pp. 8 plates. 1 figure. 4 maps.*

Smooha, Sammy. Israel: Pluralism and Conflict. *About 320 pp.*

SOCIOLOGY AND PHILOSOPHY

Barnsley, John H. The Social Reality of Ethics. *A Comparative Analysis of Moral Codes. 448 pp.*

Diesing, Paul. Patterns of Discovery in the Social Sciences. *362 pp.*

● **Douglas, Jack D.** (Ed.) Understanding Everyday Life. *Toward the Reconstruction of Sociological Knowledge. Contributions by Alan F. Blum. Aaron W. Cicourel, Norman K. Denzin, Jack D. Douglas, John Heeren, Peter McHugh, Peter K. Manning, Melvin Power, Matthew Speier, Roy Turner, D. Lawrence Wieder, Thomas P. Wilson and Don H. Zimmerman. 370 pp.*

Gorman, Robert A. The Dual Vision. *Alfred Schutz and the Myth of Phenomenological Social Science. About 300 pp.*

Jarvie, Ian C. Concepts and Society. *216 pp.*

● **Pelz, Werner.** The Scope of Understanding in Sociology. *Towards a more radical reorientation in the social humanistic sciences. 283 pp.*

Roche, Maurice. Phenomenology, Language and the Social Sciences. *371 pp.*

Sahay, Arun. Sociological Analysis. *212 pp.*

Sklair, Leslie. The Sociology of Progress. *320 pp.*

Slater, P. Origin and Significance of the Frankfurt School. *A Marxist Perspective. About 192 pp.*

Smart, Barry. Sociology, Phenomenology and Marxian Analysis. *A Critical Discussion of the Theory and Practice of a Science of Society. 220 pp.*

International Library of Anthropology

General Editor   Adam Kuper

Ahmed, A. S. Millenium and Charisma Among Pathans. *A Critical Essay in Social Anthropology. 192 pp.*

Brown, Paula. The Chimbu. *A Study of Change in the New Guinea Highlands. 151 pp.*

Gudeman, Stephen. Relationships, Residence and the Individual. *A Rural Panamanian Community. 288 pp. 11 Plates, 5 Figures, 2 Maps, 10 Tables.*

Hamnett, Ian. Chieftainship and Legitimacy. *An Anthropological Study of Executive Law in Lesotho. 163 pp.*

Hanson, F. Allan. Meaning in Culture. *127 pp.*

Lloyd, P. C. Power and Independence. *Urban Africans' Perception of Social Inequality. 264 pp.*

Pettigrew, Joyce. Robber Noblemen. *A Study of the Political System of the Sikh Jats. 284 pp.*

Street, Brian V. The Savage in Literature. *Representations of 'Primitive' Society in English Fiction, 1858–1920. 207 pp.*

Van Den Berghe, Pierre L. Power and Privilege at an African University. *278 pp.*

International Library of Social Policy

General Editor Kathleen Jones

Bayley, M. Mental Handicap and Community Care. *426 pp.*

Bottoms, A. E., and **McClean, J. D.** Defendants in the Criminal Process. *284 pp.*

Butler, J. R. Family Doctors and Public Policy. *208 pp.*

Davies, Martin. Prisoners of Society. *Attitudes and Aftercare. 204 pp.*

Gittus, Elizabeth. Flats, Families and the Under-Fives. *285 pp.*

Holman, Robert. Trading in Children. *A Study of Private Fostering. 355 pp.*

Jones, Howard, and **Cornes, Paul.** Open Prisons. *About 248 pp.*

Jones, Kathleen. History of the Mental Health Service. *428 pp.*

Jones, Kathleen, with **Brown, John, Cunningham, W. J., Roberts, Julian,** and **Williams, Peter.** Opening the Door. *A Study of New Policies for the Mentally Handicapped. 278 pp.*

Karn, Valerie. Retiring to the Seaside. *About 280 pp. 2 maps. Numerous tables.*

Thomas, J. E. The English Prison Officer since 1850: *A Study in Conflict. 258 pp.*

Walton, R. G. Women in Social Work. *303 pp.*

Woodward, J. To Do the Sick No Harm. *A Study of the British Voluntary Hospital System to 1875. 221 pp.*

International Library of Welfare and Philosophy

General Editors Noel Timms and David Watson

● **Plant, Raymond.** Community and Ideology. *104 pp.*

● **McDermott, F. E.** (Ed.) Self-Determination in Social Work. *A Collection of Essays on Self-determination and Related Concepts by Philosophers and Social Work Theorists. Contributors: F. P. Biestek, S. Bernstein, A. Keith-Lucas, D. Sayer, H. H. Perelman, C. Whittington, R. F. Stalley, F. E. McDermott, I. Berlin, H. J. McCloskey, H. L. A. Hart, J. Wilson, A. I. Melden, S. I. Benn. 254 pp.*

Ragg, Nicholas M. People Not Cases. *A Philosophical Approach to Social Work. About 250 pp.*

● **Timms, Noel,** and **Watson, David** (Eds). Talking About Welfare. *Readings in Philosophy and Social Policy. Contributors: T. H. Marshall, R. B. Brandt, G. H. von Wright, K. Nielsen, M. Cranston, R. M. Titmuss, R. S. Downie, E. Telfer, D. Donnison, J. Benson, P. Leonard, A. Keith-Lucas, D. Walsh, I. T. Ramsey. 320 pp.*

Primary Socialization, Language and Education

General Editor Basil Bernstein

Adlam, Diana S., *with the assistance of Geoffrey Turner and Lesley Lineker.* Code in Context. *About 272 pp.*

Bernstein, Basil. Class, Codes and Control. *3 volumes.*
  1. *Theoretical Studies Towards a Sociology of Language. 254 pp.*
  2. *Applied Studies Towards a Sociology of Language. 377 pp.*
● 3. *Towards a Theory of Educatiomal Transmission. 167 pp.*

Brandis, W., and **Bernstein, B.** Selection and Control. *176 pp.*

Brandis, Walter, and **Henderson, Dorothy.** Social Class, Language and Communication. *288 pp.*

Cook-Gumperz, Jenny. Social Control and Socialization. *A Study of Class Differences in the Language of Maternal Control. 290 pp.*

● **Gahagan, D. M.,** and **G. A.** Talk Reform. *Exploration in Language for Infant School Children. 160 pp.*

Hawkins, P. R. Social Class, the Nominal Group and Verbal Strategies. *About 220 pp.*

Robinson, W. P., and **Rackstraw, Susan D. A.** A Question of Answers. *2 volumes. 192 pp. and 180 pp.*

Turner, Geoffrey J., and **Mohan, Bernard A.** A Linguistic Description and Computer Programme for Children's Speech. *208 pp.*

Reports of the Institute of Community Studies

● **Cartwright, Ann.** Parents and Family Planning Services. *306 pp.*
  Patients and their Doctors. *A Study of General Practice. 304 pp.*

Dench, Geoff. Maltese in London. *A Case-study in the Erosion of Ethnic Consciousness. 302 pp.*

● **Jackson, Brian.** Streaming: *an Education System in Miniature. 168 pp.*

Jackson, Brian, and **Marsden, Dennis.** Education and the Working Class: *Some General Themes raised by a Study of 88 Working-class Children in a Northern Industrial City. 268 pp. 2 folders.*

Marris, Peter. The Experience of Higher Education. *232 pp. 27 tables.*
  Loss and Change. *192 pp.*

Marris, Peter, and **Rein, Martin.** Dilemmas of Social Reform. *Poverty and Community Action in the United States. 256 pp.*

Marris, Peter, and Somerset, Anthony. African Businessmen. *A Study of Entrepreneurship and Development in Kenya. 256 pp.*

Mills, Richard. Young Outsiders: *a Study in Alternative Communities. 216 pp.*

Runciman, W. G. Relative Deprivation and Social Justice. *A Study of Attitudes to Social Inequality in Twentieth-Century England. 352 pp.*

Willmott, Peter. Adolescent Boys in East London. *230 pp.*

Willmott, Peter, and Young, Michael. Family and Class in a London Suburb. *202 pp. 47 tables.*

Young, Michael. Innovation and Research in Education. *192 pp.*

●Young, Michael, and McGeeney, Patrick. Learning Begins at Home. *A Study of a Junior School and its Parents. 128 pp.*

Young, Michael, and Willmott, Peter. Family and Kinship in East London. *Foreword by Richard M. Titmuss. 252 pp. 39 tables.*
The Symmetrical Family. *410 pp.*

Reports of the Institute for Social Studies in Medical Care

Cartwright, Ann, Hockey, Lisbeth, and Anderson, John L. Life Before Death. *310 pp.*

Dunnell, Karen, and Cartwright, Ann. Medicine Takers, Prescribers and Hoarders. *190 pp.*

Medicine, Illness and Society

General Editor W. M. Williams

Robinson, David. The Process of Becoming Ill. *142 pp.*

Stacey, Margaret, *et al*. Hospitals, Children and Their Families. *The Report of a Pilot Study. 202 pp.*

Stimson, G. V., and Webb, B. Going to See the Doctor. *The Consultation Process in General Practice. 155 pp.*

Monographs in Social Theory

General Editor Arthur Brittan

●Barnes, B. Scientific Knowledge and Sociological Theory. *192 pp.*

Bauman, Zygmunt. Culture as Praxis. *204 pp.*

●Dixon, Keith. Sociological Theory. *Pretence and Possibility. 142 pp.*

Meltzer, B. N., Petras, J. W., and Reynolds, L. T. Symbolic Interactionism. *Genesis, Varieties and Criticisms. 144 pp.*

●Smith, Anthony D. The Concept of Social Change. *A Critique of the Functionalist Theory of Social Change. 208 pp.*

Routledge Social Science Journals

The British Journal of Sociology. *Editor – Angus Stewart; Associate Editor – Leslie Sklair. Vol. 1, No. 1 – March 1950 and Quarterly. Roy. 8vo. All back issues available. An international journal publishing original papers in the field of sociology and related areas.*
Community Work. *Edited by David Jones and Marjorie Mayo. 1973. Published annually.*
Economy and Society. *Vol. 1, No. 1. February 1972 and Quarterly. Metric Roy. 8vo. A journal for all social scientists covering sociology, philosophy, anthropology, economics and history. All back numbers available.*
Religion. Journal of Religion and Religions. *Chairman of Editorial Board, Ninian Smart. Vol. 1, No. 1, Spring 1971. A journal with an interdisciplinary approach to the study of the phenomena of religion. All back numbers available.*
Year Book of Social Policy in Britain, The. *Edited by Kathleen Jones. 1971. Published annually.*

Social and Psychological Aspects of Medical Practice

Editor   Trevor Silverstone

Lader, Malcolm. Psychophysiology of Mental Illness. *280 pp.*
● **Silverstone, Trevor,** and **Turner, Paul.** Drug Treatment in Psychiatry. *232 pp.*

Printed in Great Britain by Unwin Brothers Limited
The Gresham Press Old Woking Surrey
A member of the Staples Printing Group